W9-AYQ-467

This book provides the most comprehensive analysis of one of the most important issues in China today: the tensions between the Chinese Communist Party and the Chinese state legislative, judicial, administrative, and military institutions. Taking the "neo-institutionalist" approach, the author suggests that the Communist Party in post-1949 China faces an institutional dilemma: The Party cannot live with the state and it cannot live without the state.

This study makes three contributions to the field of scholarship. First, it demonstrates that it is not only conceptually constructive, but analytically imperative to distinguish the state from the Communist Party. Second, it integrates a detailed study with broader generalizations about Chinese politics, thus making efforts to overcome the tendency toward specialized scholarship at the expense of a comparative and systemic understanding of China. Third, it opens a new dimension of Chinese politics – the uncertain and conflictual relationship between the Communist Party and the Chinese state.

This work is quite timely because China is currently undergoing a dramatic transformation and faces an uncertain future.

Party vs. State in Post-1949 China

Cambridge Modern China Series

Edited by William Kirby, *Harvard University*

Party vs. State in Post-1949 China

The Institutional Dilemma

SHIPING ZHENG
University of Vermont

CAMBRIDGE
UNIVERSITY PRESS

PUBLISHED BY THE PRESS SYNDICATE OF THE UNIVERSITY OF CAMBRIDGE
The Pitt Building, Trumpington Street, Cambridge CB2 1RP, United Kingdom

CAMBRIDGE UNIVERSITY PRESS
The Edinburgh Building, Cambridge CB2 2RU, United Kingdom
40 West 20th Street, New York, NY 10011-4211, USA
10 Stamford Road, Oakleigh, Melbourne 3166, Australia

© Shiping Zheng 1997

First published 1997

Printed in the United States of America

Typeset in Times Roman

Library of Congress Cataloging-in-Publication Data
Zheng, Shiping, 1955–
Party vs. state in post-1949 China : the institutional dilemma /
Shiping Zheng.
p.   cm. – (Cambridge modern China series)
Includes bibliographical references and index.
ISBN 0-521-58205-9 (hb). – ISBN 0-521-58819-7 (pb)
1. Chung-kuo kung ch' an tang. 2. China – Politics and
government – 1949–   I. Title. II. Series.
JQ1519.A5Z49   1997
324.251'075 – DC21   96-50078
                                 CIP

*A catalog record for this book is available from
the British Library.*

ISBN 0-521-58205-9 hardback
ISBN 0-521-58819-7 paperback

To my wife,
Yi Shen,
and our children,
June and Jim Zheng

Contents

Contents

Part III
State-building under a Reformist Party:
The Deng Xiaoping Era

Contents

Tables

Acknowledgments

Without the support of many organizations and individuals, the completion of this book would have been impossible. My initial research was made possible by a scholarship from Harvard-Yenching Institute in 1988–89. In 1990 a scholarship from Tsai Shao-Hua Scholarship Foundation enabled me to spend a year at Harvard University. A research grant from Yale Center for International and Area Studies in 1991 enabled me to gather data on China's administrative reform. In 1993 a research grant from the University of Vermont Committee on Research and Scholarship enabled me to collect data on new central and provincial leaders in China.

I wish to express my special gratitude to Professor Joseph LaPalombara, who has been my mentor and great source of inspiration since I entered Yale in 1986. His insights have broadened my perspectives and his wisdom will benefit my research for many years to come. Professor David Mayhew at Yale introduced me to comparative political parties and American politics, which has kept me fascinated with the comparisons of Chinese and American political institutions. I also drew my initial inspiration from the courses I took with Professor Stephen Skowronek and from his book on American administrative state-building.

Professor Roderick MacFarquhar of Harvard University has been my friend and adviser for many years. His remarkably detailed knowledge of the Chinese elite politics has impressed me more than anything else. My book has benefited from his work on the origins of the Cultural Revolution and from his lectures at Harvard College, where I once served as his teaching fellow. Working with him has been the greatest academic experience for me.

I am also grateful to Professors Miles Kahler, Susan Shirk, and Tun-jen Cheng for reading and commenting on my original research proposal. My thanks also extend to Professors Suzanne Ogden and Merle Goldman for offering constructive comments on the draft chapters. I am particularly grateful to Professors Brantly Womack, Barry McCormick, and William Kirby for offering invaluable comments and suggestions for revisions of the original manuscript.

I also thank Eugene Wu of the Harvard-Yenching Library and Nancy Hearst of the Fairbank Center library of Harvard for helping me locate needed books and materials. Special thanks go to Dr. John Watt and Dr. Anne Watt for suggesting improvements of the draft chapters. Thanks are due to my colleagues at the University of Vermont, Professors Peter Seybolt, John Burke, George Moyser, Carolyn Elliott, and Joshua Forrest, who have read parts of the manuscript or otherwise offered valuable advice.

Finally, I want to thank my wife, Yi Shen. This book would not have been possible without her constant support and encouragement. To her, my gratitude is profound.

Abbreviations

CCP	Chinese Communist Party
CMC	Central Military Commission
CPGC	Central People's Government Council
CPPCC	Chinese People's Political Consultative Conference
CPSU	Communist Party of the Soviet Union
FBIS-CHI	*Foreign Broadcast Information Service, Daily Report: China*
GAC	Government Administrative Council
GPD	General Political Department
KMT	Kuomintang (Nationalist Party)
NPC	National People's Congress
NDC	National Defense Council
PCG	Party core group
PLA	People's Liberation Army
PLAC	Political and Legal Affairs Committee
PRC	People's Republic of China
ROC	Republic of China

Part I

INTRODUCTION

1

Understanding the State and Party in China

THE collapse of the Communist regimes in Eastern Europe and the Soviet Union highlights the issue of state-building in today's world politics. As one quickly discovers, building the state institutions after Communism is anything but easy. Newly elected leaders in the former Communist countries have faced formidable challenges, as they realized how much still needed to be done in this "third wave of state formation."[1] Decades of Communist rule seem to have contributed little, if anything, to institutional development. Everything has to start from scratch: negotiating the rules of the game, establishing political authorities, defining power relationships, learning how to convene parliaments as well as how to behave like a parliamentarian. Meanwhile, from the pointless bombardment of the parliament in Russia to the senseless ethnic war in former Yugoslavia, and from escalating lawlessness in the center to rising outcry for breakup in the periphery, we have witnessed in recent years the devastating consequences of state institutional breakdown.

Against this background, China seems to be doing very well: At an average of 9 percent per year over the past sixteen years, the Chinese economy was the fastest growing in the world; market reform had been deepening, despite or perhaps because of the tragedy in Tiananmen Square in 1989; foreign investments poured in and Chinese products rushed out. Much of the booming economy, of course, hinges upon the Communist Party's grip on power in China. What will happen if or when the Chinese Communist Party (CCP) also collapses? Will China face similar dangers of breakup as we have seen in the former Soviet Union and Yugoslavia? Can the Chinese state institutions survive the end of the Communist Party's rule? Will China remain a unified country after Communism? These are fundamental, yet difficult, questions about the future of China.

---

[1] This is a rephrasing of Daniel S. Papp's term of "Third Proliferation of States." Daniel S. Papp, *Contemporary International Relations: Frameworks for Understanding,* 4th edition (New York: Macmillan College Publishing Company, 1994), pp. 41–3.

3

Looking beyond the booming economy, we may find that not all is comforting in China. Indeed, China today is facing a deep institutional crisis. This is so not just because the old guard of the revolution is going to "see Marx," nor just because official corruption is rampant or the official ideology is rapidly losing its currency or relevance. First, the death of a paramount leader undoubtedly has a great impact on the Chinese polity. It jolts the political system and pushes all the elements of the existing power structure into disequilibrium. However, China has had this kind of shakeup before. In imperial China, emperors came and went but the dynastic rule continued. In post-1949 China, the regime has also endured the death of its founding fathers, such as Mao Zedong and Zhou Enlai. Second, today's rampant corruption suggests that something is seriously wrong with the system and may even signal the approaching end of the regime.[2] Yet, runaway corruption is only the symptom of a much deeper crisis. Corruption happens all the time and in all political systems. It is what has led to uncontrollable and widespread official corruption in China that warrants our attention. Third, because China lacks a broadly held religious belief and a civic culture has yet to develop, the ideology of Marxism-Leninism-Mao Zedong Thought functioned as an important integrating instrument for keeping the Party together. The erosion of the ruling ideology, therefore, is bound to weaken the regime's ability to govern. Nonetheless, we have to note that the official ideology began to lose its appeal in the later years of the Mao Zedong era, long before the current crisis loomed large. An eroding ideology exacerbates the crisis, but is not the crisis itself.

China is in crisis because the Party organization that has controlled the country since 1949 is now in disarray, and the Chinese state institutions have yet to prove their ability to organize 1.2 billion people. Due to the devastating attack on Party officials during the Cultural Revolution of the 1960s and 1970s and because of the profound impact of "loosening up" and "getting rich first" on the morale of Party members during the reforms of the 1980s and 1990s, the discipline and cohesion of the Communist Party organization has irremediably declined. As the Party becomes weak, the lack of capacity of Chinese state institutions becomes increasingly noticeable.[3] After more than four decades of existence, the state of the People's Republic of China (PRC) has yet to develop

---

[2] For a comparative study of the role of corruption in effecting the collapse of Communist systems, see Leslie Holmes, *The End of Communist Power* (New York: Oxford University Press, 1993).

[3] "Beijing Losing Control: China in Transition: No Law, No Order," *Far Eastern Economic Review* (June 9, 1994), pp. 22–30.

the necessary and adequate abilities to handle major political, social, and economic problems. In many ways, the Chinese state institutions can hardly function independently of the Party organization. China — a country that invented the civil service system many centuries ago — still lags behind many others in establishing a government civil service in modern times. In a dramatic way, the forty-nine-day standoff between the demonstrating students and the government in Tiananmen Square in the spring of 1989 and the loss of control by the government in the escalating tensions, seemed to prove the inability of the state to act even in a crisis. The dispatch of field armies to the capital to suppress the defenseless students and civilians further bore testimony to the inability of the legal and police apparatus to maintain law and order.[4]

Sixteen years of economic reform in China have unleashed both constructive and destructive forces, and set free both angels and devils. Amidst stock market speculation and business activities, organized crime and violence is on the rise, tax evasion or tax resistance is widespread, and smuggling has become epidemic, often ignored, if not aided, by local officials.[5] The official corruption has become so pervasive that Party General Secretary Jiang Zemin warned that the corruption will bury the Party, the regime, and the modernization program if it is unchecked.[6] There is nothing surprising here compared with what we have seen in Russia and other former Communist countries. What is revealing, however, is that all this is happening in China where the world's largest Communist Party is still in power!

Both the Chinese rulers and their critics have recognized the dangers of an institutional breakdown in China. As early as in 1981, Deng Xiaoping warned: "Without Party leadership there definitely will be nationwide disorder and China would fall apart."[7] After the 1989 Tiananmen Square Incident, the Party leaders have recycled Deng's argument many times in an attempt to deter Chinese and Westerners alike from trying to weaken the Party's rule. Mean-

---

[4] Bringing the military forces to the capital was the last thing the imperial Chinese rulers wanted in peacetime. This, however, has happened at least twice in the history of the People's Republic of China. What Deng Xiaoping did in May–June 1989 resembled what Mao Zedong did in July–August 1968 when he ordered the People's Liberation Army to terminate the Red Guard movement.

[5] Chinese Vice Premier Li Lanqing warned, "The PRC might become the kingdom of smugglers." The *People's Daily,* August 4, 1993.

[6] Jiang made this comment at the Second Plenum of the CCP Central Disciplinary Committee in August 1993. *Zhongguo jingji tizhi gaige* (Reform of the Chinese Economic System) (September 1993), p. 21.

[7] Deng Xiaoping, *Selected Works of Deng Xiaoping 1975–1982* (Beijing: Foreign Languages Press, 1984), p. 369.

while, the aging "Long March" veterans, who are literally racing against the clock, have tried everything they can to make sure that the Party will survive after they leave the political scene. Yet, in a dramatically changed world, neither the dying veteran revolutionaries nor the new Party leaders are likely to find a magic formula for revitalizing the Communist Party. On the other hand, opponents to the Communist rule in China are faced with the challenge of providing an alternative to the CCP if the fundamental changes they advocate are to come. Despite their strenuous efforts to search for an alternative discourse, there is little indication that an organizational alternative to the CCP will soon materialize. Thus, approaching the end of the twentieth century, China is again facing a crisis of institutional disintegration, much like the one she faced at the century's onset. China's crisis today is less about leadership, discipline, ethics, or ideology than it is about institutions. Chinese institutional breakdown or rebuilding has again become an urgent issue that deserves our attention.

This is a study of the issue of state-building in post-1949 China. By comparing the Mao Zedong era (1949–76) and the Deng Xiaoping era (1978–95), I want to find out what has happened after a strong revolutionary party won the civil war and established a new state. What did a revolutionary party mean to the process of state-building? What are the problems, difficulties or dilemmas that a revolutionary party has in its relations with the state? By exploring these issues of state-building, we may better understand the institutional challenge China faces today and the direction in which China might be heading in the future.

THE QUESTION OF STATE-BUILDING

Organizing China has never been easy because of the sheer size of its land and population. The problem of governance became all the more acute after the imperial institutions that had ruled China for thousands of years collapsed at the beginning of this century. That is why one of the most important issues in the twentieth century has been how to reorganize China. Contemporary Chinese history is full of struggles over establishment, abolition, reestablishment, restoration, or reform of political institutions.[8] It is no coincidence that Sun Yat-sen and Mao Zedong, two key figures in contemporary Chinese poli-

---

[8] The Chinese efforts at creating political institutions in the first half of the twentieth century are detailed in William L. Tung, *The Political Institutions of Modern China* (The Hague, Netherlands: Martinus Nijhoff, 1968).

tics, recognized this problem early on in their revolutionary careers. Sun complained that China had become like a "sheet of loose sand."[9] Mao urged his countrymen to "get organized!"[10]

The pre-1949 Chinese struggles to reorganize China have captured much attention from historians and comparative theorists in the West. Studies of the successes or failures of the pre-1949 Chinese state-building are abundant.[11] State-building in post-1949 China, however, has not been a major concern until recently.[12] It seemed as if the century-long problem of state-building in China had been solved in no time after the Communists had taken over the mainland. Studies of Chinese political history usually stopped short of looking further at how the new state evolved after the revolution, whereas research on post-1949 Chinese politics often began with the assumption that the state was already an established institution and a given condition.[13]

Neglect in China studies of the post-1949 state-building problem is attributable to several factors. First, there is a long-held assumption that China has a strong "statist" tradition. Whereas studies of American political development have pointed to the weakness or absence of the state as "the great hallmark of American political culture,"[14] the state is often taken for granted in studies of Chinese political development. After all, some scholars would argue, how could China not have a strong state? The Chinese empire had existed for thousands of years. The imperial bureaucracy was perhaps the oldest and most

---

[9] Dr. Sun Yat-sen, the founding father of the 1911 Chinese Republic, made this complaint in 1924. Sun Yat-sen, *San Min Chu I* (The Three Principles of the People), translated by Frank W. Price (Shanghai: China Committee of the Institute of Pacific Relations, 1927), p. 5.

[10] Mao made this call in November 1943. Mao Zedong, *Selected Works of Mao Tse-tung,* vol. 3 (Beijing: Foreign Languages Press, 1965), p. 153.

[11] The most influential books are: Theda Skocpol, *States and Social Revolutions: A Comparative Analysis of France, Russia and China* (New York: Cambridge University Press, 1979); John King Fairbank, *The Great Chinese Revolution, 1800–1985* (New York: Harper & Row, 1987); and Jonathan D. Spence, *The Search for Modern China* (New York: W. W. Norton & Company, 1990).

[12] Recent scholarship on the post-1949 state-building problems in China includes: Stuart R. Schram, ed., *Foundations and Limits of State Power in China* (London: The School of Oriental and African Studies, University of London, 1987); Vivienne Shue, *The Reach of the State: Sketches of the Chinese Body Politic* (Stanford, CA: Stanford University Press, 1988); and Gordon White, *The Chinese State in the Era of Economic Reform: The Road to Crisis* (Armonk, NY: M. E. Sharpe, 1991).

[13] This is what Joseph W. Esherick calls "the 1949 barrier." Joseph W. Esherick, "Ten Theses on the Chinese Revolution," *Modern China* 21, no. 1 (January 1995), p. 48.

[14] Stephen Skowronek, *Building a New American State: The Expansion of National Administrative Capacities 1877–1920* (New York: Cambridge University Press, 1982), p. 3.

sophisticated in world history. The official ideology dominated Chinese culture and philosophy. If one finds the American political tradition "stateless,"[15] the Chinese political tradition must look very "statist" by comparison. The long existence in China of a strong state, therefore, must be the rule, whereas the institutional disorder between the last imperial dynasty and the first people's republic is the exception.

Second, the issue of Chinese state-building is overshadowed by the course of revolution. In the literature on modern Chinese history, the dominant theme can be briefly summarized as follows: In the last one hundred years or so, China underwent a great social revolution that ultimately buried the long-existing imperial dynasty. The revolution started with the collapse of the old state and ended with the founding of a new state.[16] The process of revolution in China is thus simultaneously a process of state-rebuilding. Even though the revolutionaries were determined to smash the old state structure, the revolution resulted in "a much larger, more powerful and more bureaucratic new political regime."[17] Under the shadow of the revolution, the formation of a modern Chinese state is seen as a natural result of the revolutionary process.

Third, the key role played by the revolutionary parties further obscured the issue of state-building. Ever since the Alliance Society toppled the last imperial dynasty in 1911 and founded the Republic of China, the revolutionary parties occupied a central role in social and political changes. If the Chinese revolution is a continuous process consisting of successive phases,[18] then the revolutionary parties were seen as the major protagonists, and the state played only a minor role. Thanks to the "revolution" paradigm that once dominated China studies, the dynamics and causes of revolutions were given much more attention than their consequences.[19] The impact of the revolutionary parties on state-building was seldom qualified to be a legitimate topic.[20] This, coupled

---

[15] J. P. Nettl, "The State as a Conceptual Variable," *World Politics* 4 (July 1968), p. 569.

[16] This theme is most explicitly developed in Skocpol, pp. 236–81.

[17] Ibid., p. 263.

[18] Fairbank divides this process into the Republican Revolution of 1911–12, the Nationalist Revolution of 1925–28, and the Communist Revolution of 1945–49. Fairbank, 1987, pp. 37–45.

[19] For a discussion of the "revolution" paradigm, see Thomas A. Metzger and Ramon H. Myers, "Sinological Shadows: The State of Modern China Studies in the US," in Amy Auerbacher Wilson, Sidney Leonard Greenblatt, and Richard W. Wilson, eds. *Methodological Issues in China Studies* (New York: Praeger Publishers, 1983), pp. 14–50.

[20] Some exceptions are A. Doak Barnett, *Cadres, Bureaucracy, and Political Power in Communist China* (New York: Columbia University Press, 1967); Harry Harding, *Organizing China: The Problem of Bureaucracy, 1949–1976* (Stanford, CA: Stanford University Press, 1981); and

with the ideological preference for a limited state in liberal democracies, had often led us to think more of problems caused by the state than of problems caused to the state.

Conceptually, there has long been a tendency to equate the Chinese Communist Party with the post-1949 Chinese state. Prevailing in China studies is the view that it is of no analytical significance to distinguish the Party from the state, because the Party organization has deeply penetrated the state apparatus and the Party leadership has tightly controlled the state bureaucracy.[21] This is best exemplified by the conception of a "party-state" that denotes a type of state in which the Communist Party organization, as the core of the state, monopolizes state power over the direction and control of society. Although not everyone is comfortable with the conceptual marriage of the state and the Party, the party-state image is so prevalent as to make analytical distinctions between the Party organization and the state institutions theoretically appealing to only a few researchers. Studies of post-1949 Chinese politics, though varying in their focuses, share much in accepting the party-state argument. Convinced of the strong statist tradition in China and trapped by the revolution paradigm, we have often taken the party-state concept for granted too easily.

The party-state conception was undoubtedly influenced by the "totalitarian" model.[22] Once popular in comparative studies of Communism, the totalitarian model emphasizes, among other things, the central role of the Communist Party in the state of the Communist countries.[23] To be sure, an over-simplistic

Tang Tsou, *The Cultural Revolution and Post-Mao Reforms: A Historical Perspective* (Chicago: The University of Chicago Press, 1986), pp. 259–334.

[21] This view is summarized in Kenneth Lieberthal and Michel Oksenberg, *Policy Making in China: Leaders, Structures, and Processes* (Princeton, NJ: Princeton University Press, 1988), pp. 4–6.

[22] Theories of political order also seem to have supported the "party-state" concept. According to Samuel Huntington, in many developing countries, "[w]eak political institutions, particularly the lack of a strong political party, contributed to military coups and political instability." Thus a strong party organization like the CCP could be the most important provider of political stability. "The party is not just a supplementary organization; it is instead the source of legitimacy and authority." Samuel P. Huntington, *Political Order in Changing Societies* (New Haven, CT: Yale University Press, 1968), p. 5, 91.

[23] Some of the major books on "totalitarianism" include Carl J. Friedrich and Zbigniew Brzezinski, *Totalitarian Dictatorship and Autocracy* (Cambridge, MA: Harvard University Press, 1956); Zbigniew Brzezinski, *The Soviet Bloc: Unity and Conflict* (Cambridge, MA: Harvard University Press, 1960); Raymond Aron, *Democracy and Totalitarianism: A Theory of Political Systems* (Ann Arbor: The University of Michigan Press, 1965); Sigmund Neumann, *Permanent Revolution: Totalitarianism in the Age of International Civil War*, 2nd edition (New York: Praeger Publishers, 1965); and Leonard Schapiro, *Totalitarianism* (New York: Praeger

Orwellian depiction of an omnipotent totalitarian Communist state fits the Chinese case poorly because of the backward communication facilities in a vast peasant society. Nonetheless, attempts at modifying the totalitarian model to make it applicable to the Chinese case are not rare.[24]

The totalitarian perception of a party-state in China was greatly shaken by the events of the Cultural Revolution of the 1960s, when the Chinese officials at all levels were attacked by the young Red Guards and rebel workers. In the early 1970s, a shift away from the totalitarian image of the Chinese state was already discernible.[25] By the late 1970s, observation of the chaos in the 1960s began to bear certain theoretical fruit, and new perspectives on the Chinese state mushroomed.[26] Taking the initial shot at the totalitarian model, revisionist scholars discovered the weakness of the Chinese state. They argued that the state in China might not be as strong and monolithic as was previously thought, largely because of the practical difficulty the Communist Party organization had in maintaining an effective command of the state machine.[27] Meanwhile, studies of the Chinese revolution began to offer some new thoughts. Rather than praising the achievements of the revolutionaries, many have chosen to examine the long-term consequences of the revolution.[28] As one reviewer points out: "In sum, recent scholarship has begun to consider the numerous specific uncertainties, difficulties, and ambiguities involved in the revolution's course, rather than simply continuing to debate the overall causes of its ultimate success."[29]

Publishers, 1972).

[24] Tang Tsou's analysis of the revolutionary "feudal" totalitarian trend in China is perhaps the best of such attempts. See "Back from the Brink of Revolutionary-'Feudal' Totalitarianism," in Tsou, pp. 144–88.

[25] Two examples are Chalmers Johnson, ed., *Change in Communist Systems* (Stanford, CA: Stanford University Press, 1970), and Lucian W. Pye, *China: An Introduction* (Boston: Little, Brown, 1972).

[26] A good source of these new perspectives on the Chinese state is Victor Nee and David Mozingo, eds., *State and Society in Contemporary China* (Ithaca, NY: Cornell University Press, 1983).

[27] Ibid., pp. 17–24.

[28] For examples, see Chen Yung-fa, *Making Revolution: The Communist Movement in Eastern and Central China, 1937–1945* (Berkeley: University of California Press, 1986), and Steven I. Levine, *Anvil of Victory: The Communist Revolution in Manchuria, 1945–1948* (New York: Columbia University Press, 1987). See also the symposium on "Rethinking the Chinese Revolution," organized by Philip C. C. Huang, *Modern China* 21, no. 1 (January 1995), pp. 3–143.

[29] Stephen C. Averill, "The Chinese Revolution Reevaluated," *Problems of Communism* (January–February 1989), p. 83.

These two developments have led to the replacement of a totalitarian or monolithic image of party-state with a limited or fragmented image of party-state.[30] For instance, after examining the relations between the state center and the peasant periphery, Vivienne Shue argues that the reach of the state in the Mao Zedong era was limited because of the existence of "*the honeycomb pattern of the polity* – a highly localized, highly segmented, cell-like pattern" – that characterizes the way social and economic life came to be organized in the Chinese countryside in the 1950s and 1960s.[31]

The party-state concept, however, has survived all the revisions. Recent scholarship on the Chinese state has begun to challenge the revolution paradigm, but remained enslaved by the party-state conception. Even the revisionist scholars are not yet ready to reject the party-state concept. Instead, they tend to rest content with showing how a party-state may become weak, in contrast to the earlier literature that emphasized the strength of a party-state. Many studies of Chinese politics still depend on the basic assumption, as a point of departure, that the Communist Party constitutes the core of a modern Chinese state.

The party-state concept is persistent because it is difficult to change. To distinguish the Party from the Chinese state is no easy job. That the Party organization has penetrated the state institutions so deeply can easily discourage the effort. It also incites questions of whether the exercise has any value. The party-state concept is prevalent because it is easy to use. It seems to describe the Chinese state without a need for further explanation. We tend to believe that by putting the Party organization and the state institutions together, we can largely control the variable of the state in our analysis, which in turn enables us to focus on social and economic factors. An insistence on an analytical distinction between the Party organization and state institutions will perhaps make our job more difficult or even weaken some of the basic assumptions with which we have already become so comfortable.

However, the compound noun *party-state* usually brings us more confusion than convenience. As an analytical tool, the party-state concept is inherently a problematic one, because it often blurs rather than reveals the structural conflicts that beset the Party organization and the state institutions. By accepting

---

[30] The view of a "fragmented" authoritarian state in China is presented by Kenneth Lieberthal and David M. Lampton in *Bureaucracy, Politics, and Decision Making in Post-Mao China* (Berkeley: University of California Press, 1992), pp. 1–12.

[31] Shue, pp. 130–37.

the party-state assumption, we are led to believe that the organizational interests of the Party and the state institutions not only coexist but are one and the same thing. This then leads to the belief that insights into Chinese politics can be gained without having to probe into actual, as well as potential, conflicts between the Party and the state. As such, the party-state concept is at best inadequate and at worst misleading.

The basic premise of this study is that it is not only conceptually constructive, but analytically imperative to distinguish the state from the Party. In this study, the state and Party are regarded as two different types of political organization, each with distinctive organizational logic. In post-1949 China, the tensions between them have constituted one of the most important dimensions of Chinese politics.

AN INSTITUTIONAL PERSPECTIVE

To raise questions about the validity of the party-state concept is only the beginning. We face the challenge of how to approach the issue of state-building in post-1949 China. In this respect, Marxist perspectives seem to offer little help. A class view of state allows no distinction between state institutions and other political organizations. As Karl Marx declared: "The executive of the modern state is but a committee for managing the common affairs of the whole bourgeoisie."[32] For Lenin, too, the state was nothing but "a machine for the oppression of one class by another." This being so, the state must be smashed by the revolutionary party. So Lenin predicted: "The state will disappear as a result of the coming social revolution."[33] For Lenin, the state was the problem, whereas the revolutionary party was the solution. In the theoretical arsenal of the Leninist party, there is a lot about party-building, but not much about state-building. The state is to be destroyed, not built.

A modified version of the bureaucratic model in China studies correctly points to the structural constraints on political actors.[34] Nevertheless, when conflicts of interests between the Party and the state are acknowledged within this conceptual framework, they are often treated to a large extent in terms of the competition among different bureaucratic agencies for a larger share of

---

[32] Cited in Jon Elster, *Making Sense of Marx* (New York: Cambridge University Press, 1985), pp. 416–18. Karl Marx did suggest, though, in *The Eighteenth Brumaire* that the state's behavior does not necessarily follow the interests of the dominant class.

[33] V. I. Lenin, *State and Revolution* (New York: International Publishers, 1971), pp. 17–20.

[34] For the application of the bureaucratic model to China studies, see Lieberthal and Oksenberg.

power. That is, the conflict is conceived merely as the tension between one type of bureaucracy (the Party) and another type of bureaucracy (the state).[35] Yet, the Party is a mass revolutionary organization that infiltrates, manages, and controls all the state institutions. The Party is in the state institutions, but it is also above and around the state institutions. In this sense, the Party is not another bureaucracy of the state. It is not even another key institution of the state. The Party's rules of the game are often beyond the explanatory power of the bureaucratic model.[36]

A state-society approach that has been productive for many research subjects provides a general framework for analyzing the state-building problem in China. When we come down to the specific relationship between the Party organization and the state institutions, problems begin to emerge. Studies in this area generally focus on social variables to explain changes in the state-society relationship – arguing, for example, that the nature of the Chinese society makes it difficult for the state to penetrate. The existence of the Chinese state, on the other hand, is often assumed. In fact, for the state-society perspective to operate, a state *has* to be there as a given. Research that moves along this dimension often starts with the premise that there is a state, or even a powerful state, vis-à-vis society. Once we follow this framework of analysis, it becomes almost impossible to ask whether the assumed powerful state is indeed so. As long as an analytical distinction is not made between the Party organization and the state institutions, discussion of a Chinese state-society relationship could easily turn into a practice of muddling through, for it is not clear whether the Party or the state or both of them serve as an explanatory variable.

As illuminating as they are, the aforementioned perspectives do not carry us very far in understanding the state-building problem in post-1949 China. To proceed beyond where a few scholars have gone along this particular road, I have applied an institutional approach to the Chinese state-building.[37] From an

---

[35] Ibid., pp. 21–2.

[36] For instance, Graham Allison argues that one's position on policy issues is determined by one's bureaucratic interests. Thus, "where you stand depends on where you sit." Graham T. Allison, *Essence of Decision: Explaining the Cuban Missile Crisis* (Boston: Little, Brown, 1971), pp. 162–84. In China, however, the opposite seems true. In numerous political campaigns, it is one's stand or political attitude that determines where one would be given a seat or whether one would go upward or downward in the official hierarchy. More often than not, "where you sit depends on where you stand."

[37] The institutional perspective here derives from the new Institutionalism literature that emerges largely in the studies of American politics and international political economy. For a summary of the literature, see James G. March and Johan P. Olsen, "The New Institutionalism: Organiza-

institutional perspective, a state may be defined as a set of differentiated and autonomous government institutions, distinguishable from nongovernmental organizations, which represent state sovereignty – the sole authority to make and implement, with the backing of force, the binding rules for all the people within a given territory.[38] This definition includes the traditionally accepted defining elements of state (such as territory, population, and monopoly of force), but it emphasizes the aspect of the state's institutions. In other words, the state is a set of sovereign, differentiated, and autonomous institutions and those officials who run these institutions.

The process of state-building may be seen as one of establishing state institutions that are staffed by state functionaries and controlled by a centralized state leadership in order to meet challenges of political and economic development.[39] An institutional perspective on state-building may include the following propositions:

1. Changes in the economic, social, or international environment challenge the ruling elite's ability to govern and create the need of state institution-building. Certain organizational innovations or adaptations must occur, without which disorder, chaos, violence, or even war are likely to follow.[40]
2. Institutional changes do not take place automatically whenever changes in the broader socioeconomic environment call for them. Much depends upon the political elite (human agent) who may respond, or fail to respond, to changes. Because their choices or collective actions are constrained by the institutions and organizational environment in which they are operating, the political elite usually seek strategies consistent with the organizational environment to maximize their gain or at least minimize their loss.[41]

tional Factors in Political Life," *The American Political Science Review* 78 (1984), pp. 734–49. See also James G. March and Johan P. Olsen, *Rediscovering Institutions* (New York: The Free Press, 1989).

[38] According to Gianfranco Poggi, "The modern state is perhaps best seen as a complete set of institutional arrangements for rule operating through the continuous and regulated activities of individuals acting as occupants of offices." Gianfranco Poggi, *The Development of the Modern State: A Sociological Introduction* (Stanford, CA: Stanford University Press, 1978), p. 1.

[39] For an analysis of how a public administrative system evolved in several Western countries, see Joseph LaPalombara, "Values and Ideologies in the Administrative Evolution of Western Constitutional Systems," in Ralph Braibanti, ed., *Political and Administrative Development* (Durham, NC: Duke University Press, 1969), pp. 166–219.

[40] Joseph LaPalombara, "Penetration: A Crisis of Government Capacity," in Leonard Binder et al., eds., *Crises and Sequences in Political Development* (Princeton, NJ: Princeton University Press, 1971), pp. 205–07, 219. As Stephen Skowronek suggests, "State building is a process basic to any nation's political development." Skowronek, p. 6.

[41] March and Olsen, "The New Institutionalism: Organizational Factors in Political Life." For

3. The sequences of development are crucial to an understanding of institutions. Institutional innovations made by human agents at a previous stage may later become an integrated part of the institutional framework and organizational norms, thus affecting the options at the next stage. Choices made at one historical juncture may limit the range of choices to be made at subsequent junctures. Past historical experiences, especially successful ones, weigh heavily in the minds of those participants and thus disproportionately shape their perceptions of what changes may be desirable at a later time.[42]

4. As much as they influence human agents, organizational norms and practices also reflect the will and preferences of the founders. Although this is true in every organizational situation, it is particularly so in systems where institutionalization is either absent or weak.[43] In such cases, a few supreme leaders can play an extremely important role in defining and redefining the organizational environment. They are the symbols and essence of the organizations they build. In a fundamental sense, they are the organizations.[44]

In sum, state-building is a continuous process that involves not one but many stages. As the economic, social, or international environment is ever changing, demands for institutional innovations keep emerging. Yet, whether or how human agents respond to changes depends on their maximizing strategies consistent with their organizational environment and institutional configurations formed or consolidated at the earlier times.

BASIC THEME AND ARGUMENTS

The analysis in this book unfolds around a basic theme: *The Communist Party that had brought China out of civil wars has become a major obstacle to state-building in post-1949 China.* First, I try to argue that a revolutionary party is not necessarily conducive to state-building, for state-building is not the same as waging revolution. The Communist Party's winning the civil war does not necessarily mean it will be successful in rebuilding the state. How to build state

application of rational-choice theory to area studies, see Daniel Little, "Rational-Choice Models and Asian Studies," *The Journal of Asian Studies* 50, no. 1 (February 1991), pp. 35–52.

[42] A sequential model, or what is sometimes called a "branching" model, of political development can be found in Binder et al.

[43] The contrast between the institutional leadership and the personal leadership is elaborated in Neumann, 1965, pp. 44–72.

[44] Thus Lenin and Leninism stood for the Bolshevik Party in Russia, Stalin and Stalinism stood for the post-Lenin Communist regime in the Soviet Union, and Mao and Mao Zedong Thought stood for the Communist Party in China.

institutions under a single strong revolutionary party is a much more serious issue than the existing literature has recognized. Second, I intend to show that the post-1949 Chinese state-building involves conflicts between the Party organization and the state institutions. Because the Party and the state are two sets of political institutions with different organizational logic and tasks, attempts at building state institutions while strengthening the Party control over the state inevitably cause contradictions and tensions.

As a revolutionary organization surviving decades of military warfare, the Chinese Communist Party has developed a set of organizational features. Much cherished by the veteran revolutionaries, these organizational features mainly include: a revolutionary ideology that upholds the concept of a "vanguard party" and calls for continuous class struggle; the Leninist organizational principle of democratic centralism, which is supported by the political rewards and punishments; and a mobilizational style of work that translates into frequent mass campaigns and a built-in tendency against state bureaucracy.[45] After the civil war was over, the enemies suppressed, and the victory won, the revolutionary nature of the Party's political ideology, the Leninist feature of the Party organization, and the mobilizational style of the Party's work, which spelt the CCP's success before 1949, became increasingly irrelevant to the new tasks of national economic and political development. Should the revolutionary ideology continue to dominate the political institutions in China? Could the Party's organizational principle of democratic centralism be justified in peacetime? Could mass campaigns and political mobilizations serve as efficient and effective means of economic development?

As the Party elite pondered these questions, the changing social and economic environment posed serious challenges for institutional innovations. First was the changing basis of legitimacy. Unlike its imperial predecessors, the CCP as a revolutionary party could not establish its legitimacy by the heredity. Unlike bourgeois revolutionary parties in the West, the CCP did not seek to build its legitimacy on a natural order or a "social contract." Consequently, the CCP's dominance in Chinese political life has to be attributed to its success in waging a revolution. However, legitimacy based on revolutionary tradition was likely to decrease simply because of the universal Thermidorian phenomenon

---

[45] There are numerous Chinese sources of the CCP documents and propaganda handbooks that describe the official ideology, the organizational principle, and the work style of the CCP. One useful book in English on Mao's revolutionary ideology is John Bryan Starr, *Continuing the Revolution: The Political Thought of Mao* (Princeton, NJ: Princeton University Press, 1979).

that, after a long process of revolution, people grow tired of revolution.[46] A younger generation that had no direct experience of the revolution found it hard to understand, let alone appreciate, the struggles waged by the veteran revolutionaries. Thus, the Party faced a choice of whether to continue evoking the revolutionary tradition as the basis of legitimacy or to shift to a constitutional order and build up legitimacy on policy performance. As the political events in the post-1949 China suggest, this was not an easy choice for the Party to make.

Second, there was the challenge of organization. Large-scale, complex societies like China are characterized by equally complex organizations. A revolutionary movement that has embraced many social and political organizations is only the result of unusual revolutionary circumstances. After the revolutionary war, there is a natural tendency for every social and political organization to assume a certain autonomy from the Party's control. Here nothing is more crucial than the Party's relations with the state institutions. To create a favorable environment for production and economic growth, legal order and judicial process had to be established, government administration strengthened, and national defense forces regularized. This process of state-building, however, raised questions of whether the Party leaders should obey laws, whether the Party organization should render its supremacy to legislatures, whether the Party should surrender its control over the government administration, and whether the Party should turn over the command of the military to state institutions. Again this was a difficult choice for the Party to make.

Third, there was the challenge of defining an organizational purpose for a revolutionary party after the revolution. As the environment changed from war and revolution to construction, a revolutionary party organization faced the danger of either being submerged into state institutions or losing much of its relevance and thereby its dominance. If the focus of the Party's work was to shift from waging a war to managing an economy, and a party of revolution was to become a party of production, why couldn't the Party and state simply merge into one after the revolution? After all, the tasks and missions of the state and Party were supposed to become identical. If the state institutions were to be created and their capacities to be enhanced for achieving the collective goals of organizing the country and managing the economy, what was left for the Party organization to do? It was how the Party leaders responded to these three challenges that had shaped the Party–state relations in post-1949 China.

[46] Peter R. Moody, Jr., *The Politics of the Eighth Central Committee of the Communist Party of China* (Hamden, CT: The Shoe String Press, 1973).

I analyze the state-building problem along three dimensions: the legal system, government administration, and the military. My dependent variable is the development of the state institutions, and I mainly focus on three sets of factors for explanations.

    1. *Environmental factors.* I characterize the general social and economic environment where state-building had to occur as either a "revolution situation" or a "construction situation." I examine the challenges each situation posed to the political elite and see how they responded, or failed to respond, to changes in the environment.

    2. *Normative factors.* As the political elite tried to respond to changes in the environment, they looked for normative guidelines and organizational principles. So here I examine the interactions between different norms and principles involving the Party and state. Specifically, they are: (1) rule of Party or rule of law; (2) Party's unified leadership or separation of the Party from the government; and (3) army of the Party or army of the state.

    3. *Institutional factors.* Here I analyze how the Party institutions, once established, served to constrain the political elite, and to promote or impede certain organizational principles. Such institutions include the Party's Political and Legal Affairs Committee, which supervises the state legal apparatus, Party core groups in state institutions and Party work departments that parallel government administrative agencies, and the Party Central Military Commission that controls the military.

The "state" in this study refers to the Chinese legislative, judicial, administrative, and military institutions, and those who manage these institutions. More specifically, the state institutions mean the National People's Congress (NPC), and provincial people's congresses and their functional committees; the courts and procuratorates at various levels; the central and provincial government administration; and the state military command. In terms of the official Chinese classification of cadres, the state functionaries include those who work in *lifa xitong* (legislative system), *sifa xitong* (judicial system), *xingzheng xitong* (administrative system), and *jundui xitong* (military system).[47]

The "Party" in our study has several meanings. First, it may refer to all the CCP members – totaling 57 million in 1996. This all-encompassing definition, however, may not be very useful, for we can hardly judge one's political

---

[47] Those who work in the Party and mass organizations–*dangqun ganbu*–are excluded. Also excluded are those who work in enterprises and noneconomic institutions because these areas are beyond the scope of this study, although it can be argued that factory directors, company managers, and university presidents were part of the state bureaucracy, at least before the economic reform began in the 1980s.

preferences by merely identifying his or her membership in the Party. One case in point is that during numerous political campaigns, many among the accused "anti-Party elements" were Party members. Being a Party member does not tell us whether one is liberal or conservative, pro-central planning or pro-market reform. Being a Party member, however, does subject one to major constraints that a non-Party member normally does not have to deal with. This brings us to the second meaning of Party – as a set of rules of the game that underscore the Party's political ideology, organizational principle of democratic centralism, and the revolutionary tradition of guerrilla warfare and mass mobilization. Party ideology, principles, and tradition cannot be sustained without organizational backing. Thus a third meaning of Party covers a rather complicated organizational structure and those holding important positions in it. More specifically, it refers to the Party's central and provincial committees and their work departments, Party core groups in state institutions, the Politburo and its Standing Committee, and all the key members in these Party units.

Through the enforcement by various Party organizational units, Party ideology, principles, and tradition created an organizational environment where an individual Party member found himself or herself located. Those who adjusted or adapted themselves well to this organizational environment got rewarded. Official language describes them as *dangxing qiang* (strong in Party spirit). We might as well call them "Partymen." Those who remolded themselves less satisfactorily were ignored, and those who deviated were punished. Periodically, the top Party leadership felt a strong need to launch a Party rectification campaign to speed up the process of rewarding the most fit, warning the less fit and weeding out the least fit.

Generally, it is not too difficult to distinguish the Party organization in the state from the state institutions. For instance, Party core groups, as their organizational titles rightly suggest, should be viewed as part of the Party organization, although they are located in central and provincial government agencies. Making a clear distinction between Party officials and state functionaries, however, is not easy. I mainly follow two criteria. First, members of legislatures, judges and procurators, central ministers and provincial governors, and military commanders are treated as part of the state, even though the majority of them are CCP members. The assumption, as mentioned earlier, is that membership in the Party has less bearing than one's assumed responsibility and institutionally generated role on one's political preferences.

Second, when one individual concurrently holds major official posts in both the Party and government, I prefer to take the individual's primary (and sometimes exclusive) responsibility as the main factor to determine his or her institutional identity. For instance, almost as a rule in post-Mao China, a provincial governor is concurrently a deputy secretary (often ranked the first among the deputy secretaries) of the provincial Party committee. Nonetheless, I treat this individual as part of the state functionaries. It is reasonable to believe that, as the governor of a province, this individual bears primary and foremost responsibility for certain areas of work in the province. If anything goes wrong in these areas, it is the governor's fault. On the other hand, as the deputy Party secretary, this individual functions as part of a collective decision-making body that consists of several secretaries and members. The governor as a deputy Party secretary does not have to bear the sole responsibility for what goes wrong in the provincial Party organization. Thus, this individual is more likely to see his or her role primarily as the governor and act accordingly. The same holds true for military commanders who are concurrently deputy Party secretaries of the Party committees in their military units.

Undoubtedly, the post-1949 Chinese state is more dependent on the CCP and less autonomous than an ideal type of modern state would suggest. It is, however, this distance from the ideal type that allows us to analyze the progress or lack of it in Chinese state-building. Also, the extent to which the Chinese state institutions and functionaries are differentiated from, and autonomous of, the Party organization varies at different points in time. Thus we may pinpoint some best and worst moments in Chinese state-building since 1949. For instance, the Mao Zedong era is generally hostile, and the Deng Xiaoping era more favorable, to state-building. Mao's China was largely preoccupied with class struggle and political campaigns; Deng's China was directed at reforms and economic development. One was when politics finally took command; the other was when economics ultimately prevailed.

Yet, even during the Mao era, there were some promising moments of state-building, such as the adoption of the first PRC constitution in 1954, and some devastating attacks on the state institutions, such as the Anti-Rightist Campaign in 1957 and the Cultural Revolution in 1966–69. During the Deng era, state institution-building has acquired both legitimacy and urgency, yet the process is by no means smooth and noncontroversial. Expectations were raised in 1980, when Deng Xiaoping delivered a major speech on political reform and in 1987, when Zhao Ziyang presented an unprecedented package of political reform to the Thirteenth Party Congress. High expectations, however, were often met with frustrating outcomes. In other words, although the Mao and Deng eras are different in many ways, they also bear important resemblances.

Both of them started with ambitious calls for economic modernization. Both periods have raised hope for, and produced frustration, with the state-building. Most importantly, both periods give testimony to the recurring structural conflicts between the Party organization and state institutions.

STRUCTURE OF THE BOOK

In Chapter 2, I provide a historical background for understanding the state-building problem in post-1949 China. I discuss the imperial state institutions and their relevance to modern Chinese state-building. I analyze the fall of the imperial state and the rise of revolutionary parties in contemporary Chinese politics. I also discuss the relevance of the Nationalist state-building efforts and the CCP's experience in the Jiangxi/Yan'an base areas in the pre-1949 period, as it shaped the CCP's approaches to the state.

Part II of the book deals with the issue of state-building in the Mao Zedong era. I seek to find out why a successful revolutionary party had to build state institutions after the revolution and how the tensions between the growing state and expanding Party led to the Party's attack on the state. In Chapter 3, I examine the efforts to construct a legislative and judicial system, beginning with the first PRC constitution in 1954, and the Party leaders' varying responses. I particularly analyze the Anti-Rightist Campaign in 1957 as a turning point in legal development during this period. In Chapter 4, I look at the parallel development of the state administration and the Party's mechanisms of control. The Great Leap Forward movement in 1958–60 is analyzed to highlight the tensions. In Chapter 5, I discuss the army's initial efforts at military modernization. I analyze the emerging power relationship between the Chinese army and the Party and the inherent political risk for the military. In Chapter 6, I discuss the unprecedented assault on the Chinese state institutions in the early stages of the Cultural Revolution and various attempts at institutional rebuilding in the later stages. I also analyze the role of mass campaigns in recreating a revolutionary environment.

Part III of the book deals with the issue of state-building in the Deng Xiaoping era. I seek to explain why and how the post-Mao modernization and reform programs affected the process of state-building. In Chapter 7, I trace the Deng regime's move from lawlessness to rule by law, the rationale behind it, and how significant and fragile the legal reform was. I discuss the Tiananmen Square Incident in June 1989 to illustrate some legal challenges to the Party's grip on the state power. In Chapter 8, I look at some recurring problems in seeking administrative efficiency while maintaining the Party control. I also explore the difficulties of organizing the central government and its civil service, and discuss the emerging tensions between the center and provinces. In Chapter 9, I analyze the military modernization programs in the 1980s and 1990s and the continuing tensions in the Party–army relations, highlighted by the involvement of the military in the 1989 Tiananmen Square crackdown and helped by the increasing economic role and political autonomy of the army. Finally, I attempt to summarize the findings of this study and conclude by offering some perspectives on the future of the Chinese state.

2

Where Did the Chinese State Come from?

STATE institutions are not built overnight, nor does a state come from nowhere. Scholars of international relations often trace the beginning of the modern state to 1648 when the Peace of Westphalia began the end of the Holy Roman Empire. In England, the year 1648 witnessed the climax of the civil war between the king and Parliament, an event that signified the modern institution-building in England. In France, the 1789 Revolution represented a direct challenge by the Third Estate in the National Assembly to King Louis XVI's power and his great great-grandfather's claim, "L'état, c'est moi!" France since then has experienced several alternations between empires and republics, coupled with revolutions and wars. The American state-building has also gone through what Stephen Skowronek describes as "patchwork" during 1877–1900 and as "reconstruction" during 1900–20.[1] All this suggests that state-building is a long and often bloody process.[2]

China came late to this process of state-building. In the 1640s, the Manchu rulers of the Qing dynasty had just begun their reign of more than two centuries in China. By the late eighteenth century, the Qianlong emperor, while reaching the end of his reign, was still capable of waging wars against Vietnam and Nepal and of suppressing a series of rebellions at home.[3] Since the mid-nineteenth century, however, China had entered a long period of political chaos, national disintegration, foreign invasion, and civil wars. Indeed, in view

---

[1] Stephen Skowronek, *Building a New American State: The Expansion of National Administrative Capacities 1877–1920* (New York: Cambridge University Press, 1982).

[2] For the role of violence and war in state formation in Western Europe, see Charles Tilly, "Revolutions and Collective Violence," in Fred I. Greenstein and Nelson W. Polsby, eds., *Handbook of Political Science,* vol. 3 (Reading, MA: Addison-Wesley, 1975), pp. 483–556; and Charles Tilly, ed., *The Formation of National States in Western Europe* (Princeton, NJ: Princeton University Press, 1975).

[3] Jonathan D. Spence, *The Search for Modern China* (New York: W. W. Norton & Company, 1990), pp. 110–16.

of the difficulties of state formation in other countries, there is no reason to believe that the modern Chinese state-building could be easy.

In this chapter, I try to put the issue of the post-1949 Chinese state-building in a historical perspective. I am mainly interested in the question, "Where did the Chinese state come from?" Specifically, I address the questions of whether the statist tradition of imperial China facilitated the state-building in modern times, whether the post-1949 state was a natural result of the revolutionary process in the first half of the twentieth century, and what might be the impact of the pre-1949 Nationalist regime and the CCP's base areas on the post-1949 state-building. The purpose here is not to carry out the impossible mission of presenting the political history of China in one chapter, but to bring attention to the historical background of the post-1949 state-building.

THE IMPERIAL TRADITION OF CHINA

To say that tradition continues is one thing and to argue that tradition regenerates is another. Before we can answer the question of whether the assumed strong statist tradition of imperial China is the womb for the modern Chinese state, we need to take a look at the imperial institutions. Basically, the Chinese imperial rule was constructed upon three main pillars: emperor, ruling ideology, and bureaucracy.[4] Connecting the three pillars was the system of civil service examination on Confucian moral principles, through which the emperors recruited their officials. Claiming to be the "Son of Heaven," the emperor was the center of all powers. His rule was justified by the official ideology – Confucianism – which began as a means for bringing social order out of chaos. Confucian ideology provided the basis of legitimacy and the instrument of rule for the imperial system. The Chinese empire was managed by a bureaucracy often seen as one of the most thoroughly developed and sophisticated in the world.

Although the date of birth of the imperial statehood in China remains debatable, John Fairbank held the view that the central authority in China emerged during the Xia dynasty (2200–1750 B.C.).[5] The absolute power of the emperor, however, was not established until one of the Warring States, the Qin,

---

[4] In trying to understand the Chinese imperial institutions, I benefited greatly from Professor Roderick MacFarquhar's lectures while working as his teaching assistant for the Harvard College Core Course: "The Chinese Cultural Revolution" in 1990–91.

[5] John King Fairbank, *China: A New History* (Cambridge, MA: The Belknap Press of Harvard University Press, 1992), pp. 31–9.

defeated its rivalries and unified China in 221 B.C. The king of the Qin dynasty, under the self-proclaimed title of First Emperor, quickly and ruthlessly imposed upon his empire a centralized government system managed by a bureaucracy consisting of centrally appointed civil governors, military commanders, and county magistrates.[6]

With a despotic rule and severe punishments following the doctrine of Legalism, the First Emperor contributed as much to the fall as to the rise of his dynasty. The emperor of the succeeding Han dynasty (206 B.C.–220 A.D.) subsequently turned to the teachings of Confucius that prescribed a "government by the good," in which the emperor, as the Son of Heaven, should strive to become a sage king and set a model of virtue for his subjects, and the officials should assume moral responsibility.[7] The Han emperor's amalgamation of the Legalist "rule by force" and Confucian "rule by virtue" produced what Fairbank called "Imperial Confucianism."[8]

The official status of Confucianism was not uncontested. During the next five hundred years or so, as different dynasties inevitably rose and fell, the teachings and institutions of Buddhism and Daoism introduced alternatives to Confucianism. It was only during the Song dynasty (960–1279 A.D.) that Confucianism, now transformed through reinterpretations by the neo-Confucian scholars, became the established ideology of the state, thanks to no small extent to the invention of printing technology, mushrooming land-granting schools, and the institutionalization of the civil service examination as a major source of official recruitment.[9] The examination system, being a crucial link between the emperor and bureaucrats, and between the imperial center and local gentry, ultimately became a mechanism of "political reproduction" that served to prolong the triangular system of the emperor, Confucian ideology, and bureaucracy.[10]

In imperial China, there was no clear distinction between the state and society, nor any clear boundary separating the spheres of "public" and "private." In many ways, the state was like an extended family, and the family was

---

[6] Ibid., p. 56.

[7] Cheng F. Zhang, "Public Administration in China," in Miriam K. Mills and Stuart S. Nagel, eds., *Public Administration in China* (Westport, CT: Greenwood Press, 1993), pp. 4–5.

[8] Fairbank, 1992, p. 62.

[9] Ibid., pp. 93–101.

[10] For an analysis of the reproductive functions of the imperial civil service system, see Benjamin A. Elman, "Political, Social, and Cultural Reproduction via Civil Service Examinations in Late Imperial China," *The Journal of Asian Studies* 50, no. 1 (February 1991), pp. 7–28.

like a small state. What was taught and practiced in the family could be immediately applied to managing state affairs. The relationship between the ruler and his subjects was paternalistic, similar to the one between parents and their children. As in a family, where children listened and father or grandfather dictated, subjects must obey and revere the emperor. A display of disloyalty to the emperor or unfiliality to parents was equally regarded as the most serious crime one could possibly commit. The emperor had his obligations as well. According to Confucian teachings, the emperor must take good care of his people. A breach of this obligation could result in a termination of the paternalistic relationship and justify the overthrow of the ruler. Whereas Aristotle, the ancient Greek philosopher, suggested rule in common interest or in self-interest as a way to distinguish between a monarch and a tyrant, Confucian scholars drew the line between a benevolent ruler and a tyrant on the basis of whether the emperor fulfilled his parental obligations.

Bureaucrats in imperial China were the servants of the emperor rather than the servants of the public. When the Confucian state institutions were initially established during the Han dynasty, the administrative department had managed the affairs of both the imperial family and the state. It was not until the Sui (589–618 A.D.) and Tang (618–907 A.D.) dynasties that these two functions were differentiated.[11] But because the emperor was the head of the bureaucracy (outer court) as well as of the imperial household (inner court), a clear distinction between these two functions was often difficult to make. It was not uncommon for the bureaucrats to intervene in the emperor's family business, nor was it rare for the emperor's wives, concubines, relatives, and eunuchs to interfere in state affairs. Hence one could argue that the Chinese imperial state was like a "family-state" and the Chinese term for state – *Guojia* – indeed consists of two characters, *Guo* (state) and *Jia* (family).

Imperial China depended on a system of ethical rather than legal codes. Contrary to the idea of original sin embedded in Christian tradition in the West and in Legalist philosophy in China, Confucianism stressed that men were born to be good and essentially educable. Thus it was the responsibility of emperors and officials to set moral examples and teach their subjects virtues and proper behavior. There should be a government by goodness and a rule of benevolence. If everyone behaved properly according to Confucian moral principles, harmony would be achieved within family and society, and all would be calm

---

[11] Fairbank, 1992, p. 78.

under heaven. Laws, often seen as instruments of punishment and signs of failed moral teaching, were of much less importance. The concepts of citizenship, individual rights, rule of law, and constitutional order also found little chance to come into bloom.

Since the Chinese imperial state was an empire of Confucian culture, its political meaning was ambiguous at best. In the Chinese language, the character *Guo* could refer to "clan," "king," "principalities," "society," "nation," and "state" or "kings," "princes," "dukes," "ministers," and "emperors."[12] Conversely, there are many alternative terms to refer to the imperial state, such as *Tianxia* (under heaven), *Sheji* (the god of the land), *Huangshi* (imperial family), and *Chaoting* (imperial court). The ambiguity of the Chinese state as reflected in the language continues into contemporary China where the identity of the state is often confused with those of "nation," "country," or "regime."[13] For instance, *Zhongguo* (China or Middle Kingdom) could refer to the People's Republic of China, mainland China, mainland China plus Taiwan and Hong Kong, or the Chinese nation. The exact meaning of the Chinese state has remained obscure.

Chinese dynasties were no strangers to such crises as sudden deaths of emperors, peasant uprisings, and alien conquests, but the imperial rule had managed to continue even though the imperial rulers had changed. For instance, after rebellious peasant leaders succeeded in bringing down the old regime and established their new dynasty, more often than not, they revived the political structures of the old dynasty.[14] Even Mongol and Manchu conquerors found it necessary to rely on the Chinese political system to consolidate their dynasties.[15]

Of course, this brief discussion of a system that was thousands of years in the making can hardly do any justice to its subtleties and complexities. Over centuries, the imperial system had undergone many changes. Here the Qing Dynasty whose political legacy continues to be relevant in the twentieth century deserves some special attention. The Manchus defeated the Chinese Ming

---

[12] Yue Qingping, *Jiaguo jiegou yu zhongguoren* (Family-State Structure and the Chinese) (Hong Kong: Zhonghua shuju, 1989), p. 26.

[13] For a recent study of the Chinese identity crisis, see Lowell Dittmer and Samuel S. Kim, eds., *China's Quest for National Identity* (Ithaca, NY: Cornell University Press, 1993).

[14] John King Fairbank, *The United States and China,* 4th and enlarged edition (Cambridge, MA: Harvard University Press, 1983), pp. 80–105.

[15] Ibid.

dynasty on horseback, but they quickly supplemented their military power with the Confucian political system and indeed copied many institutions of the previous Chinese dynasties.[16] The consolidated Qing central government consisted of three categories of agencies: Principal Offices that included the Grand Secretariat, the Grand Council, and the Six Boards (Personnel, Revenue, Rites, War, Punishments, and Public Works) and constituted the essential organs of the central government; Coordinate Offices that included such agencies as the Censorate, the Court of Judicature and Revision, the Office of Transmission, and the Hanlin Academy; and Imperial Departments such as the Imperial Household, the Court of State Ceremonial, the Imperial Medial Department, and the Banqueting Court.[17]

Although adapting to the Chinese form of government, the Manchu rulers introduced several major institutional innovations. First, they adopted a "device of synarchy" (joint administration by two or more parties), whereby Manchus and Chinese were jointly appointed to be the heads of the Six Boards of the central government and to be governors-general and governors, respectively, in the provinces.[18] Second, the Qing legal system, although still subordinate to morality, was more sophisticated and elaborate. With 436 main statutes and 1,900 substatutes, the great Qing code was believed to contain specific penalties for specific crimes.[19] In addition to the system of criminal law, a system of administrative law was also developed to make the Qing bureaucracy functional.[20] Qing rulers also improved the Ming system of personnel evaluation by setting up a system of rewards and punishments directly related to an official's performance, particularly in tax collection and criminal prosecution.[21] Third, to minimize the danger of usurpation of power by the inner court, a new institution – the Imperial Household Department – was established to manage the imperial family's domestic affairs, income, and prop-

---

[16] Susan Naquin and Evelyn Rawski, *Chinese Society in the Eighteenth Century* (New Haven, CT: Yale University, 1987), p. 5.

[17] Immanuel C. Y. Hsü, *The Rise of Modern China,* 4th edition (New York: Oxford University Press, 1990), pp. 47–55.

[18] Fairbank, 1992, pp. 148–49.

[19] Ibid., pp. 183–86.

[20] For an excellent study of the subject, see Thomas A. Metzger, *The Internal Organization of Ch'ing Bureaucracy: Legal, Normative, and Communication Aspects* (Cambridge, MA: Harvard University Press, 1973).

[21] Naquin and Rawski, p. 9.

erty.[22] Fourth, while making the imperial palace affairs relatively institutional-ized, the Qing emperors struggled to escape from the bureaucratic procedure of the outer court.[23] The Grand Secretariat, an institution the Qing inherited from the Ming dynasty, soon became ill suited for the Qing emperors. Kangxi was known for relying on his personal secretaries in the Imperial Study. Yongzheng went further and set up in 1729 a secret Office of Military Finance, which later evolved to replace the Grand Secretariat as "the most important organ in the central government," known as the Grand Council.[24] Fifth, the Qing emperors, particularly Kangxi, Yongzheng, and Qianlong, often reviewed and com-mented on a tremendous amount of documents in order to keep themselves informed and bureaucrats under check. To facilitate the emperor's work, the Office of Transmission was assigned to handle the "routine memorial" from the provincial governments while the Chancery of Memorials was authorized to handle special "palace memorials" from senior civil and military officials.[25]

Overall, however, the institutional innovations during the Qing dynasty were not aimed at making the government "a rational institution."[26] Dual appoint-ments, secret channels of information and reports, and expansion of the inner court agencies were primarily designed to make the imperial bureaucracy more controllable than efficient and to help the emperor maintain his absolute per-sonal rule. Whereas the process of state formation in the West had generally proceeded through city-states, empires, principalities, and nation-states, the political structure in China had remained dynastic. Whereas the English in the seventeenth century and French in the eighteenth century were fighting wars over the power of parliament versus the monarchy and over republics versus empires, the political struggles in China were over who would be the legitimate supreme ruler, *not* what political institutions should be the supreme organs of power. It therefore remains highly arguable whether the often-assumed statist tradition of China carries within itself the seeds of a modern state.

[22] Ibid., p. 7; see also Frederic Wakeman, Jr., *The Fall of Imperial China* (New York: The Free Press, 1975). pp. 93–4.

[23] Fairbank, 1992, pp. 150–1.

[24] Hsü, p. 51. For a detailed study of the origin and functions of the Grand Council, see Beatrice S. Bartlett, *Monarchs and Ministers: The Grand Council in Mid-Ch'ing China, 1723–1820* (Berkeley: University of California Press, 1991). See also Wakeman, pp. 98–100.

[25] Hsü, pp. 54–5.

[26] Ch'ien Mu, *Traditional Government in Imperial China: A Critical Analysis,* translated by Chün-tu Hsüeh and George O. Totten (Hong Kong: The Chinese University Press, 1982), pp. 126–32.

FALL OF THE IMPERIAL STATE AND RISE OF THE REVOLUTIONARY PARTY

The Chinese search for a modern state began in the nineteenth century when two major sources of disorder overwhelmed the imperial institutions: domestic disintegration and foreign invasion. Between the eighteenth and nineteenth centuries, Chinese population had doubled and redoubled.[27] The problem of population explosion created tremendous pressure on the limited farm land to provide a sufficient food supply. For economic, religious, or ethnic reasons, peasant uprisings began to erupt. Moreover, beginning with the Opium War of 1839–42, the imperial army suffered a series of defeats at the hands of the industrial powers of the West. The image of a shattering imperial dynasty accelerated rebellion and dissolution within China, exemplified by the Taiping Rebellion of 1851–64 that nearly toppled the Qing dynasty.[28]

Reforms and Failures

Shocked by the massive peasant rebellions and humiliated by the Western powers, the Qing rulers sought various solutions to domestic crisis and foreign threat, focusing their initial efforts on developing military technology. During the Self-Strengthening Movement of 1861–95, the Qing reformers tried to rescue the imperial dynasty without fundamentally changing the political structure. These efforts, however, failed terribly, as manifested in another defeat in 1894–95, this time at the hands of the neighboring Japanese who had adopted a more positive attitude toward the challenge from the West. During the next round of reform, institutional change rather than technical innovation became the focus. Persuaded by his scholar advisers, the young Guangxu emperor went so far as to consider forming a parliament during the "Hundred Days" Reform of 1898.[29] In the end, though, the proposed institutional reforms proved to be too much for the conservatives, who abruptly aborted the reform program by placing the young emperor under house arrest and beheading six of his top advisers.

---

[27] Fairbank, 1992, p. 169.

[28] Ibid., p. 206.

[29] The need for institutional reform was best expressed by Kang Youwei, the Guangxu emperor'stop adviser. When challenged in January 1898 by high officials who insisted: "The institutions inherited from the ancestors cannot be changed," Kang replied: "We cannot preserve the realm of the ancestors. What is the use of their institutions?" Fairbank, 1987, p. 134.

Nevertheless, facing the harsh reality of continuing decline of the imperial power, the conservative rulers were forced within a decade to realize that institutional change was critically needed. They had to revive the reform program that was aborted earlier and to tolerate the Constitutional Movement in 1905–6. Among the most significant changes was the abolition of the civil service examination system in 1905, which virtually cut off the connections among the emperor, the ruling ideology, and the official gentry.[30]

The reform measures in the first decade of this century were aimed at replacing dynastic rule with a new form of government. This time the imperial rulers hoped to save themselves, if not "the institutions inherited from the ancestors," by experimenting with some new institutional adaptations. Perhaps they believed that reforms similar to the Meiji Restoration in Japan might reinvigorate the dying regime, but a revolution was already imminent, thanks to those Chinese students who had returned from abroad with ideas so devastating to the imperial rule. As the old regime lay dying, a once unified China disintegrated into an institutional vacuum.

The unprecedented institutional crisis in the beginning of the twentieth century hastened the Chinese search for alternative means of reorganizing China.[31] Since the last dynasty collapsed, construction of a modern Chinese state had been the goal shared by many Chinese modernizers. For them, this lofty goal meant that China could one day stand in the world community on an equal footing with other member states. It meant a strong and prosperous nation under a unified government. In 1912, Liang Qichao, one of the most influential writers at the time, so warned his countrymen: "Historically, China had been a cultural empire rather than a sovereign state; now it was imperative that she transform herself into a modern state with a complex government structure, in order to survive in an age of power politics."[32]

If the first two decades of this century saw China in chaos, they also produced a "free" intellectual environment. A country in a vacuum of state power

---

[30] It is not surprising that since then China has seen a rapid increase in the number of students going abroad to study.

[31] Some most influential figures in this search include: Liang Qichao, Yen Fu, and Zhang Binglin. See Chang Hao, *Liang Chi'-ch'ao and Intellectual Transition in China, 1890–1907* (Cambridge, MA: Harvard University Press, 1971); Benjamin I. Schwartz, *In Search of Wealth and Power: Yen Fu and the West* (Cambridge, MA: The Belknap Press of Harvard University Press, 1964); and Wong Young-tsu, *Search for Modern Nationalism: Zhang Binglin and Revolutionary China, 1869–1936* (New York: Oxford University Press, 1989).

[32] Chester C. Tan, *Chinese Political Thought in the 20th Century* (Newton Abbot: David & Charles, 1971), p. 32.

was paradoxically full of new ideas and new experiments. From Social Darwinism to Kropotkin's anarchism to socialism, and from autocracy to democracy to dictatorship and to democratic dictatorship, Chinese scholars debated almost every Western concept that was known to them.[33] If the Chinese nation was in total crisis, Chinese intellectuals were in total hunger for solutions.[34] Some supported a revived monarchy, and others sought a constitutional system of the American type. Some preferred a parliamentary system, whereas others favored a presidential system. Within a decade or two, China in search of a modern state had experienced a remarkable shift of attention from monarchy to presidency, to parliament, and to revolutionary party.

Formation of the KMT and CCP

China between 1912 and 1921 witnessed the formation of the two largest parties in modern Chinese history. The Chinese Nationalist Party, or Kuomintang (KMT), was formed in 1912 as a coalition of five factions within the Alliance Society that overthrew the Qing dynasty. The Chinese Communist Party (CCP) came into existence nine years later. It was only in the wake of the 1917 Bolshevik Revolution in Russia that the ideas of Karl Marx and Lenin began to appeal to the educated Chinese.[35]

Unfortunately, the Chinese parties stepped into the arena of politics when the newly installed constitutional framework was falling apart. In the 1910s and 1920s, efforts to establish a national government under a Western-style parliamentary system were aborted by fierce fighting among politically ambitious warlords.[36] Without an institutionalized political order, Chinese party

---

[33] Chi Wen-shun, *Ideological Conflicts in Modern China: Democracy and Authoritarianism* (New Brunswick: Translation Books, 1986).

[34] One reflection of the Chinese intellectuals' desperation is their total negation of the Chinese traditional culture. See Lin Yu-sheng, *The Crisis of Chinese Consciousness: Radical Antitraditionalism in the May Fourth Era* (Madison: University of Wisconsin Press, 1979).

[35] Thanks to the guidance from Gregory Voitinsky, a representative from the Communist International to China, Communist groups were formed in Peking, Canton, Shanghai, and Hunan in 1920–1. Benjamin I. Schwartz, *Chinese Communism and the Rise of Mao* (Cambridge, MA: Harvard University Press, 1951), pp. 32–4.

[36] For Chinese warlord politics, see Chi Hsi-sheng, *Warlord Politics in China, 1916–1928* (Stanford, CA: Stanford University Press, 1976); Jerome Ch'en, *The Military-Gentry Coalition: China Under the Warlords* (Toronto: University of Toronto–York University, Joint Centre on Modern East Asia, 1979).

politics quickly turned into a deadly game.[37] By the spring of 1927, with help from the Soviet Union and the Chinese Communists, the KMT had defeated the warlords during the Northern Expedition. After the victory, however, the KMT turned its back on its former ally and used military means to establish a single-party dictatorship.[38] Even though the Nationalists and the Communists had cooperated in the war against the warlords and both of them had been influenced by the same Leninist principle of party-building, the two parties were thereafter engaged in political and military struggles for twenty-eight years. Successive wars and political divisions that had plagued the nation created insurmountable difficulties to any serious attempt at state-building.

The Chinese dream of building a modern state seemed to have come true when Mao Zedong, the chairman of the Communist Party, proclaimed in Tiananmen Square in October 1949 that the People's Republic of China (PRC) was founded. Although how exactly the CCP won and the KMT lost the mainland is still a matter of dispute and is subject to many interpretations,[39] there is no doubt that by the 1950s the CCP had become the only organizational force in China. With the victory of the Communists, a new political order seemed to be emerging, in which the Party organization became the main mechanism of control. For millions of Chinese, a new China was born. Gone were the old days when their country was humiliated by military powers from abroad and ruined by political divisions at home. At last China could now hope to become a strong and prosperous nation in the world.

---

[37] For party politics in this period, see George T. Yu, *Party Politics in Republican China: The Kuomintang, 1912–1924* (Berkeley: University of California Press, 1966). For political assassinations in this period, see K. S. Liew, *Struggle for Democracy: Sung Chiao-jen and the 1911 Chinese Revolution* (Berkeley: University of California Press, 1971).

[38] Among the best studies of the KMT regime during the 1930s are Tien Hung-mao, *Government and Politics in Kuomintang China, 1927–1937* (Stanford, CA: Stanford University Press, 1972), and Lloyd F. Eastman, *The Abortive Revolution: China Under National Rule, 1927–1937* (Cambridge, MA: Harvard University Press, 1990).

[39] Various interpretations of the CCP's success and the KMT's failure on the mainland before 1949 can be found, for example, in Chalmers A. Johnson, *Peasant Nationalism and Communist Power; The Emergence of Revolutionary China* (Stanford, CA: Stanford University Press, 1962); Mark Selden, *The Yenan Way in Revolutionary China* (Cambridge, MA: Harvard University Press, 1971); Tetsuya Kataoka, *Resistance and Revolution in China: The Communists and the Second United Front* (Berkeley: University of California Press, 1974); Chen Yung-fa, *Making Revolution: The Communist Movement in Eastern and Central China, 1937–1945* (Berkeley: University of California Press, 1986); and Steven I. Levine, *Anvil of Victory: The Communist Revolution in Manchuria, 1945–1948* (New York: Columbia University Press, 1987).

Given the organizational strength of the CCP, the new regime quickly established its control over the country. Compared with the pre-1949 KMT state that was beset by divisions and wars or with many Third World states where political order was fragile, government institutions weak, and military coups frequent, the Chinese Communist regime appeared capable of maintaining stability and order.[40] In the early 1950s, the CCP regime seemed to have managed several crises simultaneously.[41] With the unification of the mainland and the end to foreign domination of China, the CCP offered the Chinese people a new political identity. The final victory after a long and difficult revolution gave the new regime sufficient legitimacy. With the expansion of the CCP organizational units, the Party facilitated political integration. Land reform and mass political campaigns provided ample opportunity for poor peasants to participate in politics. The CCP also adopted policies aimed at promoting an egalitarian distribution of the national wealth.

Although there is no question that the CCP had taken over the mainland by the 1950s, it is far from clear whether a new state had indeed emerged as a result of the revolution. In the early 1950s, however, few in China could have had the courage or foresight to question whether the new revolutionary regime of the CCP represented a proper form of modern Chinese state. With the advance of the revolutionary armies, the CCP organization expanded into various sectors of the society. Everywhere, war-hardened CCP cadres were sent to take over administration and fill key positions in the newly set up state agencies. As the new rulers quickly consolidated their control over mainland China, everyone had to learn to accept the Party leadership, willingly or otherwise. Besides, nationalist pride and patriotic feeling drove the Chinese, regardless of their ideological preferences, to look to the CCP for the realization of long-sought national goals of becoming prosperous and strong. For many who lived far away from the center, it was not a modern state that they cared about. What really mattered was that by now there was a new "emperor" in the capital city and a new leader in their village. The rulers of China had changed and that was it. Political traditions had taught people to pay respect to authority no

---

[40] Joel S. Migdal, *Strong Societies and Weak States: State–Society Relations and State Capacities in the Third World* (Princeton, NJ: Princeton University Press, 1988).

[41] Comparative political scientists have generally identified five crises of political development, namely, identity, legitimacy, participation, distribution, and penetration. For a discussion of these crises, see Leonard Binder et al., eds., *Crises and Sequences in Political Development* (Princeton, NJ: Princeton University Press, 1971).

matter who exercised it and to show loyalty to leaders no matter what they were called.

Yet, before long, the CCP's rule had become one of the most controversial issues. Those who dared to speak out in 1957 and consequently suffered did not assume that a strong Communist Party organization meant a strong state.[42] But before we begin to deconstruct the party-state and to suggest that a strong revolutionary party organization might turn out to be a major obstacle to state-building after the revolution, we need to take a look at how the political situation in pre-1949 China shaped the post-1949 state-building.

NANJING, JIANGXI, OR YAN'AN

While there is not much debate about Mao Zedong arriving in Beijing (Peking) in September 1949 as the ultimate victor of the Chinese civil war, there have been different interpretations as to where Mao's road to Beijing began. Some researchers stress the continuity rather than the breakaway between the pre- and post-1949 Chinese states and argue that both the successes and failures of the KMT regime in Nanjing (1928–37) have laid down the foundation for the post-1949 state-building. Others prefer to put more emphasis on the CCP's experience in managing its base area governments such as the Jiangxi Soviet in 1931–34 and Yan'an during the Anti-Japanese War. In other words, Mao's road to Beijing could begin in Nanjing, Jiangxi, or Yan'an.

The CCP Rebels and the KMT Regime

Since its founding in 1921, the CCP had been a rebellious political force. It was an antisystem party, a party against the existing state. Dictated by the Party's revolutionary goals, the 1921 Party constitution set strict restrictions on Party members participating in the existing state bureaucracy: "Except in cases of legal necessity or with special permission from the Party, Party members are not allowed to become members of the government or members of the parliament, except as soldiers, policemen, and office workers."[43] After the CCP–KMT alliance against the warlords was strangled by Chiang Kai-shek's decision to suppress the Communists in April 1927, the CCP Politburo soon set

---

[42] This is discussed in detail in Chapter 3 of this book.

[43] *Zhongguo gongchandang dangwu gongzuo dacidian* (Dictionary of Chinese Communist Party Work) (Beijing: Zhongyang dangxiao chubanshe, 1990), p. 728.

even tougher restrictions: "Without permission from the Party, no Party member is allowed to assume any position in the state organs."[44]

Despite the CCP's antistate approach, some analysts have found a lot in common between the KMT and CCP regimes. Robert E. Bedeski suggests that the KMT's success in assembling a unified military force, its partially successful efforts at national political integration under a party dictatorship, and its failure to establish a constitutional government "created an incomplete set of political structures which served as a 'rough draft' for the PRC."[45] Others have pointed to the same Leninist feature of the Party organization, political control of the army, censorship over culture and the press, resort to the appeals of nationalism and anti-imperialism, establishment of a national educational system, and economic planning, as examples of the continuities between the two antagonistic regimes. The PRC was thus built on the foundations of the KMT regime.[46]

If we add a little order to this list of examples, we may find that most of the continuities fall into three categories: the establishment of a single-party rule, national unification, and implementation of economic and social programs. In these areas, similarities and continuities do appear to be striking. But in terms of how to organize national and provincial legislatures, how to establish a legal system, how to build an effective government administration, and how to define the power relations between the center and localities, we are much less convinced that the continuity does exist.[47]

Jiangxi/Yan'an Experience

Having adopted a hostile stance toward the KMT regime, various Communist forces in China had worked to establish their own "state" within the existing state. The most analyzed cases are the Chinese Soviet Republic in the rural Jiangxi in 1931–4 and the united front government in the CCP-controlled Yan'an area during the Anti-Japanese War of 1937–45. Although these CCP

---

[44] Ibid., p. 740.

[45] Robert E. Bedeski, *State-Building in Modern China: The Kuomintang in the Prewar Period* (Berkeley: Institute of East Asian Studies, University of California, 1981), p. ix.

[46] Joseph W. Esherick, "Ten These on the Chinese Revolution," *Modern China* 21, no. 1 (January 1995), pp. 47–8.

[47] For instance, Kevin O'Brien finds little institutional continuity between the KMT's Legislative Yuan and the National Assembly and the CCP's National People's Congress. See Kevin J. O'Brien, *Reform Without Liberalization : China's National People's Congress and the Politics of Institutional Change* (New York: Cambridge University Press, 1990), pp. 17–20.

regimes were on a small scale and located in the poor countryside, they nevertheless provided the Communists with direct experience in government administration.

The Jiangxi Soviet Republic afforded the Communists the first opportunity to test their ability to govern. It was during this period that the CCP convened two National Congresses of the Soviet Republic, passed a few laws, organized elections, and established the government administration, thereby formally creating a state of its own.[48] As Derek J. Waller suggests, the Jiangxi Soviet Republic of 1931 was symbolically important in that it represented an "alternative way" to the existing state. The first Soviet Republic in China was also organizationally important because it was the only case in CCP history in which Mao Zedong deliberately used the Jiangxi Soviet Republic to counterbalance his opponents who were in control of the Party organization.[49] It may be the first example of "state against Party," but it surely is not the last one, in view of the continuing tensions between the Party organization and state institutions after 1949. The Jiangxi Soviet Republic, however, did not last long, and Mao's dominance of it was even shorter. In less than two years after the First National Congress in 1931, Mao lost effective control over the government to his opponents in the Party leadership.[50] The brief institution-building experience during the Jiangxi Soviet period therefore must have a very limited impact on the post-1949 state-building.

In examining the structures and processes of the base areas of the Jiangxi Soviet, Ilpyong J. Kim finds some concepts and organizational techniques more continuous and enduring, namely, Mao's idea of "mass line" and the Party's work style of mass mobilization.[51] Mark Selden's now classic study of the "Yan'an Way" certainly confirms this organizational continuity. Selden finds the CCP's social and economic programs in the Yan'an period populist and participatory.[52] Kenneth Lieberthal summarizes the "Yan'an complex" as consisting of elements of decentralized rule, ideological work, leadership by generalists, mass line, and egalitarianism, which was different from the Soviet centralized, functionally specialized, hierarchical, and command-oriented sys-

---

[48] Derek J. Waller, *The Kiangsi Soviet Republic: Mao and the National Congresses of 1931 and 1934* (Berkeley: Center for Chinese Studies, University of California, 1973).

[49] Ibid., p. 50.

[50] Ibid., p. 113.

[51] Ilpyong J. Kim, *The Politics of Chinese Communism, Kiangsi under the Soviets* (Berkeley: University of California Press, 1973).

[52] Selden, 1971.

tem.[53] The Yan'an style of mobilizational politics had its terrible consequences. The Party Rectification campaign in 1942–3 often employed the methods of false accusations, torture, and forced confession.[54] The dark side of the Yan'an Way included "political scapegoating, personality cult, repression, and manipulation."[55]

What we have seen here was the maturing of a revolutionary party organization that relentlessly pursued its ideological purity, with an organizational principle of democratic centralism supported by iron discipline and with a mobilizational style of work that frequently called for mass campaigns. Furthermore, through the years of the Jiangxi Soviet and Yan'an, certain organizational principles were gradually established concerning the relationship between the CCP and its own government. In November 1928, when discussing the relations between the Party and the Communist-led government in the base areas, Mao criticized the practice of the Party directly interfering in the work of the government.

> The Party enjoys immense prestige and authority among the masses, the government much less. The reason is that for the sake of convenience the Party handles many things directly and brushes aside the government. There are many such instances. . . . From now on the Party must carry out its task of giving leadership to the government; with the exception of propaganda, the Party's policies and measures it recommends must be carried out through the government organizations. The Kuomintang's wrong practice of directly imposing orders on the government must be avoided.[56]

Mao's position was formalized by the CCP Politburo in a document issued in September 1942, which laid out the two principles concerning the Party–state relations that largely constituted the CCP's answers to the similar problems in the post-1949 period:

1. The Party committee is the highest leading organ, and it should exercise a unified leadership over all the other organizations, including government, army, and mass organizations.

[53] Kenneth Lieberthal, *Governing China: From Revolution Through Reform* (New York: W. W. Norton & Company, 1995), p. 51.
[54] Ibid.
[55] Mark Selden, "Yan'an Communism Reconsidered," *Modern China* 21; no. 1 (January 1985), pp. 8–44.
[56] Mao, 1965, vol. 1, p. 92.

2. The Party leadership means that the Party should decide on policies, but not directly interfere in, or take care of, every matter that is within the jurisdiction of the government.[57]

It is fair to say that neither stories of success nor tales of terror of the Jiangxi Soviet and Yan'an period could establish the premise that a modern Chinese state originated in the mountains of Jiangxi or caves of Yan'an. The CCP's experience in Jiangxi and Yan'an was, however, relevant because it greatly conditioned the CCP elite's mindset and limited their choices of institutional innovation after 1949. The "Return to Jinggang Mountain" or "Return to Yan'an" impulse of Mao and other veteran revolutionaries constrained their perspectives as they faced new challenges in a changing environment. Indeed, it was precisely the success of Mao's politics of campaigns in the Yan'an period that created difficulties to the state institution-building after 1949.

PREMATURE BIRTH OF THE PRC STATE

Whether it was Nanjing, Jiangxi, or Yan'an that guided Mao's road to Beijing, ultimately it was the CCP's victory on the battlefield that paved the way. In retrospect, Mao's proclamation of the new Chinese state in 1949 was hasty under the circumstances. As of October 1, half of China was yet to be taken over by the People's Liberation Army (PLA), including such important areas in south and southwest China as Guangdong, Guangxi, Fujian, Yunnan, Guizhou, Sichuan, Hainan, and Xinjiang.[58] Moreover, although the Communist troops had entered Nanjing, Chiang Kai-shek and his troops had yet to retreat to Taiwan. In many parts of the country, the war went on. Furthermore, at the time Mao proclaimed the founding of the PRC in Tiananmen Square, the new central government was barely functioning. It was on October 19, 1949, that the central government ministers were appointed and on October 21 that the Government Administrative Council (GAC) — the executive branch of the central government — was formed.[59] At the regional, provincial, and local

---

[57] *Dangshi jiaoxue cankao zhiliao* (Reference Materials for Teaching the CCP History), vol. 3 (Beijing: Renmin chubanshe, 1979), p. 29.

[58] The KMT forces in Xinjiang negotiated a settlement with the CCP and declared a peaceful insurrection on September 25, 1949. The PLA troops did not begin to enter Xinjiang until October 12, 1949.

[59] Some Chinese scholars claim that the newly established national government did not begin to function until December 1949. Xiao Xiaoqin and Wang Youqiao, eds., *Zhonghua renmin gongheguo sishi nian* (Forty Years of the People's Republic of China) (Beijing: Beijing shifan xueyuan chubanshe, 1990), p. 8.

levels, the task of establishing an administrative control was even tougher because of the vast size of China. It took more than one year after the founding of the PRC to set up all the governments in the six administrative regions and thirty-two provinces (including administrative districts equivalent to a province). It took two more years to complete the process of organizing the new government administration in 160 cities, 2,174 counties (including administrative units equivalent to a county), and about 280,000 *xiang*.[60]

The premature decision to proclaim the founding of a new Chinese state was prompted by the fact that in 1949 the KMT regime collapsed much more quickly than anyone had expected. The civil war between the Nationalists and the Communists began on a national scale in July 1946. Within a year, the Communist forces, which had now grown into a total of 1.95 million, had reportedly eliminated 1.12 million KMT soldiers.[61] On the basis of this victory, Mao suggested in July 1947 that the CCP should plan to defeat the KMT within five years (beginning from July 1946).[62] According to this calculation, the Communist forces would have taken over China in 1951.

However, developments on the battlefield within the following sixteen months surprised both the Nationalists and Communists. After the Jinan Campaign (September 12–24, 1948) reportedly wiped out 84,000 KMT soldiers, the civil war was going extremely well for the Communists.[63] By November 2, 1948, the Communist forces had reportedly eliminated 555,000 more KMT soldiers in another crucial battle – the Liaoxi-Shenyang Campaign – and had taken over northeast China.[64] Mao could hardly conceal his surprise and excitement. In a telegram to the Party Central Bureaus and the Party Committees of the PLA Field Armies on November 11, 1948, Mao happily admitted that the original estimate made in early September (before the Jinan Campaign) "appeared to be outdated because of the great victories in September and October."[65] On November 14, 1948, Mao suggested: "The original estimate was that the reactionary Kuomintang government could be completely over-

---

[60] Ibid., pp. 9–10. *Xiang* may be literally translated as "township." *Xiang* governments were the rural administrative units under county governments, and they constituted the lowest level and furthermost reach of the Chinese state.

[61] *Zhongguo renmin jiefangjun liushinian dashiji* (A Chronology of Sixty Years of the People's Liberation Army) (Beijing: Junshi kexue chubanshe, 1988), p. 16.

[62] *Zhongguo gongchandang lishi dashiji* (A Chronology of the Chinese Communist Party) (Beijing: Renmin chubanshe, 1989), p. 160; *Dangde wenxian* (Party Documents) (May 1989), p. 13.

[63] *Zhongguo renmin jiefangjun liushinian dashiji*, p. 436.

[64] Ibid., p. 443.

[65] *Dangde wenxian* (May 1989), p. 15; *Zhongguo gongchandang lishi dashiji*, p. 172.

thrown in about five years, beginning from July 1946. As we now see it, only another year or so may be needed to overthrow it completely."[66] The rapid development on the military front allowed the Communists little time to prepare for state-building. Having initially expected to establish a new Chinese state in 1951, the CCP leadership in 1948 suddenly found themselves en route to becoming the new rulers of this vast country. As the KMT government collapsed, an increasingly widening vacuum of power pushed the victors on the battlefield to put a new government in place.

Political Patchwork

The organization of the People's Republic was based on the Organic Law of the Central People's Government and the Common Program, a constitution-like document passed by the Chinese People's Political Consultative Conference (CPPCC) convened in September 1949. Summoned by the Communists, the delegates to the CPPCC quickly endorsed the Central People's Government Council (CPGC) as the highest organ of state power, with Mao Zedong as its chairman. Under the CPGC, there was the Government Administrative Council (GAC) as the executive organ in charge of government administration. Chaired by Zhou Enlai and consisting of thirty ministries and general administrative agencies, the GAC was empowered to manage state affairs.

Unlike some of its counterparts in 1945–8 Eastern Europe,[67] the CCP did not have to share political power with any other political parties or groups. The CCP organization was much stronger and had a much longer history of political and military struggle. The CCP also had its own Red Army to help consolidate and defend the political power that the Party had gained. Compared to the CCP's overwhelming political and military strength, the non-Communist parties in China were simply outclassed.

Yet, the CCP leaders made strenuous efforts to form a broad "united front." All the political parties and groups that had opposed the KMT one-party dictatorship were invited to join the process of organizing a new Chinese state. Altogether 134 delegates representing twenty-three non-Communist parties

---

[66] Mao Zedong, *Selected Works of Mao Tse-tung,* vol. 4 (Beijing: Foreign Languages Press, 1961), p. 288.

[67] For the Communists' difficulties in consolidating their power in Poland, Bulgaria, Czechoslovakia, Hungary, and East Germany in 1945–48, see Teresa Rakowska-Harmstone, ed., *Communism in Eastern Europe,* 2nd edition (Bloomington: Indiana University Press, 1984).

and groups were able to attend the first session of the CPPCC.[68] As a result, the CPPCC was made into "an assembly representing all areas, political organizations, and interest groups except those in direct enmity to the revolution."[69] The CCP also appointed a disproportionate percentage of non-Communists to high positions in the new government: three vice chairmen of the CPGC (out of a total of six); one vice chairman of the National Defense Council (out of a total of five); two vice premiers (out of a total of four), ten ministers (out of a total of thirty-eight), and thirty-two deputy ministers (out of total of fifty-five) in the GAC.[70] Since the non-Communist parties altogether had fewer than 20,000 members compared to 4.48 million CCP members, these arrangements were very generous for the non-Communists. This level of "power-sharing" has never since been surpassed.

There were two reasons why the CCP in the early 1950s was willing to share some power with non-Communists. First, even though as many as two million KMT personnel finally followed Chiang Kai-shek to Taiwan,[71] there were still many former KMT officials, government functionaries, and surrendering troops left over on the mainland. A "united front" government that included former KMT political and military leaders seemed to be the only way to secure the former KMT personnel's cooperation with the new regime. Second, the CCP had its own weaknesses. The Party, army, and cadre corps consisted mainly of peasants often poorly educated and unskilled. This was the inevitable result of the CCP's past concentration in the countryside and Mao Zedong's strategy of "gathering strength in the villages, using the villages in order to surround the cities and then taking the cities."[72] Two decades after they had been driven out of the cities by the KMT, the CCP leaders in 1949 found the Party back in the cities again, but a Party much different from what it was when

---

[68] *Zhou Enlai zhuan, 1898–1949* (A Biography of Zhou Enlai, 1898–1949) (Beijing: Renmin chubanshe and Zhongyang wenxian chubanshe, 1989), pp. 765–79.

[69] Jack Gray, *Rebellions and Revolutions: China from the 1800s to the 1980s* (New York: Oxford University Press, 1990), p. 287.

[70] Ma Yuping and Huang Yuchong, eds., *Zhongguo zuotian yu jintian, 1840–1987 nian guoqing shouce* (China's Yesterday and Today: Handbook of National Conditions: 1840–1987) (Beijing: Jiefangjun chubanshe, 1989), pp. 705–16; *Zhonggong dangshi zhong de shijian yu renwu* (Events and Personages in the History of the Chinese Communist Party) (Shanghai: Shanghai renmin chubanshe, 1983), pp. 742–51; Li Weihan, *Huiyi yu yanjiu* (Recollections and Research) (Beijing: Zhonggong dangshi ziliao chubanshe, 1986), p. 791.

[71] Tien Hung-mao, *The Great Transition: Political and Social Change in the Republic of China* (Stanford, CA: Hoover Institution Press, Stanford University, 1989), p. 18.

[72] Mao, 1961, vol. 4, p. 363.

it left the cities.[73] The composition of the Party membership made it difficult for the Party to manage the cities and the national economy directly. As far as economic development was concerned, the CCP needed help and cooperation from non-Communists and intellectuals, at least for the time being.

Ruling the Country on Horseback

Although the 1949 state structure was hastily put together during the civil war, was meant to be temporary,[74] and indeed proved to be short lived, the initial years of the Chinese state-building under a revolutionary party heralded certain state-building problems that would only become more obvious later. The new government faced enormous difficulties. The national economy had been devastated by eight years of war against the invading Japanese, followed by four more years of civil war. The task of postwar consolidation was no less formidable than that of winning the war. In the cities, high inflation had to be halted, unemployment reduced, prices stabilized, industrial production organized, and economic recovery stimulated.[75] In the countryside, agrarian reform needed to be furthered and completed, especially in the newly liberated areas. This was of vital importance not only for maintaining support for the CCP among the peasantry, but also for restoring and promoting the agricultural production that could in turn support industrialization. In many ways, economic recovery became the first testing ground of the Communists' ability to govern on a national scale. Realistic or not, the people expected the new rulers to improve the economic situation quickly. Thus Mao Zedong warned the Party in March 1949:

[73] Some CCP leaders like Liu Shaoqi had lived in the urban areas for years. Nonetheless, they were mainly experienced in organizing underground revolutionary activities in the cities and lacked necessary skills of managing national production, commerce, distribution, finance, and banking.

[74] The Organic Law stipulated that the CPPCC would function in lieu of a national legislature until a National People's Congress convened, after which the CPPCC would exist only as a united front organization. The Common Program also stipulated: "In all places where military operations are completely ended, agrarian reform thoroughly carried out and people of all circles have been fully organized, elections based on universal franchise shall be held immediately for the purpose of convening local people's congresses." These documents are translated in Albert P. Blaustein, ed., *Fundamental Legal Documents of Communist China* (South Hackensack, NJ: Fred B. Rothman & Company, 1962).

[75] Harry Harding, *Organizing China: The Problem of Bureaucracy, 1949–1976* (Stanford, CA: Stanford University Press, 1981), p. 32.

If we know nothing about production and do not master it quickly, if we cannot restore and develop production as speedily as possible and achieve solid successes so that the livelihood of the workers, first of all, and that of the people in general is improved, we shall be unable to maintain our political power, we shall be unable to stand on our feet, we shall fail.[76]

On the political front, the job was no less demanding than the economic recovery. Although the PLA had crossed the Yangtze River, the Communist ideology had not. Although the Communists controlled the land, they had yet to control the mind. The people in south and southwest China, especially the urban residents, intellectuals, and industrialists, had yet to be convinced that socialism was the answer to the problems of China. As the Communists entered the cities, Communist ideological revolution had just begun.

While the economic and political tasks were challenging, the war on the battlefield continued. According to Chinese sources, there were in 1950 nearly 2 million "armed bandits," 600,000 KMT agents, and 600,000 core members of various anti-Communist groups on the mainland, who were engaged in all types of sabotage activities against the new regime.[77] Before the new regime could hope to suppress any armed resistance, the Korean War suddenly broke out. Although the war caught the Chinese by surprise and was the last thing they wanted, once Mao Zedong committed himself to supporting Kim Il Sung, the whole country was mobilized.[78] In October 1950 a war-torn China was again dragged back into warfare, this time with the United States.[79]

---

[76] Mao, 1961, vol. 4, p. 365.

[77] Xiao Xiaoqin and Wang Youqiao, p. 17; *Dangdai zhongguo de gongan gongzuo* (China Today: Public Security Work) (Beijing: Dangdai zhongguo chubanshe, 1992), p. 2.

[78] Although Mao was told in advance of Kim Il Sung's plan to invade the South, it was clear that China was not prepared for fighting the war. On January 9, 1950, Mao approved a report by Lin Biao and the CCP Northeast Regional Bureau to move 100,000 men from the Fourth Field Army into production in Northeast China. In another instruction to the military leaders, written on April 21, 1950, about two months before the Korean War started, Mao expressed the hope that the Central South Military Region would demobilize 530,000 to 600,000 soldiers, "so as to cut down the expenditures for a total of four months from September to December, and partly reduce the food and tax burden on the people." Following Mao's instruction, a Central Demobilization Commission was established to take charge of military reorganization and demobilization. *Jianguo yilai Mao Zedong wengao, 1949, 9–1950, 12* (Mao Zedong's Manuscripts Since the Founding of the People's Republic of China: September 1949–December 1950), vol. 1 (Beijing: Zhongyang dangan chubanshe, 1987), pp. 222–3, 310, 359. For a recent study on the subject, see S. N. Goncharov, John W. Lewis, and Xue Litai, *Uncertain Partners: Stalin, Mao, and the Korean War* (Stanford, CA: Stanford University Press, 1993).

[79] In early July 1950, China began to mobilize the military forces (four armies and three artillery

Thus, the new regime faced three formidable challenges: reconstructing the economy, consolidating the revolution, and continuing to fight wars both at home and abroad. Given these enormous tasks and the primitive nature of the new state institutions, it should come as no surprise that the CCP leaders in the early 1950s heavily relied on two organizations that were already available to them to get the job done, namely, the army and the Party. From 1949 to 1952, the country, for all practical purposes, was under military control. Four of the five regional governments were headed by Military Administrative Committees, which controlled a total of twenty provinces.[80] In November 1952, when all the military operations in the country had ended and the political and economic situation stabilized, the Military Administrative Committee was transformed into the Administrative Committee. The Communist Party organization assumed a more active role, although high-ranking military leaders continued to chair some of the Regional Administrative Committees, at least nominally.[81] As Dorothy Solinger points out, "Institutionally, the availability of a disciplined, unified party and army made the central direction of development possible, and helped to strengthen central power in the localities."[82]

China's political and economic programs were carried out through mass mobilization by the revolutionary party. In June 1950, an agrarian reform movement was initiated following the promulgation of the Land Reform Law. After Chinese troops entered the Korean War in October 1950, the Chinese people were mobilized into a nationwide "Resist-America and Aid-Korea" campaign. In December 1950, a mass campaign was launched to suppress counterrevolutionaries. In 1951, a "Three-Anti" campaign was initiated against waste, bureaucratism, and corruption in the Party and government

divisions – a total of 255,000 soldiers) into the China-Korean border area, following the decision made at the meeting of the Central Military Commission on July 7, 1950. The Chinese forces formally entered the Korean War on October 12, 1950. *Jianguo yilai Mao Zedong wengao,* vol. 1, p. 428.

[80] China was divided into six Great Administrative Regions: North China, Northwest, East China, Central-South, Southwest, and Northeast regions. Except North China, which was under the direct jurisdiction of the central government, all the Great Administrative Regions had their own regional governments. For a case study of the Great Regional Government in Southwest China, see Dorothy J. Solinger, *Regional Government and Political Integration in Southwest China, 1949–1954: A Case Study* (Berkeley: University of California Press, 1977).

[81] Peng Dehuai was the chair of the Northwest Regional Administrative Committee; Lin Biao, the Central-South; and Liu Bocheng, the Southwest. It is important to note that all of these senior military leaders concurrently held central government positions.

[82] Solinger, p. 257.

institutions. In 1952, a "Five-Anti" campaign was carried out against bribery, theft of state property, theft of state secrets, cheating on contracts, and tax evasion by private merchants and industrialists. During 1951–2, a "Thought Reform" movement was organized among the intellectuals and non-Communists. This campaign style of work by the new Chinese regime again should come as no surprise. After all, the army and revolutionary party were best at organizing mass campaigns, military or otherwise. Mass campaigns provided a link between the CCP's experiences in waging wars and its present task of managing state affairs. This is important in that it set the tone for many later mass mobilization campaigns by the CCP.

The state of PRC during 1949–53 was therefore built upon a temporary "united front" among various political forces. Its existence and functions were dependent on a strong political control at the local levels by the army and Party organization. Its tasks were carried out in the form of mass mobilization. Although these features betrayed the immaturity of the new state institutions, they were largely the product of historical circumstances. It can be argued that, had it not been for the organizational support of the Party, the new government could have hardly met the challenge and survived the difficulties. As unprepared as anybody else, the CCP leaders in the early 1950s began the process of state-building amid war, revolutionary mobilization, and struggles for economic survival. The Chinese revolutionaries had fought for a new political system on horseback. Now they had to rule the country on horseback.

In sum, we tend to conclude that the legacy of the imperial state, although influential in several ways, did not provide an easy answer to the question of how to build a modern Chinese state. Furthermore, a discussion of the revolution in twentieth century China highlights the rise of the revolutionary parties following the demise of the imperial rule, but gives no support to the argument that a modern Chinese state had naturally emerged as a result of the revolution. A further examination of the Jiangxi and Yan'an experience points to a revolutionary party maturing in ideological manipulation, organizational control, and mass mobilization, which was only to create problems for post-1949 state institution-building. Finally, an analysis of the military-revolutionary regime in the early 1950s leads us to believe that the new state institutions of the PRC during this period were immature, incomplete, and dependent. The assumption that there was a strong Chinese state after the Communist victory in 1949 defies logic and history. It is probably fair to say that the PRC founded in October 1949 was essentially symbolic. With the risk of stretching Benedict Anderson's concept, we may call this new state "an imagined community."[83] Surely the Chinese state institutions did not come into being all of a sudden. With Mao's announcement in Tiananmen Square, the vision of a new Chinese state was projected, but that vision had yet to be realized in the years to come.

WHY THE STATE? WHY THE PARTY?

By 1949, the CCP was already twenty-eight years old. Mao Zedong figuratively described the Party in the following way: "Like a man, a political party has its childhood, youth, manhood and old age. The Communist Party of China is no longer a child or a lad in his teens but has become an adult."[84] Unlike the Russian Bolsheviks, who, after a successful coup in 1917, faced a hostile government bureaucracy, an army of the old state, and a resisting peasantry in the countryside, the Communists in China had by 1949 developed a huge pool of political and military personnel who had deep roots in the countryside. Their organizational assets included a party of 4.48 million members, an army of 3.57 million, or a civilian cadre corps of 720,000.[85] Given these advantages, it was conceivable that the Chinese Communists could simply run the country with the Party organization. Why, then, did they bother to create state institutions after taking over the mainland? Why did a single strong revolutionary party need to build a state at all?

Perhaps a state could perform certain functions that even a successful revolutionary party was simply not capable of doing. First, the state of the People's Republic represented a much larger political entity than the Communist Party, which, by claiming to be a vanguard party of the working class, necessarily consisted of only a small proportion of the Chinese population.[86] Second, a state based on a constitution could legitimize the Communist Party's rule. To the revolutionaries, a state constitution surely did not mean something like a contract that a democratic government makes with society or an agreement on how political power should be divided and shared. Nonetheless, the fact that

---

[83] Benedict Anderson, *Imagined Communities: Reflections on the Origin and Spread of Nationalism* (London: Verso, 1983).

[84] Mao, 1961, vol. 4, p. 411.

[85] Figures are from Ma Yuping and Huang Yuchong, p. 536; *Zhongguo guoqing baogao* (Report on the National Conditions of China) (Shenyang: Liaoning renmin chubanshe, 1990), p. 930.

[86] In 1949, the CCP members accounted for only 0.8 percent of the Chinese population. Over the next decade, the CCP had recruited nearly ten million new members, but it still accounted for only 2.1 percent of the total population in 1959. For more information about the CCP membership changes, see Appendix A in this book.

the CCP leaders wanted to finalize the victories of their revolution and lay out their future work in the form of a constitution – "the fundamental law," as Mao called it – suggests a recognition, though only vaguely expressed, of sovereignty inherently embedded in a state, something even a successful revolutionary party could not hope to possess.[87] Third, a state would also enhance the coercive and administrative capacities of the regime. In June 1949, to the question, "Don't you want to abolish state power?" Mao answered:

> Yes, we do, but not right now; we cannot do it yet. Why? Because imperialism still exists, because domestic reaction still exists, because classes still exist in our country. Our task is to strengthen the people's state apparatus – mainly the people's army, the people's police and the people's courts – in order to consolidate national defense and protect the people's interests.[88]

What Mao implied here was a sense of legitimate organization of coercive power through the state apparatus. To the extent that the Party disciplinary rules could only be applied to Party members, the state institutions, such as a national legislature, a centralized government, and a legal system, provided the Party leaders with the tools and means necessary for managing a big country like China.

If, for all these reasons, a state was necessary, why did a revolutionary party need to continue after the revolution? Presumably, the CCP leaders could gradually turn their organizational assets into a state bureaucracy. The CCP leaders could assume the roles of state leadership by occupying the government offices both at the central and provincial levels. The cadre corps of 720,000 men and women could immediately fill the middle- and lower-ranking

---

[87] Mao Zedong, *Selected Works of Mao Tse-tung,* vol. 5 (Beijing: Foreign Language Press, 1977), p. 145.

[88] Mao, 1961, vol. 4, p. 418. Stalin made a similar point ten years earlier. Speaking at the Eighteenth Congress of the Communist Party of the Soviet Union in 1939, Stalin argued that Friedrich Engels's proposition that the state withered away when there were no longer any antagonistic classes required modification: It was only true once the revolution had triumphed all over the world. Stalin stressed that in the capitalist encirclement in which the USSR found itself, the state would continue to exist even in the present stage, where socialism had been achieved, and no antagonistic classes, let alone exploiters, remained. Indeed, the state could continue to exist even after the USSR had progressed to the next and higher phase, communism, so long as capitalist encirclement was a fact. Joseph Stalin, *Problems of Leninism,* cited in Leonard Schapiro, *The Communist Party of the Soviet Union,* 2nd edition (New York: Vintage Books, 1971), p. 473. I am grateful to Professor Joseph LaPalombara for bringing to my attention this similarity.

official positions and millions of Party members could readily become the state workers. Meanwhile, the Party as a revolutionary organization might gradually "wither away" as it merged into the state institutions.

Yet, instead of gradually disappearing or becoming submerged in the state bureaucracy, the CCP as a revolutionary organization was not only kept alive after 1949, but became more active and distinctive. A war-hardened Party organization not only coexisted with the state, but also expanded parallel to the growing state.[89] Paradoxically, before 1949, the CCP was determined to build a new state of its own. After it had founded its own state, however, the CCP strongly resisted any tendencies for the Party to be absorbed into the state institutions.[90] In the early 1950s, several Party rectification campaigns were launched to keep the Party organization as revolutionary and antibureaucratic as possible.[91] Indeed, as we will see later, Mao had constantly expressed hostility toward the formal bureaucracy. In his never-ending pursuit of the transformation of the land and the mind, Mao depended on the Party for organizing mass campaigns.

Patterns of the Party–State Relationship

The parallel development of the state institutions and a revolutionary party after 1949 inevitably raised some key questions regarding their relations. How would a revolutionary party deal with its own state? What would be the role and status of a revolutionary party in the state? Conceivably, these questions could be answered by at least three formulas:

1. "A or B" (either party or state);
2. "A & B" (both party and state); and
3. "A = B" (party supersedes state).

---

[89] By the end of 1949, the Party had about 4.48 million members. During 1950–54, the Party membership grew at an average rate of 7.8 percent, which translated into 400,000 new members each year. During 1955–57 when the process of state-building gained new momentum, the Party organization expanded even more rapidly. By 1957 it had reached 12.7 million. See Appendix A in this book.

[90] As Franz Schurmann observes, "The Chinese Communists in particular have sharply fought any tendencies toward bureaucratization of the Party, and so have had a strong material interest in maintaining the ideological principle that the Party is not part of the apparatus of the state." Franz H. Schurmann, *Ideology and Organization in Communist China,* 2nd and enlarged edition (Berkeley: University of California Press, 1968), p. 111.

[91] Harding suggests that rectification and mass campaigns are the Party's remedial approaches to the "bureaucratic dilemma." Harding, pp. 327–59.

The first approach – "A or B" – suggests a hostile relationship between the Party and the state. Obviously, this was the approach of the CCP toward the existing state in the pre-1949 period. Since the KMT regime was seen as a repressive bourgeois state, the goal of the CCP was to mobilize the masses to overthrow it. The second approach – "A & B" – suggests a harmonious relationship in which the Party and the state not only coexist, but function according to certain rules regarding divisions of labor. This was the Communists' preferred approach to handling the relations between the Party and their own state, an approach that was first suggested in the Jiangxi Soviet period and later endorsed in the Yan'an period. The "A & B" approach, while maintaining that the Party's unified leadership over policies of the government is necessary, suggests that the direct interference by the Party in government work should be avoided. The experience of the PRC, however, would soon prove that it was at least difficult to define a clear-cut boundary between a unified leadership over policies on the one hand, and no interference in every government matter on the other. Consequently, upholding the first principle was certain to impede the achievement of the second principle. This ultimately led to the "A = B" situation, revealing a basic dilemma facing the Party after it had established its own state.

The CCP leaders had long insisted that the revolutionary party organization was not the same thing as the state and that the Party simply could not rule the country without the state institutions. Yet an emphasis on the Party's unified leadership often led to a situation in which the Party organization increasingly took over the authority and functions of the state. As the Party organization penetrated and took the place of the state institutions, its revolutionary traditions and mobilizational style only made the management of state affairs extremely difficult. Furthermore, as more and more Party members became officials and functionaries of the state, they were caught up in an impossible process of playing their roles both as bureaucrats of the state and as members of a political organization that was revolutionary, mobilizational, and anti-bureaucracy. Thus we have the institutional dilemma in post-1949 China: The Party cannot live without the state and it cannot live with the state. This dilemma reflects the fundamental institutional conflicts between the Party and state.

Part II

STATE-BUILDING UNDER A REVOLUTIONARY PARTY: THE MAO ZEDONG ERA

Revolution, Laws, and Party

MODERN state-building is more than designing a national flag, choosing a national anthem, and designating a capital city. Establishing a legal system and building legislative and judicial institutions are some of the essential innovations that modern state-building requires. In the 1950s, the Chinese Communists were no strangers to this thinking. After all, constitutionalism had already been debated and experimented with in China for decades. The state of the Nationalists before 1949 had established an elaborate and sophisticated legal system. The Communist regimes in the Soviet Union and Eastern Europe had also installed a constitutional and legal system. Furthermore, laws and regulations seemed to have a magic appeal to many sectors of the society that the CCP's ideology and organization did not have. Yet, by definition, revolution and law must be the two most incompatible ideas in human conceptualization. Hence, how the CCP as a revolutionary organization dealt with a legal system of its own is our main focus. This chapter begins with the CCP's initial efforts at establishing a new legal system in the early 1950s. It analyzes how the legal development challenged the power and privileges of the CCP and how a major crisis led to a fundamental reversal in the late 1950s.

"DESTROYING THE OLD AND ESTABLISHING THE NEW"

The construction of a new legal system for the People's Republic began with the destruction of the constitution, laws, and judicial system of the regime that preceded it. In early 1949, the CCP leaders decided to abolish the old legal system of the KMT. A Party directive issued in February 1949 ordered the Six Legal Codes of the Nationalist government to be repealed, including the 1947 constitution; civil, criminal, and commercial laws; and civil and criminal procedure.[1] The Common Program that served as the temporary constitution of

---

[1] Zheng Qian et al., eds., *Dangdai zhongguo zhengzhi tizhi fazhang gaiyao* (Outline of the

the PRC until 1954 called on the people to "repeal all the laws, regulations and judicial system that the reactionary KMT government had used to suppress the people" and to "formulate the laws, regulations to protect the people and establish the people's judicial system."[2] Following the CCP's directive and the Common Program, a mass political struggle was launched to destroy the institutions of the KMT's legal order.

The CCP's hostility toward the KMT's legal system is not difficult to understand. The Chinese Communists, like almost all the Communists, accepted Karl Marx's class interpretation of the nature of law. As part of the superstructure, law reflected the economic base and protected the dominant class. Hence, the working class must overthrow the laws of the oppressing class. Besides the ideological reason, the way the CCP developed also affected its attitude toward the KMT's legal system. As a revolutionary organization, the CCP was labeled "rebellious" and "bandit" by the Nationalist government. The Communists knew only too well how laws and regulations were formulated by the KMT regime as a legal weapon against them. Now that the Communists had taken over the mainland, they wanted nothing of the KMT's legal system. This was a political revenge or retaliation against enemies. The Marxist class view of law and the revolutionary tradition of the CCP had thus constrained the post-1949 leaders in their efforts to build a new legal system.

The 1949–53 Legal System

By late 1949, the KMT's legal system on the mainland had been largely dismantled. To fill the legal vacuum, the new regime mainly relied on Party directives and orders from military control commissions. Meanwhile, the Party leaders appeared just as enthusiastic in establishing a new legal system as in burying the old legal system. The Chinese central government in 1949–53 included the Supreme People's Court and Supreme People's Procuratorate, which functioned, respectively, as the highest judicial and procuratorate organs of the state. Under the Government Administrative Council, there was the Ministry of Public Security, the Ministry of Justice, and the Legislation Com-

---

Development of Contemporary Chinese Political System) (Beijing: Zhonggong dangshi zhiliao chubanshe, 1988), p. 24.

[2] *Zhongguo guoqing daiquan* (Comprehensive Book of Chinese National Conditions) (Beijing: Xuewang chubanshe, 1990), p. 269.

mission. Courts, procuratorates, and judicial administrative agencies were also established at the provincial and local levels. To coordinate the work among civil affairs, public security, administration of justice, procuratorates, and courts, a Political and Legal Affairs Committee was formed in the central, regional, and provincial governments. Several important laws were promulgated, including the Marriage Law (April 1950), the Land Reform Law (June 1950), and the Trade Union Law (June 1950).

The formation of a legal system depended on the development of legislative institutions. Although it was only a temporary arrangement hastily made during the last few years of the civil war, the central government nominally acquired all the powers, including legislative, executive, judicial, and military. The central government was composed of the State Administrative Council, the People's Revolutionary Military Commission, the Supreme People's Court, and the Supreme People's Procuratorate. Local governments, whose leaders were directly appointed by the central government, were organized in the similar fashion, combining legislative and administrative powers in one.

In using the word "nominally," what I mean is that the state power was actually controlled by the Party leaders. Party Chairman Mao Zedong was concurrently the chairman of the Central People's Government, the chairman of the Central People's Revolutionary Commission, and the chairman of the Political Consultative Conference, which supposedly exercised the oversight power over the central government. Like the old term "emperor," the new term "chairman" symbolized the center of the political power. This kind of arrangement makes one wonder whether any division of power among the state institutions mattered at all, since the Party was to control all the powers anyway. Nevertheless, the Party leaders seemed to be genuinely concerned about the nonelected central government with undifferentiated responsibilities of legislation and administration. For one thing, the Party's claim of "people's democracy" would appear less convincing. For another, this state structure would look quite similar to the KMT state, implying that nothing had really changed.

Before the First National People's Congress (NPC) was convened, the restructuring of the national government could hardly proceed. The Party leadership, however, had come to foresee a formal power relationship between the legislative and executive agencies. In June 1950, while discussing the role of the people's representatives conference (predecessor of the people's congress), Mao stressed, "All the important work of the people's government must be discussed and decided upon by the people's representatives conferences."[3] In February 1951, Party Vice Chairman Liu Shaoqi also pointed out, "The People's Governments of all levels should report their work and activities to these conferences [People's Representatives Conferences], answer their questions, and open themselves to their investigations. The most important work and activities should first be discussed and decided on by these conferences."[4]

Establishing a new legal system certainly was not as easy as destroying the old. The most obvious difficulty was lack of enough qualified judges and legal staff to run the newly established legal institutions; there were even fewer lawyers to initiate the legal procedures. The legal personnel of the new regime mainly consisted of two groups: those recruited directly from the army and the "retained personnel" (*liuyong renyuan*) from the KMT regime. The learning process was anything but easy for both groups. The former had to appreciate that the revolutionary war was over, and the latter had to realize that the revolutionary struggle had just begun. One group must be convinced that laws worked more effectively than guns in maintaining public order; the other had to learn how to practice law under a revolutionary regime. To help the retained personnel adjust, a nationwide legal reform movement was launched in 1952–53 to denounce the "old legal viewpoints and judicial style," to "draw a clear line between the old and new legal systems," and to rectify and purify the legal institutions. Those found unfit were removed from the legal system. Here the CCP's revolutionary experience and ideological campaigns began to define an organizational environment to which the legal personnel of the new republic had to conform.

Mass Justice and Party Leadership

Given the Party's rich experience in mobilizing the peasants in wars and land reform, a revolutionary legal system was to be built upon mobilization of the revolutionary masses. The judicial system in the initial period of the PRC clearly reflected the CCP's revolutionary legacy of the Jiangxi Soviet and Yan'an. It could be characterized as a system of mass justice under Party leadership. Mass justice was carried out in frequent mass campaigns, first against the counterrevolutionaries, then against the industrialists and mer-

---

[3] Mao Zedong, *Selected Works of Mao Tse-tung,* vol. 5 (Beijing: Foreign Languages Press, 1977), p. 19.

[4] Liu Shaoqi, *Collected Works of Liu Shao Ch'i: 1945–1957* (Hong Kong: Union Research Institute, 1969), p. 248.

chants, and finally against the corrupt elements in the Party, government, and army. In one campaign after another, most judicial personnel had to take an active part. As mass campaigns quickly built up a sense of urgency, the normal work and procedure of the judicial system had to be halted. For a while, five judicial agencies in the central government – the Political and Legal Affairs Committee, the Supreme People's Court, the Supreme People's Procuratorate, the Ministry of Justice, and the Legislation Commission – simply merged into one so that they could handle the cases more effectively during mass campaigns.

The most exemplary application of mass justice was the so-called people's tribunals at the county and city levels. This was a special court separate from, and independent of, the regular court of criminal and civil justice. Presided over by leaders of a work unit and consisting of political activists as judges, the people's tribunals had enormous judicial powers, ranging from summons for interrogation, arrest, and detainment, to passing sentence and awarding the death penalty. The people's tribunals emerged during the campaign of "suppressing the counterrevolutionaries" as a speedy way to deal with mounting cases. During the "Three-Anti" and "Five-Anti" movements, the practice of people's tribunals was further extended to handle cases of corruption and violations of economic regulations. Although the people's tribunals proved to be only temporary, the tradition of mass justice has continued through the next four decades of the PRC legal history, as manifested in public trials, sentencing at mass rallies, and the parade of the convicted.

During the mass campaign of suppressing the counterrevolutionaries in 1951, the CCP had established a strictly enforced system called the "internal review and approval" (*neibu shenpi*) or "prior review and approval within the Party" (*dangnei shenpi*). Under this system, before any legal judgment concerning arrests, sentencing, and particularly use of the death penalty was handed down, it had to first be approved by Party committees at the appropriate levels or by Party core groups in the judicial institutions.[5] Major cases had to be approved by the Party center. Under the circumstances, the direct interference by the Party in handling the legal cases was perhaps inevitable, if not ideal, given the incompleteness of the newly established judicial system and legal procedure. But the problem is that the system of *neibu shenpi* or *dangnei shenpi* has since become deeply entrenched in the Chinese judicial system. Once established, the practices of mass justice and Party direct interference in

---

[5] Party core group system is discussed in detail in Chapter 4 of this book.

legal affairs has continued beyond the special circumstances that could justify their existence.

1954: The Moment of High Expectations

In July 1953, a truce was finally signed to end the Korean War. By late 1953, resistance activities against the new regime had been essentially suppressed and military operations on the mainland were ended. If the unusual conditions in the previous years could justify the harsh rule of the new regime, it now became possible for the Chinese leaders to resort to laws, regulations, and administrative orders rather than mass campaigns and guns to run the country. The economic construction under the First Five-Year Plan also called for law and order, for people were most productive when they were free from fear of physical danger. To help create a political and social environment conducive to economic production, the legal system had to be strengthened, laws had to be respected, and crimes had to be dealt with by legal means.

A class view of laws, however, prohibited the Chinese judges and jurists from learning from the Western legal experience or from inheriting the legal traditions from the KMT regime. With no precedents to follow and no legal traditions to rely on, China could only copy the constitutional and legal system of the Soviet "big brother." Just as the American aid to non-Communist countries in Asia after World War II had a great impact on the state-building process in these countries, the Soviet model is often seen by the Chinese scholars as one of the three major sources of influence on the post-1949 Chinese political system.[6] As China leaned to the Soviet side, the CCP leaders came to realize that the state-building involved more institutional details and sophistication than just convening meetings, announcing appointments, and issuing decrees.

The year 1954 was a major turning point in the development of the Chinese legal system, symbolized by the adoption of the constitution of the PRC. The CCP leaders appeared serious about the constitution-writing. From March to June 1954, a draft constitution prepared by the CCP was discussed by more than 8,000 representatives from the non-Communist parties, mass organiza-

---

[6] The other two sources of influence are the CCP's pre-1949 experience in managing the revolutionary base areas and the Chinese political traditions. See Nie Gaomin et al., eds., *Guanyu dangzheng fenkai de lilun tantao* (Theoretical Discussion on Separating the Party from the Government) (Beijing: Chunqiu chubanshe, 1987).

tions, and social groups. Then the revised draft constitution was discussed nationwide by reportedly 150 million people for two more months.[7]

As originally stipulated in the Common Program of the Chinese People's Political Consultative Conference, elections would be held for people's congresses when the conditions were ripe. Thus, in June 1953, the first nationwide census in the PRC was conducted, and elections were subsequently held, following the promulgation of the Electoral Law. On September 15, 1954, the First National People's Congress of 1,226 delegates was convened in Beijing and approved the first state constitution. Reporting to the NPC, Liu Shaoqi stressed: "Formulating the Constitution of the People's Republic of China is an event of great historical significance in the life of the state in our country."[8] Mao must have meant it when he said that after the draft constitution was rectified,

> it will be the formal constitution. We should be getting ready now to enforce it. Once it is approved, the whole nation, one and all, should observe it. . . . To fail to observe the constitution is to violate it. . . .
> An organization has to have a charter. A country must also have a charter. The constitution is an overall charter; it is a fundamental law.[9]

In addition to the constitution, the first NPC also passed several organic laws for restructuring the national legislature (the NPC); the central administration (the State Council); the judiciary (the People's Court and the People's Procuratorate); and provincial and local governments. The constitution and organic laws thus established the Chinese state that we have become familiar with in the following decades.

Compared with the primitive state structure of 1949–53, the state in 1954 contained several important institutional changes and consolidations. First was the installation of formal legal authority in the national legislature. The constitution stipulated that the NPC was "the highest organ of state authority." The NPC was also the "only legislative authority" in the country because the political system in China was a unitary one and all powers derived from the central authority. According to the articles of the constitution, the powers of the

---

[7] Xiao Xiaoqin and Wang Youqiao, eds. *Zhonghua renmin gongheguo sishi nian* (Forty Years of the People's Republic of China) (Beijing: Beijing shifan xueyuan chubanshe, 1990), p. 48.

[8] Liu Shaoqi, *Liu Shaoqi xuanji* (Selected Works of Liu Shaoqi), vol. 2 (Beijing: Renmin chubanshe, 1988), pp. 138–9.

[9] Michael Y. M. Kau and John K. Leung, eds., *The Writings of Mao Zedong: 1949–1976*, vol. 1 (Armonk, NY: M. E. Sharpe, 1986), p. 458; Mao, 1977, vol. 5, pp. 145–7.

NPC would be almost unlimited. The NPC had sovereign powers in adopting and amending the state constitution, in declaring war and peace, and general amnesties, and in deciding the status and boundaries of all the provincial and local governments. It had financial powers to approve the state budget, national economic plans, and other financial reports. It had appointment and removal powers over all high-ranking state officials, including the state chairman and the vice chairman of the PRC, the premier and vice premiers and ministers of the State Council, the president of the Supreme People's Court, and the chief procurator of the Supreme People's Procuratorate. It also had implied powers, for the NPC could "exercise such other functions and powers as the National People's Congress considers necessary."[10] The NPC was also to be differentiated from the central government that now referred solely to the State Council – the highest state administrative organ. The national, provincial, and local people's congresses were entrusted with the powers to elect, supervise, and remove government leaders at the same levels.

Second, a complete judicial system was established, following the promulgation of the Organic Law of the People's Court and People's Procuratorate. The 1954 constitution and two organic laws defined the structures, functions, jurisdiction, and legal methods of the court and procuratorate and therefore established a legal basis upon which the judicial activities could be regularized and institutionalized. Below the Supreme People's Court, a three-level court system was set up at the basic, middle, and high levels. Certain people's tribunals still existed, but they no longer had the separate and special judicial powers they used to exercise.

Third, important judicial principles were announced in the 1954 constitution and the organic laws, such as judicial independence and equality of citizens before the law.[11] By July 1957, a total of 4,108 laws, legal codes, regulations, and rules had been approved. In the meantime, criminal law, criminal procedure, civil law, and civil procedure were also being drafted.[12] Despite the initial obstacles, the legal institution-building of the PRC got off to a good start in 1954. Chinese legal scholars optimistically predicted that the PRC's legal development had entered a "new historical stage."[13]

---

[10] For the English text of the 1954 Constitution, see William L. Tung, *The Political Institutions of Modern China* (The Hague, Netherlands: Martinus Nijhoff, 1968), Appendix H, p. 370.

[11] Ibid., pp. 33–4.

[12] *Zhongguo guoqing daiquan,* pp. 271–2.

[13] Wu Lei, ed., *Zhongguo sifa zhidu* (The Chinese Judiciary System) (Beijing: Zhongguo renmin daxue chubanshe, 1988), p. 32.

In September 1956, Party Vice Chairman Liu Shaoqi told the delegates to the Eighth Party Congress:

[T]he period of revolutionary storm and stress is past, new relations of production have been set up, and the aim of our struggle is changed into one of safeguarding the successful development of the social productive forces; a corresponding change in the method of struggle will consequently have to follow, and a complete legal system becomes an absolute necessity.[14]

The Party officials seemed to agree with Liu's assessment, for a resolution passed by the Eighth Party Congress stressed:

As the socialist revolution is basically over and the main task of the country has shifted from liberation of productive forces to protection and development of productive forces, we must further strengthen the legal system of the people's democracy and consolidate the order of socialist construction. The state must gradually formulate and perfect laws according to needs.[15]

In January 1957, Mao also affirmed that

the law must be observed and the revolutionary legal system must not be undermined. Our laws form part of the superstructure. Our laws are made by the working people themselves. They are designed to maintain revolutionary order and protect the interests of the working people, the socialist economic base and the productive forces.[16]

In February 1957, in a speech to the Eleventh Session of the Supreme State Conference, Mao also proclaimed that in "the country as a whole, the bulk of the counterrevolutionaries has been cleared out. Our basic task has changed from unfettering the productive forces to protecting and expanding them in the context of the new relations of production."[17] These major policy speeches by Mao and Liu and the resolution by the Eighth Party Congress suggest that the CCP leadership in early 1957 had concluded that China was no longer in a

---

[14] Liu Shaoqi, 1969, p. 386.

[15] *Dang de shiyijie sanzhong quanhui yilai zhengzhi tizhi gaige de lilun yu shijian* (Theories and Practices of Reform of the Political System Since the Third Plenum of the Eleventh Party Congress) (Beijing: Chunqiu chubanshe, 1987), p. 50.

[16] Mao's statement was quoted in Party leader Peng Zhen's speech to the NPC in June 1979. Peng Zhen, "Explanation of Seven Laws," *Beijing Review* 28 (July 13, 1979), p. 16.

[17] Mao, 1977, vol. 5, p. 397.

"revolutionary situation." The traditional methods of revolutionary struggle needed to be replaced by a legal system more appropriate for economic construction.

Unfortunately, no one at the Eighth Party Congress in September 1956 had expected the process of legal development to be drastically reversed within only eight months. Talking about the legal system and new relationships of production, even Mao had not expected a relatively peaceful and stable situation to turn into a major political crisis. Yet, when many legal workers and non-Communist legislators later criticized the Party for ignoring the constitution and legal procedures, Mao and his veteran revolutionaries had no hesitation or mercy in striking back through the Anti-Rightist Campaign. Slipping back into the revolutionary mentality proved so easy whereas moving forward in establishing a constitutional order and legal institutions proved so difficult.

THE ANTI-RIGHTIST CAMPAIGN OF 1957

In February 1956, Khrushchev's "secret speech" to the Twentieth Congress of the Communist Party of the Soviet Union (CPSU) ushered in a process of "de-Stalinization" in the Soviet Union. The secret speech also sent shock waves throughout the socialist countries. In China, Mao seemed to have his own version of the "thaw."[18] Some liberal policies were announced for intellectuals shortly before Khrushchev's speech, but the shocking event in the Soviet Union impelled Mao "to devote more attention to the question of the party's relationship to the people as a problem in its own right."[19] On April 25, 1956, Mao proposed a policy to "Let a hundred flowers bloom and let a hundred schools contend" with the intention to encourage intellectuals and non-Communists to speak freely.

Although Mao's idea of the thaw aroused opposition from the Party officials, particularly those in charge of Party propaganda work,[20] the "Hundred Flowers" policy made no significant progress in improving relations between the Party and the non-Communists and intellectuals. Tensions continued to run high, especially at the same time that such international events as the "Polish October" and the "Hungarian Revolt" were unfolding. In China, cases of

[18] Roderick MacFarquhar, *The Origins of the Cultural Revolution, I: Contradictions Among the People 1956–1957* (New York: Columbia University Press, 1974), pp. 33–8.

[19] Ibid., p. 48.

[20] Roderick MacFarquhar, Timothy Cheek, and Eugene Wu, eds., *The Secret Speeches of Chairman Mao, From the Hundred Flowers to the Great Leap Forward* (Cambridge, MA: Council on East Asian Studies, Harvard University, 1989), pp. 7–8.

workers' strikes, student boycotts of classes, and peasant riots were reported in a few cities and some areas in the countryside. For instance, in 1956, the All-China Federation of Trade Unions alone handled eighty-six cases of strikes and petitions. During the six months from late August 1956 to January 1957, there were thirty cases of class boycotts and petitions by students in colleges and vocational schools. About 100,000 workers were involved in strikes, 100,000 students boycotted classes, and there were peasant riots in several dozens of counties.[21] As Roderick MacFarquhar suggests, the strikes in China made Mao Zedong conclude that a Party rectification campaign was needed soon.[22]

An Unusual Spring

The spring of 1957 was indeed "an unusual" one as one editorial of the Party newspaper, the *People's Daily,* called it.[23] On February 27, 1957, Mao addressed an enlarged session of the Supreme State Conference on the conflicts and tensions existing in China. Entitled "On the correct handling of contradictions among the people," his speech was designed to lay down a theoretical justification for the upcoming Party rectification campaign.[24] If Mao and other Party leaders could agree that a Party rectification was necessary to prevent events like the Hungarian Revolt from occurring in China, they reached no agreement on how the Party rectification campaign was to be carried out. Such campaigns , of course, were not new to the Party, having been first carried out in Yan'an in 1942, and then in 1947–48 and 1950. Initially, the Party leadership was prepared to begin such a rectification campaign in 1958. What had bothered many of Mao's colleagues, however, was that this time Mao wanted to invite people outside the Party, mostly the non-Communists and the intellectuals, to criticize the Party publicly.

Perhaps Mao sincerely believed that allowing the non-Communists and intellectuals to criticize the Party was the best way to reduce tensions. Perhaps he simply miscalculated, by underestimating the discontent against the Party and overestimating his reputation. Whatever the reason, Mao himself spearheaded this unusual assault on the Party's mistakes. In March 1957, the Party center convened the National Conference on Propaganda Work during which Mao made several speeches to Party propaganda officials and non-

---

[21] Xiao Xiaoqin and Wang Youqiao, pp. 109–10.
[22] MacFarquhar, Cheek, and Wu, p. 10.
[23] The *People's Daily,* June, 22, 1957.
[24] MacFarquhar, Cheek, and Wu, p. 9.

Communist intellectuals, attempting to sell his idea about a Party rectification campaign.[25] During the following month, Mao undertook a lecture tour in the country, this time trying to persuade provincial Party officials to accept his justification and method for a Party rectification campaign.[26] On April 27, after fending off much doubt, reservation, and even opposition from his colleagues in the Party leadership, Mao finally made the Party center issue a "Directive Concerning the Rectification Campaign" against what the directive condemned as the "Kuomintang style of work," namely, the "three evils" of "bureaucratism, sectarianism, and subjectivism."[27] Meanwhile, the hesitant non-Communists and intellectuals needed to be convinced of the genuine willingness of the Party to let them speak out. So on April 30, Mao summoned the leaders of the non-Communist parties for a final effort at persuasion.[28]

The Party rectification campaign finally started on May 2, with the *People's Daily* carrying an editorial entitled "Why Do We Need a Rectification?"[29] On May 8, the CCP's United Front Department opened forums and invited the leaders of the non-Communist parties to criticize the Communist Party. The United Front Department also invited the industrialists and businessmen to air their criticism. Similar forums were provided by Party organizations at both provincial and municipal levels and in government institutions and universities for non-Communists and intellectuals to lodge their complaints or criticism.

Issues of Party–State Relations

During about a month of "blooming and contending," some fundamental issues about the Party–state relations were raised. First, there was the question about the relations between the Party and the legislature: "Who makes laws, the Party or the National People's Congress?" One critic asked,

> Whose words count in connection with state affairs? The Constitution lays down that the words of the National People's Congress and its Standing Committee count, but actually the National People's Congress is nothing but a mud idol while all power is in the hands of the

---

[25] Xiao Xiaoqin and Wang Youqiao, p. 110.

[26] For the draft transcripts of Mao's talk in Tianjin, Shandong, Jiangsu, and Shanghai, see MacFarquhar, Cheek, and Wu, pp. 275–362.

[27] Roderick MacFarquhar, ed., *The Hundred Flowers* (London: Stevens, 1960), p. 36; *Zhongguo gongchandang lishi dashiji* (A Chronology of the Chinese Communist Party) (Beijing: Renmin chubanshe, 1989), p. 229.

[28] For the draft transcript of Mao's talk, see MacFarquhar, Cheek, and Wu, pp. 363–72.

[29] The *People's Daily,* May 2, 1957.

CCP Central Committee. The National People's Congress merely carries out the formality of raising hands and passing resolutions.[30]

This criticism was substantiated by one member of the Standing Committee of the NPC: "On many occasions when major matters were under discussion often only the democratic personages spoke, whereas the party members declined to utter a word. Does this indicate that the party has already discussed and made its decisions on the matters concerned?"[31] Many pointed out that the situation at the provincial and local levels was even worse. After conducting inspection of work at the lower levels, the legislators from the NPC often reported that people at the local levels generally did not know who the county magistrate or provincial governor was. People knew only the Party, not the government.[32]

Second, there was the question about the relations between the Party and the legal system: "Which is superior, the Party or the law?" Whether the Party was above the law was undoubtedly the most crucial issue that had been around for several years. In 1957, this issue was publicly debated for the first time. One critic pointed out:

Although the constitution has come into force, yet there are still a section of the leaders who take a nihilist standpoint toward law, maintaining that it is only natural for the Party to take the place of the Government, that the Party's orders are above the law; and words of Party members are regarded, by themselves, as 'golden rules and jade laws.' This is a contravention of the legal system. . . . [33]

Many judges and legal officials took the opportunity to voice their strong support for judicial independence and argued that "leadership of the court by party committee interfered with the independence of the law."[34] They suggested that the campaign of suppressing the counterrevolutionaries was not correctly handled and that interference by the Party was one of the reasons for so many innocent people wrongly accused.[35]

---

[30] MacFarquhar, 1960, p. 108.

[31] Ibid., p. 42.

[32] The *Guangming Daily* May 31, 1957; The *People's Daily*, June 3, 1957.

[33] MacFarquhar, 1960, p. 114.

[34] The *People's Daily*, September 17, 1957; October 23, 1957.

[35] Ibid., September 7, 1957; September 15, 1957; September 20, 1957; September 24, 1957; October 14, 1957; October 23, 1957; and October 28, 1957.

Third, there was the question about the relations between Party organization and government administration: "Who runs the country, the Party committee or the government?" Several critics exposed the role assumed by Party core groups.

> Now the general situation is that in every government institution, the Party core group is in charge. The system of the Party is the actual command system while the administrative system has become powerless. Party core groups in government institutions directly give instructions about work to the lower levels and replace the administrative system. They actually give orders in the name of the Party core groups.[36]

One critic asked, "If the state is led by the working class, why not use these state institutions instead of weakening their authority by establishing a Party system in addition to the state?"[37] One vice chairman of the NPC Standing Committee criticized the practice of the CCP and the State Council jointly issuing directives. He stressed: "This is a violation of the 1954 constitution. It also makes one believe that only jointly issued instructions are important. An instruction issued only by the State Council is less important. Thus the party has weakened the power of the State Council."[38]

Finally, there was the question about the CCP's status in the Chinese state. All the criticism of the CCP ultimately boiled down to one essential question: "Whose state is it anyway, the Party's or the people's?" Several non-Communists blasted the CCP's unwillingness to sanction the practices of sharing state power with non-Communists. At the provincial and local levels, non-Communist vice governors and county magistrates did not have much authority to do their assigned government work. Many things had already been done by the Communist cadres before anyone reported to the non-Communist governors.[39]

Some members of the non-Communist parties further criticized the CCP for treating the Chinese state as its private property and argued that the Party belonged to only a small group of people, but the Chinese state belonged to every member of the people.

> The Communist Party has 12,000,000 members, less than 2 percent of the total population. The 600 million people are to become the obe-

---

[36] MacFarquhar, 1960, p. 277. [37] The *People's Daily,* June 6, 1957.
[38] The *Guangming Daily,* May 17, 1957. [39] The *People's Daily,* June 3, 1957.

dient subjects of these 2 percent of people. What sort of principle is this! The absolute leadership of the Party must be done away with. The privilege of the Party members must be done away with.[40]

Chu Anping, who in 1954 had written a much-read article to hail the new regime, now sharply criticized the Party.

> Where is the key to the problem? In my opinion, the key lies in the idea that "the world belongs to the Party". . . . [I]sn't it too much that within the scope of the nation, there must be a Party man as leader in every unit, big or small, whether section or subsection; or that nothing, big or small, can be done without a nod from a Party man? . . . I wonder if the Party acts this way because it entertains the idea that "every place is royal territory" and therefore has created the present monochromatic, one-family-empire appearance.[41]

One comment seemed to have best summarized the tensions: "[T]he revolution was worse than a change of dynasties and living in such a society is heartbreaking. The intellectuals are more and more timid every day, and they are living less peacefully than during the Japanese occupation or Kuomintang rule. . . ."[42]

The Party Strikes Back

The United Front Department of the CCP organized altogether thirteen such forums at which most of the criticism of the CCP was voiced. These forums continued until June 3, long after Mao Zedong and other Party leaders had lost their interest in listening to the criticism. It is now clear that only two weeks after the Party rectification campaign was formally launched, Mao changed his mind. On May 15, 1957, Mao wrote an article entitled "The Situation Is Changing" and circulated it among Party officials. Mao told them: "Now we should begin to pay attention to criticizing revisionism."[43] Mao estimated that there were 1 percent, 3 percent, 5 percent, up to 10 percent of the non-Communists and intellectuals who were "Bourgeois Rightists" attacking the Party. Mao also warned that there was a proportion of new intellectual mem-

---

[40] MacFarquhar, 1960, p. 57.
[41] Ibid., pp. 51–2.   [42] Ibid., p. 57.
[43] John K. Leung and Michael Y. M. Kau, eds., *The Writings of Mao Zedong: 1949–1976* (Armonk, NY: M. E. Sharpe, 1992), vol. 2, p. 548.

bers in the Party who echoed "Rightists" outside the Party. Mao described them as "so-called Communist Party members" and "rightist elements within the Communist Party – the revisionists."[44] But to draw out the opposition, Mao instructed the Party leaders not to act immediately and to wait for a while. "We shall let the Rightists run amuck for a time and let them reach their climax. The more they run amuck, the better for us."[45]

On May 19, students began to put up wall posters on university campuses to air their views and criticism. This made Mao Zedong increasingly worried. On May 25, when receiving the delegates to the Third National Congress of the New Democratic Youth League, Mao sent out warnings, particularly to the young people. "The Chinese Communist Party is the core of the leadership of the whole Chinese people. Without this core, the cause of socialism cannot be victorious. Any word or deed at variance with socialism is completely wrong."[46] Around May 30, several provincial Party committees held emergency meetings and sent telegrams to the Party Central Committee, urging the top leadership to launch a counterattack before the situation got out of control.[47] On June 8, the *People's Daily* formally announced a struggle against anyone who had dared to criticize the Party. The Party rectification campaign was quickly reversed into a nationwide political campaign against the Rightists both inside and outside the Party.[48] Party committee secretaries at various levels were overjoyed by the Party center's decision, and many Party organizational branches enthusiastically fulfilled or overfulfilled the quota of Rightists to be exposed in their work units.[49] According to official figures published more than twenty years later, 552,877 people nationwide were designated as Rightists in 1957–58.[50] They were subsequently subjected to criticism, attack, demotion, or dismissal from office. Many of them ultimately were forced out of their home cities into labor camps in the remote rural and mountain areas, having to suffer political humiliation and economic hardships for as long as twenty-two years.

---

[44] Mao, 1977, vol. 5, p. 440.
[45] Ibid., pp. 441–2.   [46] Ibid., p. 447.
[47] *Mingfang huiyi* (Recollections of Blooming and Contending) (Hong Kong: *Zhanwang* Magazine, 1966), p. 36.
[48] By Mao's definition, the "bourgeois Rightists are the bourgeois reactionaries . . . who oppose the Communist Party, the people and socialism." Mao, 1977, vol. 5, p. 455.
[49] *The Nineties* (Hong Kong) (April 1988), p. 108.
[50] Ma Yuping and Huang Yuchong, eds., *Zhongguo zuotian yu jintian, 1840–1987 nian guoqing shouce* (China's Yesterday and Today: Handbook of National Conditions: 1840–1987) (Beijing: Jiefangjun chubanshe, 1989), p. 751.

THE TURNING POINT IN PARTY–LEGAL RELATIONS

The Anti-Rightist Campaign went on largely in urban areas, universities, re-search institutes, and Party and government institutions where most of the intellectuals had been working.[51] Intellectuals therefore constituted the largest group among the victims of the campaign (about 57 percent).[52] However, the impact of the Anti-Rightist Campaign on the Chinese legislative and judicial institutions was equally, if not more, devastating. It was the single most impor-tant event before the Cultural Revolution that fundamentally changed the Party–legal relations.

The campaign was the first most serious trample on the constitutional rights of the Chinese citizens. Once someone was designated as a Rightist, he or she immediately lost any and every right granted by the 1954 constitution. There was no legal protection whatsoever, nor any legal procedure to appeal one's case. On many occasions, Rightists were randomly picked up to meet the quotas imposed by the higher authorities. At the central government level, the immediate victims of the campaign were three non-Communist ministers ac-cused of being Rightists – Zhang Naiqi (Minister of Food), Zhang Bojun (Minister of Communications), and Luo Longji (Minister of Timber Industry). On January 31, 1958, all three were dismissed from office. In February 1958, one more non-Communist minister lost his job (Zhang Xiruo, Minister of Education). A month after the Minister of Timber Industry was dismissed, the entire Ministry of Timber Industry was abolished. Although it must seem bizarre to suggest that a whole ministry had to be abolished because its minister was accused of being a Rightist, no other explanation was available.

Not only did the constitutionally granted rights or the ministerial status in the central government fail to protect one from random political attack in the campaign, but even the Chinese national legislature failed to provide sanctuary to its members. Thirty-eight legislators in the National People's Congress were labeled as Rightists, including three members of the NPC Standing Committee. Subsequently they were all disqualified from attending the NPC meetings and lost their jobs.[53]

---

[51] Theodore H. E. Chen, *Thought Reform of the Chinese Intellectuals* (Hong Kong: Hong Kong University Press, 1960); Merle Goldman, *China's Intellectuals: Advise and Dissent* (Cam-bridge, MA: Harvard University Press, 1981).

[52] Chen Xuewei, *Sishi nian huigu* (Remembrance of Forty Years) (Beijing: Zhongyang dangxiao chubanshe, 1990), p. 171.

[53] *Quanguo renda jiqi changweihui dashiji, 1954–1987* (A Chronology of the NPC and Its Standing Committee, 1954–1987) (Beijing: Falü chubanshe, 1987), p. 99.

The official figure released in the post-Mao period shows that during the Anti-Rightist Campaign, as many as 6,284 state officials working in the central government institutions were designated as Rightists.[54] In the military 5,799 were accused of being Rightists and about 11,000 were labeled "middle-Rightists."[55] This alarming figure, of course, does not include the many more officials working in the provincial and municipal government institutions who were purged or removed from office. For instance, in 1957–58, four governors and eighteen vice governors from fourteen provincial governments (out of a total of twenty-nine) were dismissed from their office (see Table 3.1). Some of them were accused of being "Rightists within the Party." Others were denounced for "trying to break away from the Party leadership." Suggesting that the Party be separated from the government turned out to be politically fatal for Sha Wenhan. As governor of Zhejiang provincial government, Sha argued that if the provincial Party committee issued orders to the district Party committees, and the district Party committees issued orders to the county Party committees, the administrative system of the provincial government would become redundant. He suggested that the provincial government should take command. Not surprisingly, he was accused of "opposing the Party leadership over government work."[56] Sha and his associate, Yang Siyi, became the first victims among the provincial government leaders. At a conference in Hangzhou in January 1958, Mao disdainfully described Sha Wenhan and Yang Siyi as "something else."[57]

With the launching of the Anti-Rightist Campaign, efforts to consolidate a constitutional and a legal system were suddenly halted. In many ways, the newborn national legislature was crippled and the legal system was damaged. Government agencies of justice and supervision were abolished and not restored until decades later. Important legal procedures were abandoned. The magnitude of the devastation the Chinese legal institutions suffered during the Anti-Rightist Campaign has yet to be analyzed.

---

[54] Ma Yuping and Huang Yuchong, p. 751.

[55] *Guanyu xinshiqi jundui zhengzhi gongzuo de jueding zhushiben* (The Annotated Book for the Resolution Concerning the Political Work in the Military in the New Era) (Beijing: Jiefangjun chubanshe, 1987), p. 160.

[56] *The Nineties* (Hong Kong) (February 1988), p. 109.

[57] MacFarquhar, Cheek, and Wu, p. 380.

Table 3.1. *Provincial governors dismissed, 1957–58*

Province	Name	Post	Date of dismissal
Zhejiang	Sha Wenhan	Governor	12/1957
	Yang Siyi	Vice Governor	12/1957
Qinghai	Sun Zuobin	Governor	3/1958
Guangxi	Chen Zaili	Vice Governor	3/1958
Shaanxi	Han Beie	Vice Governor	7/1958
Hunan	Cheng Xingling	Vice Governor	7/1958
Guangdong	Gu Dacun	Vice Governor	9/1958
	Feng Baiju	Vice Governor	9/1958
Guizhou	Ou Baichuan	Vice Governor	9/1958
Anhui	Li Shinong	Vice Governor	11/1958
Gansu	Sun Diancai	Vice Governor	11/1958
	Liang Dajun	Vice Governor	11/1958
	Chen Chengyi	Vice Governor	11/1958
Shandong	Zhao Jianmin	Governor	11/1958
	Wang Zhuoru	Vice Governor	11/1958
	Yuan Ziyang	Vice Governor	11/1958
Yunnan	Gong Zizhi	Vice Governor	11/1958
Henan	Zhang Zhen	Vice Governor	12/1958
Xinjiang	Iminov	Vice Governor	Unknown
	Ashad	Vice Governor	Unknown
Liaoning	Du Zheheng	Governor	Unknown
	Li Dao	Vice Governor	Unknown

Sources: Shou Xiaohe, Li Xiongfan, and Sun Shuyu, eds., *Zhongguo sheng shi zizhiqu ziliao shouce* (Handbook of Reference of the Provinces, Municipalities and Autonomous Regions in China) (Beijing: Shehuikexue wenxian chubanshe, 1990); Donald W. Klein, and Anne B. Clark, eds., *Biographical Dictionary of Chinese Communism 1921–1965,* (Cambridge, MA: Harvard University Press, 1971); Frederick C. Teiwes, *Politics and Purges in China: Rectification and the Decline of Party Norms, 1950–1965,* 2nd edition (Armonk, NY: M. E. Sharpe, 1993), p. 275.

Attack on the National Legislature

In the U.S. Congress, the congressional committee and subcommittee system plays such a crucial role that one can hardly imagine how the Congress could work without these committees. In 1954, the Chinese national legislature did not yet have a committee system. In the autumn of 1956, Liu Shaoqi, the chairman of the NPC Standing Committee (like House Speaker), suggested

Table 3.2. *Bills proposed in the National People's Congress, 1954–63*

Year	Dates	Congress	Session	Bills proposed
1954	9/15–9/28	First	First	39
1955	7/5–7/30	First	Second	214
1956	6/15–6/30	First	Third	176
1957	6/6–7/15	First	Fourth	243
1958	2/1–2/11	First	Fifth	81
1959	4/18–4/28	Second	First	80
1960	3/30–4/10	Second	Second	46
1962	3/27–4/16	Second	Third	163
1963	11/17–12/3	Second	Fourth	172

Source: Compiled by the author from information in *Quanguo Renda jiqi Changweihui Dashiji 1954–1987* (A Chronology of the National People's Congress and Its Standing Committee, 1954–1987) (Beijing: Falü Chubanshe, 1987).

that the NPC establish several work committees. Later that year, Peng Zhen, the vice chairman of the NPC Standing Committee and secretary-general of the NPC, led a delegation to the Soviet Union and several Eastern European countries. One important mission of the trip was to observe how the legislatures in these countries were organized. After the trip, proposals were made to establish NPC work committees of Political and Legal Affairs, Finance and Trade, Heavy Industry, Light Industry, Agriculture, Education, and Foreign Affairs. Clearly these committees would correspond to the division of work of the ministries in the State Council, thus promising an active role in legislating and supervising the work in these areas. However, the Anti-Rightist Campaign soon began and these proposals got nowhere.[58] As a result, the first work committee of the NPC was not formed until 1979, thirty-five years after the first NPC was convened.

Political attacks on the thirty-eight legislators also had a chilling effect on the entire body of the NPC. Those who survived the campaign had to be cautious in their speeches in the legislature, and few had the courage to express opinions different from the Party's line. Because there wasn't much one dared to say, there wasn't much to propose. The number of the bills proposed by the legislators to the NPC declined drastically from 243 in 1957 to 81 in 1958, 80

[58] *Quanguo renda jiqi changweihui dashiji, 1954–1987,* p. 10.

72

in 1959, and 46 in 1960 (see Table 3.2). The NPC not only legislated much less, but also had fewer and fewer meetings. As the NPC gradually turned into a rubber-stamp, the sessions of the Standing Committee of the NPC had decreased from thirty-nine in 1957 to twenty-two in 1960, and fourteen in 1961.

Attack on the Judicial System

Between March and August 1958, a series of meetings were held in the judicial institutions to expose the "primary danger" of Rightist mistakes, which included: (1) "ignoring the struggle against the enemy and putting undue emphasis on the democratic rights of the people"; (2) "ignoring the class and mass nature of the legal system"; (3) "upholding bourgeois legal viewpoints" and "wholesale copying of the Soviet experience"; and (4) "ignoring the absolute leadership by the Party" and even "asserting independence from the Party."[59] The legal principles that were clearly stipulated in the 1954 constitution, such as equality of citizens before the law, independent trial by courts, and the procuracy exercising its authority independently, were criticized during the campaign as erroneous ideas, the "legal viewpoints of the bourgeois," and "using the law against the Party."[60] After the campaign, it was taken for granted that Party committees at various levels would directly review and approve legal cases and that the courts and the procuratorates would simply carry out Party committees' decisions through legal formalities. Mao was even less interested in legal procedures. In August 1958, Mao was quoted as saying that laws could not be expected to rule the majority of people. Most people had to develop good habits. Mao argued that every resolution and meeting of the Party could substitute for laws. Later the Party theorists admitted that, beginning in 1957, "rule of man, not rule of law" was widely advocated and had become the fundamental principle in judicial activity.[61]

Before the campaign, the national legislature had already begun to draft a criminal law, a civil code, police regulations, and regulations for the punishment of public functionaries. By June 1957, the draft criminal law had gone through dozens of revisions. With the sudden outbreak of the campaign, however, all the work was stopped. In a report to the Politburo, the Party's Central Leading Group of Political and Legal Affairs said it all: "The principle we have

---

[59] Zheng Qian et al., p. 97.
[60] Ibid.
[61] *Quanguo renda jiqi changweihui dashiji*, pp. 13–4; *Zhongguo guoqing daiquan*, p. 277.

agreed upon is that any law that is inappropriate must not be formulated." "According to the actual conditions in our country, it is no longer necessary to formulate criminal code, civil code and procedural laws."[62] Consequently, China did not enact such basic laws as a code of criminal law and a code of criminal procedure until more than two decades later. Also, it was not until 1983 that China began to experiment with civil procedural law. In 1980, Deng Xiaoping admitted: "Though we tried repeatedly to draw up such a code and it went through more than 30 drafts, nothing ever came out of the project."[63]

During the campaign, the Supreme People's Court and the Supreme People's Procuratorate were accused of "breaking away from the Party leadership" and "showing Rightist tendencies."[64] Beyond the verbal attack, the Chinese legal system underwent a major structural change. The "dual rule" that had been applied to government administration was now extended to legal institutions. Whereas before the people's courts and the people's procuratorates at the provincial and local levels were all under the direct jurisdiction of the Supreme People's Court and the Supreme People's Procuratorate, now they were placed under the direct leadership of Party committees at the same level. This lateral slicing of the judicial and procuratorate authority by the Party organization deprived the Supreme People's Court and the Supreme People's Procuratorate of their authority in legal affairs.

The Party Takes Over

The Anti-Rightist Campaign greatly consolidated the Party's organizational control of the judicial administration. In July 1957, the Party center convened the Qingdao Conference attended by provincial and municipal Party committee secretaries to further plan the counterattack on the Rightists. Mao stressed, "The politics and law, as well as culture and education departments of local governments, must receive instructions from provincial, municipal or autonomous regional Party committees and provincial, municipal or autonomous regional people's governments, provided there is no violation of the policies

---

[62] Zheng Qian et al., p. 99.

[63] Deng Xiaoping, *Selected Works of Deng Xiaoping, 1975–1982* (Beijing: Foreign Languages Press, 1984), p. 227. Deng, however, should blame himself as well because he was in charge of the Party's Anti-Rightist Campaign in 1957–58.

[64] Chen Xuewei, *Lishi de qishi: shi nian jianshe yanjiu, 1957–1966* (Revelations of History: Research on the Ten Years of Construction, 1957–1966) (Beijing: Qiushi chubanshe, 1989), p. 76.

and regulations of the center."[65] The directives or opinions of the Party committees thus became the highest law in judicial activities and normal legal procedures were simply pushed aside. From making arrests to trials to sentencing, all the legal decisions had to be made by the Party committees at the same level or by the Party core groups in the judicial institutions.

On September 18, 1957, the editorial of the *People's Daily* pointed out, "The attack by the Rightists shows that in certain areas the leadership over state power by the proletarian class is still not consolidated. The proletarian class has not yet really established its leadership over certain organs of state power and cultural and education organizations."[66] The logical conclusion then was to further strengthen the Party leadership in these areas. In a report sent to the CCP Central Committee on November 30, the Party core group of the Supreme People's Court and the Ministry of Justice expressed their determination to "resolutely carry out Chairman Mao's instructions." They further affirmed that the people's courts at all levels must absolutely place themselves under the leadership of the Party committee.

> Not only in principles and policies, but also in their entire judicial activity, the people's courts must resolutely obey the Party leadership and accept the Party's supervision. The Party core groups in the people's courts must frequently and on their own initiative seek instructions from and report to Party committees at the same level.[67]

Since then, there had been established a direct line of authority between the Party center and the Supreme People's Court and between the local Party committees and local people's courts. Views that judicial organs were "the tractable tool of the Party" and that there should be "no separation of Party and law" began to prevail in the entire Chinese judicial system.

Ironically, the expressed determination by the Ministry of Justice to uphold the Party leadership did not help to save the ministry. In 1959, all the agencies of the Ministry of Justice, from the central office in Beijing down to the bureaus in provinces, were simply abolished. No official explanation was given as to why the Ministry of Justice, an important component of the Chinese state, had to be abolished. During the "blooming and contending period," the Minister of Justice, who was a non-Communist, came out to defend the CCP's policy and practice in legal affairs. Nevertheless, because many judges and

[65] Zheng Qian et al., p. 88.
[66] The *People's Daily,* September 18, 1957.
[67] Zheng Qian et al., p. 89.

legal officials working in the Ministry of Justice strongly criticized inter-ference in legal work by Party committees, it would not be too difficult to believe that the Party leaders must have found the Ministry of Justice trouble-some at best and dangerous at worst.

The case of the Ministry of Supervision was also telling. During the cam-paign, the Ministry of Supervision was severely criticized for "breaking away from the Party leadership." Judging from the number of Rightists being ac-cused, there seemed to be some elements of truth to this accusation. In the ministry, one deputy minister, three deputy bureau chiefs, and one division chief were accused of being Rightists. In some provinces, about 20 percent to 30 percent of the officials in the Bureau of Supervision were accused of being Rightists.[68] In October 1957, the Party core group in the Ministry of Supervi-sion sent a report to the Party Central Committee in which it ironically admit-ted the mistake of "breaking away from the Party leadership" since the begin-ning of the PRC. The solution, the Party core group suggested, was to merge the Ministry of Supervision into the Party's Commission of Supervision. In April 1959, the NPC, following the Party's decision, abolished the Ministry of Supervision.[69] Party committees literally took over the state's authority to manage administrative supervision and the Ministry of Supervision was not restored until 1988.

In November 1960, the Party center approved a report by the Party's Central Leading Group of Political and Legal Affairs to further simplify the central judicial institutions. According to the approved plan, the Ministry of Public Security, the Supreme People's Court, and the Supreme People's Procuratorate would simply work together, with the Ministry of Public Security calling the shots.[70] Most judges and procurators would report to work in the Ministry of Public Security. The Supreme People's Court itself was allowed to retain about fifty people and one office, and the Supreme People's Procuratorate was al-lowed to retain twenty to thirty people and one office. On December 9, 1960, the Office of Political and Legal Affairs of the State Council was abolished and the Party's Central Leading Group of Political and Legal Affairs became responsible for formulating policies and guidelines for judicial work. This completed the takeover of the state legal institutions by the Party organization.

During the three years of economic adjustment (1960–62) following the serious economic crisis caused by the failed Great Leap Forward policy, the

---

[68] The *Nineties* (Hong Kong) (May 1988), p. 109.
[69] Zheng Qian et al., p. 138.
[70] Ibid.

legislative institutions were among the first to get the ax. The NPC and its Standing Committee, already damaged during the Anti-Rightist Campaign, were further weakened by the efforts to cut government budgets and reduce the central state apparatus. The national legislature of a country of 700 million people finally ended up having just over one hundred staff members.[71] Naturally, both "the quantity and quality of legislation declined drastically and the legislative process was often paralyzed."[72] By 1962 the damage to the Chinese legal system had proved to be so severe that even Mao had to admit: "We cannot live without laws. We not only need a criminal code, but also a civil code. Now the situation has become absolutely lawless. We cannot live without laws. We must formulate a criminal law and a civil code. We should not only make laws, but also compile legal cases."[73]

The criticism of the Party in 1957 was sharp and sometimes harsh, but the Party's massive counterattack was hardly justified. After all, it was Mao who had painstakingly persuaded the initially reluctant and timid non-Communists and intellectuals to "bloom and contend." Second, the criticism voiced in the spring of 1957 largely reflected the existing problems and tensions. Similar views had been previously expressed by the top Party leaders as well. Third, it was exactly the problems criticized during the "blooming and contending" period that had convinced Mao that a Party rectification campaign was needed.

The Anti-Rightist Campaign was not just an overreaction by the Party against its critics, many of whom were long-time supporters of the Party. Nor was it an attack and counterattack by the non-Communists and Communists, for many of the CCP members were also accused of being Rightists during the campaign. In the most fundamental sense, the campaign was a political punishment carried out by the Party organization against anyone who dared to challenge the Party's role and status in the Chinese political system.

In conclusion, we can perhaps stress three major points. First, during the "unusual spring" of 1957, the CCP's war-hardened revolutionary spirit, the principle of the Party's unified leadership, and the Party's control of the state legislative and judicial institutions were seriously challenged. Even at this early stage of the People's Republic, the institutional tensions between rule of

---

[71] Ibid., p. 15. The figure of the Chinese population was for 1964.

[72] Li Fuyu, Tang Jian, and Zhang Xuelian, eds., *Zhongguo xingzheng guanli jiangzuo* (Lectures on the Administrative Management in China) (Shenyang: Liaoning renmin chubanshe, 1985), pp. 37–8.

[73] Wu Lei, p. 37; *Zhongguo guoqing daiquan*, p. 271.

Party and rule of law were high and deep. The cracks in the so-called party-state were enormous.

Second, the massive attacks on the legislative and judicial institutions during the Anti-Rightist Campaign suggests that the CCP as a revolutionary organization could be just as decisive and destructive in dealing with its own legal system as with the KMT's legal system. For Party committees at various levels, carrying out the Anti-Rightist Campaign in 1957–58 was just like mobilizing the masses into warfare or land reform before 1949. For many Party officials, purging their colleagues in the legislative and judicial institutions was no different than attacking the retained personnel of the KMT regime or than eliminating the counterrevolutionaries. The CCP again proved to be more capable of destruction than construction.

Third, the dramatic shift from optimism in legal development in 1954 to devastation of the legal system in 1957 powerfully illustrates an impossible choice a revolutionary party faced in state-building. Unlike a national flag and national anthem, a legal system, once established, could begin to have its own life and develop its own logic. If the state constitution was the highest law of the land, then words by any individual or by any party surely were not. If everyone was equal before the law, then Party leaders were no exception. On the other hand, if Party leaders had no intention to place themselves beneath the laws, then it might serve them better if they had not bothered to promulgate those laws in the first place. If legal nihilism and total destruction of the legal system were the organizational purpose of the CCP, the Party could also forget about benefits associated with a system of law and order. Mao then should have no reason to complain about the "absolutely lawless" situation in 1962. All the inconsistencies and contradictions can only point to the institutional dilemma that the Party faced: It could not hope to rule the country effectively without a legal system, and yet it could practically lose its dominance if a legal system was fully developed.

4

Party Leadership and State Administration

B Y late 1953, the economic situation in China had significantly improved. A three-year period (1950–52) of economic recovery enabled the new regime to get national finance and the economy under control. Gross industrial and agricultural production had not only surpassed the level of 1949, but the highest recorded level in history.[1] As China's First Five-Year Economic Plan was soon to be put into effect,[2] efforts had to be made to enhance state capacities, particularly regarding the management of the national economy. To a large extent, China's economic growth was contingent on a strong administrative state.

As a centralized government administration developed, however, the Party's organizational control also expanded. A growing state and an expansionist Party then raised questions about who should administer state affairs and how economic production would be organized. This chapter examines the structure of "dual role" in the central and provincial government, analyzes the emerging tensions between the Party organization and government agencies, particularly during the Great Leap Forward in 1958–60, and offers a new perspective on the issue of central–local relations by emphasizing an analytical distinction between the Party and state.

GROWING STATE AND EXPANSIONIST PARTY

Under the 1954 constitution, the central administration was given an upgraded status. The newly established State Council, which now solely represented the Chinese central government, was constitutionally defined as "the highest ad-

---

[1] Xiao Xiaoqin and Wang Youqiao, eds., *Zhonghua renmin gongheguo sishi nian* (Forty Years of the People's Republic of China) (Beijing: Beijing shifan xueyuan chubanshe, 1990), p. 33.
[2] Although the Five-Year Plan was discussed as early as 1951 and was supposed to cover a five-year period from 1953 to 1957, it was finally approved by the National People's Congress and implemented by the State Council in 1955.

ministrative organ of the state." According to the new constitution and the Organic Law of the State Council, the premier who presided over the plenary sessions of the State Council was responsible for the daily work of the central government. The premier and vice premiers were to lead all the agencies of the central government. Every ministry, commission, and administrative bureau followed a responsibility system under which the highest administrative official of each agency assumed total responsibility for that agency. Under this mandate, the State Council expanded rapidly. In 1954, it established sixty-four agencies (including offices, ministries, commissions, and administrative bureaus), compared to thirty-five in 1949 and forty-four in 1953. The agencies of the State Council further increased to seventy in 1955 and eighty-one in 1956.[3]

Revolutionaries or Bureaucrats

The Chinese state institution-building in 1954–55 looked impressive with its newly built institutions and constitutionally assigned roles. This seemed to point to the beginning of a process of normalization and bureaucratization of governance. Yet, from the very beginning, this process of state-building encountered serious difficulties, one of which was the lack of qualified personnel to fill 2.7 million positions in the new Chinese state institutions.[4]

As I mentioned earlier, the new Communist regime in China did not lack revolutionaries and political activists to seize power or to launch mass campaigns. But when it came to management of state affairs and organization of the national economy, many of the CCP cadres were hardly qualified. In 1951, the CCP had 1.75 million cadres in addition to 1 million military officials and 1.1 million teachers and cultural personnel. The CCP cadres mainly came from six groups: old cadres, former KMT officials, old intellectuals, young intellectuals, demobilized soldiers, and worker and peasant activists.[5] Among the 1.75 million cadres who worked in state institutions, about 600,000 were old cadres who joined the revolution before 1949. About 400,000 were retained personnel from the old regime.[6] Another large group of cadres was that of worker and

[3] *Zhongguo guoqing baogao* (Report on the National Conditions of China) (Shenyang: Liaoning renmin chubanshe, 1990), p. 919.

[4] Hong Yung Lee, *From Revolutionary Cadres to Party Technocrats in Socialist China* (Berkeley: University of California Press, 1991), pp. 48–9.

[5] Ibid.

[6] These figures were provided by An Ziwen, then director of the CCP Organization Department. See An Ziwen, *An Ziwen zuzhi gongzuo wenxuan.* (Selected Works by An Ziwen on Organization Work) (Beijing: Zhonggong zhongyang dangxiao chubanshe, 1987), p. 32.

peasant activists.[7] Yet, even when the CCP claimed to be a party of the proletariat, only less than 10 percent of the party members were industrial workers, whereas more than 80 percent of the CCP's 4.5 million members in 1950 were peasants who lacked adequate administrative skills.[8]

Facing a severe shortage of qualified cadres to manage the new state institutions, the CCP leaders did try to recruit more intellectuals and train young people to be qualified government workers. However, one political campaign after another in the 1950s removed an increasing number of qualified administrators from the state institutions. The first group of people to go was that of retained personnel from the old regime. For instance, in the 1955–57 campaign to expose the so-called hidden counterrevolutionaries in the government and army institutions, more than 40 percent of the retained personnel were under investigation. In some areas, 98.5 percent of the retained personnel were under investigation.[9] Then during the Anti-Rightist Campaign, more than half a million intellectuals, professionals, and government administrators were purged, including 6,284 government officials working in the central government and many more in the provincial governments. Because many engineers, scientists, and administrators were dismissed from their positions in government, political activists known more for their political zeal than their professional qualifications were recruited to fill the vacuum.

Here the CCP leaders had certainly missed a great opportunity to transform a revolutionary movement into building an administrative state. If Lenin in the earlier years of the USSR believed that ordinary citizens could be readily put into bureaucratic jobs and run the state, Mao and other CCP leaders seemed to conclude that the national economy and state affairs could be managed the way a revolutionary war was organized – by mobilizing thousands of worker and peasant activists in campaigns. Needless to say, the events in the USSR and China proved both Lenin and Mao to be wrong.

The System of "Dual Rule"

Before the new state institutions were established, the Chinese central administrators had recognized that learning how to adjust the relations between the Party and the state was not going to be easy. In April 1950, Premier Zhou Enlai pointed out, "Due to the long-term war conditions in the past, we have developed a habit of often issuing orders in the name of the Party. It was

---

[7] Hong Yung Lee, p. 52.   [8] An Ziwen, p. 5.
[9] Ibid., p. 93.

especially so in the army. Now that we have entered a peaceful period and established our national regime, we should change this habit."[10] He also argued, "There are connections, but also differences between the Party and the government. The principles and policies of the Party must be carried out through the government and the Party organization should guarantee the implementation."[11]

Dong Biwu, vice premier of the Government Administrative Council, also emphasized:

> The Party must exercise its leadership over the organs of the state power, but it does not mean that the Party should directly manage state affairs. . . . The Party must achieve its leadership through the work of Party members in the organs of state power and by making the state organs accept the policies of the Party. . . . Under no circumstances, should the Party mix the functions of the Party organs with those of the state organs. The Party must not take over the work of the state organs simply because it exercises the leadership over them.[12]

In a letter to Rao Shushi, the first secretary of the CCP East China Regional Bureau, Dong suggested that it would be inappropriate for the Party to be directly involved in day-to-day government management, although the Party should direct the work to establish government agencies at the lower levels. Mao Zedong seemed to agree to Dong's suggestion, for he instructed all the CCP regional bureaus to "pay attention to this matter."[13] Clearly these leaders favored an A & B approach to the Party–administration relations. Under this format, the Party center would make major decisions regarding the state affairs, whereas the government administration would assume full responsibility for implementing the Party's directives and policies.

The A & B scenario, however, did not materialize. The state administrative institution-building was structurally incapacitated by a system called dual rule. As Franz Schurmann explains, "The general functional principles on the allocation of authority to government agencies are those of vertical rule and dual

---

[10] Zhou Enlai, *Selected Works of Zhou Enlai* (Beijing: Foreign Languages Press, 1981), pp. 174–5.

[11] Ibid.

[12] Dong Biwu, *Dong Biwu xuanji* (Selected Works of Dong Biwu) (Beijing: Renmin chubanshe, 1989), pp. 190–1.

[13] Michael Y. M. Kau and John K. Leung, eds., *The Writings of Mao Zedong: 1949–1976*, vol. 1 (Armonk, NY: M. E. Sharpe, 1986), p. 227.

rule." Vertical rule means "single channels of command and information" between a lower-echelon agency and a higher-echelon agency. In contrast, dual rule means multiple channels of command and information, under which an agency is subjected to control from a higher-echelon agency and also subjected to "another body on the same administrative level."[14] Since 1949, a system of dual rule had been quickly put in place under which the government agencies at various levels, while reporting vertically to their superiors in the state hierarchy, also had to subject themselves to horizontal control by Party committees at the same level. The central government was under the control of the CCP Politburo, and provincial and local governments were under the control of Party committees at the same level. Clearly, vertical rule would strengthen the authority of central government agencies whereas dual rule would increase the power of Party committees.[15]

The system of dual rule under which the party organization exercised horizontal control over government was not unique to China. In the Soviet Union, the same system had existed for several decades. Nor was the system unique to Communist parties. The Chinese Nationalist Party or KMT had also installed a similar control system on the mainland in the 1930s and 1940s and has continued the tradition in Taiwan since the 1950s. However, the CCP control system was more comprehensive than that attainable by merely setting up party organizational units parallel to government agencies. The CCP's most important organizational devices included: (1) Party core groups in the state institutions;[16] (2) Party work departments that overlapped government departments at the same level; and (3) Party and government jointly issued directives.

Party Core Group (PCG)

In November 1949, the CCP Politburo decided to form Party core groups in the newly established state institutions. The PCGs were also set up at the local

---

[14] Franz H. Schurmann, *Ideology and Organization in Communist China,* 2nd and enlarged edition (Berkeley: University of California Press, 1968), pp. 188–9.

[15] Ibid., p. 191.

[16] The party core group system was scarcely mentioned in the early studies of Chinese politics and government. Recent discussion of the system can be found in Susan L. Shirk, *The Political Logic of Economic Reform in China* (Berkeley: University of California Press, 1993), pp. 55–69; Kenneth Lieberthal, *Governing China: From Revolution Through Reform* (New York: W. W. Norton & Company, 1995), pp. 213–4; and Carol Lee Hamrin and Suisheng Zhao, eds., *Decision-Making in Deng's China: Perspectives from Insiders* (Armonk, NY: M. E. Sharpe, 1995), especially chapter 13.

level once the municipal governments had been established. Their mission was to "ensure as well as strengthen the Party leadership of the government."[17] The PCGs usually consisted of three to five Party members who assumed leading roles in the government agencies. In a ministry in the State Council, for instance, a PCG would include a minister, vice ministers, and one or two bureau chiefs. There would be one secretary from each PCG and, if necessary, one deputy secretary. If the minister happened to be a non-Communist, as was true in several ministries in the early 1950s, then a Communist vice minister would be the secretary of the PCG and the actual power-holder in that ministry. The same pattern held true at the provincial and local governmental levels. Secretaries and members of PCGs were appointed by a Party committee at the same or higher level and those at the central level were appointed by the CCP Politburo (and its Secretariat). The 1949 Decision particularly stressed, "Party core groups must see to it that all the decisions by the CCP Central Committee concerning the government work are carried out and that no violations occur."[18]

The history of the PCG dated back to June 1927. The amended Party constitution stipulated that in any non-CCP organization or institution (such as the Nationalist government, trade unions, and peasant unions), "Party core groups should be organized wherever there are more than three CCP members. The aim of Party core groups is to strengthen the Party influence in every aspect and to carry out the Party's policies among the non-Communist masses."[19] Back then this decision seemed logical, for the CCP did not control the KMT state and Chiang Kai-shek had already begun a massive purge of the Communists about a month earlier. The CCP had to make sure that its members in the Nationalist government and other organizations were properly organized. After that, however, the same system had continued and was further strengthened over the years. In June 1945, a decision was made at the Seventh Party Congress that PCGs were to be organized by three Party members who had assumed leading roles in non-CCP organizations.[20]

[17] *Zhongguo gongchandang shanghai shi zhuzhi shi zhiliao, 1920, 8–1987, 10* (Organizational Data of the Chinese Communist Party in Shanghai, August 1920–October, 1987) (Shanghai: Shanghai renmin chubanshe, 1991), p. 410.

[18] Chen Xuewei, *Lishi de qishi: shi nian jianshe yanjiu, 1957–1966* (Revelations of History: Research on the Ten Years of Construction, 1957–1966) (Beijing: Qiushi chubanshe, 1989), p. 61.

[19] *Zhongguo gongchandang dangwu gongzuo dacidian* (Dictionary of Chinese Communist Party Work) (Beijing: Zhongyang dangxiao chubanshe, 1990), pp. 740–51.

[20] Ibid.

If the system of the PCG was needed before 1949 to penetrate the KMT state, why was it still necessary after 1949? Could it have simply been a matter of convenience? Because there were some non-Communists in leading positions in the central government, some analysts argue, the system of the PCG was needed to ensure that major issues were reported to the Party center and that the Party's directives were properly implemented.[21] However, to suggest that the system of the PCG was aimed at controlling the non-Communist administrators is perhaps an understatement.

In the early 1950s, there was a PCG of the Government Administrative Council and a joint PCG of the Supreme People's Court and the Supreme People's Procuratorate. The PCG of the Government Administrative Council was further divided into four branches, which were in charge of political and legal affairs, finance and economy, culture and education, and supervision, respectively. In each ministry, commission, administrative bureau, and agency of the central government, there was a sub-PCG under the PCG of the Government Administrative Council. To coordinate the work among the various PCGs, there was a council of PCG secretaries. It was much like a cabinet of the central government. If this system had continued, it would have likely become an inner circle of the premier.

However, the council of the PCG secretaries was soon abolished. On March 10, 1953, in the name of opposing decentralism and, in Mao's words, "to avoid the danger of various departments of the government becoming divorced from the leadership of the Party Central Committee," the CCP Politburo decided "to strengthen the Party leadership over the government work."[22] The 1953 Decision stipulated:

> From now on, major and important principles, policies, plans and matters in government work must be discussed, decided or approved by the Party Central Committee. . . . [T]he work of Party core groups in all the agencies of the central government must be strengthened and be under the direct leadership of the Party Central Committee. Therefore, the present system of the council of Party core group secretaries in the central people's government is no longer necessary and should be abolished immediately.[23]

[21] Hsiao Pen, "Separating the Party from the Government," in Hamrin and Zhao, p. 159.
[22] Kau and Leung, p. 369.
[23] Chen Xuewei, 1989, p. 64.

"Becoming divorced from the leadership of the Party Central Committee" was a serious accusation. It appeared that Mao did not trust even his own premier and ministers, nor the state institutions he had created. Because the council of PCG secretaries in the central government was presided over by Premier Zhou Enlai, the accusation had to be targeted at none other than Zhou.

The change in 1953 was a direct assault on the authority of Premier Zhou and his State Council. Since the change, PCGs in every central government agency had directly reported to the CCP Politburo, creating an often confusing and conflicting system of dual rule. For example, on the one hand, the ministers had to report to the premier, following the Organic Law of the State Council. On the other hand, PCGs of the ministries must report to the CCP Politburo, following the Party's organizational principle. There was no clear line of responsibility and the CCP Politburo often directly gave orders to PCGs in the ministries, bypassing the premier. Surely, Zhou Enlai, as a senior member of the Politburo, was still involved in the decision-making regarding the government work. But in that capacity, Zhou was only part of a collective decision-making body, whereas as the State Council Premier, he could alone direct the government ministries and agencies.

Party Work Department

Government agencies were not only internally controlled by PCGs, they were also subject to frequent intervention from the Party work departments. These departments were units in Party committees at various levels that not only overlapped government agencies in areas of responsibilities, but also took over the daily work from their counterparts in the government. Traditionally, Party committees had propaganda, organization, and united front departments. These may be regarded as functional departments in that they were essential for Party committees to operate. Beginning in 1953, however, many more Party work departments were set up that were aimed at the government work. This change could be illustrated by the case of Shanghai (see Table 4.1).

The seemingly sudden increase of the work departments in the Shanghai Municipal Party Committee in 1956 was no accident. What constituted a watershed in the formation of Party work departments was a report in October 1955, prepared by the CCP Organizational Department under instructions from Party Secretary-General Deng Xiaoping. The report specifically recommended that the Party add to its central and provincial committees work departments of industry and transportation, finance and trade, culture and education, and poli-

Table 4.1. *Work departments of Shanghai Municipal Party Committee,*
1952–56

Year	Departments	Ad hoc committees
1952		Propaganda, industry & commerce, financial work, political & legal affairs, religion, reorganization, production supervision
1953	Heavy industry, private business	Propaganda work, industrial production, finance & economy, religious work, secrecy, neighborhood work
1954	State industry, finance & trade, school work	Art work, cadre examination, neighborhood work, urban work, private business investigation, wage research in private business
1955	State industry, finance & trade, school work	Art work, cadre examination, elimination of counterrevolutionaries, private business investigation
1956	Heavy industry, light industry, finance & trade, art work, higher education, supervision, education & public health, political & legal affairs, city transportation	Labor & wage, cadre review, elimination of counterrevolutionaries

Source: The Establishment Committee of Shanghai Municipal Government, ed., *Shanghai dangzheng jigou yange 1949–1986* (Evolution of the Party and Government Institutions in Shanghai 1949–1986) (Shanghai: Shanghai renmin chubanshe, 1988), pp. 30–70.

tical and legal affairs. County Party committees were asked to establish finance and trade, and culture and education departments. Municipal Party committees could establish more work departments.[24]

The Party work departments soon expanded their power beyond their pri-

[24] Chi Fulin et al., eds., *Zhengzhi gaige jiben wenti tantao* (Discussion on the Basic Questions in the Reform of the Political System) (Beijing: Chunqiu chubanshe, 1988), p. 66; Zheng Qian et al., eds., *Dangdai zhongguo zhengzhi fazhan gaiyao* (Outline of the Development of Contemporary Chinese Political System) (Beijing: Zhonggong dangshi zhiliao chubanshe, 1988), p. 64.

mary responsibility for managing cadres. Because the Party work departments overlapped the government agencies, this eventually led to the Party work departments taking over the government work. To supervise the work departments, there was usually a full-time Party secretary or a standing committee member who was specifically assigned to be in charge of government work. These Party officials did not hold any office in the government and yet wielded more power than their administrative counterparts. Here the Chinese central and local administrative system would easily confuse anyone, because what we have observed were not just one or two, but three, different systems: One was the administrative hierarchy of the government itself; another was the system of PCGs within the government; and the third was the Party work departments that were outside the government but overlapped the government agencies.

Jointly Issued Directives

Control over the flow of directives within a hierarchical structure is of vital importance to any organization. In a highly centralized and tightly controlled system like that in China, who sent out what directives indicated where the political power ultimately lay. The A & B approach to the Party–state relations would mean that the Party Central Committee issued its directives to provincial and local Party committees concerning Party affairs whereas the State Council issued its directives to various ministries and to provincial governments concerning the state affairs. For a few years, this seemed to be the preferred arrangement. In the early 1950s, the Party center was careful not to issue directives directly to the government. On October 30, 1949, the CCP Propaganda Department and the official Xinhua news agency sent out a circular to all the Party organizations, Party newspapers, and branches of the Xinhua news agency regarding the proper way of reporting about the Party and the government's directives. The circular pointed out:

> After the central people's government was founded, all the matters within the jurisdiction of the government should be discussed by the government, whose decisions will be promulgated in formal decrees and implemented by the government. Decrees about national affairs should be promulgated by the central government, and those within local jurisdiction should be promulgated by the local government. Decisions, resolutions or circulars of an administrative nature should

no longer be issued in the name of the Chinese Communist Party as sometimes practiced in the past.[25]

Although in reality a clear distinction was never made, the Party and the Government Administrative Council usually chose not to send out directives jointly except in one case.[26] This, however, began to change after 1955, when the Party center sent out more and more directives jointly with the State Council (see Table 4.2). The increase of jointly issued directives after 1955 points to a dilemma facing the Party. On the one hand, because PCGs in central state institutions directly reported to the CCP Politburo and the Party work departments overlapped the government agencies, it was inevitable that the Party center sent out many directives to keep the system running. On the other hand, because the new state constitution was adopted and the central state institutions were fully established, the Party had to treat the state as a more legitimate source of administrative directives concerning the state affairs. The compromised solution was to send out directives in the name of both the Party center and the State Council.

By the mid-1950s, it became clear that a process of Party substituting for the state was under way and the A & B approach to the Party–state relations was in reality being replaced by the A = B approach. As the founders of the new Chinese state, the Party leaders might have had every reason to believe that they had the right to control the state. But if "party supersedes state" was what the Party leaders wanted, then why should they bother to create a whole set of state institutions in the first place and then painstakingly set up parallel Party organizations to control them?

Contradictory as they may appear, the CCP leaders continued to emphasize the A & B approach to the Party–state relations. In his political report to the Eighth Party Congress in September 1956, Party Vice Chairman Liu Shaoqi devoted one section to discussing the nature and role of the new Chinese state. He then went on to say, "In all work the Party should and can play a leading role ideologically, politically, and in matters of principle and policy. Of course, that does not mean that the Party should take everything into its own hands, or

---

[25] CCP Propaganda Department and the Xinhua news agency, "Circular by the CCP Propaganda Department and the Xinhua News Agency: Decisions of Administrative Nature Should Be Issued by the Government," in *Xinhuashe wenjian ziliao xuanbian* (Selected Documents and Materials of the Xinhua News Agency), vol. 2, (Beijing: Xinhua chubanshe, 1987), p. 4.

[26] It was a joint decision in September 1951 by the Party and the central government to launch an ideological remolding campaign among the intellectuals.

Table 4.2. *Directives issued by the Party and central government, 1950–59*

	Number of directives									
	1950	1951	1952	1953	1954	1955	1956	1957	1958	1959
CCP	10	8	17	13	11	12	9	42	26	23
Government	14	12	4	2	1	5	4	1	0	0
Joint	0	1	0	0	0	1	4	7	18	12

Source: Zhongguo gongchandang zhizheng sishi nian (Forty Years of the Chinese Communist Party in Power) (Beijing: Zhongyang dangxiao chubanshe, 1988), pp. 581–90.

interfere in everything."[27] Party Secretary-General Deng Xiaoping also stressed:

> The Party is the highest form of class organization. It is particularly important to point this out today when our Party has assumed the leading role in state affairs. Of course this does not mean the Party can exercise direct command over the work of the state organs or discuss questions of a purely administrative nature within the Party, overstepping the necessary line of demarcation between Party work and the work of state organs.[28]

What needed to be said was said, but nothing actually happened after the Party Congress to bring about the changes that the Party leaders had envisioned. Deng's report to the Party Congress suggested that a division of labor between the Party and the government be clearly made, but not much improvement in that respect was achieved.[29] PCGs continued to play a crucial role in government work. The parallel Party work departments continued to exist. No one understood the problem better than Premier Zhou Enlai, who, in a report to the NPC on June 26, 1957, bitterly complained: "In some government institutions, the Party organization has taken over the administrative work or has directly intervened in certain concrete matters without going through the government

---

[27] Liu Shaoqi, p. 397.

[28] Deng Xiaoping, *Selected Works of Deng Xiaoping, 1975–1982* (Beijing: Foreign Languages Press, 1987), p. 22.

[29] Nie Gaomin et al., eds., *Guanyu dangzheng fenkai de li lun tantao* (Theoretical Discussion on Separating the Party from the Government) (Beijing: Chunqiu chubanshe, 1987), p. 237.

administration. These practices are neither beneficial to the government work, nor beneficial to the Party work, and should be corrected."[30] However, by then the Party had already launched a major political struggle against the Rightists. After the entire country was engulfed in the Anti-Rightist Campaign, Party–state relations further deteriorated.

PARTY LEADERSHIP IN ACTION: 1958–60

The problems of Party organization trying to run the government administration were not limited to those of redundant and cumbersome organizational procedures. The most serious danger was that a war-hardened revolutionary party organization had the natural tendency to run the country and manage the economy the way it used to organize war mobilization and conduct mass campaigns. No event could more powerfully demonstrate the Party leadership in action than the Great Leap Forward movement.

In 1958, as the CCP's "blooming and contending" policy turned into the Anti-Rightist Campaign, the issue of development strategy came to the fore. The First Five-Year Plan, which was modeled after the Soviet experience, had succeeded in laying down a foundation for Chinese industry. The success, however, came with a high price. With its emphasis on heavy industry, the plan largely ignored agriculture and light industry. Due to lack of sufficient capital and technological investment, agricultural production could no longer keep up with the rapid growth in the industrial sector. As a result, the gap between workers and peasants widened. The Communist Party leaders, now mostly living in the cities, faced the danger of losing support from their traditional constituency – the peasantry. With agricultural production lagging, feeding a growing population became increasingly difficult. According to Alexander Eckstein, between 1952 and 1957, the urban population grew by almost 30 percent. Grain production in 1957, however, increased by only 1.3 percent, a little over half the rate of the population increase in that year.[31] Neglect of light industry also caused a shortage in daily necessities in cities and the countryside, which led to widespread discontent among the populace.

The unbalanced development strategy had serious political consequences as well. Under the slogan, "Learn from the Soviet big brother," a process of wholesale copying of the Soviet model created a mentality of worshipping

---

[30] Ibid.
[31] Alexander Eckstein, *China's Economic Revolution* (New York: Cambridge University Press, 1977), p. 54.

everything Soviet. According to one Chinese source, in the early 1950s, there developed a practice of "two-whatevers": "Whatever Stalin says must not be violated and whatever the Soviet experience is must be followed."[32] This was not good news for Mao Zedong who in his revolutionary career had never managed to establish a warm relationship with Stalin.[33]

Khrushchev's denunciation of Stalin in 1956 encouraged Mao to reevaluate the Soviet model. Soon after the CPSU's Twentieth Congress, Mao asked the heads of the Chinese central ministries to do away with superstition and adopt a critical attitude toward Soviet experience. Mao argued that it was wrong to believe that Chinese economic construction was impossible without the Soviet aid.[34] Although, politically, Mao chose to come to Stalin's defense, economically, Mao decided to search for an alternative that might better fit a peasant country in which capital and technology were particularly lacking. Underscoring the change of the development strategy was the immediate concern about how to boost stagnating agricultural production while maintaining a momentum in heavy industry without massive government investment. In many ways, this was an impossible mission, but Mao believed that China could accomplish this goal by mobilizing the people – the only abundant resource China had – in a nationwide Great Leap Forward movement. As a surviving Long Marcher, Mao now concluded that managing the economy was no different or more difficult than waging wars.

The Upsurge of the Great Leap Forward Movement

The economic drive began in late 1957. At the Third Plenum of the Eighth Central Committee during September and October, Mao reaffirmed the slogan that he put forward in 1956, calling on the whole country to "undertake Socialist construction more, faster, better and more economically."[35] Mao also suggested that China plan to reach the target of producing 20 million tons of steel

---

[32] Shi Zhongquan, *Mao Zedong de jianxin kaituo* (The Arduous Path-Finding by Mao Zedong) (Beijing: Zhonggong dangshi zhiliao chubanshe, 1990), p. 149.

[33] Several years later (around early 1960), Mao had this to say: "After the liberation and during the three years of economic recovery, we were ignorant of how to carry out economic construction. Then we started our First Five-Year Plan and we were still ignorant. We basically could only copy the Soviet methods, but we always felt dissatisfied and uncomfortable." Ibid.

[34] Ibid., p. 152.

[35] Roderick MacFarquhar, *The Origins of the Cultural Revolution, I: Contradictions Among the People, 1956–1957* (New York: Columbia University Press, 1974), pp. 30–1.

within fifteen years.[36] During his second and last visit to Moscow in November 1957, Mao was impressed by Khrushchev's bold promise that the Soviet economic output would surpass the current level of the United States in fifteen years.[37] Mao quickly announced that China would overtake the United Kingdom in fifteen years in the output of iron, steel, and other major industrial products.[38] On November 13, 1957, the *People's Daily* publicly announced the launching of the Great Leap Forward movement.[39]

In March 1958, the Party's Work Conference at Chengdu produced thirty-seven documents setting high targets in industrial and agricultural output for 1958. An enlarged session of the Politburo in late August 1958 produced thirty-seven more documents covering policies about the people's commune, agriculture, industry, education, commerce, the militia, and participation in physical labor by cadres. The communiqué of the meeting called for an output of 10.7 million tons of steel in 1958, twice the output of 1957. After this meeting, an upsurge of the Great Leap Forward movement quickly swept the whole country.

The rapid formation of people's communes[40] and the mass steel production drive, plus many other mass campaigns such as water conservancy, road construction, and deep ploughing, put the normal arrangements for agricultural production and harvesting into total disarray. Confusion and disruption were inevitable. In many counties, crops were left rotting in the fields while peasants were busy making steel in "backyard furnaces." In the winter of 1958, a food crisis began to loom large in the rural areas. Due to the campaign to form people's communes and public mess halls, some peasants did not even have a place to cook or a place to live.[41] In a few areas, desperate peasants either begged or fled. Reported cases of unexpected deaths began to accumulate.

---

[36] China did reach this target figure (21.3 million tons) of steel production in 1971. In 1956, however, China produced only 4.47 million tons of steel.

[37] Roderick MacFarquhar, *The Origins of the Cultural Revolution, II: The Great Leap Forward, 1958–1960* (New York: Columbia University Press, 1983), p. 16.

[38] Ibid.

[39] *Zhongguo gongchandang lishi dashiji* (A Chronology of the Chinese Communist Party) (Beijing: Renmin chubanshe, 1989), p. 233.

[40] For instance, within a month, the number of people's communes grew from 8,730 to 26,425, or from 30.4 percent of the peasant households at the end of August to 98.0 percent at the end of September 1958. See Ma Yuping and Huang Yuchong, eds., *Zhongguo zuotian yu jintian, 1840–1987 nian guoqing shouce* (China's Yesterday and Today: Handbook of National Conditions: 1840–1987) (Beijing: Jiefangjun chubanshe, 1989), p. 751.

[41] Ibid., p. 148.

On the first day of 1959, a *People's Daily* editorial called for continuation of the Great Leap Forward movement. At the same time, the situation in the countryside continued to worsen. On January 22, in a work report to the Party center, the CCP Shandong provincial committee admitted that peasants were fleeing in large numbers from famine-stricken areas and that agricultural production was disrupted. Some efforts were now made by the Party center to modify the pace of the Great Leap Forward movement and to lower the target figures in production, although there were no signs of any immediate improvement. In early May, the Party center had to send out five urgent instructions concerning agricultural production. In late May, the Party center sent another urgent instruction requiring the Party committees to take extreme measures to relieve the shortage of cooking oil.

However, the policy dispute at the Lushan Conference in July prompted the Party leadership to reverse this recent retrenchment. In the countryside, a new mass mobilization was initiated for large projects in water conservancy, road construction, and local industry. People's communes were further expanded, and more public mess halls were opened. The so-called wind of Communism was now sweeping through the rural areas. In industrial sectors, scarce resources, manpower, and machine tools were all pulled together in concerted efforts to reach the goals for iron and steel output. Hence, from late 1959 to the first half of 1960, the whole country underwent a second upsurge of the Great Leap Forward movement in the wake of the Anti-Rightist Tendency Campaign following the Lushan Conference.

In 1959, adverse weather conditions had already hit some rural areas hard. During the following two years, bad weather continued to cause severe damage to agricultural production. In 1960 and 1961, grain output declined to only 143.5 and 147.5 million tons, respectively, going back to the level of 1951.[42] Poor harvests, food waste in the public mess halls, and high quotas for state grain purchases had contributed to the worst food shortages in the history of the PRC. On July 16, 1960, the Soviet government suddenly decided to withdraw all Soviet advisers and canceled 257 scientific and technical cooperation projects. The Soviet punitive actions against Mao's deviance further worsened an already devastating situation caused by mismanagement of the national economy fueled by political campaigns. In the end, between thirty and forty million people perished because of hunger or malnutrition.[43]

There is no question that Mao had to be blamed for the disastrous conse-

[42] Ibid., p. 583.   [43] Xiao Xiaoqin and Wang Youqiao, p. 165.

quences of the Great Leap Forward movement.[44] The movement was not a well-calculated and carefully thought-out development strategy. It was another long march with a compass but no maps. It was a mass mobilization driven by political imperatives over common economic sense. However, if we were to hold Mao solely responsible, we would grossly underestimate the role of the Party. Mao was able to launch the Great Leap Forward movement because he had the entire Party organization mobilized, which in turn precipitated a national frenzy. In many ways, the Great Leap Forward movement looked like a process going out of control. Yet, unlike the institutional chaos during the initial years of the Cultural Revolution, the Great Leap Forward movement was tightly controlled by the Party committees at various levels. This was not a period of the Party's organizational breakdown. Instead, the Party greatly expanded its organizational control during the movement, particularly over the management of the national economy.

Political Mobilization

Mao's mobilization of the Party began with a national tour in early 1958. As bitter winter arrived in Beijing, Mao as usual liked to go down south. Also, as Mao's mass line and the Party's work style dictated, an inspection of the situation at the basic levels was necessary before an all-out mass campaign could be launched. However, Mao's intention for the tour this time was not just to escape cold Beijing, nor just to survey the local situation. He was going to mobilize the provincial and local Party committees to pressure his opponents in Beijing. Since early 1956, Premier Zhou Enlai, Vice Premier Chen Yun, and Finance Minister Li Xiannian had fought hard against *maojin* – "reckless advance." Being in daily charge of the national economy, these central administrators had to be worried about many economic dislocations caused by imbalances, too much investment in basic construction, and unrealistically high target figures. But Mao had different concerns. In October 1957, Mao seized the opportunity to ride the political wind of the Anti-Rightist Campaign to attack his opponents. Mao sharply criticized them for "promoting retrogression" and "showing a rightist tendency."[45]

---

[44] Some analysts believed that given China's limited access to foreign capital and technology, Mao's emphasis on mobilizing human resources was not necessarily irrational. See Victor D. Lippit, "The Great Leap Forward Reconsidered," *Modern China* 1 (January 1975), pp. 92–115.

[45] Mao Zedong, *Selected Works of Mao Tse-tung,* vol. 5 (Beijing: Foreign Languages Press, 1977), pp. 491–2.

During Mao's tour in early 1958, Party meetings were convened wherever he went, at which provincial Party officials listened to Mao's criticism of central administrators and economic planners for their typically cautious attitude toward an economic leap. At the Nanning Conference (January 11–22) attended by the first Party secretaries from eleven provinces, Mao launched a direct attack against Zhou Enlai and Chen Yun's efforts in 1956 to halt reckless advance. Mao alleged that his colleagues were "only 50 meters from the rightists."[46] At this conference, Zhou was forced to engage in a self-criticism.[47] Still this was not enough for Mao, for he continued to denounce the anti-reckless advance policies at the Chengdu Conference in March and at the Second Session of the Eighth Party Congress in May 1958.[48]

While holding his opponents under check, Mao used one meeting after another to push the Party organization into a great leap. During the first eight months of 1958, the CCP uncharacteristically held ten top-level meetings, each adding more fuel to the already overheated engine of the Great Leap Forward movement.[49] At every meeting, Mao's ideas ultimately prevailed and were accepted as the Party's line. Mao certainly did not lack enthusiastic followers. Every time Mao made a proposal or even a casual comment, he could be assured that some provincial Party officials would immediately join him and carry his ideas even further. To name a few, during the people's commune movement, the provincial Party committees of Henan, Sichuan, Anhui, Hebei, Hubei, Gansu, and Shandong were among the "activists." In the mass steel production drive, the first Party secretaries of Shanghai and the Henan Province stood at the fore.[50]

---

[46] Frederick C. Teiwes, *Politics and Purges in China: Rectification and the Decline of Party Norms, 1950–1965,* 2nd edition, (Armonk, NY: M. E. Sharpe, 1990), p. lii.

[47] Jiang Huaxuan et al., eds., *Zhongguo gongchandang huiyi gaiyao* (Summaries of the Chinese Communist Party Conferences) (Liaoning: Shenyang chubanshe, 1991), p. 388; Xiao Xiaoqin and Wang Youqiao, p. 134. For a draft transcript of part of Mao's criticism, see Roderick MacFarquhar, Timothy Cheek, and Eugene Wu, eds., *The Secret Speeches of Chairman Mao, From the Hundred Flowers to the Great Leap Forward* (Cambridge, MA: Council on East Asian Studies, Harvard University, 1989), pp. 393–6.

[48] Jiang Huaxuan et al., pp. 389–99.

[49] From 1954 to 1964 the CCP on average held four top-level meetings each year, but in 1958 alone the Party convened as many as ten top-level meetings. See Jiang Huaxuan et al., pp. 319–511.

[50] The two provincial Party first secretaries who had been recently elevated to the CCP Politburo were among the most enthusiastic defenders of the Great Leap Forward at the Lushan Conference. They were Ke Qingshi of Shanghai and Li Jinquan of Sichuan. See MacFarquhar, 1983, p. 251; and Li Rui, *Lushan huiyi shilu* (True Record of the Lushan Plenum) (Beijing: Chunqiu chubanshe and Hunan jiaoyu chubanshe, 1989), pp. 183–4.

The case of the steel drive is particularly telling. During the First Five-Year Plan, Chinese steel output increased rapidly at an average rate of 36.8 percent a year. Nonetheless, even with the Soviet technical assistance and large amounts of government capital investment, China still produced only 4.47 million tons of steel in 1956 and 5.35 million tons in 1957. At the Party's Nanning Conference in January 1958, the target figure of steel production for 1958 was set at 6.20 million tons. In February, the NPC settled on the figure of 6.24 million tons, which represented an increase of 890,000 tons over the output of 1957. At the Party's Chengdu Conference in March, however, the figure was raised to 7 million tons.[51] When Wang Heshou, Minister of Metallurgical Industry, reported to Mao that the actual steel production in 1958 could reach 8 million tons, Mao asked whether it was possible to double the figure of 1957 to 10.7 million tons. Wang expressed his doubt, but Ke Qingshi, first Party secretary of Shanghai, upon learning about Mao's ambition, quickly proposed setting the target figure for 1958 at 11 million tons. Under the pressure from the provincial Party officials, the Ministry of Metallurgical Industry began to adjust the target figures. In a report to the CCP Politburo in mid-June, the Party core group of the Ministry of Metallurgical Industry proposed to set the target figure for 1958 at 8.2 million tons. The Party core group of the State Economic Commission estimated in its report to the Politburo that the steel production could reach 10 million tons in 1957. Mao responded by suggesting to raise the figure to 11 million tons.[52] A few days later, the Party core group of the Ministry of Metallurgical Industry reported to the Politburo that the steel production could reach 30 million tons in 1959 and above 80 or 90 million tons in 1962.[53] After several months of this numbers race, the Party leaders at the Beidaihe meeting in August finally concluded that the target figure of 8 to 8.5 million tons of steel production for 1958 "is still low" and set the new target figure at 10.7 million tons.[54]

When the Beidaihe meeting was over, it was already the end of August, and the whole country had produced only a little more than 4.5 million tons of steel so far.[55] It stretches imagination to the limits to believe that China could produce 6.2 million more tons of steel within the remaining four months. Yet,

[51] Wen Lü, ed., *Zhongguo "zuo" huo* (The "Leftist" Calamities in China) (Beijing: Zhaohua chubanshe, 1993), p. 307.

[52] Ibid., p. 308.

[53] Jiang Huaxuan et al., pp. 407–8.

[54] MacFarquhar, 1983, p. 91; Wen Lü, p. 308.

[55] Xiao Xiaoqin and Wang Youqiao, p. 140.

Mao and some Party leaders believed that a mass steel production drive with a strong Party leadership could produce miracles. From the end of August, the *People's Daily* carried a series of editorials calling for everyone to get mobilized immediately to accomplish the task of doubling iron and steel output. Steel Production Headquarters were set up all over the country and Party secretaries took command. During the four months from September to December of 1958, as many as 90 million people were involved in the mass steel production drive.[56] On December 22, a *People's Daily* editorial rejoiced that the "great call of the Party has been fulfilled."[57] However, out of the reported 5.35 million tons of increased iron and steel output, 3 million tons turned out to be "essentially useless,"[58] and it was later revealed that the actual steel output in 1958 was 8 million tons. Although not a small achievement, this was far below the figure set at the Beidaihe meeting. Steel output in 1960 did reach the record level of 18.6 million tons, but because the national economy in general and heavy industry in particular were so exhausted that steel target figures had to be set at much lower levels in the following years (8.7 million tons in 1961, 6.7 million tons in 1962, and 7.6 million tons in 1963).[59] Chinese steel production did not again reach the 1960 level (18.6 million tons) until ten years later. The mass steel production drive was not only a big waste of manpower and economic resources, but also an ecological disaster, for the more than 600,000 furnaces all over the country consumed many trees and caused serious problems of environmental pollution.

CENTRALIZATION AND DECENTRALIZATION

The Great Leap Forward movement underscored another major issue of the Chinese state-building, namely, how to strike a balance between the central control and local initiatives. Governing a big country like China is not easy by any means and governing a big country with a highly centralized system is even more difficult. Throughout history, the Chinese empire chronically suffered from the vicious circles of "unification–separation." In the twentieth century, localism and warlordism have been a constant threat to attempts to gain control by the center. Since 1949, the Chinese Communist leaders have

[56] Ibid.
[57] The *People's Daily*, December 22, 1958. Because December 26 was Mao's birthday, it is conceivable that the *People's Daily* announced this news as a birthday present to Mao.
[58] Xiao Xiaoqin and Wang Youqiao, p. 142.
[59] Ma Yuping and Huang Yuchong, pp. 580–1.

been trying to solve the "contradiction between the center and localities." In 1958, when the visiting Field Marshal Montgomery of England asked Mao Zedong about the latter's experience in managing a big country like China, Mao responded, "I have no experience but one, that is, when it is over-centralized, I decentralize it, and vice versa."[60] Mao's simple answer summarized the constant shift of power back and forth between the center and localities without making much headway toward solving the "contradiction."

The state-society perspective suggests that the problem lay in the fact that the Chinese leaders had not decentralized enough power to the society. As Franz Schurmann points out, there are two kinds of decentralization: Decentralization I that shifts power from the central government to provincial governments and Decentralization II that transfers power from the state to society. The CCP's failed decentralization in the 1950s and 1960s mainly fell into the category of Decentralization I, so power was still concentrated in the hands of the government.[61] However, if we introduce an analytical distinction of the Party and the state into the discussion, we will find that the decentralization efforts in the 1950s and 60s actually represented the power shift from the central ministries to provincial Party committees, not to provincial governments, let alone to social and economic organizations. When the previously decentralized power was later recentralized, it often did not return to where it used to belong, but was taken over by the Party committees at higher levels instead. A general discussion of the power shift between the center and localities would miss this important dimension of power relations.

Cycles of "Centralization–Decentralization–Recentralization"

In the first three years of the PRC, China was governed by a three-level administrative system: the central government, the provincial government, and the regional government in between. The regional government was the highest administration at the subnational level, although it also served as the representative of the central government to supervise the provincial governments. This was a relatively decentralized system, for the regional governments had certain authority and autonomy in matters of finance, local industry, and economy.

---

[60] Cited in Li Yichang, "An Insider's Perspective: The Development of Chinese Administrative Science," in Miriam K. Mills and Stuart S. Nagel, eds., *Public Administration in China* (Westport, CT: Greenwood Press, 1993), p. 139.
[61] Schurmann, pp. 175–8.

In late 1952, the first round of centralization began. In view of the upcoming economic reconstruction, the Party center decided to strengthen the central control by transferring the Party secretaries of the CCP Regional Bureaus (who were usually the chairs of the regional governments) to Beijing and by gradually reducing the size and authority of the regional governments. In November, the regional governments were changed into administrative councils that no longer functioned as one level of government, but solely as representatives of the central government. The administrative agencies at the regional level were drastically reduced to only four committees: political and legal affairs, finance and economy, culture and education, and supervision. Other departments were turned over to the central ministries.

The Gao-Rao incident in 1953 gave the Party center particular reasons to worry about the regions seeking independence[62] and prompted a nationwide political campaign against localism. Any attempt to expand local administrative autonomy was criticized as a tendency toward building an "independent kingdom." Mao was unequivocal on this issue. He laid down the leadership principle of "monopolize the major powers and disperse the minor powers." Mao was also unambiguous about who should monopolize the major powers. "The Party committee makes decisions and all others carry out the decisions."[63] On June 19, 1954, the central government decided to abolish the regional governments, thus removing one level of administration between the center and the localities. The official statement explained: "As the country enters a period of planned economic construction, it requires further strengthening of a centralized and unified leadership."[64] Subsequently, China was administratively divided among twenty-nine provincial governments that were under the direct control of the central government.

Yet, in less than two years the decentralization began. In spring of 1956, Mao concluded that the Chinese political system had two main drawbacks: (1) power was overcentralized in the center; and (2) organization was unwieldy. Mao suggested to "give the localities more independence and let the localities do more things."[65] On April 25, 1956, Mao proposed, "[W]e must oppose

---

[62] This was the first major power struggle in the CCP leadership since 1949. For an analysis of this incident, see Frederick C. Teiwes, *Politics at Mao's Court: Gao Gang and Party Factionalism in the Early 1950s* (Armonk, NY: M. E. Sharpe, 1990).

[63] Zheng Qian et al., p. 89.

[64] *Shanghai dangzheng jigou yange, 1949–1986* (The Evolution of the Party and Government Institutions in Shanghai, 1949–1986) (Shanghai: Shanghai renmin chubanshe, 1988), p. 49.

[65] Mao, 1977, vol. 5., p. 297.

bureaucracy and a cumbersome apparatus. I propose that the party and government organs should be thoroughly streamlined and cut by two-thirds provided that no person dies and no work stops."[66] A two-thirds cut in the central Party and government apparatus was nothing short of radical. This perhaps indicated Mao's growing dissatisfaction with the highly centralized and hierarchical Soviet model of administration. It might also reflect Mao's belief in spontaneity and voluntarism among the masses and his well-known dislike of routines, formalities, and above all, bureaucracy.

Following Mao's proposal, the State Council spent the next few months figuring out how to streamline. In September, provincial governments were notified of the State Council's decision to decentralize the administrative authority. According to the plan, the central government would be mainly responsible for managing the food industry, railways, and civil aviation, whereas the provincial governments would be mainly responsible for managing the rest of the economic sectors, including industry, agriculture, forestry, water resources, transportation, post and telecommunication, commerce, culture and education, and public health.[67]

Decentralization accelerated as the Great Leap Forward movement unfolded. On June 2, 1958, the Party center approved a further decentralization plan and demanded that by June 15 all the decentralization work must be completed. A major shift of administrative authority was made almost overnight. When it was completed, 885 out of the 1,165 enterprises and noneconomic institutions that belonged to the nine central ministries of industry were transferred to the local authorities. The Ministry of Textiles had transferred all of its directly managed 201 enterprises and noneconomic institutions to the local authorities. The Ministry of Light Industry had transferred 96.2 percent; the Ministry of First Machinery Industry, 81.7 percent; and the Ministry of Chemical Industry, 91 percent.[68] The city of Shanghai alone suddenly acquired the management authority over 150 industrial enterprises and noneconomic institutions with 90,000 employees.[69] This decentralization represented the largest transfer of power from Beijing to the provinces that China had ever seen, causing enormous confusion and chaos in the administrative system.[70] For example, in a report to the Politburo on November 11, 1960, the Party core group of the Finance Ministry admitted that because the government

---

[66] Ibid.   [67] *Shanghai dangzheng jigou yange,* pp. 55–6.
[68] Zheng Qian et al., p. 83.   [69] *Shanghai dangzheng jigou yange,* p. 86.
[70] Bo Yibo, *Ruogan zhongda juece yu shijian de huigu* (Some Major Policy-Decisions and Events in Retrospect), vol. 1 (Beijing: Zhonggong zhongyang dangxiao chubanshe, 1991), p. 489.

tax agencies were merged and the number of tax officials was greatly reduced, in many areas there was no one to collect tax any more for the state.[71]

The decentralized authority, however, did not fall into the hands of administrators in the provincial and local governments. Before this decentralization began, Mao had encouraged the provincial Party committees to resist the central ministries.

> The localities have the right to resist all impracticable, unrealistic, and subjectivist orders, directives, instructions, and forms that various ministries of the Central Government may send down to them. It doesn't matter if the localities exercise a little too much resistance. The right is only given to the provincial and municipal [Party] committees (which are comparatively mature politically).[72]

The Party's Chengdu Conference in March 1958 also put forward the slogan of "Party secretary takes command," which meant that Party secretaries at all levels were to take charge of all the work.[73] With the massive transfer of administrative authority over hundreds of enterprises and noneconomic institutions, the provincial Party committee began to act as provincial government. Again take Shanghai for an example. In September 1958, the Shanghai Municipal Party Committee decided to combine the municipal government work with that of the Party committee in the name of strengthening the Party's unified leadership. The Shanghai Municipal Party Committee's circular stipulated:

1. From now on, all the bureaus of the municipal government must directly report to the commissions or departments of the municipal Party committee. All the district and county governments must directly report to the district and county Party committees, not to the municipal government.
2. All the documents drafted by the bureaus and agencies of the municipal government must be sent to the commissions or departments of the municipal Party committee for approval before they can be issued in the name of the municipal government. Documents concerning major issues must be sent to the municipal Party committee for discussion and decision.

---

[71] *Shanghai dangzheng jigou yange,* pp. 94–5.

[72] John K. Leung and Michael Y. M. Kau, eds., *The Writings of Mao Zedong: 1949–1976,* vol. 2 (Armonk, NY: M. E. Sharpe, 1992), p. 69.

[73] *Dang de shiyijie sanzhong quanhui yilai zhengzhi tizhi gaige de lilun yu shijian* (Theories and Practices of Reform of the Political System Since the Third Plenum of the Eleventh Party Congress) (Beijing: Chunqiu chubanshe, 1987), p. 44.

3. The municipal government will no longer convene the district and county magistrates' conference or administrative conference, nor will the mayor convene any work conference under normal circumstances.

4. To continue to overcome bureaucratism, streamline state institutions, and improve work efficiency, the size of the general office of the municipal government will be reduced by two-thirds. The staff and secretarial support for all the deputy mayors will be canceled and the office secretaries will report to work in the municipal Party committee.[74]

The decision by the Shanghai Municipal Party Committee clearly suggests that the decentralization in the late 1950s was in essence a transfer of power from the central government ministries to municipal and provincial Party committees. After the decentralization, provincial local Party committees became the highest administrative authorities in their respective provinces, prefectures, counties, or districts. They had power to decide on all the major policy issues of a local nature and, through Party work departments, frequently took over the work of the government agencies. During the Great Leap Forward movement, therefore, the State Council as a whole lost decision-making power over economic matters to the CCP's Politburo, and the central ministries lost management power over enterprises and economic institutions to provincial Party committees.

In January 1961, the Ninth Plenum of the Eighth Central Committee discussed the administrative system and concluded that too much power had been transferred to the localities. To assure the success in economic adjustment in the wake of the disastrous Great Leap Forward movement, it was decided to strengthen the central leadership, and a new round of centralization was initiated. The "Temporary Regulations Concerning Adjustment of Management System" issued by the Party center reaffirmed Mao's principle, "monopolize the major powers and disperse the minor powers." It stressed that the administrative authority over personnel, finance, commerce, and industry that had been inappropriately transferred from the central ministries to provincial and local authorities must all be recentralized.

The recentralization in the early 1960s, however, did not return the power back to the central ministries. Instead, it was concentrated in the hands of the newly established CCP regional bureaus. The Ninth Plenum endorsed the Politburo's decision to reestablish the CCP central bureaus in six regions. But, this time, they were not meant to allow a certain local autonomy, but to

---

[74] *Shanghai dangzheng jigou yange,* p. 114.

strengthen the Party center's control over provincial Party committees. The Party's 1961 "Temporary Regulations" pointed out that "the major powers of economic management should be concentrated at the levels of Party Central Committee, central bureaus in the regions, and provincial Party committees. In the next two or three years, more powers should be concentrated in the Party center and central bureaus."[75] The 1961 recentralization strengthened the central control, but did not change the Party–government relations. The central government now reported directly to the CCP Politburo via the Party core groups in the State Council and central ministries. At the local level, provincial Party committees, now superseding the government agencies, reported to the Party center via the six central bureaus. Most of the government work was carried out by means of the Party center sending out documents and issuing directives. Decentralization or recentralization, the Party's organizational control over the government administration had continued to expand.

Building a strong government administration is perhaps what every state-builder desires. Even the Chinese Communist revolutionaries seemed to be no exception. The efforts at building the state administrative institutions in the early 1950s in China were no less ambitious nor insincere than in many other countries. What distinguished China from many others was that a strong Party organization already existed by the 1950s. The analysis in this chapter suggests that the CCP as a revolutionary party had tremendous difficulty to come up with a viable solution to the problem of organizing China after 1949. On the one hand, a strong revolutionary party experienced in mass mobilization and land reform was neither qualified nor capable of managing the economy without the state administrative institutions. When the Party organization did try to take over state affairs and organize the economic production the way it mobilized masses into military and political campaigns, the outcome was often disastrous. On the other hand, as the government administration grew, a system of dual rule had been firmly put in place. The existence of Party core groups and Party work departments suggests that the CCP leadership did not even trust its own administrators (most were Party members). The structure of dual rule was cumbersome and inefficient, and only served to weaken the administrative capacities of the Chinese state. A more sensible answer to the Chinese administrative problems would have been if the Party had allowed the state administration to manage state affairs. Or the answer would have been less compli-

---

[75] Zheng Qian et al., p. 131.

cated if the Party had not bothered to build the state administrative institutions in the first place and then tried to control them. The fascinating thing about the Chinese state-building in the Mao era was that the CCP leaders had accepted neither of these two answers and had struggled in vain to find an alternative one.

5

Army-Building and Revolutionary Politics

THE founding of the People's Republic of China in 1949 signified a fundamental change in the status of the People's Liberation Army (PLA). From
now on, the PLA was no longer a group of rebel or guerrilla forces scattering
all over the country and only loosely coordinated by the Communist Party
leaders hiding in isolated areas. It was a national standing army under a new
central government. Its main mission was no longer harassing the official
troops, attacking the government facilities, and sabotaging the public order. As
the pillar of the new political order, the PLA was commissioned to defend the
country and safeguard the national interests. As such, the PLA was to become
more like any official army in other countries, and it would have to meet the
standards of such an official army. This chapter examines the PLA's modernization programs in the 1950s and the emerging tensions between building a
modern standing army and maintaining the traditional control by the revolutionary party. It analyzes the intricate historical and structural linkage between
the Party and the army and underscores the inherent danger of the PLA's
political role.

MILITARY REORGANIZATION AND MODERNIZATION

The first eight years of the PRC had witnessed a vigorous program to reorganize and modernize a peasant army now operating in a new environment. The
military modernization program included streamlining the ground force; establishing the navy, air force, and technical services; upgrading weapons and
equipment; setting up military academies; promoting education and military
training; and formulating military regulations, rules, and ranks.

Reorganization

By April 1950, the total number of the PLA forces had already reached 5.5
million. Because the civil war was about to end and the situation in the country

106

was returning to normality, maintaining such a large army with its huge expense was neither necessary nor practicable. The new regime, therefore, decided to reduce the total size of the army to 4 million by demobilizing 1.5 million soldiers in order to help balance the government budget. Demobilization began in May 1950, but was soon halted when the Korean War broke out. After the war ended in 1953, the PLA was again urged to reduce its size, making military budget cuts to meet the more pressing need for economic development. Between 1954 and 1958, the PLA underwent two major waves of streamlining. The first one was accomplished in 1955, which reduced the size of the PLA by 23.3 percent. In 1958, the second wave of streamlining further reduced the size of the PLA by 36 percent on top of the reduction in 1955. Military spending also declined dramatically. During 1953–55, the average annual military spending was 27.36 percent of the total government expenditure. It had remained high even after the Korean War ended. In September 1956, however, Mao stressed that "reducing the military and administrative cost is an effective method of accumulating capital for the socialist construction," and he demanded that the military and administrative expenditures be reduced. In January 1957, the enlarged meeting of the Party Central Military Commission (CMC) decided to slash the military expenditure by more than 50 percent, from 23.39 percent of the government expenditure during the First Five Year Plan period to only 10.7 percent during the Second Five-Year Plan period.[1]

Reflecting a general awareness among the Party leaders and military generals of the shift from guerrilla warfare to modern warfare, the PLA had also drastically reorganized its troops. While reducing the total size of the ground force, the new regime had established or reinforced the navy, air force, and technical corps. On March 24 and September 21, 1949, Mao twice stressed that China must not only build a strong army, but also a strong air force and a strong navy in order to have a strong national defense force.[2] Within the first two years of the PRC, the PLA quickly formed the air force (November 1949), navy (April 1950), artillery corps (August 1950), and armored corps (September 1950). By 1953, the PLA had largely accomplished the major transition from a single-service army to an army of multiple armed and technical services. By the end of the decade, the navy, air force, and all the technical

---

[1] *Dangdai zhongguo jundui de junshi gongzuo* (China Today: The Military Work of the Chinese Army) (Beijing: Zhongguo shehui kexue chubanshe, 1989), pp. 43–5.

[2] Ibid., p. 38–9.

services of the army had accounted for 32 percent of the total size of the PLA.[3] Although the PLA had remained a ground force for many years to come, what the PLA's reorganization had accomplished in the 1950s was nonetheless impressive.

Modernization

In the early 1950s, the PLA's military weaponry and equipment were not only short in quantity, but poor in quality. The Chinese industry had yet to recover from many years of devastation. Mao complained that China could not make one automobile, one airplane, one tank, or one tractor.[4] In early 1950, China could still buy some vessels from some Western countries through Hong Kong.[5] After the Korean War broke out and the U.S. imposed an embargo on China, this source of military supply was essentially cut off.[6] Some vessels that were already in Hong Kong could not be delivered to mainland China. As the Korean War further consumed the already constrained military supplies, the problem became all the more serious. China could look to no country other than the Soviet Union for help. In May 1951, the Chinese government sent a high-ranking military procurement delegation to Moscow. After four months of tough negotiation, the two sides finally signed an agreement under which the Soviet Union would sell up to sixty divisions of military equipment to the Chinese army. By October 1954, all the purchased military equipment had finally arrived in China. Although they discovered that some weapons were World War II models, the Chinese generals were nonetheless impressed with the firepower of the Soviet weaponry. Meanwhile, China speeded up her own process of weapon production. The First Five-Year Plan assigned great importance to the development of defense industry and defense science and technology. Under the plan, seventy-nine large military industrial factories were to be built, whose mission was to mass produce military weapons and equipment by utilizing Soviet technology and by copying the Soviet models. By the end of 1955, using imported and China-made weaponry, the PLA was able to equip 9 subdivisions of the Navy fleet and 186 divisions in the infantry, cavalry, air

---

[3] Ibid., p. 43.

[4] Mao Zedong, *Selected Works of Mao Tse-tung,* vol. 5 (Beijing: Foreign Languages Press, 1977), p. 130.

[5] Altogether, China bought forty-eight aging vessels made in the United States, Britain, and Japan.

[6] *Dangdai zhongguo jundui de junshi gongzuo,* p. 69.

force, artillery and antiaircraft corps, air defense, tank force, armored, and border patrol corps.[7]

Education

To train a large number of military personnel capable of organizing modern warfare, the Party CMC decided in June 1950 to reorganize and establish a number of military academies. In January 1951, the PLA Military Academy was established and Mao praised this event as a major turning point in the PLA's history of army-building. In the next two years, the army schools mushroomed; by the end of 1952, there were already two hundred or so army schools at different levels.[8] By the end of the decade, the PLA had established military academies for every armed and technical service, including the Academy of Logistics (1952), the General Advanced Infantry School (1953), the Academy of Military Engineering (1953), the Academy of Political Work (1956), the Academy of Artillery Corps (1958), the Naval Academy (1958), the Academy of Military Science (1958), the Academy of Armored Corps (1959), and the Air Force Academy (1959).

As a peasant army, the PLA was also in urgent need of improving the basic education of its soldiers. In the early 1950s, 80 percent of the PLA officers and soldiers were either illiterate or had received only primary education. In 1950, Mao specifically instructed the Party CMC to launch education programs.[9] The Korean War delayed this effort for a year or two, but large-scale cultural and educational campaigns occupied much of the PLA's training agenda during 1952–53. After June 1954, following Mao's instruction to strengthen the PLA's fighting capacity in modern wars through formal military training, the PLA shifted its focus in training from cultural education to formal military drill aimed at enhancing the PLA's combat effectiveness. Formal military training programs, modeled after the Soviet Red Army, were carefully designed with specific targets and requirements. Military training goals were set and adjusted every year. For instance, the 1956 training program was aimed at preparing the PLA for "active defense." The training principle for 1957 was to go beyond the PLA's military traditions to command modern military technology and to train

---

[7] Ibid., p. 43.

[8] Ibid., p. 37.

[9] *Jianguo yilai Mao Zedong wengao, 1949, 9–1950, 12* (Mao Zedong's Manuscripts Since the Founding of the People's Republic of China: September 1949–December 1950) (Beijing: Central Archives Publishers, 1987), pp. 446–9.

for carrying out joint military actions by multiarmed services in the night and under adverse climate.[10] For several years after 1956 annual military exercises had also become a routine way of training.

Regularization

Reorganization and modernization of the PLA had to follow certain centrally formulated rules and regulations in place of the existing fragmented rules for different army units in various regions. The effort in this regard, again heavily dependent on the model of the Soviet Red Army, led after two years of experiment to the formal issuance of Regulations of Interior Service, Regulations of Formation, and Regulations of Discipline in May 1953. The abolition of the egalitarian supply system in favor of a hierarchic salary system in the army in 1955 and the passing of the Law of Compulsory Military Service by the NPC in the same year began to transform the traditional guerrilla forces into a modern standing army. Military specialization and standardization were further reinforced by the introduction of the Soviet-styled military rank system into the PLA in February 1955. There were altogether four grades (Captain, Colonel, General, and Marshal) that were further divided into fourteen classes.[11] For the first time in PLA history, military personnel at different ranks in various armed services could be easily identified. Officers in their new uniforms with epaulettes clearly distinguished themselves from the rank and file. On September 23, 1955, ten senior PLA military leaders were promoted to the rank of marshal. Four days later, several hundred military officers were promoted to the rank of general (10 senior generals, 55 generals, 175 lieutenant generals, and 801 major generals).[12] On National Day (October 1), 1955, newly ranked marshals and senior generals, wearing their dress uniforms with military decorations and medals of honor, appeared in full array to review the military parade. It was undoubtedly the most glorious and glamorous moment for the army.

---

[10] *Dangdai zhongguo jundui de junshi gongzuo,* p. 45.

[11] *Zhongguo renmin jiefangjun liushinian dashiji* (A Chronology of Sixty Years of the People's Liberation Army) (Beijing: Junshi kexue chubanshe, 1988), pp. 545–6.

[12] Between 1956 and 1965 when the military rank system was abolished, the Party CMC appointed 2 more generals, 2 more lieutenant generals, and 559 more major generals. Altogether, there were 10 marshals, 10 senior generals, 57 generals, 177 lieutenant generals, and 1,359 major generals. Ma Yuping and Huang Yuchong, eds., *Zhongguo zuotian yu jintian 1840–1987 nian guoqing shouce* (China's Yesterday and Today: Handbook of National Conditions: 1840–1987) (Beijing: Jiefangjun chubanshe, 1989), p. 785.

THE PLA COMMAND AND CONTROL SYSTEM

The literature of civil–military relations, as pioneered by Samuel Huntington, suggests that power relations between civilian leaders and military generals are essentially conflictual – a zero-sum game, that civilian control of the military is preferable, and that military intervention in politics should be discouraged.[13] Scholars of the civil–military relations in developing nations and of Party-army relations in Communist countries have long cast doubt to the Huntingtonian model based on the experience of Western liberal democracies. The obvious difficulty in applying the Huntingtonian model to China is how to define who is "civilian" and who is "military."[14] Before 1949, the Communist army was in many ways indistinguishable from the Communist Party, for the army was the political tool of the Party and the Party was practically a fighting force. Many Party (civilian?) leaders therefore had military experiences. For instance, as the Chinese premier for twenty-seven years, Zhou Enlai managed the Chinese government administration from 1949 until he died in 1976.[15] Yet, Zhou's military career extended much longer than his government administrative career. As early as 1927, Zhou had begun to take charge of the CCP's military affairs and he had remained a major player in the military affairs ever since. It is worth noting that during the most critical years of the civil war (1947–48) Zhou Enlai was chief of the Communist army's General Staff.

Hence, when the military ranks were introduced to the PLA from the Soviet Red Army in 1955, the initial proposal recommended that Mao Zedong be ranked as Grand Marshal; Zhou Enlai, Liu Shaoqi, and Deng Xiaoping as Marshals; and Li Xiannian (finance minister), Tan Zhenlin (Party deputy secretary-general), Deng Zihui (head of the CCP Rural Work Department) and Zhang Dingcheng (procurator-general) as Senior Generals. Mao, however, decided that he did not want to be Grand Marshal and asked Zhou, Liu, Deng, and others to give up the idea as well.[16] If these Party leaders had been granted military ranks and attended the National Army Day in uniforms, we would probably have found it impossible to refer to them as civilian leaders.

---

[13] Samuel P. Huntington, *The Soldier and the State: The Theory and Politics of Civil–Military Relations* (Cambridge, MA: The Belknap Press of Harvard University Press, 1957), pp. 80–97.

[14] Harlan W. Jencks, "Watching China's Military: A Personal View," *Problems of Communism* (May–June 1986), p. 77.

[15] Zhou was concurrently Chinese foreign minister between 1949–58.

[16] Song Renqiong, "Chairman Mao Refused to Be the Grand Marshal" (Maozhuxi bu dang dayuanshuai), *Minzhu yu fazhi* (December 1993), pp. 8–9.

Party and Guns

The difficulty in analyzing the Party–army relations in terms of the orthodox civil-military model lies beyond the mixed political/military careers of the first generation of the Chinese Communist elite. There are structural reasons as well. Indeed, the organizational linkage between the CCP and PLA was so entrenched that the military seemed to be necessarily part of the Chinese political process. The CCP began to set up its military affairs department in 1925. Later the military affairs department was upgraded into the Party CMC. In August 1937, the Party CMC was reorganized after the Long March to reinforce Mao's rising influence in the Party. During the Anti-Japanese War when the CCP's military forces were nominally submerged into the Nationalist forces, the Party CMC appeared to cease its active role. On the eve of the Civil War, however, the Seventh Party Congress in 1945 reestablished the CMC as the Party's highest command of the military.

After the founding of the People's Republic, the issue of whether the army should belong to the Party or to the new state began to surface. At first, though, the CCP leaders seemed satisfied with the institutional arrangement under which the Party controlled the state and thereby commanded the army, even though the formal command of the gun was turned over from the Party to the state. In November 1949, the central government set up the People's Revolutionary Military Commission. With Mao as its chairman, this commission was to command all the military forces in China. Meanwhile, the Party CMC ceased to exist. In 1954, the first state constitution of the PRC established the National Defense Council (NDC) in place of the People's Revolutionary Military Commission. The newly installed state chairman of the PRC, who concurrently served as the chairman of the NDC, was to be in command of the Chinese military forces. The new constitutional arrangement seemed to promise the state's control of the army through the NDC, even though the state chairman of the PRC and chairman of the NDC was none other than Party Chairman Mao.

As soon proved to be the case, however, the NDC assumed only an advisory role in military matters. On September 28, 1954, one week after the state constitution was ratified, the CCP Politburo adopted a resolution to reestablish the Party CMC. Mao assumed the chairmanship of the Party CMC, and Marshal Peng Dehuai, the only vice chairman of the Party CMC, was entrusted with taking charge of the daily work of the PLA. The next day, Peng was appointed the Defense Minister. The Party CMC quickly took charge of the military affairs. Three months later, it was the Party CMC, not the NDC of the state, that made decisions on such issues as compulsory military service, military ranks, and pay scale for military officers.[17]

The Party CMC in 1954 consisted of all the ten PLA marshals-to-be, plus Mao Zedong and Deng Xiaoping. It was the same group of people who comprised the leadership of the NDC except for four former KMT generals.[18] However, to suggest that the Party CMC was set up to exclude the four KMT generals from actual military decision-making is missing the point. The Party CMC that was reestablished after the state constitution went into effect was to become a major institutional obstacle to moving the army under state control.

Who Managed the Army?

The military reorganization in the 1950s abolished the headquarters of the PLA field armies and the entire country was divided into six, and later (February 1955) twelve, major military regions. They were the Shenyang, Beijing, Jinan, Nanjing, Guangzhou, Wuhan, Chengdu, Kunming, Lanzhou, Xinjiang, Inner Mongolia, and Tibet military regions.[19] Each major military region directly commanded several armies and divisions. Within each major military region, there were several provincial military districts, military subdistricts, garrisons (in major cities), and people's military departments at county and city levels. Maintaining a unified and centralized management of an army more than four million strong in so many military regions and districts was a tough challenge for the Party leadership.

The PRC Ministry of Defense is ranked second in the government hierarchy only after the Ministry of Foreign Affairs. Yet it is no secret that, unlike the U.S. Defense Department, the PRC Defense Ministry does not manage the troops. This, of course, does not mean that the Defense Minister plays a minor role in Chinese military affairs. On the contrary, the Defense Minister has always been a prominent military leader in active duty. Also, without exception, the Defense Minister has always been a member of the Party CMC. But the institutional power of the Defense Ministry is overshadowed by the PLA General Headquarters – the General Staff, the General Political Department,

---

[17] *Zhongguo gongchandang zhizheng sishi nian* (Forty Years of the Chinese Communist Party in Power) (Beijing: Zhongyang dangxiao chubanshe, 1988), p. 584.

[18] They were Cheng Qian, Zhang Zhizhong, Fu Zuoyi, and Long Yun. *Zhongguo renmin jiefangjun liushinian dashiji,* pp. 538–9.

[19] In 1956, the thirteenth military region, Fuzhou Military Region, was added to the list.

and the General Logistics Department.[20] Under the direct command of the Party CMC, the PLA general departments supervised various armed services and major military regions. They are parallel in status to the Defense Ministry in the central government, but maintain actual control over the PLA troops.

Because the CCP had been engaged in military struggles many years before the PRC was founded, the general department system had a much longer history than the relatively young Defense Ministry. After 1954, however, the general departments could in theory be transferred to the Defense Ministry of the PRC. In the first five years of the PRC, this seemed to be the case as the general departments were gradually placed under the People's Revolutionary Military Commission. If this trend had continued, we would have probably found a pattern similar to that in the former Soviet Union where the Defense Ministry evolved to be the central command of the Soviet Red Army and the commanders of the military services almost automatically became deputy defense ministers.

Yet, after the first state constitution established the PRC Ministry of Defense in 1954, the military management system turned backward. On October 11, 1954, the general departments all changed their organizational titles. For instance, "the General Staff of the People's Revolutionary Military Commission" became "the General Staff of the People's Liberation Army." Back then, this might have been seen as just one of the many name-changing games following the adoption of the first state constitution. Some recently available documents, however, suggest that there was more to it than met the eye. On October 6, 1954, Defense Minister Peng Dehuai sent a report to Mao concerning the proper organizational titles of the general departments. Peng explained that the general departments should not be placed under the NDC because the NDC played "only an advisory role." Nor should they be placed under the Defense Ministry, for if the general departments were to become part of the executive organ of the state, it would prohibit members of the national legislature from assuming leading positions of these departments.[21] Peng further explained that it was not appropriate for the Party CMC to declare a direct affiliation with the

---

[20] Between 1954 and 1958, following the model of the Soviet army, five other general departments (cadre, training supervision, finance, military machinery, and supervision of military forces) were created in the PLA headquarters. In July 1958, as China was turning away from the Soviet model of economic development, the PLA returned to the traditional system of three general departments. *Dangdai zhongguo jundui de junshi gongzuo,* pp. 42–3.

[21] This, however, sounds like an excuse instead of a justification. As of 1954, only one Marshal, Luo Ronghuan, was the vice chairman of the Standing Committee of the National People's Congress and concurrently the director of the General Political Department.

general departments because the Party's military command could not publicly put its signature on many military documents and orders. After this painstaking reasoning, Peng proposed to put "PLA" into the organizational titles of the general departments.[22] Thus, "the General Staff, the General Political Department, and the General Logistics Department of the People's Revolutionary Commission" became "the General Staff, the General Political Department, and the General Logistics Department of the PLA."[23] Although the General Staff of the PLA sounds similar to the General Staff of the U.S. Army, the crucial difference is that the Chinese General Staff is not under the Ministry of Defense, but under the Party's CMC. In this way, the Party could maintain its organizational control over the military through the PLA general departments without having to appear too obvious. On October 8, 1954, Mao informed Peng that the CCP Secretariat had approved the proposal.[24] Since then we have never heard any suggestion for changing these appellations.

Through the Party CMC, the military had acquired a special status. The Party CMC was separate from, but equal to, the Party Central Committee. It was also free from intervention from the powerful functional departments of the Party Central Committee, such as the Organization and Propaganda departments. Although major military policies had to be approved by the Party Politburo and sometimes by its secretariat, matters concerning the PLA were generally left to the generals in the Party CMC.

The emphasis on the Party CMC, however, does not reveal the whole picture. The military leaders in the Party CMC theoretically had to listen to the Chairman of the CMC. Yet mere assumption of the chairmanship of the Party CMC guarantees no actual control over the military generals. In the final analysis, the military generals listened to whoever proved to be able to command them. Since the Long March in 1934–35, the Chinese Communist army had essentially listened to one man: Mao Zedong. So the answer to the simple question of "Who commands the gun?" is a little bit complicated: The gun in China was commanded by the paramount leader through the military generals in the Party CMC. The institutional arrangements of Party–army relations were therefore dictated by this factor.

---

[22] Peng had consulted with Liu Bocheng, He Long, Luo Ronghuan, Nie Rongzhen, and Ye Jianying. These military leaders were all conferred the military rank of Marshal in 1955.

[23] *Jianguo yilai Mao Zedong wengao, 1953, 1–1954, 12* (Mao Zedong's Manuscripts Since the Founding of the People's Republic of China: January 1953–December 1954), vol. 4 (Beijing: Zhongyang dangan chubanshe, 1990), p. 562.

[24] Ibid.

The 1954 constitution stipulated that the state chairman of the PRC commanded the military forces. Since Mao was both the state chairman and Party chairman, this did not appear to be a major problem. Although a new Ministry of Defense was set up, it was clear that Mao exercised the command over the military through the Party CMC. A structural problem began to emerge, however, when Mao resigned from his post as the state chairman in 1959 and senior Party Vice Chairman Liu Shaoqi became the State Chairman. Even though Liu's new role as the state chairman could only strengthen the Party's organizational control over the military, Mao concluded that the existence of two chairmen not only caused confusion in titles, but also threatened his own command over the military. After Liu was purged in 1968, Mao was so determined not to repeat his mistake of having two chairmen that Lin Biao's insistence in 1970 for the reinstallation of the state chairman eventually led to Lin's demise.

Who Controlled the Military?

Through decades of wars and revolution, the Party had formed a complicated system of political control over the military. This included an inclusive policy of recruiting soldiers into the Party, the system of political commissar and political department, and the Party committee system. Political control over the soldiers first seemed assured by a disproportionately high percentage of Party membership in the military. The CCP is the only political party one can join while in the military, as none of the eight satellite parties is allowed to recruit its members from military personnel.[25] As a rule of thumb, any soldier eligible for promotion to the rank of platoon leader must be admitted into the Party first or join the Party soon after the promotion. To be sure, granting Party membership to military officers is no guarantee of political loyalty, however it is defined. But being a Party member does subject one to many organizational constraints that a non-Party member normally does not have to deal with. These include, among others, attending regular Party study meetings, following the Party's organizational disciplines, internalizing the Party's norms and ideals, and responding to the Party's calls for political campaigns and mass work.

Following the Soviet advice, the PLA also established a commissar sys-

---

[25] Tan Fangzhi, *Dang de tongzhan gongzuo cidian* (Dictionary of the Party's United Front Work) (Beijing: Zhongguo zhanwang chubanshe, 1988), p. 552.

tem.[26] Political commissars at the regiment level and above and political instructors below the regiment level functioned parallel to commanders in the military hierarchy. Their main duties were to countersign, except in case of emergency, orders given by commanders of their units; to propagate Party ideology and policy; and to organize educational and cultural studies for soldiers. For the regiment level up to the PLA General Headquarters, a political department was also set up, which, under the instruction of political commissars at the same level, was responsible for carrying out the Party's directives and rules pertaining to political work in the military. The political commissars functioned as the political part of the PLA and friction inevitably occurred between military commanders on the one hand and commissars and political workers on the other. However, we must be careful not to exaggerate this friction. The political commissar system started in revolutionary Russia when the Bolsheviks tried to send loyal Communist Party supporters to supervise former Tsarist military personnel in the Red Army. In China, political commissars were assigned not so much to supervise military commanders as to organize political propaganda and educational work.[27] The Chinese revolution that had lasted for more than two decades before 1949 was essentially an armed struggle. As a result, political commissars inevitably became war-hardened soldiers and military commanders ultimately became experienced revolutionaries. Indeed, many military commanders often assumed more importance in the Party hierarchy than their political counterparts. The relations between military commanders and political commissars might be best described as one between the left hand and right hand. One might accidentally hurt the other, but the two essentially cooperated.

An essential component of the political work system was the Party committee set up at the regiment level and above.[28] This system was initially established in the Red Army by Mao in December 1929 and was subsequently consolidated in 1954. It contained three major elements: (1) The Party exercised a unified leadership over every aspect of the military; (2) Except in cases of emergency, all major decisions had to be discussed and made collec-

---

[26] For a discussion of the evolution of the political commissar system in China, see Cheng Hsiao-shih, *Party–Military Relations in the PRC and Taiwan: Paradoxes of Control* (Boulder, CO: Westview Press, 1990), especially chap. 2, pp. 11–32.

[27] John Gittings, *The Role of the Chinese Army* (New York: Oxford University Press, 1967), p. 101; Cheng Hsiao-shih.

[28] David Shambaugh, "The Soldier and the State in China: The Political Work System in the People's Liberation Army," *The China Quarterly* (September 1991), p. 539.

tively by the Party committee. No individual or individuals were allowed to decide arbitrarily; and (3) commanders were responsible for carrying out the decisions made by the Party Committee pertaining to military matters, and political commissars, the political work.[29] Military commander and political commissar could be either the secretary or deputy secretary of the Party committee, but what really matters was not who assumed what post, but that every major issue must be brought up in the Party committee meetings and a collective decision made. The CCP therefore tried to keep the military under control not by employing the tactics of "divide and rule," but by bringing the commanders and commissars together into the Party.

DANGER OF REVOLUTIONARY POLITICS

The intricate structural linkage of the PLA with the Party subjected the military to Party politics – revolutionary style. During numerous political campaigns, the PLA was neither immune to political upheavals nor exempt from them. As political power struggles factionalized the Party leadership, they inevitably divided the army. Power struggles and political campaigns produced victims and victimizers in the army as well as in the Party. The PLA as an institution had both suffered and benefited from its structural participation in revolutionary politics of the CCP. Before the Cultural Revolution in the late 1960s, the struggle against the "bourgeois military line" in 1958 and the "Anti-Rightist Tendency" campaign in 1959 are two of the best examples that illustrate the political dilemma of the PLA.

Opposing the "Bourgeois Military Line" in 1958

In 1958, the PLA's modernization efforts began to encounter strong resistance. In May, a fierce political struggle was initiated by the newly appointed Party Vice Chairman Lin Biao against the bourgeois military line, officially defined as a tendency to copy wholesale the Soviet model of army-building; to deemphasize the role of the political commissar and Party committee in the army; and to oppose the leadership of the Party CMC.[30] These were serious accusations, as were the struggle meetings and purges that followed. Marshal

---

[29] *Guanyu xinshiqi jundui zhengzhi gongzuo de jueding zhushiben* (The Annotated Book for the Resolution Concerning the Political Work in the Military in the New Era) (Beijing: Jiefangjun chubanshe, 1987), pp. 486–9.

[30] Jiang Huaxuan et al., eds., *Zhongguo gongchandang huiyi gaiyao* (Summaries of the Chinese Communist Party Conferences) (Liaoning: Shenyang chubanshe, 1991), pp. 400–3.

Liu Bocheng, who in late 1950 volunteered to take up the responsibility for supervising the newly established PLA Military Academy, was now condemned for engaging in a bourgeois military line against the correct military line of the Party. Despite his illness, Liu was carried to the struggle meeting to make self-criticism. He was subsequently dismissed from his posts as commandant and political commissar of the Military Academy. Marshal Ye Jianying was relieved of his responsibility for military training and education. Other military leaders in charge of military training were also affected. Senior General Su Yu, chief of the PLA General Staff, was demoted to vice commandant of the PLA Academy of Military Science. Generals Xiao Ke and Li Da not only lost their posts as deputy defense ministers, but were forced out of the army. General Xiao was later assigned the post of deputy minister in the Ministry of Agriculture and Forestry and General Li became a deputy minister in the State Commission of Physical Culture and Sports.[31] Their power base – the PLA General Training Department – was abolished. After this struggle, the process of military regularization and modernization was largely halted. Several regulations and codes of behavior issued only two or three years earlier were now abolished.[32] To counter the Soviet influence, the PLA also launched a major campaign to study Mao Zedong's military writings. By 1959 when the study movement fully unfolded, as many as 180,000 military officers above the level of platoon commander had participated in the study movement.[33]

What was wrong with the military modernization in the early 1950s? Did Mao initially oppose it in favor of the revolutionary tradition of guerrilla warfare? Mao's own words seem to suggest otherwise. In January 1953, when giving instructions to the students at the opening ceremony of the PLA General Advanced Infantry School, Mao stressed:

> To keep our motherland free from invasions by the imperialists, it is
> no longer adequate to rely on our past and relatively backward equip-
> ment and tactics that we used to fight against our domestic enemies.
> We must master the newest equipment and subsequently the newest
> tactics that are associated with it.[34]

In his congratulatory note to the first graduating class of the PLA Military Academy in July 1953, Mao further suggested that the PLA had now entered a

---

[31] Ibid., p. 403.

[32] *Dangdai zhongguo jundui de junshi gongzuo,* p. 48.

[33] Ibid., p. 402.

[34] *Zhongguo renmin jiefangjun liushinian dashiji,* p. 525.

higher stage of army-building, that is, the stage of mastering modern technology. He said:

> In step with the modernization of [our armed forces'] equipment, there is a demand that the establishment of the troops become regularized; this means the implementing of a unified command, a unified system, organization, discipline and training [for all the troops], that is, the materialization of closely knit coordinated actions on the part of all the various arms of the services.[35]

Mao seemed to have concluded that the PLA's guerrilla warfare tradition was obsolete, for he went on to say, "[T]he decentralization, lack of unity and phenomena of lassitude and simplicity in discipline, as well as the guerrilla mentality and practices, which might have been appropriate and correct in the past but are no longer appropriate and correct today, must be overcome. . . ."[36] Following Mao's instructions, the Party CMC held an enlarged meeting in December–January at which it was decided that the PLA should spend the next five to ten years to achieve the following goals: modernization of military equipment; rationalization of the military establishment; standardization of training of officer corps; and regularization of the military system and military training.[37]

In the early 1950s, there was a deeply felt need among the top Party and military leaders to modernize the PLA. This was reinforced by the PLA's performance in the Korean War. The war had exposed some fatal problems in the PLA, particularly regarding weaponry, technical training, logistical supply, air power, command, and communication systems.[38] Although many PLA generals remained proud of their revolutionary tradition of "relying on millet plus rifles" to defeat the Japanese and the Nationalists and then to fight the Americans to a standstill in Korea, they also realized there was a huge human cost associated with the tactics of the "human wave." Mao's instructions for military modernization undoubtedly reflected this consensus.

Was Mao opposed to learning from the Soviet Red Army? The answer depends on the period. The arrival of large numbers of Soviet military advisors

---

[35] Michael Y. M. Kau and John K. Leung, eds., *The Writings of Mao Zedong, 1949–1976,* vol. 1 (Armonk, NY: M. E. Sharpe, 1986), p. 273.

[36] Ibid.

[37] *Dangdai zhongguo jundui de junshi gongzuo,* pp. 40–2.

[38] Jacques Guillermaz, *The Chinese Communist Party in Power, 1949–1976,* translated by Anne Destenay (Boulder, CO: Westview Press, 1976), p. 161.

in the early 1950s opened Chinese eyes to an alternative way of building the army up to international standards, and the Chinese army-building up to 1958 mainly followed the Soviet model.[39] It is hard to imagine that the PLA's movement to "learn from the Soviet big brother" could proceed if Mao opposed it from the very beginning. In fact, Mao specifically instructed the Chinese military in January 1951:

> We must learn every bit of the advanced experiences of the Soviet Union in order to change our armed forces from their condition of backwardness and construct our armed forces into a most superior modernized military force [in the world], so as to be able to assure ourselves of the ability to defeat, in the future, the invasion of the imperialists' armies.[40]

In his instructions to the Academy of Military Engineering on August 26, 1953, Mao again stressed:

> It is a fine tradition in our history of army building to learn from the Soviet Union. . . . We must learn from the Soviet advanced science and technical knowledge; the Soviet rich experience in developing military engineering; the Soviet advisors' study and work attitude; and their high spirit of patriotism and internationalism.[41]

Unless Mao did not mean what he said, one would have to conclude that Mao later (after 1958) changed his mind when he decided to move away from the Soviet experiences and back toward the Chinese revolutionary tradition. Unfortunately, military generals such as Liu Bocheng, who had faithfully followed Mao's calls for military modernization, paid a price for Mao's inconsistency, whereas others such as Lin Biao took advantage of the changing political climate to gain influence. This, however, was only the beginning of the troubled Party–army relations.

The Confrontation at Lushan in 1959

The most significant political event that affected the military before the Cultural Revolution was the confrontation at Lushan in 1959. Ironically, the

---

[39] For instance, between October 1949 and December 1950, 711 Soviet military advisors arrived in China to help build the Chinese Navy. *Dangdai zhongguo de haijun* (China's Navy Today) (Beijing: Zhongguo shehui kexue chubanshe, 1987), pp. 48–9.

[40] Kau and Leung, p. 157.

[41] *Jianguo yilai Mao Zedong wengao: 1953, 1–1954, 12,* vol. 4, 1990, p. 309.

Lushan Conference was scheduled to discuss nineteen problems, but military issues were not even on the agenda.[42] Yet the Chinese army suffered as a result of a top-level conflict over economic policies. On July 2, 1959, the CCP Politburo convened an enlarged meeting at Lushan to discuss the economic situation. The meeting was designed to assess the ongoing Great Leap Forward movement and make policy adjustments, if necessary. Thus evaluations or even criticism of current policies were encouraged. Party and government officials attending the meeting were divided into small discussion groups so they could feel free to report on the situation in their provinces. During the exchanges of views on the economic situation in the small group sessions, some expressed deep concerns about the Great Leap Forward whereas others remained optimistic. Some debates were recorded, but overall the atmosphere was relaxed.[43]

On July 11, all the participants were notified that the meeting would end on July 15, and they were asked to arrange for their transportation back home. No resolution or important document emerged from the conference, except a summary of small group discussions. At this moment, Peng Dehuai, defense minister and China's second highest-ranking marshal, wrote a long personal letter to Mao to offer his critique of the Great Leap Forward. The Letter of Opinion was presented to Mao on July 14. The next morning, it was suddenly announced that the Lushan Conference would be prolonged for an indefinite period and that all participants were to stay in Lushan. Copies of Peng's personal letter to Mao were distributed to every participant for discussion.

For ten days, many participants were asked to air their views on Peng's letter. Mao did not lack strong defenders of the Great Leap Forward policies, but many participants had either come to conclusions similar to Peng's or shared his worries. Some openly expressed their support for Peng's assessment, whereas others carefully indicated their sympathy. More politically sensitive participants suspected that something big was coming, but few had expected this policy debate to become a major confrontation.

On July 23, Mao finally spoke. He warned that the CCP was "under com-

---

[42] Li Rui, *Lushan huiyi shilu* (True Record of the Lushan Plenum) (Beijing: Chunqiu chubanshe and Hunan jiaoyu chubanshe, 1989), pp. 26–33.

[43] One participant recalled that in the evening, dance parties and movie shows were arranged. Some aging Politburo members found the leisure to write poems while younger Party and government officials took the opportunity to play their favorite Mahjong until late in the night. Mao Zedong even took time off and swam in a nearby reservoir down the mountain. Li Rui, pp. 19–25.

bined attack from within and outside the Party" and from "the rightists and wavering elements."[44] Mao sent out a clear message: mistakes were made in the Great Leap Forward, but those who opposed the Great Leap Forward were "on the verge of becoming rightist." Mao laid out an impossible choice before the audience:

> But if we do ten things and nine are bad, and they are all published in the press, then we will certainly perish, and will deserve to perish. In that case, I will go to the countryside to lead the peasants to overthrow the government. If those of you in the Liberation Army won't follow me, then I will go and find a Red Army, and organize another Liberation Army. But I think the Liberation Army would follow me.[45]

After Mao made his position clear, many of Peng's sympathizers quickly switched sides. On July 31 and August 1, Mao, now joined by the members of the Politburo Standing Committee, began to blast Peng's views about the Great Leap Forward as well as all Peng's mistakes in the past. Old scores were dug up one after another in an attempt to prove that Peng was the representative of the bourgeoisie.

During August 2–16, the Lushan Conference was changed into the Eighth Plenum of the CCP Eighth Central Committee. In his opening speech, Mao accused Peng and his associates of organizing a "right opportunist antiparty clique" and a "military club."[46] Under high political pressure from Mao and other senior Party leaders, Peng had no choice but to accept whatever accusations had been made against him and to offer to resign from his posts.[47] The attack on Peng Dehuai and his associates, however, went beyond the Lushan. On August 18, 1959, an enlarged meeting of the Party CMC was convened to criticize Peng's "anti-Party crimes" and "bourgeois military line." One hundred and forty top army leaders were asked to attend the meeting. During the group discussions, many of them, although expressing their support for the

---

[44] Ibid., pp. 131–2.

[45] Ibid., p. 139.

[46] Xiao Xiaoqin and Wang Youqiao, eds., *Zhonghua renmin gongheguo sishi nian* (Forty Years of the People's Republic of China) (Beijing: Beijing shifan xueyuan chubanshe, 1990), p. 161. Mao's accusation was endorsed in the formal resolution passed by the Plenum. For the English translation of the Resolution of the CCP Central Committee, see Harold Hinton, ed., *Government and Politics in Revolutionary China: Selected Documents, 1949–1979* (Wilmington, DE: Scholarly Resources, 1982), pp. 98–100.

[47] *Peng Dehuai zhuan* (Biography of Peng Dehuai) (Beijing: Dangdai zhongguo chubanshe, 1993), pp. 633–4.

Party's decision to oppose the "Rightist tendency," did not believe that Peng and his associates had intended to attack Mao and the Party. The meeting was getting nowhere. At the suggestion of his followers, Mao decided to expand the session from 140 delegates to an unprecedented level of 1,070.[48] On August 21, eighteen airplanes departed to bring the delegates from all over the country to the meeting hall in Beijing.

On August 22, the enlarged meeting of the Party CMC began. A new momentum was gradually built up by Mao's followers, but several army leaders still tried to defend Peng. The most dramatic episode came when Lin Biao, who presided over the meeting, began to accuse Peng of trying to eliminate Mao's troops during the Long March. General Zhong Wei, chief of staff of the Beijing Military Region, suddenly stood up and cited his personal experience to rebuff Lin Biao's accusation. He called Lin's accusation "nonsense" and denounced Lin and others for "fabricating rumors to mislead people." Zhong Wei shouted, "You have already declared the formation of a 'military club' by Peng Dehuai. You can declare me to be a member of this club and send me to execution by shooting now!" With this, the entire meeting hall burst into an uproar. Within five minutes, General Zhong was handcuffed and hurried out of the meeting hall by two fully armed soldiers. Although he was not executed, General Zhong Wei was deprived of his military rank and sent back to his home town for physical labor. He was not rehabilitated until after 1976.[49]

Still the meeting got nowhere, and several senior Party leaders, including Liu Shaoqi, Zhou Enlai, Chen Yun, and Li Fuchun, had to be called to the struggle meeting to put more pressure on the military leaders. Marshal Zhu De was forced to engage in self-criticism because of his sympathy for Peng at the Lushan Conference. Other marshals spent most of the time discussing trivial matters in their relations with Peng. Liu Shaoqi, the senior vice chairman of the Party, again attacked Peng as he did at Lushan. Zhou Enlai offered a moderate criticism of Peng as well as a self-criticism of himself. Chen Yun was the only Politburo member who managed to remain silent as he had been since the Lushan Conference.[50] On the final day, Mao himself had to come to bring the struggle meeting to an end. A resolution was finally passed to launch a campaign against the bourgeois military line and "Right Opportunists" in the army.

---

[48] Ibid., p. 638.
[49] Ma Ge, Pei Pu and Mao Taiquan, *Guofang buzhang fucheng ji* (The Rise and Fall of the Defense Minister) (Beijing: Kunlun chubanshe, 1988), pp. 119–20.
[50] Ibid., p. 126.

Table 5.1. *Military leaders purged in 1959–60*

Name	Military rank	Post(s)
Peng Dehuai	Marshal	Defense Minister
Huang Kecheng	Senior General	Chief, PLA General Staff
Hong Xuezhi	General	Director, PLA General Logistics Dept.
Deng Hua	General	Deputy Chief, PLA General Staff Commander, Shenyang Military Region
Zhou Huan	General	Commissar, Shenyang Military Region
Wan Yi	Lt. General	Head, PLA Dept. of Equipment Planning
Zhong Wei	Major General	Chief-of-Staff, Beijing Military Region

Sources: Compiled by the author from biographical information in the following sources: *Who's Who in China: Current Leaders* (Beijing: Foreign Languages Press, 1989); Donald W. Klein and Anne B. Clark, eds. *Biographical Dictionary of Chinese Communism 1921–1965* (Cambridge, MA: Harvard University Press, 1971); Jiang Huaxuan, Zhang Weiping, and Xiao Shen, eds., *Zhongguo gongchandang huiyi gaiyao* (Summaries of the Chinese Communist Party Conferences) (Liaoning: Shenyang chubanshe, 1991).

As a result of the subsequent massive purge in the military, several senior army leaders were dismissed from their posts (see Table 5.1).

Of course the number of the senior military generals purged represented only the tip of an iceberg.[51] Within a month from mid-September to mid-October, 847 military officers were singled out for criticism and denunciation. By the end of November 1959, 1,848 military personnel were designated as Right Opportunists, among whom 195 were at or above the rank of regimental commander. Between 1959 and 1960, altogether 17,212 persons in the military were declared to be Right Opportunists, to have committed "Right Opportunist errors," or to have political problems.[52]

---

[51] The treatment of some of the purged military leaders, though, was interesting. Peng Dehuai was allowed to keep his seat on the Politburo. Accused of being "anti-Party and anti-Mao," General Deng Hua was forced to leave the army, but was later appointed a vice governor of Sichuan Province in charge of agricultural machinery. *Zhongguo renmin jiefangjun jiangshuai minglu* (Biography of the People's Liberation Army Marshals and Generals), vol. 7 (Beijing: Jiefang-jun chubanshe, 1988), pp. 48–9.

[52] Jiang Huaxuan et al., p. 441; Wen Lü, ed., *Zhongguo "zuo" huo* (The "Leftist" Calamities in China) (Beijing: Zhaohua chubanshe, 1993), p. 358; *Guanyu xinshiqi jundui zhengzhi gongzuo de jueding zhushiben,* p. 160.

Mao and Party Politics

In the West, some studies suggest that Peng had violated the "consensus" in presenting his views.[53] Some characterized this incident as an "open attack" by Peng and a faction of the military on Mao and the Party.[54] Others argued that the purge of Peng "was surgical, and barely cut out an isolated few who had challenged Mao's majority on domestic policy."[55]

Did Peng violate the rules of the game within the CCP in presenting his views? Peng had criticized the Great Leap Forward policies at a few meetings before the Lushan Conference. It is true that on one such occasion, Mao half-jokingly and half-seriously accused Peng of overstepping his authority.[56] Yet, before Mao began to attack Peng on July 23, none of the Party leaders had accused Peng of violating procedure or discipline within the Party. Indeed, it is within the CCP organizational rules for the Party Central Committee members to write letters to Party leaders.[57] Peng was a senior member of the Party Politburo and vice premier of the State Council. It was not at all inappropriate for Peng to express his views on economic policy. Even as defense minister, Peng had reasons to be worried about national economic conditions. The worsening economic situation in the countryside inevitably demoralized the PLA's rank and filers, as most of them came from peasant families.

Ironically, Peng could have avoided this confrontation. Because of his other responsibilities, Peng was absent from several Party meetings leading to the Lushan Conference. When the conference was about to begin, Peng had just come back from a trip to eight foreign countries. Had it not been for a direct

---

[53] For a discussion of this issue, see Marcia R. Ristaino, "China's Leaders: Individual or Party Spokesmen?" *Problems of Communism* (July–August 1990), pp. 100–6.

[54] Such a characterization of the Peng incident is common in the literature. See, for instance, Victor Nee and David Mozingo, eds., *State and Society in Contemporary China* (Ithaca, NY: Cornell University Press, 1983), p. 92; Jürgen Domes, *Peng Te-huai: The Man and the Image* (Stanford, CA: Stanford University Press, 1985).

[55] Gerald Segal, "The Military as a Group in Chinese Politics," in David S. G. Goodman, ed., *Groups and Politics in the People's Republic of China* (Armonk, NY: M. E. Sharpe, 1984), p. 87.

[56] Ma Ge, Pei Pu and Mao Taiquan, p. 20.

[57] On January 7, 1948, the CCP Central Committee issued a directive for establishing a report system. The directive clearly stipulated that every member and alternate member of the Party Central Committee had the right and obligation to report separately to the Central Committee and its chairman on the current situation and to express his or her views. Feng Zhibin et al., eds., *Zhongguo gongchandang jianshe quanshu, 1921–1991* (Encyclopedia of the Construction of the Chinese Communist Party, 1921–1991), vol. 6 (Shanxi: Shanxi renmin chubanshe, 1991), pp. 1,049–50.

phone call from Mao himself, Peng would have stayed at home to rest, for he had already asked for a leave of absence.[58] When Peng arrived at Lushan, it seemed almost inevitable that he would stand up to criticize the Great Leap Forward policy again, given his reputation for being outspoken. Still, Peng carefully calculated what to do. After much hesitation,[59] Peng decided to take an indirect approach to express his views to Mao by writing a personal letter. Peng had no intention of offending Mao, let alone challenging Mao's power.[60] Under the circumstances, it seemed that no one could have done better than Peng except by turning a blind eye to the problems – unfortunately, nor could anyone have expected Mao to be so intolerant.[61]

Was Mao's prestige so overwhelming that only a few dared to challenge him?[62] Recently published memoirs by the participants to the Lushan Conference suggest that no matter what personality cult or charisma Mao might have developed by then, it surely was not enough to keep his critics silent at first.[63] Many participants, particularly junior officials, did not shy from criticizing Mao's Great Leap Forward policy. Before Mao revealed his attitude toward Peng's letter, many senior Party leaders also shared Peng's views. But when Mao threatened to "go to the countryside to lead the peasants to overthrow the government," the top Party leadership quickly sided with Mao at the expense of Peng and many others. In his fierce attack on Peng, Mao clearly abused his power, but senior Party leaders, including Liu Shaoqi and Zhou Enlai, did nothing to discourage Mao from purging Peng and his associates.[64]

Mao's ultimate power over his colleagues lay in his perceived vital importance to the Party organization. Ever since the Zunyi Conference in 1935 when

---

[58] Wen Lü, p. 329. Two other sources suggest that Peng went to Lushan because of the persuasion of a colleague. Ma Ge, Pei Pu, and Mao Taiquan, pp. 25–6; *Peng Dehuai zhuan,* p. 584.

[59] Peng's seemingly painful deliberation of whether to talk to Mao directly or to write to him indirectly is detailed in Ma Ge, Pei Pu, and Mao Taiquan, pp. 44–53.

[60] Frederick C. Teiwes, *Politics and Purges in China: Rectification and the Decline of Party Norms, 1950–1965,* 2nd edition (Armonk, NY: M. E. Sharpe, 1993), pp. xxxiii–xxxiv.

[61] In his analysis of the crisis at Lushan, Teiwes suggests that it was not Peng, but rather Mao who violated the "norms of inner Party democracy." Ibid., pp. l–lvi.

[62] Marcia R. Ristaino, "China's Leaders: Individual or Party Spokesmen?" pp. 102–3.

[63] In fact, Mao's prestige among his colleagues had seriously suffered due to his miscalculations about the "Hundred Flowers" campaign and the Great Leap Forward movement.

[64] Li Rui, Mao's former secretary and a victim at the Lushan Conference, described his sad feeling in the following way: "To be frank, I had been in an extremely complicated mental situation during the meetings of more than ten days. I felt very pessimistic. I wondered: This is the Party Central Committee. This is the meeting of the highest leadership of our Party. How come there is not even one person who dares to come out to say a word in fairness?" Li Rui, pp. 318–9.

127

Mao maneuvered to regain his leading position, Mao had come to be known as the only Party leader who could lead the Communist revolution to victory. Myth or truth, Mao's rescue of the Party and Red Army during the Long March became the legend in the official history of the Party. Thus the CCP simply could not afford to dump Mao the way the CPSU under Khrushchev dumped the late Stalin, for Mao was both Lenin and Stalin in China. To challenge and possibly depose Mao ran the risk of trashing the entire history of the Party since 1935 and undermining the legitimacy of the CCP.[65]

Second, whereas Mao had been portrayed as leading the Chinese revolution from victory to victory, most of his colleagues were burdened by their historical records of failed opposition to Mao. This gave Mao plenty of ammunition and Mao had an instinct for bringing up old scores. Since only Mao could most authoritatively interpret the Party history, every CCP leader was ultimately at the mercy of Mao's interpretation of their personal record and political career. In this sense, Mao had become the Party and the Party was Mao.

Third, Mao's supreme power lay in his ability and potential to destroy the Party, a unique weapon that no other Party leader had mastered. Whenever Mao threatened to resign and leave the Party, thus inevitably causing the Party to split, the CCP leadership had to cave in. In a major confrontation between Mao and his colleagues, the Party could afford to sacrifice any of its top leaders, but not Mao. Otherwise the Party would face a real danger of breaking apart.

Finally, Mao knew how to justify the purges of his opponents by use of the Party's ideology and organizational norms. Here a brief comparison between Chiang Kai-shek and Mao Zedong could be illuminating. Both men demanded loyalty from their generals and yet neither man's command over the military was absolute. Chiang's generals dared to put him under house arrest and forced him to sign something he didn't want; Mao's generals dared to challenge him on major policy issues. What made Mao different from Chiang, however, is that Mao's command of the military was both personal and organizational. For Chiang, dismissal was the end of his dissenting generals. For Mao, dismissal was just the beginning of yet another political campaign. Mao let his generals enjoy freedom and autonomy within the framework of a revolutionary organization. PLA generals could challenge Mao to a certain extent, but once Mao declared his opponents to be the enemy of the Party and revolution, any dissenting voice quickly lost legitimacy, let alone support.

[65] Teiwes, 1993, p. 331.

Many years ago, Samuel Huntington perceptively pointed out: "Politics is beyond the scope of military competence. . . ."[66] If history has taught us anything, it is that military engagement in politics is like playing with fire. What has made the PLA's situation even more difficult is that the content of Party politics kept changing, even under the same paramount leader. Being "politically correct" has meant different things under different circumstances. To follow Mao's call to regularize and modernize the army in the early 1950s was condemned in the late 1950s as pursuing a bourgeois military line and ignoring revolutionary politics. Peng Dehuai's invited participation in re-evaluating the Party's economic policy at Lushan in 1959 was attacked as being "anti-Party and anti-Mao."

The political attacks on Senior General Tan Zhen in 1960 and Marshal Luo Ronghuan in 1961 further illustrate the arbitrary and dangerous nature of Party politics. As Ellis Joffe pointed out, Tan opposed "mechanically" copying the Soviet experience as early as in 1956. As director of the PLA General Political Department (GPD), Tan was also a strong advocate of Party control of the military.[67] In other words, Tan had been politically correct and he obviously did not object to Mao's attack on Peng at Lushan. Yet, when Tan disagreed with Lin Biao on how (not whether) to promote Mao's ideas in the PLA in March–April 1960, Lin orchestrated a major struggle meeting for thirty days against the "Tan Zhen anti-Party faction."[68] Tan was dismissed from his posts and later (1965) forced to leave the military to take up a job as vice governor of Fujian Province.[69] The case of Tan Zhen raises questions about the basic assumption of the "politicization versus professionalism" model. If Liu Bocheng, Peng Dehuai, Su Yu, and others were on the "wrong side" for promoting "military professionalism" (perhaps the Soviet style) in the PLA, why then were Tan Zhen and his associates who had been advocating Party control of the military also purged? It is worth noting that Tan and his associates faced the same

---

[66] Huntington, 1957, p. 71.

[67] Ellis Joffe, *Party and Army: Professionalism and Political Control in the Chinese Officer Corps, 1949–1964* (Cambridge, MA: The East Asian Research Center of Harvard University, 1965), pp. 43, 76–8.

[68] Jiang Huaxuan et. al., pp. 446–8.

[69] Along with Tan Zhen, those purged were Liu Qiren, director of the organization department of the GPD; Jian Shiyi, director of the propaganda department of the GPD; Ou Yangwen, chief editor of the *Liberation Army Daily;* and Bai Wenhua, secretary-general of the GPD. Fu Zhong and Gan Shiqi, two deputy directors of the GPD, were also criticized. *Luo Ronghuan zhuan* (Biography of Luo Ronghuan) (Beijing: Dangdai zhongguo chubanshe, 1991), p. 572.

accusations as Peng did: "opposing the Party and Mao, and implementing bourgeois military line."[70]

After the purge of Tan Zhen, Marshal Luo Ronghuan reassumed his directorship of the GPD. Like Tan, Luo had long insisted that learning from the Soviet experience must follow the Chinese conditions. As early as in 1950, Luo ran into disputes with the Soviet military advisers over this issue. In 1953, Luo said to Peng Dehuai,

> Some comrades now believe that the political work system is outdated, that the political commissar can no longer play an important role, and that we should learn from the Soviet one-man leadership. If so, isn't it going to abandon the tradition of political work we had established since the Jinggangshan period?[71]

However, Luo's seemingly "Maoist," or politically correct views did not spare him from political trouble. When he ran into serious disagreements with Lin Biao in 1961 on how to organize soldiers to study Mao's writings, Lin Biao did not hesitate to attack Luo. Lin Biao and Luo Ronghuan were commander and political commissar of the Fourth Field Army, respectively, but Luo's field army connection with Lin had no relevance this time. In fact, Lin Biao even had this to say: "What's the Lin and Luo connection? Lin and Luo must be separated. Lin and Luo have never been together."[72] Luo could have become another victim of Party politics had it not been for his serious illness and Mao's ambivalence toward this attack.[73]

The military reorganization and modernization programs after the founding of the People's Republic provided the PLA with a golden opportunity to transform itself from a guerrilla force into a modern standing army. Yet, the historical and structural linkage between the PLA and the revolutionary party organization made the modern army-building difficult. Having built the army themselves, the CCP leaders refused to let the PLA be placed under the command of the new state institutions. The National Defense Council and the Ministry of Defense in the State Council were established in 1954, and yet they exercised no control over the military. The armed forces reported only to the PLA General Headquarters under the Party CMC. Moreover, even the Party Central Committee had little control over the Party CMC. It was the paramount leader who actually commanded the guns through his loyal generals in the

---

[70] Ibid.   [71] Ibid., pp. 526–8.
[72] Ibid., p. 605.   [73] Luo Ronghuan died in 1963.

Party CMC. Furthermore, the PLA's unique and intricate linkage with the revolutionary party inevitably subjected the military institution to the danger of unpredictable Party politics. During the political struggles, neither seniority nor military achievements could save marshals or generals from humiliation and purges. More often than not, the Party elite simply watched their long-time comrades-in-arms fall from grace and did nothing, for fear of jeopardizing their own political career. Finally, Mao was the one who initiated the ambitious program in the early 1950s to build a strong and modern army. Yet, when the decade ended, the PLA was deeply factionalized and seriously weakened by the massive political purges. This must be the greatest irony of army-building in the Mao Zedong era.

6

Politics of Campaigns: The Cultural Revolution

THE mass assault on the authorities and state institutions that swept China three decades ago has few parallels in this century.[1] Its impact on the Chinese society and polity has been profound, and its causes are still debated by both Chinese and Western scholars. Depending on one's level of analysis and source of information, the Cultural Revolution can be viewed as a Chinese great purge masterminded by Mao Zedong; a showdown between Mao's romantic revolutionary ideals and Liu Shaoqi's strict organizational control; a life-and-death power struggle among various political factions, including Lin Biao's military, Zhou Enlai's government apparatus, and the radical group headed by Mao's wife, Jiang Qing; or a social movement that included the Red Guard rebellion and workers' revolts.[2] This chapter takes as the main issue the

---

[1] Harry Harding, *Organizing China: The Problem of Bureaucracy, 1949–1976* (Stanford, CA: Stanford University Press, 1981), p. 148.

[2] There now exists a huge literature on the Chinese Cultural Revolution. See, among others, Edward Rice, *Mao's Way* (Berkeley: University of California Press, 1972); Lowell Dittmer, *Liu Shao-ch'i and the Chinese Cultural Revolution: The Politics of Mass Criticism* (Berkeley: University of California Press, 1974); Thomas W. Robinson, ed., *The Cultural Revolution in China* (Berkeley: University of California Press, 1971); Hong Yong Lee, *The Politics of the Chinese Cultural Revolution: A Case Study* (Berkeley: University of California Press, 1978); Anita Chan, *Children of Mao: Personality Development and Political Activism in the Red Guard Generation* (Seattle: University of Washington Press, 1985); Anita Chan, Richard Madsen, and Jonathan Unger, *Chen Village: The Recent History of a Peasant Community in Mao's China* (Berkeley: University of California Press, 1984); David Zweig, *Agricultural Radicalism in China, 1968–1981* (Cambridge, MA: Harvard University Press, 1989); Lynn T. White III, *Policies of Chaos: The Organizational Causes of Violence in China's Cultural Revolution* (Princeton, NJ: Princeton University Press, 1989); and William A. Joseph, Christine P. W. Wong, and David Zweig, *New Perspectives on the Cultural Revolution* (Cambridge, MA: Council on East Asian Studies, Harvard University, 1991). Also, for a Mao-centered interpretation of the Cultural Revolution, see Kenneth Lieberthal, *Governing China: From Revolution Through Reform* (New York: W. W. Norton & Company, 1995), pp. 111–21. For the analysis of the political events leading to the outbreak of the Cultural Revolution, see Roderick MacFarquhar, *The Origins of the Cultural Revolution, I: Contradictions Among the People 1956–1957* (New York: Columbia University Press, 1974), *The Origins of the Cultural Revolution, II: The Great*

institutional destruction and rebuilding during the Cultural Revolution. It discusses the unprecedented assault on the Chinese state institutions in the early stages of the Cultural Revolution, Mao's failed attempts to establish alternative ways of reorganizing China, and the role of the military and mass campaigns.

MAO AND MORE CLASS STRUGGLE

Historians in China have suggested that class struggle during the Mao era escalated four times, leading to the political upheaval of the Cultural Revolution: the Anti-Rightist Campaign in 1957, the purge of Peng Dehuai in 1959, the Tenth Plenum of the Eighth Party Central Committee in 1962 that confirmed class struggle as the Party's basic line, and the Socialist Education Campaign in 1964–65.[3] In early 1961, having recognized his responsibility for the disastrous consequences of the Great Leap Forward movement, Mao decided to retreat to the "Second Front," focusing on theoretical and ideological issues. Pragmatic leaders like Zhou Enlai, Chen Yun, and Deng Xiaoping now played a more important role in managing the national economy. In May 1961, in Mao's absence, the CCP Politburo Standing Committee decided to take a series of drastic measures that would constitute a reversal of what had been called for in the Great Leap Forward. The peasants were to be compensated, light industry supported, and government deficits reduced. Those targeted and accused in the political campaigns of the previous years were to be rehabilitated.[4] To rescue agriculture and the national economy from disaster, pragmatic Party leaders played down ideology. In July 1962, Party Secretary-General Deng Xiaoping reportedly said, "Whether cats are white or black, so long as they can catch mice, they are all good cats."[5] In this spirit, measures were adopted to redistribute land to peasant households and to permit the expansion of private plots, free markets, and sideline production.

Leap Forward 1958–1960 (New York: Columbia University Press, 1983), and Frederick C. Teiwes, *Politics and Purges in China: Rectification and the Decline of Party Norms, 1950–1965,* 2nd edition (Armonk, NY: M. E. Sharpe, 1993).

[3] *Dangshi yanjiu yu jiaoxue* (Research and Teaching of Party History), vol. 79, p. 80.

[4] The available data from twenty-three provinces show that by the end of August of 1962, more than 2.5 million Party members and cadres who were wrongly accused in the past had been rehabilitated. See Xiao Xiaoqin and Wang Youqiao, eds., *Zhonghua renmin gongheguo sishi nian* (Forty Years of the People's Republic of China) (Beijing: Beijing shifan xueyuan chubanshe, 1990), p. 178.

[5] Cited in Stephen Uhalley, Jr., *A History of the Chinese Communist Party* (Stanford, CA: Hoover Institution, Stanford University, 1988), p. 133.

After a temporary retreat of several months, however, Mao concluded that the country was heading in the wrong direction under the guidance of his pragmatic colleagues. As the national economic situation was improving, Mao believed that deviations from revolutionary goals had become the main problem. At the Party Work Conference in August 1962, Mao began to denounce the policies of economic adjustment. Mao warned his colleagues of the "danger of capitalism and revisionism." He asked, "The KMT collapsed after being in power for twenty-three years. How many years are left for us?"[6] At this conference, Mao criticized certain central ministries and commissions for doing things without consultation with "the Party center" beforehand and for not reporting to the Party center afterward.[7] Mao sarcastically suggested that "the Ministry of Commerce should change its name to 'Ministry of Sabotage.'"[8] In September 1962, at the Tenth Plenum of the Eighth Central Committee, Mao put forward a new Party line of "taking class struggle as the key link" and warned the whole Party: "Never forget class struggle." Mao stressed:

> We must acknowledge that classes will continue to exist for a long time. We must also acknowledge the existence of a struggle of class against class, and admit the possibility of the restoration of reactionary classes. . . . Therefore, from now on we must talk about this every year, every month, every day. We will talk about it at congresses, at party delegate conferences, at plenums, at every meeting we hold, so that we have a more enlightened Marxist-Leninist line on the problem.[9]

The Party Central Committee, as always, accepted Mao's analysis without much resistance. Many would have disagreed with Mao, but to minimize their risks in an increasingly dangerous political environment of class struggle, members of the Party Central Committee simply obeyed Mao.[10] In February

---

[6] Jiang Huaxuan et al., eds., *Zhongguo gongchandang huiyi gaiyao* (Summaries of the Chinese Communist Party Conferences) (Liaoning: Shenyang chubanshe, 1991), p. 487.

[7] Ibid., p. 488. Here "the Party center" should read as "Mao."

[8] Ibid.

[9] Mao, "Speech at the Tenth Plenum" in Stuart R. Schram, ed., *Chairman Mao Talks to the People* (New York: Pantheon Books, 1974), pp. 189–90.

[10] Twenty years later, the Party Central Committee offered a belated official assessment of Mao's mistakes: "At the Tenth Plenary Session of the party's Eighth Central Committee in September 1962, comrade Mao Zedong widened and absolutized the class struggle, which exists only within certain limits in socialist society, and carried forward the viewpoint he had advocated after the anti-rightist struggle in 1957 that the contradiction between the proletariat and the

1963, at a CCP central work conference, Mao further affirmed, "Class struggle is the key link and everything else hinges on it."[11] The conference decided to launch a new "Five-Anti" campaign in the cities and a Socialist Education Movement in the countryside. The movement began in the spring of 1963, and by 1964 thousands of Party work teams and more than one million Party and government officials had been sent down to the villages to mobilize the masses. Because class struggle now became the "key link," problems in economic management at the basic levels were seen as a reflection of class struggle within the Party and government. Many lower-ranking cadres were criticized or purged.[12] All these attacks, however, paled greatly when compared with the massive destruction of lives and institutions during the Cultural Revolution, which is undoubtedly the darkest episode in the history of the People's Republic. If in the Anti-Rightist Campaign of 1957 the Party officials prevailed over their critics, the ensuing Cultural Revolution turned on the Party itself. Without a minimum guarantee of the basic constitutional rights of individuals, the logic of political campaigns eventually made victimizers victims as well.

Mass Assault and Power Seizure

The post-Mao leaders defined the Cultural Revolution as a decade-long turmoil (1966–76), although the upsurge of the Cultural Revolution lasted from 1966 to 1969, when the authorities at all levels were "bombarded" and the Party and state institutions were swept away in a series of power seizures by rebel students and workers. The mass assault on the authorities and state institutions roughly consisted of three stages: the agitation of the urban youth by Mao against social values and cultural authorities, the attack on the government and Party officials, and a nationwide power seizure by rebel organizations. At each stage, the rebel youth and workers had received approval and praise from Mao and his radical associates. Although the society did have

bourgeoisie remained the principal contradiction in our society. He went a step further and asserted that throughout the historical period of socialism, the bourgeoisie would continue to exist and would attempt a comeback and become the source of revisionism inside the party." *Resolution on the History of the Chinese Communist Party (1949–81)* (Beijing: Foreign Languages Press, 1981).

[11] *Zhongguo gongchandang lishi dashiji* (A Chronology of the Chinese Communist Party) (Beijing: Renmin chubanshe, 1989), p. 264.

[12] *Shanghai dangzheng jigou yange, 1949–1986* (Evolution of the Party and Government Institutions in Shanghai, 1949–1986) (Shanghai: Shanghai renmin chubanshe, 1988), p. 100.

much grievance and anger to unleash, the call for a new revolution against the Communist Party and the government authority came from the very top.

The Red Guard movement officially began on August 18, 1966, when Mao received nearly one million high school and college students in Tiananmen Square. During the next few weeks, the Red Guards rampaged in major cities, smashing and destroying the so-called Four Olds – old ideas, culture, custom, and habits. The destructive acts of the rebellious youth could continue not only because they were encouraged by Mao himself and received official endorsement from the Party newspaper, but also because the law enforcement agencies were not allowed to take action. On August 22, 1966, the Party center and the Ministry of Public Security sent out specific instructions strictly forbidding the police from "suppressing revolutionary student movement."[13] Meanwhile, the military was asked to help organize Red Guard rallies in Tiananmen Square and provide logistical support for those Red Guards who traveled all the way to Beijing from other provinces to see Mao.

Around September–October, 1966, the Red Guard movement entered a second stage as Beijing Red Guards began to surround the central government office buildings and demanded that several government officials come out to face mass struggle meetings. Red Guards' threats and personal attacks against high-ranking officials again received encouragement from Mao, Lin Biao, and the Party magazine, *Red Flag.* Before long, waves of denunciation and bombardment engulfed many central and provincial government institutions. Mao welcomed the massive dismantling of the Party and state apparatus. On his seventy-third birthday on December 26, 1966, Mao congratulated the Red Guards on "waging an all-out civil war."[14]

Then came the third stage. In early January 1967, Red Guards and rebel workers in Shanghai declared a nonrecognition of Cao Diqiu as the city's mayor and a takeover of the municipal government. Within a week, Mao approved this power seizure and hailed it as "a great revolution."[15] On January 22, 1967, the *People's Daily* editorial called on the rebels to seize power from "those in authority who are taking the capitalist road."[16] Following the January power seizure in Shanghai, a nationwide power seizure took place, and by September 5, 1968, all the provincial and local governments had been replaced by the revolutionary committee.

---

[13] Wen Lü, ed., *Zhongguo "zuo" huo* (The "Leftist" Calamities in China) (Beijing: Zhaohua chubanshe, 1993), p. 415.
[14] Ibid., p. 429.   [15] Ibid., p. 430.
[16] Ibid.

Victims of the Cultural Revolution

The Red Guard movement and the ensuing mass violence encouraged by Mao's radical associates had devastating consequences for Chinese officials as well as for the Party and government institutions. Except for Mao Zedong, his protégé, Lin Biao, and a few of their followers, almost all the Chinese leaders were attacked or paraded in public if they were lucky, and tortured or imprisoned if they were not. By 1968, 71 percent of the members and alternate members of the CCP Eighth Central Committee had been accused of being "traitors," "enemy agents," and "antiparty elements."[17] Among the high-ranking officials (above the rank of deputy minister or vice governor), 75 percent were placed under special investigation by rebel masses. In the central government agencies, 29,885 officials were persecuted.[18] When the political rehabilitation process began in 1978, as many as 300,000 victims of the Cultural Revolution were identified. Deng Xiaoping, who had miraculously survived two purges during the Cultural Revolution, gave the estimate that as many as 2.9 million people had suffered political persecution during this period.[19]

In the national legislature, 60 of 115 members of the NPC Standing Committee, including the chairman and five vice chairmen, were accused of being enemy agents, traitors, counterrevolutionary revisionists, capitalist roaders, and anti-Party, anti-socialism, and anti-people elements.[20] On July 7, 1968, the Standing Committee of the Third NPC met for the last time and decided to postpone the Second Session of the Third NPC indefinitely. The postponed meeting never convened. In fact, during the eight years from 1966 to 1975, the entire NPC and its Standing Committee did not have a single meeting and virtually ceased to function. During this period, the only reported NPC activities were of Guo Moruo, the vice chairman of the NPC Standing Committee and Mao's protégé, meeting with foreign delegations (mostly Japanese).[21]

On August 7, 1967, Xie Fuzhi, the Minister of Public Security and a member of Jiang Qing's radical group, became the first one to openly call for "thoroughly smashing the public security, procuratorate and courts." In the central

---

[17] *Zhongguo gongchandang lishi dashiji,* p. 299.

[18] Wen Lü, p. 428.

[19] Sources are quoted in James C. F. Wang, *Contemporary Chinese Politics: An Introduction,* 5th edition (Englewood Cliffs, NJ: Prentice Hall, 1995), p. 30.

[20] *Quanguo renda jiqi changweihui dashiji 1954–1987* (A Chronology of the National People's Congress and Its Standing Committee, 1954–1987) (Beijing: Falü chubanshe, 1987), p. 18.

[21] Ibid., pp. 202–16.

office of the Ministry of Public Security in Beijing, 225 officials were accused of being enemy agents, traitors, or counterrevolutionaries, among whom forty-seven were put in jail. Except Xie Fuzhi and another vice minister, all the officials at the ministerial rank in the Ministry of Public Security were arrested or detained. Nationwide, 34,400 policemen, procurators, judges, and judicial workers were persecuted. Among them, 1,100 died and 3,600 were seriously injured or crippled.[22] Under the revolutionary terror of class struggle, judicial institutions were smashed by the revolutionary rebels, who then formed various special case groups to detain, interrogate, and punish their targets with no regard for legal procedure.

During the Cultural Revolution, the State Council also came under heavy attack. In the name of "better troops and simpler administration" and of preparing for war, twenty-eight out of fifty-four central ministries and commissions of the State Council were abolished on June 22, 1970.[23] The agencies of the State Council were reduced from a total of seventy-eight to only thirty-two, among which only nineteen were under the direct authority of Zhou Enlai, the premier of the State Council, thirteen were taken over by the military under Lin Biao, and three were placed under the Party's Cultural Revolutionary Group headed by Mao's radical associates.

The mass assault on the Party and state institutions took a heavy toll on human lives as well. Although no reliable figures are available as to exactly how many people committed suicide or were tortured to death during the Cultural Revolution, one official source revealed in 1981 that about 34,000 died due to political persecution, among whom was Liu Shaoqi, the state chairman of the People's Republic. In 1968, Liu was denounced as "China's Khrushchev" by the Red Guards in the street, and as "renegade, traitor and scab" by his colleagues in the Party plenum's resolution. When Liu finally realized that he could hope for no one to rescue him, he resorted to a copy of the Chinese constitution and his official title as the state chairman in a failed attempt to save himself.[24] In November 1969, Liu Shaoqi died in disgrace in a secluded place away from Beijing and from his wife and children.

---

[22] Wen Lü, pp. 460–1.

[23] *Zhonghua renmin gongheguo quanguorenda zhongyang he difangzhengfu quanguozhengxie lijiefuzeren renming lu* (Directory of the Former Responsible Persons of the National People's Congress of the People's Republic of China, the Central and Local Government, and the National People's Political Consultative Conference) (Beijing: Renmin chubanshe, 1984), p. 64.

[24] Kevin J. O'Brien, *Reform Without Liberalization: China's National People's Congress and the Politics of Institutional Change* (New York: Cambridge University Press, 1990), pp. 56–7.

Mao and the Party Leadership

It can be debated whether the Chinese revolution somehow could have been institutionalized after 1949 if it had not been for Mao's insistence on continuing the revolution.[25] It can certainly be argued that had it not been for Mao, the Cultural Revolution would not have happened.[26] Mao was undoubtedly responsible for many mass campaigns after 1949. Nonetheless, as this study demonstrates, most of the Party leaders for most of the time followed Mao either enthusiastically or passively. Such enthusiasm can be found in the various campaigns of the early 1950s, in the Anti-Rightist Campaign of 1957–58, in the Great Leap Forward movement of 1958–60, and even in the initial months of the Cultural Revolution. Focusing on the Cultural Revolution, some historians in the CCP History Research Department have reached a similar conclusion. They argued that Mao should be held primarily, but not exclusively, responsible for the mistakes of the Cultural Revolution. For one thing, the Party leadership had accepted Mao's wrong ideas and passed them as the collective resolutions of the Party Central Committee. For another, when it was still not too late to act decisively to prevent Mao from launching the Cultural Revolution, the Party Central Committee failed the test.[27]

Mao was powerful not necessarily because he commanded the personal loyalty of his colleagues, but because he was capable of creating a revolutionary organizational environment from which the CCP leaders found it difficult to escape. In this organizational environment, there could be no personal enemy of Mao, only a public enemy of the Party. Mao became the Party, and whoever opposed Mao was anti-Party. Without this organizational context, it would be difficult to imagine that Mao, with the support of his radical associates, could have forced the entire Party and state leadership to yield. Mao did not have a formidable secret force behind him. He did mobilize millions of the masses, but only because the Party organization was there doing the mobilization work. During the early stage of the Cultural Revolution, Mao did have Lin Biao's army on his side, but only because the army was just as divided as the Party on the issue of the Cultural Revolution. In fact, if the PLA marshals and

[25] Peter R. Moody, Jr., *The Politics of the Eighth Central Committee of the Communist Party of China* (Hamden, CT: The Shoe String Press, 1973), pp. 1–28.

[26] Harry Harding, "The Chinese State in Crisis, 1966–9," in Roderick MacFarquhar, ed., *The Politics of China, 1949–1989* (New York: Cambridge University Press, 1993), p. 235.

[27] *Xuexi lishi jueyi zhuanji* (Studies of the Resolution on the CCP History) (Beijing: Research Department of the Chinese Communist Party History, the Chinese Communist Party Central Committee, 1982), pp. 158–9.

senior generals had pulled themselves together, they could have prevented Lin Biao from building up his political stock in the army.

Having worked for the Party for several decades, however, few in the Party and army had the courage to oppose Mao at the risk of splitting the Party. To them, Party meant everything, which invariably meant that Mao was everything. Party gave them a sense of identity and belonging. Through working for the Party, they had gained power, prestige, and privilege. Were they to leave the Party, it would not only bring disgrace, but also denial of their values and existence. A few CCP leaders, such as Wang Ming and Zhang Guotao who chose to split with Mao, had been constantly condemned in the Party documents and history books, serving as bad examples for no one to follow. If the CCP leaders did not necessarily believe what Mao did was right, at least they rationally calculated the benefits of standing on Mao's side and the costs of challenging him. Mao might be argued with or even criticized. But when Mao threatened to leave the Party, thus inevitably causing the Party to split and indeed throwing the entire political system into total disarray, Party leaders simply had no choice but to follow him. Anyone who defied this unwritten law would be certain to face strong opposition from within the Party. In any confrontation between Mao and his colleagues, the Party leadership concluded that they could sacrifice any of its members, but not Mao.

The more senior the Party leaders were, the more afraid they were of being abandoned by the Party. If necessary, they preferred to admit their "mistakes" much against their own will, rather than become "Partyless." On many occasions, Party leaders had to accept as correct what was obviously wrong, admit mistakes they did not commit, and twist their personalities and consciences to meet Mao's demands. The Party leaders were afraid to stand up to Mao, even when Mao was on the wrong track. Senior Party leaders like Zhou Enlai and Liu Shaoqi became model yes-men to the Party as well as to Mao. They concluded that they simply had to put up with Mao for the sake of the Party and thereby their own power and career.

The partyman mentality certainly did not mean that Chinese leaders under Mao had all lost their individual characters. On the contrary, on many occasions these leaders tried to express their views, protect their institutional interests, and emphasize their priorities. In other words, they tried to be their own men insofar as they could. Only when their ideas, interests, and tactics were in conflict with the highest organizational goal – the existence of the Party – did they have to bend their personalities or twist their consciences in order to avoid a disaster for the Party.[28] Even Mao's victims could not escape the partymen mentality. Ever since he had been purged by Mao, Peng Dehuai was waiting for Mao to change his mind. When Mao agreed to see Peng in September 1965 and told him, "Maybe the truth is on your side," Peng was deeply moved, even though Mao did not formally rehabilitate him as Peng had wished.[29] Thus, although the Chinese Communists created a party organization to liberate their countrymen; in the end, they themselves had become the slaves of that organization.

QUESTION OF REORGANIZATION

In many ways, Mao Zedong's attack on Chinese officialdom during the Cultural Revolution of 1966–69 is like Stalin's assault on Soviet officialdom during the Great Purge of 1936–39. Yet there is a major difference. As some Soviet specialists point out, by physically eliminating virtually the entire Party elite, Stalin's terror literally destroyed the old Bolshevik Party as a ruling class.[30] "After the purges swept away at least one million of its members between 1935 and 1939," Stephen Cohen suggests, "the primacy of the Party – 'essence' of Bolshevism-Leninism, in most scholarly definitions – was no more. . . . Even in its new Stalinist form, the Party's political importance fell below that of the politics, and its official esteem below that of the state."[31] "The soldier of the Party" was replaced by "the soldier of Stalin."

---

[28] The tensions between one's conscience and the Party policy, or between one's individuality and his or her official role have been well recorded in the biographies of the Chinese Communist elites. For instances, see Jürgen Domes, *Peng Te-huai: The Man and His Image* (Stanford, CA: Stanford University Press, 1985); Yang Zhongmei, *Hu Yaobang: A Chinese Biography* (Armonk, NY: M. E. Sharpe, 1988); and Ching Hua Lee, *Deng Xiaoping: The Marxist Road to the Forbidden City* (Princeton, NJ: Kingston Press, 1985). A review of these books is in Marcia R. Ristaino, "China's Leaders: Individual or Party Spokesmen?" *Problems of Communism* (July–August 1990), pp. 100–6.

[29] *Peng Dehuai zhuan* (A Biography of Peng Dehuai) (Beijing: Dangdai zhongguo chubanshe, 1993), pp. 697–700.

[30] Robert C. Tucker, *The Soviet Political Mind: Stalinism and Post-Stalin Change,* revised edition (New York: W. W. Norton & Company, 1971), p. 135; for a recent study of the Great Purges, see J. Arch Getty, *Origins of the Great Purges: The Soviet Communist Party Reconsidered, 1933–1938* (New York: Cambridge University Press, 1985).

[31] Stephen F. Cohen, "Bolshevism and Stalinism" in Robert C. Tucker, ed., *Stalinism: Essays in Historical Interpretation* (New York: W. W. Norton & Company, 1977), p. 18.

Mao, however, was not primarily interested in physical elimination. Although Mao had to be held responsible for the loss of many lives during the Cultural Revolution, there is no evidence for suggesting that Mao personally ordered his political opponents to be executed.[32] Rather, Mao was motivated by an ideological goal of remolding the Party and state bureaucracy. His mass campaign was aimed at making his revolutionary experience and ideals part of the post-revolutionary generation. Whereas Stalin used the state machine (particularly the secret police) to destroy Lenin's Bolshevik Party, Mao used his "masses of people" to shake the Party and state apparatus. After the Great Purge, therefore, the dilemma for Stalin was: how to trust the institution of terror that had ruthlessly eliminated his political opponents? After the mass assault on the Party and state authorities, the dilemma for Mao was: how to control the masses that had mercilessly smashed his political institutions?

Mao initiated the Red Guard movement by encouraging high school and college students to "bombard the headquarters" and by telling them "To rebel is justified!" This reminds one of Mao's unreserved praise for the rioting peasants in his home province, Hunan, in 1927. "Pretty soon," Mao had proclaimed, "several hundred million peasants will rise like a mighty storm, like a hurricane, a force so swift and violent that no power, however great, will be able to hold it back."[33] In the summer of 1966, Mao might very well have been in the same mood. However, Mao the "Great Helmsman" in 1966 was not the Mao of 1927, irritated and marginalized by an urban-oriented CCP leadership. Back then, Mao had nothing but radical ideas; in 1966, Mao not only had radical ideas, but also a country to run. In 1927, Mao encouraged his countrymen to overthrow the local landlord class; in 1966, what the Red Guards and rebel workers were about to destroy were the very Party and state institutions that Mao had built. If the mass assault was swift and violent like a hurricane in smashing the old political structure, it could do very little in creating a new political system. Anyone who experienced the Chinese Cultural Revolution would perhaps testify to the greatest irony revealed during its most turbulent years: There were so many political organizations, and yet the society was in institutional chaos; there were so many self-proclaimed headquarters of authorities, and yet there was little authority and order.

---

[32] Harding, "The Chinese State in Crisis, 1966–9," p. 243.

[33] Mao Zedong, *Selected Works of Mao Tse-tung* (Beijing: Foreign Languages Press, 1965), vol. 1, pp. 23–8.

Searching for Alternatives

At the beginning of the Cultural Revolution, there were four institutions of political authority at the top, each trying to represent the interests of their own constituencies.[34] The Party Central Committee supervised the Party committees at various levels and millions of Party members. The State Council managed the central and provincial administration and government administrators. The Party Central Military Commission controlled the PLA General Headquarters and more than four million soldiers. The Central Cultural Revolution Group was to direct the organization of Red Guards and rebel workers.

The Party Central Committee was once tightly controlled by Liu Shaoqi and Deng Xiaoping, but by October 1966, Liu and Deng had lost much of their authority over the Party organization. After February 1967, the Politburo of the Party Central Committee had practically ceased to function. While rebel organizations with support from Jiang Qing's Central Revolutionary Group seized power from the Party committees at all levels, Lin Biao's military also dealt severe blows to the Party organizational authority. Zhou Enlai's State Council barely survived the initial attacks on the state institutions, but only because Zhou had conceded much of his institutional base to Jiang Qing's radical group and Lin Biao's military forces.

On August 8, 1966, the Eleventh Plenum of the Eighth Central Committee adopted a sixteen-point decision to formally launch the Cultural Revolution. The decision called for organizing the Cultural Revolution committees in grass-roots units as "a mechanism for popular participation."[35] These mass revolutionary organizations were supposed to serve as a vehicle for the education of the masses "under the leadership of the Communist Party," as a "bridge to keep our Party in close contact with the masses," and as "organs of power" for conducting the movement.[36] But they were not to replace the Party committees.[37] Mao as the Party chairman did not intend to destroy the Party as a useful organizational instrument but to "shake the party to its foundations to rid it of revisionism."[38]

---

[34] Harding, "The Chinese State in Crisis, 1966–9," pp. 215–6.

[35] Ibid., p. 180.

[36] John Bryan Starr, "Revolution in Retrospect: The Paris Commune Through Chinese Eyes," *The China Quarterly 49* (January/March 1972), p. 115.

[37] Harding, "The Chinese State in Crisis, 1966–9," p. 180.

[38] Uhalley, p. 158.

As of January 1967, Mao still had romanticism about, and confidence in, mass movement. When rebel workers and Red Guards seized the power from the Shanghai Municipal Party Committee and government, Mao praised the action as "a great revolution."[39] The Party newspaper and journal carried editorials praising the radicals in Shanghai and calling for the revolutionaries all over the country "to resolutely seize power from the handful of people within the Party who are in authority and are taking the capitalist road."[40]

Mao's encouragement for the mass assault on the Party authorities quickly crippled the Party's organizational control. Mass movement, as destructive as it could be, soon proved to be a bad form of reorganization even for Mao. On February 6, 1967, the radical leaders in Shanghai proclaimed the formation of a new governing body – the "Shanghai People's Commune" – modeled after the Paris Commune of 1871. This, however, turned out to be too much for Mao. In a meeting with the radical leaders from Shanghai on February 18, Mao angrily scolded them:

> If everything were changed into a commune, then what about the Party? Where would we place the Party? . . . There must be a party somehow! There must be a nucleus, no matter what we call it. Be it called the Communist Party, or Social Democratic Party, or Kuomintang, or I-kuan-tao, there must be a party.[41]

Mao's strong objection to forming of the Shanghai Commune and insistence on keeping a party must have been a great surprise to the radical leaders who had until now received Mao's unequivocal support for waging assaults on the Party authorities. Also, it was Mao himself who in August 1966 glorified the model of the Paris Commune by characterizing the antiauthority big character posters on Beijing University campus as a declaration of a "Beijing Commune for the sixth decade of the twentieth century."[42]

Mao's change of mind seemed to have to a lot to do with his own confusion and ambivalence about the direction of the Cultural Revolution. In early February 1967, there were signs that Mao was getting disappointed with the inability of the rebels to discipline themselves. In a meeting with foreign visitors on February 3, 1967, Mao denounced the slogan, "Doubt everything and over-

---

[39] *Zhongguo gongchandang lishi dashiji,* p. 291.
[40] Ibid.
[41] Harding, "The Chinese State in Crisis, 1966–9," p. 223.
[42] Starr, "Revolution in Retrospect: The Paris Commune Through Chinese Eyes," p. 117.

throw everything," as reactionary and "extreme anarchist."[43] Encouraged by Mao's message, a group of veteran Party and government leaders challenged Lin Biao's and Jiang Qing's radical associates at several top-level meetings held between February 14 and 16, 1967. They stressed that the mass movement should be led by the Party, that not all the veteran cadres should be purged, and that the army should be stabilized. Marshal Ye Jianying questioned Zhang Chunqiao, the radical leader from Shanghai: "You organized the power seizure in Shanghai and changed the name to Shanghai Commune. And you did it without a discussion by the Politburo on such important issues concerning the system of the state. What are you up to this time?"[44] On the evening of February 18, reading somewhat distorted secret reports about these meetings prepared by his radical associates, Mao angrily denounced his senior colleagues. Yet, at the same time, Mao also repudiated the idea of the Shanghai Commune and ordered the ban on the formation of the commune. Mao's tactics of keeping factional balance notwithstanding, this suggests that Mao neither allowed the veteran leaders to stop the Cultural Revolution nor encouraged his radical associates to turn China into another Paris Commune.

After the short-lived Shanghai Commune, what Mao endorsed as an alternative way of reorganizing China was the "revolutionary committee" – a "three-in-one" combination that incorporated representatives of rebel organizations, the PLA, and "re-educated" Party and government officials.[45] But the military officers were to play an increasingly important role in creating and running the revolutionary committees. Until late 1967, the PLA was not allowed to intervene to restore political order and stop mass violence.[46] As the Red Guard movement turned increasingly factionalized, violent, and chaotic, Mao became frustrated with the radical urban youth. After September 1967, the PLA was ordered by Mao to terminate the Red Guard movement and take over administration of China. While millions of Red Guards were sent down to the countryside, nearly one million PLA representatives were sent to schools, factories, government offices, hospitals, and many other urban units.[47]

In October 1967, Mao issued instructions for reconstructing the Party organ-

[43] *Zhongguo gongchandang lishi dashiji,* p. 292.
[44] Jiang Huaxuan et al., pp. 542–3.
[45] For an analysis of the "three-in-one" revolutionary committee, see Harding, "The Chinese State in Crisis, 1966–9," pp. 198–205.
[46] Ibid., p. 297.
[47] Lieberthal, 1995, pp. 115–6.

ization.[48] However, given its rising power, the military appeared to have taken over many reorganized provincial Party committees. Lin Biao's officers had not only administered the Chinese economy and society, but also built up their power base in the Party leadership. Among the first secretaries of 29 provincial Party committees, 22 were PLA officers.[49] At the central level, there were 12 military representatives in the 21-member Party Politburo (52 percent). Of the 279 members (170 full members and 109 alternates) of the Ninth Central Committee, 47.5 percent were from the PLA.[50]

The Party is Back

A military takeover was neither what Mao's Cultural Revolution was about, nor what Mao had believed to be the appropriate way for reorganizing China. Although Mao had no choice but to bring in the military to restore order, he had no intention of letting the military run the country for long. Yet, having mobilized the masses to attack the Party and state institutions first and then having to rely on the military to stop mass violence, Mao now had to face the challenge from the military. The confrontation between Mao and Lin Biao came at the Party's Lushan Plenum in August–September 1970, when Lin's associates launched what Mao characterized as a "surprise attack" and demanded the reinstallation of the abolished post of the state chairmanship with an intention to further Lin's power base in the central government. Outraged by Lin Biao's blatant challenge to his objection, Mao quickly maneuvered to undermine Lin's power base in the military. In desperation, Lin decided to take military action to seize power. When all failed, Lin and his followers made a hasty attempt to escape from Beijing.[51]

Lin Biao's death in 1971 removed a major obstacle to restoring the Party control. The Party had come back, "reeducated" perhaps, but not much different from what it had been before as far as the Party organization was concerned. In fact, the Party was now to take control of everything. The Party organizational principle in the later stage of the Cultural Revolution became

---

[48] Roderick MacFarquhar, "Succession to Mao and the End of Maoism," in *The Politics of China, 1949–1989*, ibid., p. 255; *Zhongguo gongchandang lishi dashiji,* p. 295.

[49] MacFarquhar, "Succession to Mao and the End of Maoism," p. 256.

[50] Ibid., p. 251.

[51] For the documents and analysis of the Lin Biao incident, see Michael Y. M. Kau, *The Lin Biao Affair: Power, Politics and Military Coup* (White Plains, NY: International Arts and Sciences Press, 1975).

Table 6.1. *Provincial interlocking directorates, 1949–78*

Province	Pre-1955	Post-1955	Cultural Revolution
Anhui	1952–55		1971–77
Beijing	1951–54	1955–66	1972–78
Fujian	1949–54	1955–59	1971–79
Gansu			1971–77
Guangdong	1949–53	1955–57	1970–78
Guangxi	1949–55	1961–67	1967–77
Guizhou		1955–64	1971–77
Hebei	1952–54	1955–58	1971–79
Heilongjiang	1952–53	1956–58	1971–74
Henan		1958–61	1968–78
Hubei	1949–54		1971–73, 1975–78
Hunan			1970–77
Inner Mongolia	1947–54	1955–66	1971–78
Jiangsu			1970–77
Jiangxi			1970–72, 1974–79
Jilin			1971–77
Liaoning			1971–73, 1975–78
Ningxia	1949–51	1961–67	1971–77
Qinghai	1952–54		1971–77
Shaanxi	1950–52		1971–78
Shandong	1949–50	1961–63	1971–79
Shanghai	1950–54	1958–65	1971–76
Shanxi	1949–52		1971–79
Sichuan	1952–55		1971–79
Tianjin	1949–52	1955–58	1967–78
Tibet			1971–79
Yunnan			1971–77
Xinjiang			1971–78
Zhejiang	1949–52		1971–77

Sources: Compiled by the author from biographical information in the following: Malcolm Lamb, *Directory of Officials and Organizations in China: A Quarter-Century Guide* (Armonk, NY: M. E. Sharpe, 1994); *Zhonghua renmin gongheguo dang zheng jun qun lingdaoren minglu* (Directory of the Leaders of the Party, Government, Military and Mass Organizations in the People's Republic of China) (Beijing: Zhonggong dangshi chubanshe, 1990).

popularized as: "Whether it is in the East, West, South, North or the middle, and among the Party, the government, the military, the civilian and schools, the Party should exercise its leadership over everything." The revised Party constitution in 1975 and 1978 simply stipulated that the Party chairman commanded all the military forces in China. Mao also eliminated the formal division of labor between the Party and government by merging the Party functionaries and state bureaucracies. As Table 6.1 indicates, among the twenty-nine provincial governments (twenty-two provinces, five autonomous regions and three municipalities under the direct jurisdiction of the central government), eleven had interlocking directorates for most of the time before the Cultural Revolution; seven had interlocking directorates before 1955, but not after; two had interlocking directorates after 1955; and nine never had interlocking directorates before the Cultural Revolution. Beginning in 1970–71, all the provincial governments set up interlocking directorates under which the first secretary of a provincial Party committee was concurrently the head of the provincial revolutionary committee. Thus, by the early 1970s, Mao had come full circle back to square one to rely on the Party organization more than ever for organizing the country.

ARMY AND POWER STRUGGLE

The Cultural Revolution had dramatically exposed the dilemma of the Party–army relations. Mao began to take actions against his chief lieutenants in the Party only after he was assured of the allegiance of the army under Lin Biao's control. When Mao's young Red Guards got out of control, it was the intervention by the army that rescued Mao's revolution. Meanwhile, not only had the Party leadership given way to the military, but the army had practically taken over the country from the devastated Party organization and government institutions. By bringing in the army to deal with an essentially political crisis, even Mao himself had to make certain concessions and face assassination attempts by Lin Biao's officers. Finally, it was a quasi-military coup that ended the Cultural Revolution when the central security guards swiftly put Mao's wife and her radical associates under house arrest weeks after Mao's death. Yet, the PLA as an institution suffered as well as benefited from its active political engagement during the Cultural Revolution. The political power struggle not only factionalized the army, but also led to the purges and even deaths of many senior military leaders. By the end of the Cultural Revolution, the PLA's reputation had been tarnished, the command system crippled, and both officers and rank and file demoralized.

The Rise of Lin Biao

Although the political role of the PLA at the early stages (1966–68) of the Cultural Revolution was not so well defined, Lin Biao's role was very clear. If it can be argued that without Mao, the Cultural Revolution would not have happened, it might also be argued that without Lin Biao, Mao's Cultural Revolution would not have gone the way it did. The rise and fall of Lin Biao best illustrates the organizational incentives for military generals to play CCP politics to strengthen their power base and the inherent danger associated with this game of revolutionary politics.

Marshal Lin Biao built up his career almost exclusively as a combat commander. His contributions to the CCP's winning of the civil war in 1946–49 facilitated his rise in the military hierarchy. This was demonstrated by the fact that Lin was ranked the third among the ten Chinese marshals conferred in 1955, after Zhu De and Peng Dehuai. Nonetheless, Lin had kept a low profile for several years after 1949, partly due to his poor health. When the People's Revolutionary Military Commission was formed in 1949, Lin was not included. Like some other PLA generals, Lin was assigned to be in charge of the regional government in central southern China. Then quite suddenly, Lin Biao became very "active" both physically and politically after he was appointed the vice chairman of the Party Central Committee on May 25, 1958. Two days after his new appointment, Lin secured Mao's consent and orchestrated the struggle against Marshal Liu Bocheng. At the Lushan Conference in July 1959, Lin lodged the most serious accusation against Marshal Peng Dehuai. In August 1959, Lin directed a large-scale purge in the military of the Right Opportunists. Marshal Lin's political fortune soared after Peng Dehuai fell into disgrace. Lin Biao had taken over all the positions vacated by Peng. On September 17, 1959, Lin Biao was appointed Defense Minister. Nine days later, he became the first of the three vice chairmen of the Party CMC and was put in charge of the daily work of the military.

Lin Biao certainly knew how to play Mao's politics. In September–October 1960, Lin Biao launched a major political attack against Senior General Tan Zhen, director of the PLA General Political Department, accusing him of "deviating in political work" and "forming an anti-Party faction."[52] In May 1964, Lin edited the "Quotations from Chairman Mao," also known as the "little red book" during the Cultural Revolution. Lin ordered every soldier to study Mao Zedong Thought as was reflected in this "bible of the revolution." In December 1964, Lin further instructed the PLA to "give prominence to politics." In May 1965, the military ranks were abolished because they were politically incorrect. When his political campaign was questioned by Senior General Luo Ruiqing, chief of the PLA General Staff, Lin initiated yet another political attack to purge Luo on charges that Luo was "anti-Party and anti-Chairman Mao."[53]

It would be easy to conclude that Lin Biao was a villain, viciously attacking his colleagues all the time. Yet, without Mao's approval, Lin would not have been able to manipulate the military as he wished. In 1958, Mao was behind Lin in the political struggle against Liu Bocheng. Lin Biao was absent from the initial meetings at Lushan in 1959. Then, two weeks after Peng delivered his Letter of Opinion, Mao summoned Lin to Lushan to escalate the political attack on Peng Dehuai.[54] In late 1965, when Lin launched the attack on Luo Ruiqing, accusing the latter of downplaying the role of politics, Mao fully backed Lin: "All of us must watch out for those who do not believe in politics, who only feign agreement to putting politics in command while spreading eclectic, that is, opportunist, viewpoints."[55]

If both Mao and Lin were the "bad guys," why did the entire Party always let them prevail? It is worth noting that none of the purged military generals were secretly arrested or persecuted. All of them were first criticized publicly and then purged after the top-level meetings attended by senior Party leaders and military generals. From Liu Bocheng, Ye Jianying, Xiao Ke, and Li Da in 1958 and Peng Dehuai and Huang Kecheng in 1959, to Tan Zhen in 1960 and Luo Ruiqing in 1965, the entire Party elite watched their military colleagues fall into disgrace one after another and did nothing to stop Lin or Mao.

It would also be misleading to characterize the conflicts between Lin Biao and his victims as a "two-line struggle" between revolutionary politics and

---

[52] *Guanyu xinshiqi jundui zhengzhi gongzuo de jueding zhushiben* (The Annotated Book for the Resolution Concerning the Political Work in the Military in the New Era) (Beijing: Jiefangjun chubanshe, 1987), p. 110.
[53] Ibid., p. 113. On Lin Biao's attack on Luo Ruiqing, see Harding, "The Chinese State in Crisis, 1966–9," pp. 163–5.
[54] *Peng Dehuai zhuan,* p. 625.
[55] Ibid.

military professionalism – the familiar "Red versus Expert" problem. Lin had previously proved to be no more politically correct than any other PLA general. In fact, after the Korean War broke out in June 1950, Lin, mainly due to military concerns, did not support Mao's idea to send the Chinese troops to Korea. It must also seem paradoxical that a career military commander such as Marshal Lin was responsible for promoting Mao's revolutionary politics in the PLA, for, according to the "military professionalism" argument, Lin should have been the most likely candidate to push for military professionalism. Indeed, while promoting Mao's revolutionary politics in the PLA, Lin had not totally neglected military modernization. Having built a reputation as an excellent military commander, Lin, like many other military generals, knew the importance of military training and equipment. As the American war in Vietnam escalated, Lin Biao either approved, or consented to, several military training programs. In 1962, the Party CMC issued orders "to reorganize the army and prepare for war." The Party CMC affirmed that military training should spend more than 60 percent of the total time on military, political, and cultural training. Special military forces must spend more than 70 percent of their time on military training.[56] During Lin Biao's tenure as the Party CMC vice chairman, the PLA had greatly reinforced the fleets of the navy and the air force. The navy had expanded by 51.6 percent compared to 1958, and the Air Force had expanded by 41.8 percent.[57] China's defense expenditure increased by 34 percent in 1969, 15 percent in 1970, and more than 16 percent in 1971.[58] Thus there appears to be little empirical evidence for suggesting that there have been two trends or two lines in the PLA – revolutionary politics advocated by Mao Zedong and Lin Biao versus military professionalism represented by Liu Bocheng, Peng Dehuai, and other military generals.

To be sure, Lin Biao had his ambitions and his opponents. Then the same can be said of other military leaders. What Lin did to fulfill his ambitions and purge his opponents was to pursue a strategy most consistent with the given political environment, that is, to do what the paramount leader liked and what revolutionary campaigns called for. Initially, Lin had played this political game extremely well. Within the ten years from 1959 to 1969, Lin had risen from a relatively quiet and lonely marshal to the number two position in the Party. At

---

[56] *Dangdai zhongguo jundui de junshi gongzuo* (China Today: The Military Work of the Chinese Army) (Beijing: Zhongguo shehui kexue chubanshe, 1989), p. 53.

[57] Ibid., pp. 18, 49.

[58] *Zhongguo gongchandang lishi dashiji,* p. 302.

the peak of the Cultural Revolution, Lin was officially designated as Mao's legitimate successor at the Ninth Party Congress held in April 1969.

Purges in the Military

Whereas Lin Biao and his followers in the PLA enjoyed their heyday of political power during the Cultural Revolution, many of their colleagues paid a heavy price. Beginning in January 1967, military leaders were no longer exempt from political attacks. Their residential compounds were surrounded by the Red Guards and rebels.[59] In March 1968, Yang Chengwu (acting chief of the PLA General Staff), Yu Lijin (political commissar of the PLA air force), and Fu Chongbi (commander of the Beijing Garrison) were suddenly thrown out of office. Subsequently, the Party Central Military Commission was suspended and taken over by a work group appointed by Lin Biao.[60] Before long, eight of the ten Chinese marshals, seven of the ten senior generals, and eighteen lieutenant generals were investigated or attacked. In the PLA as a whole, more than 80,000 people were persecuted, among whom 1,169 died because of political torture and imprisonment.[61]

In the end, however, Lin Biao and his associates fared no better than their victims in revolutionary politics. In September 1971, the nation was shocked to learn that Lin Biao had died in a plane crash in Mongolia when he tried to flee to the Soviet Union after a failed attempt to assassinate Mao. After the Lin Biao incident, a major purge was immediately carried out in the military. The military under Lin Biao gained an unusual share of political influence. Now it had to pay a price. Lin's associates were all arrested, including General Huang Yongsheng (chief of the PLA General Staff), Lieutenant General Wu Faxian (deputy chief of the PLA General Staff and commander of the air force), Lieutenant General Li Zuopeng (deputy chief of the PLA General Staff and political commissar of the navy), and Lieutenant General Qiu Huizuo (deputy chief of the PLA General Staff and director of the General Logistics Department). In 1980, all of them were put on public trial — an unprecedented event in the PLA history. Politics aside, this was a total disgrace to the military institution.

---

[59] Wen Lü, pp. 456–7.
[60] Ibid., p. 448.
[61] Ibid., p. 457.

MASS CAMPAIGNS AND REVOLUTIONARY PARTY

The Cultural Revolution presents the best case to examine the role of mass campaigns in China and their significance to a revolutionary party organization. No student of Chinese politics can fail to notice the high frequency and long continuation of mass campaigns in China.[62] No study of Chinese politics would be complete without delving into the possible reasons for these campaigns throughout the history of the PRC. Before the outbreak of the Cultural Revolution, the People's Republic had already gone through more than forty mass campaigns, averaging two mass campaigns every year (see the list of campaigns in China in Appendix B in this book). The Cultural Revolution was not only the "mother of all campaigns" in China, but itself had included many political campaigns, such as the 1969 Party Rectification Campaign, the 1970 Campaign to Criticize Chen Boda and Party Rectification, the 1971–73 Campaign to Criticize Lin Biao, the 1974–75 Campaign to Criticize Confucius, the 1975 Campaign to Study the Theory of the Dictatorship of the Proletariat, and the 1975–76 Campaign against Deng Xiaoping.[63]

To be sure, not all the mass campaigns were political, but the majority of them were and every mass campaign in the Cultural Revolution was highly political. Some campaigns were nationwide, involving Party and government institutions and many sectors of the society; others were limited to Party organization, or urban areas, or certain sectors of the society. Some campaigns were aimed at certain groups of people, such as intellectuals, local cadres, or CCP members, whereas others were directed at the general population. Despite all the differences, the CCP as a revolutionary party was always involved. It may be even argued that without the Party's organizational mobilization, numerous mass campaigns in China would have been impossible. In fact, before a

---

[62] There are several studies focused on campaigns in China, for example, Charles P. Cell, *Revolution at Work: Mobilization Campaigns in China* (New York: Academic Press, Inc., 1977); A. Gordon Bennett, *Yundong: Mass Campaigns in Chinese Communist Leadership* (Berkeley: Center for Chinese Studies, University of California, Berkeley, 1976); Richard Baum and Frederick C. Teiwes, *Ssu-ch'ing: The Socialist Education Movement of 1962–1966* (Berkeley: Center for Chinese Studies, University of California, 1968). Frederick C. Teiwes' *Politics and Purges in China* is the most comprehensive analysis of the Party rectification campaigns. A brief discussion of the effects of political campaigns on the state bureaucracy is offered by A. Doak Barnett in *Cadres, Bureaucracy, and Political Power in Communist China* (New York: Columbia University Press, 1967), pp. 32–5. The CCP's political campaigns in the pre-1949 years are discussed in Mark Selden, *The Yenan Way in Revolutionary China* (Cambridge, MA: Harvard University Press, 1971), pp. 210–54.

[63] Wang, p. 220.

153

large-scale mass campaign was about to be launched, the Party often sent many work teams of cadres to the lower level to mobilize the masses and to control the direction.[64]

Political campaigns, as exemplified by the Cultural Revolution, began with editorials and articles in the official newspaper, explaining the purpose and laying out the key concepts and slogans of the upcoming campaign. This was followed by Party-organized public rallies and demonstrations to build up the momentum. Then intensive political study or struggle meetings were organized at which political activists waged relentless attacks on their victims and the rest of the participants drew lessons through criticism and self-criticism. Political campaigns usually ended with a new wave of purges.[65]

Functions of Campaigns

Campaigns performed many functions for Mao's revolutionary regime. First, they served to indoctrinate the Chinese society with Mao's revolutionary ideology – a political socialization function.[66] Examples of such campaigns include the Thought Reform Movement in 1951–52, the Campaign to Learn from Lei Feng in 1963, and the Campaign to Study the Theory of the Dictatorship of the Proletariat in 1975, among others. Second, campaigns performed the important function of policy implementation. Whether a revolutionary party organization with a work style of mass campaigns hindered the capacity of policy implementation by the state institutions or weak state institutions made mass campaigns a necessary tool for policy implementation, it seemed that the CCP could not hope to get things done without launching mass campaigns. The Steel Drive and the Campaign to Organize People's Communes in the Great Leap Forward movement of 1958–60 are some examples. Third, campaigns were the Party's traditional method of problem fixing. The political system in China lacked a regular correction mechanism, and problems were not detected or dealt with immediately until they reached a crisis point. Then a sense of urgency led to the launching of campaigns to fix certain problems. Party rectification, antibureaucracy, anticorruption, or anticrime campaigns are prime examples. Fourth, at the end of a major conflict in the Party leader-

---

[64] Ibid., p. 218.
[65] Ibid., pp. 217–8.
[66] Franz H. Schurmann, *Ideology and Organization in Communist China,* 2nd and enlarged edition (Berkeley: University of California Press, 1968), p. 48.

ship, a political campaign was often launched to purify the Party organization and educate the public.

What is most important, however, is that, by frequently launching political campaigns, Mao had artificially recreated a revolutionary environment after 1949. In a revolutionary situation, a paramount leader like Mao was not only needed but also worshipped. A revolutionary organization had also found its purpose and mission. Through numerous political campaigns, Mao's revolutionary ideology of class struggle, the Party's organizational principle, and methods of mass mobilization had been rejuvenated and reinforced. Mass campaigns had kept a revolutionary party organization vigorous. As political campaigns speeded up the process of weeding out those found "unfit" in the revolutionary organizational environment, thousands of political activists were recruited in the Party not for their professional skills but for their political enthusiasm. It is, therefore, no surprise that the Party organization thrived rather than declined in the mass campaigns. For instance, despite the initial mass assault on the Party organization, the CCP membership had greatly expanded during the Cultural Revolution. The Party membership was 14 million in 1959, and it had increased to 18.7 million before the Cultural Revolution started in 1966. By 1969, however, the Party membership had grown to 22 million, and by the time Mao died in 1976, the Party was 35 million strong (see Appendix A). During the pre-Cultural Revolution period (1949–65), the average rate of recruitment was 12.2 percent, translating into an average of about 800,000 new members each year. During the Cultural Revolution (1966–76) the rate of recruitment was 6.2 percent, translating into an average of 1 million new members each year.

Mao Zedong once pointed out: "If there is to be revolution, there must be a revolutionary party."[67] After 1949, Mao's original formulation seemed to be reversed into: "If there is to be a revolutionary party, there must be revolution." Mass campaigns, revolutionary party, and Mao proved to be mutually dependent, and it seemed neither could live without the other. In a fundamental sense, political campaigns might very well serve Mao's revolutionary regime the way the civil service examination served the imperial system. Like the examination system, political campaigns provided a crucial link between the cadres and activists and their paramount leader on the one hand and, on the other, between the Party leadership and the society. In this way, political campaigns became a mechanism of "political reproduction" for Mao's regime. They served to pro-

---

[67] Mao, 1961, vol. 4, p. 284.

long Mao's personality cult, operationalize the revolutionary ideology, and keep the Party organization function at high gear.

Consequences of Campaigns

Numerous mass campaigns have had profound consequences for Chinese society and its political life. First, mass campaigns turned the whole nation against itself. Since the early 1950s, China has been plunged into one campaign after another. "Enemies" were discovered not only in the society, but also within the Party, the government, the army, or even among the very successors chosen by the paramount leader. As mass campaigns necessarily disrupted the normal life and produced discontent, they had become the primary source of instability of the regime. The biggest irony of Mao's Cultural Revolution, therefore, was that a revolutionary party organization revived only by waging numerous political campaigns against its own people, usually the best ones. The revolutionary situation could be recreated only by artificially reproducing the enemies of the regime.

Second, politics is a process for developing a sense of purpose, and yet the political campaigns in China often degenerated into senseless and unpredictable political witch-hunts. For example, in the upsurge of the Cultural Revolution, Party Secretary-General Deng Xiaoping was denounced. In early 1975, when Mao rehabilitated Deng, those who had condemned Deng before had to switch sides quickly. But before they could complete the transition, Deng was purged again in April 1976, and whoever had supported Deng were now the targets of yet another anti-Deng campaign. However, those who had followed the Party's call to criticize Deng in 1976 found themselves in deep trouble when Deng staged another comeback in 1978. There was no rule of the game with which one could possibly draw a line. Politics of mass campaigns became a dangerous game.

Third, the Cultural Revolution and many other political campaigns dramatized the dual identity of "victim–victimizers" found in a number of Chinese leaders. During the numerous political campaigns in the past forty years, as if dictated by fate, those who had purged others before were later purged themselves. The purged, if they survived the purge physically, often went on to purge others in the following campaigns. The case of Lin Biao was a perfect example. As I have mentioned earlier, after he returned to the power center in 1958, Lin Biao orchestrated many purges in the military. In 1969, when Lin Biao's political power was at its peak, whoever disagreed with him faced persecution or, in the worst scenario, death. After Lin Biao died a tragic death in September 1971, those who had followed Lin Biao to purge his opponents in the military were themselves ruthlessly purged. Deng was another example. Although being purged twice during the Cultural Revolution, Deng was responsible for many purges before his own fall from grace, the most infamous one of which was the 1957 Anti-Rightist Campaign. Lin and Deng were not the exceptions. In fact, we can find this dual identity in many Chinese leaders who went through the Cultural Revolution. Political campaigns have produced too many victimizers-turned-victims.

The Cultural Revolution pushed to the extreme Mao's idea of "continuing the revolution under the dictatorship of the proletariat" and exposed the irony of Mao's method of mass mobilization. Mao might have had every reason for shaking up the bureaucracy and reshaping China's future, but his "shock therapy" turned out to be catastrophic for the Chinese political institutions and their leaders. The revolutionary mass movement, however, proved more destructive than constructive. Although the masses of Red Guards and rebel workers were successful institution-destroyers, they were poor institution-builders. Frustrated at being unable to bring the fighting factions to a truce, Mao had to turn to the military to restore stability and order. Having first utilized, and then abandoned, his Red Guards, Mao created a lost generation of Chinese youth who later came of age to bury Mao's revolution.

Actively engaged in the Cultural Revolution, the PLA as an institution had suffered more than it had benefited from the political engagement. The army was under frequent political and ideological pressure to serve as a model for the people in all professions and trades, a task that was often in conflict with its primary military mission. Moreover, as the military became entangled in intra-party power politics, political campaigns and factional struggles easily disrupted the training of the military and greatly affected the fate of many military leaders. The Cultural Revolution that had pushed the PLA to the center of the political power ended only in bringing devastation and humiliation to the PLA.

Furthermore, the military under Lin Biao turned out to be not only unreliable but also dangerous, as even Mao himself had to face assassination attempts. Ultimately, Mao had to rebuild the Party organization and rehabilitate the purged Party and state leaders. Thus he had come full circle in institution-destruction and -rebuilding. In the end, it was not the masses of Red Guards and revolutionary rebels or the military, but the Party organization, that had prevailed. In September 1976, when Mao died, the Party organization had grown bigger than ever but also more divided than ever by factionalism. The Party appeared in control of every state institution and socioeconomic unit but only with a much discredited leadership and a bankrupt ideology.

Part III

STATE-BUILDING UNDER A REFORMIST PARTY: THE DENG XIAOPING ERA

7

Reform, Legal System, and Party Rule

THE turmoil of the Cultural Revolution and the ensuing succession struggles created a large number of victims as well as a nation of cynics and
dissidents. When Mao died in September 1976, his revolutionary ideology
practically died with him. In February 1978, the National People's Congress
convened its first meeting after Mao's death and called on the nation to achieve
"four modernizations" in agriculture, industry, national defense, and science
and technology.[1] The modernization program gained momentum after Deng
managed to return to the power center. The Third Plenum of the Eleventh
Central Committee in late 1978 decided to abandon Mao's slogan – "Take class
struggle as the key link" – and to change the priority of the Party from political
campaigns to economic development.

Along with the call for economic modernization, the post-Mao Chinese
leaders devoted tremendous attention to reestablishing a legal system. The
Third Plenum proposed to improve the "socialist democracy" and strengthen
"socialist legality." The communiqué of the Plenum affirmed, "[I]n order to
safeguard people's democracy, it is imperative to strengthen the socialist legal
system so that democracy is systematized and written in such a way as to insure
the stability, continuity and full authority of this democratic system and the
laws: there must be laws for people to follow, these laws must be observed,
their enforcement must be strict and law breakers must be dealt with."[2] This
chapter analyzes the legal institution-building under a reformist party. It examines the progress toward, and failures in, establishing a system of rule of law
and underscores the tensions between the Party and legal institutions in a new
socioeconomic environment.

---

[1] Hua Guofeng, "Report on the Work of the Government," *Beijing Review* 27 (July 6, 1979), pp.
8–28.
[2] *The Communiqué of the Third Plenum of the Eleventh Congress of the Chinese Communist Party*
(Beijing: Foreign Language Press, 1978).

FROM LAWLESSNESS TO RULE BY LAW

In February 1979, Ye Jianying, the chairman of the NPC Standing Committee, reported that efforts were being made to formulate or revise the criminal law, law of criminal procedure, civil law, marriage law, and various kinds of economic regulations. Ye reaffirmed that the laws must be observed and strictly enforced and that violations of the law must be investigated and dealt with.[3] Reporting to the NPC in June 1979, Peng Zhen, the director of the NPC Legislative Affairs Committee, reiterated the legal principle, "Everyone is equal before the law." Peng stressed that all the Party members and cadres must set an example in obeying the law and there must be no exception made for them. He said,

> No one would be sheltered or shielded if found guilty of violating the
> law or of a criminal offense; no matter how long he had worked for
> the revolution, how high his position or how great his contributions,
> the offender would be dealt with according to law. No one had the
> privilege of being outside or above the law.[4]

Reasons for Legal Reform

Emphasis on a legal system had distinguished the post-Mao leaders from their predecessors. What motivated Deng and his associates to make legal development a top priority as they tried to modernize the economy? There are perhaps four main reasons: revulsion against the Cultural Revolution, need for new sources of legitimacy, concern about social order and stability, and economic imperatives. Although all of these factors were present during the Deng era, each gained prominence at different times.

The initial impulse for restoring the legal order in the late 1970s came as a result of disgust for the chaos and mass violence of the Cultural Revolution. Most of the post-Mao leaders had been victims of Mao's abuse of power and had suffered in a lawless situation. Like Deng, they had been rehabilitated and had returned to power only after Mao died. By the end of 1982, when the nationwide rehabilitation work was largely completed, about 3 million wrongly accused cadres had been rehabilitated, more than 470,000 had been

---

[3] *Quanguo renda jiqi changweihui dashiji* (A Chronology of the National People's Congress and Its Standing Committee, 1954–1987) (Beijing: Falü chubanshe, 1987), p. 261.

[4] Peng Zhen, "Strengthen Legal System and Democracy," *Beijing Review* 27 (July 6, 1979), p. 35.

reinstated as Communist Party members, and 120,000 had had the disciplinary measures against them lifted.[5] Through their personal experience, the rehabilitated leaders had concluded that a good legal system was needed so that something like the Cultural Revolution would not happen again. In 1980, Deng had this to say,

> Stalin gravely damaged socialist legality, doing things which Comrade Mao Zedong once said would have been impossible in Western countries like Britain, France and the United States. Yet although Comrade Mao was aware of this, he did not in practice solve the problems in our system of leadership. Together with other factors, this led to the decade of catastrophe known as the 'Cultural Revolution.' There is a most profound lesson to be learned from this.[6]

Deng of course was not totally fair to Mao. The situation of lawlessness in China did not begin with the Cultural Revolution, but with the Anti-Rightist Campaign in 1957, for which many Party leaders, including Deng, had been directly responsible.[7] The victims of the Cultural Revolution had been the victimizers ten years earlier and thus must share the blame for the unleashing of the rampage on the state constitution and laws. As long as the rehabilitated leaders were unwilling to come to terms with the dual role they had played, a revulsion against a particular type of lawlessness provided only a temporary momentum for restoring law and order.

A second factor for constructing a legal system was the changing political climate. After Mao died, it did not take long for the rehabilitated leaders to realize that social support for the Party had greatly eroded. Due to the repeated intra-party power struggles and political chaos during the Cultural Revolution, the Chinese Communist Party as the ruling Party had lost the confidence of the people. There was no way for the post-Mao leaders to reclaim legitimacy by continuing to rely on the legacy of Mao's revolution and a decaying ideology. Consequently, the new regime attempted to shift away from class struggle

---

[5] Feng Zhibin et al., eds., *Zhongguo gongchandang jianshe quanshu, 1921–1991* (Encyclopedia of the Construction of the Chinese Communist Party, 1921–1991), vol. 6 (Shanxi: Shanxi renmin chubanshe, 1991), p. 178.

[6] Deng Xiaoping, *Selected Works of Deng Xiaoping, 1975–1982* (Beijing: Foreign Languages Press, 1984), p. 316.

[7] One could also argue that the revolutionary lawlessness had begun much earlier with such campaigns as the Suppression of the Counterrevolutionaries in 1950, the "Three-Anti" in 1951 and the "Five-Anti" in 1952.

to a legal system as the new basis of legitimacy. Deng believed that to increase popular support for the new regime and to generate enthusiasm for economic modernization, more opportunities should be made available to the people to express their views and to participate in the political process. Their basic constitutional rights must be protected.[8] However, Deng's support for establishing a legal system was not unqualified. After he suppressed the "Democracy Wall" movement in March 1979, Deng laid down the "four cardinal principles," namely, upholding the socialist road, the dictatorship of the proletariat, the leadership of the Communist Party, and Marxism-Leninism and Mao Zedong Thought, thus setting the ultimate limits on legal development in China.

The third reason for legal reform was that laws and regulations could help the new regime maintain social order and stability. This was critical at a time when the Party's ideological manipulation was no longer effective and many types of crimes and corruption were rapidly increasing, thanks to economic reform and liberalization. Here the post-Mao leaders took an instrumentalist view of a legal system, a view even Mao sometimes had endorsed. The difference was that the post-Mao leaders believed that a system of rule by law could be more stable and controllable than mass campaigns.[9]

Finally, there was the economic need for legal development. As Shao-chuan Leng points out, laws and regulations are needed not only to secure a stable and orderly environment essential to the success of economic modernization, but are also necessary to regulate many new types of economic activities and relationships resulting from market reform and privatization. "Moreover, China must project itself as a stable and orderly society with effective laws to protect the interests and rights of foreigners in order to expand trade, import advanced technology, and attract international investment."[10] Deng clearly understood the connections. On January 17, 1986, Deng stated at a meeting of the Politburo's Standing Committee: "Our original idea was right: in our ef-

---

[8] Deng Xiaoping, 1984, pp. 155–8.

[9] Some scholars suggest that the differences can be analyzed in terms of the oscillations between the formal judicial and "extrajudicial" models, or between "jural" and "societal" models of law. See Jerome Cohen, "The Party and the Courts: 1949–1959," *The China Quarterly 38* (April–June 1969), pp. 131–40; Shao-chuan Leng and Hongdah Chiu, *Criminal Justice in Post-Mao China: Analysis and Documents* (Albany, NY: State University of New York Press, 1985); June Teufel Dreyer, *China's Political System: Modernization and Tradition* (New York: Paragon House, 1993), pp. 205–13.

[10] Shao-chuan Leng, ed., *Reform and Development in Deng's China* (Lanham, MD: University Press of America, 1994), p. 86.

forts to realize the modernization programme we must attend to two things and not just one. By this I mean that we must promote economic development and at the same time build a legal system."[11]

We may therefore suggest that whereas the revulsion against the lawlessness of the Cultural Revolution and attempts to seek new sources of legitimacy provided the initial momentum for the legal reforms in the late 1970s and early 1980s, it was the concern about social order and stability and need for economic regulations that sustained the legal development through the late 1980s and early 1990s, despite the officially sanctioned lawlessness characterizing the Tiananmen crackdown in June 1989.

Building a legal system after decades of Mao's class struggle and mass campaigns is anything but easy. One frequently observed problem is lack of enough qualified judges, lawyers, and legal experts. For instance, in 1988, among the cadres working in the court, procuratorate, and judicial administration, 58.3 percent had received an education below the level of junior high school. Only 3 percent had received legal training at the college level, while 43 percent had never received any training in the legal profession.[12] By the early 1990s, China still had only 380,014 judicial personnel (200,134 in courts and 179,870 in procuratorates) and 50,000 lawyers.[13]

Another often-cited problem is the lack of respect for, or indifference to, the law among the people as well as the officials – the "legal illiteracy" problem.[14] Here the blame was on the Chinese tradition that emphasized moral teaching and rule of man instead of rule of law. Yet the Chinese ancestors may have much less to do with the problem than the current leaders. The Deng regime had made great efforts to educate the people about the constitution and the laws. In 1986, a nationwide study movement was launched to popularize legal knowledge. Members of the CCP Politburo and directors of the CCP central departments took the lead to listen to lectures on laws. By the end of 1987, about 7 million cadres had listened to such lectures, including most leading cadres at the provincial, prefectural, and city levels. About 95 percent of

---

[11] Deng Xiaoping, *Selected Works of Deng Xiaoping*, vol. 3 (Beijing: Foreign Languages Press, 1993), p. 156.

[12] Wu Lei, ed., *Zhongguo sifa zhidu* (The Chinese Judiciary System) (Beijing: Zhongguo renmin daxue chubanshe, 1988), p. 229.

[13] Sources quoted in Leng, 1994, p. 90.

[14] A survey done by Chinese political scientists in 1986 revealed that Party officials and members usually did not take laws seriously. Nie Gaomin et al., eds., *Guanyu dangzheng fenkai de lilun tantao* (Theoretical Discussion on Separating the Party from the Government) (Beijing: Chunqiu chubanshe, 1987), p. 169.

elementary and middle schools had offered legal courses, teaching 180 million students. About 54 million workers and 130 million peasants had also been involved in the legal study movement. Altogether, 420 million people, more than one-third of China's population, had participated in the legal study movement by the end of 1987.[15] Why then had the legal illiteracy problem continued to such an extent that a new nationwide legal study movement had to be launched in 1994? A fully functioning legal system surely does not require everyone to become expert in legal matters. Although there was a need to publicize new economic laws and regulations, the Party-sponsored legal study movement was somewhat misdirected, if not intentionally misleading. The real problem in China was not the legal illiteracy per se, but that many people were not yet convinced that laws now weighed more heavily than power. People would not resort to legal means to challenge power-holders if they believed that such an action was only to ask for trouble, nor would they give much respect to laws if those laws were not to be applied to those who formulated and enforced them.

Judicial and Legislative Institutional Development

Deng's legal reform began with the reinstitution of the legal apparatus and judicial administration. In 1978, the people's procuracy system was restored, which was to perform the functions of "investigation, prosecution, scrutinizing trial procedures, and overseeing the execution of judgments and operation of prisons."[16] The revised Organic Law of the PRC Procuratorate promulgated in July 1979 reaffirmed that the procuratorate exercised authority and performed its functions independently, subject only to the laws and not to any interference from any administrative organs, organizations or individuals.[17] The revised Organic Law of the PRC Procuratorate also enabled the Supreme People's Procuratorate to exercise direct control over the procuratorates at all levels. The revised Organic Law of the PRC Courts reaffirmed previously condemned legal principles such as judicial independence, equality before the law, open trials, and the right to defense.[18] In September 1979, the Ministry of Justice,

---

[15] Zhang Qingfu, ed., *Fazhi jianshe shinian* (Ten Years of Legal Construction) (Beijing: Lüyou jiaoyu chubanshe, 1988), pp. 10–11.

[16] Leng, 1994, p. 87.

[17] Peng Zhen, "Strengthen Legal System and Democracy," *Beijing Review* 27 (July 6, 1979), p. 34.

[18] Leng, 1994, p. 87.

which had been abolished during the Anti-Rightist Campaign, was re-established. Subsequently, bureaus of justice in provincial governments were also restored. By the end of 1980, judicial administrative agencies at all levels had been set up. In 1980, the NPC also passed the Provisional Regulations of Lawyers in the PRC, and the system of defense by lawyers that had ended suddenly in 1957 was resurrected.

Stress on the development of the legal system led to an expansion of the legislative functions. In December 1982, a new state constitution of the PRC was promulgated.[19] A major change under the 1982 constitution was the strengthened lawmaking power of the NPC Standing Committee. Under the 1954 constitution, the NPC Standing Committee had no power to promulgate laws (only to issue regulations) and no authority to supervise the enforcement of the constitution. Only when the NPC was not in session, and when authorized by the NPC, could the NPC Standing Committee amend or revise a few laws. Under the new constitution of 1982, the NPC Standing Committee is empowered to make a wide variety of laws except the basic laws. The legislative powers of the NPC include the authority to amend the constitution, formulate and revise criminal law, civil law, organic laws of the state institutions, and other basic laws. The Standing Committee of the NPC is responsible for formulating and revising the rest of the laws.

The 1982 constitution clearly stipulates that both the NPC and its Standing Committee are the organs of the state legislative power and both can formulate laws and decrees. Thus, most of the legislative work can be done by the NPC Standing Committee. Because the NPC of more than 2,900 deputies is too cumbersome to act frequently and effectively,[20] strengthening the power of the NPC Standing Committee (about 156 members) greatly enhances the NPC's legislative functions. Moreover, the NPC and its Standing Committee jointly exercise the authority to supervise the enforcement of the constitution. Furthermore, whereas before the NPC Standing Committee could only in rare cases appoint or remove government officials, it can now, upon the recommendation

---

[19] For an early discussion of the 1982 PRC Constitution, see Byron S. J. Weng, eds., "Studies on the Constitution Law of the People's Republic of China," *Chinese Law and Government* 16, no. 2–3 (Summer–Fall 1983).

[20] The size of the NPC varies from one congress to another and between two congresses due to deaths or recalls of delegates. A general picture is as follows: First NPC (1,226); Second NPC (1,148); Third NPC (3,037); Fourth NPC (2,885); Fifth NPC (3,497); Sixth NPC (2,978); and Seventh NPC (2,903).

of the premier of the State Council, appoint or remove central ministers when the NPC is not in session.

An active legislative role demands legislative institution-building. In 1978, the Legislative Affairs Committee of the NPC was set up. The legislative committee system gained new legitimacy after the 1982 constitution authorized the NPC to establish six special legislative work committees (Nationalities Affairs; Legal Affairs; Finance and Economy; Education, Science, Culture, and Public Health; Foreign Affairs; and Overseas Chinese Affairs). They are responsible for reviewing and drafting bills under the direction of the NPC Standing Committee when the NPC is not in session.

From 1979 to 1982, the NPC was flooded with bills. Deputies to the Second Session of the Fifth NPC in 1979 proposed as many as 1,890 bills in a single session. The NPC in the following three years received even more proposed bills from its members (2,300 in 1980, 2,318 in 1981, and 2,102 in 1982).[21] Between 1979 and 1987, the NPC and its Standing Committee promulgated 57 laws and passed 112 legal decisions, including criminal law and law of criminal procedure, civil law (general principles) and civil procedure law (provisional), electoral law of the NPC and local people's congress, and various organic laws.[22] Not only did the NPC play a pivotal role in lawmaking, but the State Council also stepped up its regulative activities. Between 1978 and 1992, the State Council had issued some 900 administrative regulations and decrees.[23]

As the local economy in China became more diversified due to the regional developmental strategy and integration with the international market, provincial legislatures were also strengthened. In 1982, provincial and local people's congresses were authorized to set up special work committees. Under the new constitution, provincial people's congresses and their standing committees are empowered to institute and promulgate local laws and regulations according to specific circumstances, provided that they are not in contradiction with the state constitution or with laws and regulations issued by the NPC and the State Council. This has given provinces considerable legal autonomy in managing their own affairs. Between 1979 and 1982, provincial people's congresses and their standing committees formulated more than 860 laws and regulations of a

[21] *Quanguo renda jiqi changweihui dashiji,* pp. 273, 294, 321, 346.

[22] Ibid., p. 503. For Chinese jurists' views of the General Principles of the Civil Law, see the selection and translation of cases by William C. Jones, "Civil Law in China," *Chinese Law and Government* 18, no. 3–4 (Fall–Winter 1985–6).

[23] Leng, 1994, p. 88.

local nature.[24] Between 1988 and 1990, about 1,140 laws and regulations of a local nature were formulated.[25]

Promulgation of laws and regulations does not always mean they will be obeyed. Similarly, just because something has been written into law does not necessarily mean it will be strictly enforced. If these observations hold true in every society, then the problems might be worse in a less institutionalized system such as China. Even so, judging from the number of laws and regulations formulated in the past sixteen years, one can say that China is no longer a "lawless" society, at least so far as legislation is concerned. With so many laws and regulations in place, the behavior of power-holders would be at least judged against some publicly (and even internationally) recognized legal standards.

Change of the Electoral Law

Although multiparty competition was not what post-Mao leaders had in mind when they talked about "socialist democracy," some major changes have occurred in the way people elect their deputies to people's congresses at the county level and below. In 1979, the Fifth NPC passed the electoral law for the NPC and local people's congresses, which introduced several major changes, including more candidates than positions on the final ballot, secret ballot as the only legal method of voting, more open nominating process, and direct election of people's congress deputies at the county level.[26] In the first direct local election in 1980–81, 2,756 electoral units at the county (urban district) level elected their deputies to local people's congresses.[27] More than 400 million people reportedly participated in voting with a 96.55% voter turnout.[28] In the second direct local election in 1984, more than 84,300 electoral units at village level and 4,600 at township level were included.[29]

Despite resistance to the implementation of the electoral law at the local levels,[30] the direct local direction has become increasingly institutionalized.

---

[24] Ibid., pp. 24–5.

[25] The *People's Daily* (Overseas Edition), October 22, 1991.

[26] Brantly Womack, ed., "Electoral Reform in China," *Chinese Law and Government* 15, no. 3–4 (Fall–Winter 1982–3), p. 3.

[27] For an analysis of this election, see ibid., pp. 7–13.

[28] Zhang Qingfu ed., p. 75.

[29] Ibid., p. 78.

[30] Harry Harding, *China's Second Revolution: Reform After Mao* (Washington, DC: The Brookings Institution, 1987), p. 180.

Since 1984, four more direct local elections (1987, 1990, 1992, and 1994) have been held at the village, township, urban district, and county levels. Although rejecting Western-style democracy, Deng and other Party leaders have accepted, at least theoretically, the basic electoral principles of universal adult suffrage, equal weighting of votes, direct elections, and secret ballots. What needs to be done, according to them, is a gradual perfection and improvement of the electoral procedures. Direct local elections also held special value for Deng's regime, for they not only validated the regime's claim that China was moving toward democracy, but also provided a new source of legitimacy at the basic level.

In a big country like China with 1.2 billion people, major leadership changes through direct elections at the national level would be unthinkable if local direct elections were not implemented first, offering the Chinese voters opportunities to taste electoral democracy. Direct local elections, therefore, could prove to be the most important avenue to political democracy in China, for this is the political process in which most Chinese people can get involved. Direct local elections might be largely ritual and procedural at the beginning, but once set in motion, they are hard to turn back and inevitably lead to a series of important changes.

First, by allowing more candidates than there are vacancies to stand for election, direct local elections nurture an awareness of choice among the voters. Before too long, Chinese voters will ask why they should not freely choose their own candidates for government positions at higher levels as well. Second, direct local elections will also make voters more concerned about candidates in their own units. This inevitably leads to the ideas of constituency, responsiveness, and accountability. The Chinese voters are not yet able to use their voting power to hold provincial and national leaders accountable, but they will certainly try to make their elected representatives from their electoral districts more accountable.[31] Third, the implementation of the electoral laws could pitch directly elected local officials against indirectly elected or appointed provincial and national leaders. Local officials who have fought hard to win their positions will challenge the legitimacy of their superiors who are appointed by the higher authorities.

[31] Zhang Qingfu, ed., pp. 87–8.

WHICH IS SUPERIOR: THE PARTY OR THE LAW?

In September 1982, a new Party constitution was adopted at the Twelfth Party Congress. For the first time in the CCP history, the Party constitution stipulates that from the center to the basic level, the activities of all the Party organizational units and members must be consistent with the constitution and laws of the state. Every Party member, including the Party top leadership, must obey the laws and should have absolutely no privilege of being above the law.[32] Article 5 of the new state constitution also stipulates that "all state organs, the armed forces, all political parties and public organizations and all enterprises and undertakings must abide by the constitution and the law. All acts in violation of the constitution and law must be looked into. No organization or individual may enjoy the privilege of being above the constitution and the law."[33]

Party–Judicial Relations

The reaffirmation of constitutional supremacy and the legal principle that everyone is equal before the law was no small step in the right direction for the Deng regime to have taken. There had been some important changes in Party–legal relations since 1982. For instance, Party committees at various levels were told not to replace laws with the words of Party secretaries. Party committees also ceased to review and approve every case before a legal judgment was handed down. As a general rule, Party committees and the legal apparatus no longer jointly handled cases.

Nonetheless, legal institutions in China still have to seek political guidance from the Party on broad policy matters. Some major or complex cases still have to be reviewed and approved by Party committees.[34] Legal experts know all too well that without institutional independence and procedural guarantees, legal principles cannot be easily translated into legal reality. One major organizational device by which Party committees exercise their political control over the judicial apparatus is the Party's Political and Legal Affairs Committee (PLAC). This is undoubtedly one of the most powerful departments of Party committees. From the center to the provincial and local levels, the Party's

---

[32] Nie Gaomin et al., p. 118.

[33] An English translation of the 1982 Constitution is in *Beijing Review* 52 (December 27, 1982), pp. 10–29.

[34] Nie Gaomin et al., p. 169.

PLAC directly controls the legal apparatus, public security forces, procuratorates, and courts. Every Party committee has a secretary specially assigned to be in charge of political and legal affairs. This Party secretary for political and legal affairs serves as the ultimate guarantor, making sure that the Party's policies and intentions are observed in all legal activities.

The Central Political and Legal Affairs Committee was established in January 1980. Its responsibilities include reviewing and handling major issues in political and legal work and making recommendations to the Party Central Committee; helping the Party center handle reports sent from lower levels concerning political and legal matters; overseeing the implementation of the Party's principles and policies, state laws, and regulations; and overseeing the organizational and ideological condition of the legal apparatus.[35] Between January 1980 and May 1984, the Central PLAC was headed by Party elder Peng Zhen as the central Party secretary for political and legal affairs. Peng was later succeeded by Chen Pixian, Qiao Shi, and Ren Jianxin respectively. One deputy Party secretary, one secretary-general, and one deputy secretary-general are also appointed to the committee, suggesting that this is a fully functional rule-making body. The membership of the Central PLAC usually includes ministers of Justice, Public Security, and State Security, the president of the Supreme People's Court, and the chief procurator of the Supreme People's Procuracy. At the provincial level, the Party's PLAC usually includes the bureau chiefs of justice, public security, and state security of the provincial government, president of the Higher People's Court and procurator of the Higher People's Procuracy. The same pattern generally holds true at various local levels.

Given the legal responsibilities and composition of the Party's PLAC, three conclusions can be reached. First, it is difficult to maintain judicial independence while trying to uphold the Party's leadership. On the one hand, the enforcement of laws is supposed to be free from interference from any organizations or individuals. On the other hand, the legal apparatus must rely on guidance and direction from Party committees. The Party publications argue, sometimes painstakingly, that abiding by the law and obeying the Party leadership are compatible because the Party leadership in judicial work is over principles and policies, and the laws of the PRC are formulated under the Party leadership. Yet it must be obvious, when or if instructions given by Party

---

[35] *Zhongguo gaige dacidian* (Dictionary of Chinese Reform) (Beijing: Zhongguo guoji guangbo chubanshe, 1992), p. 465.

leaders differ from the opinions of legal experts, which one is going to prevail. Second, as the official title of the Party's Political and Legal Affairs Committee clearly indicates, politics and law are structurally inseparable. It would not be surprising if the members of the Party's PLAC let political considerations prevail over legal judgments. At the meetings of the Party's PLAC, leaders of all the judicial and public security agencies are brought together not to serve in their respective legal roles, but as members of a collective body to serve the Party's interests in political and legal affairs. Whereas in the United States every major political issue ultimately becomes a legal issue and ends up in the Supreme Court, in China every major legal issue ultimately becomes a political issue and ends up in the Party's PLAC. Third, the constitutionally stipulated legal principles such as judicial independence, equality before the law, open trials, and the right to defense are in practice implemented only as they are defined or approved by the Party's PLAC.

It is worth noting that at the Thirteenth Party Congress in October 1987, Party Chief Zhao Ziyang included in his political report a proposal to abolish the Party's PLAC along with the Party core groups at the provincial and county levels. Some changes were indeed made in a few provinces. After Zhao was purged amid the Tiananmen crisis in 1989, however, reform in this area was soon abandoned. For instance, in March 1990, the Sichuan Provincial Party committee announced its decision to restore the Party's PLAC from the county to the provincial levels.[36] By now, the system of the Party's PLAC has been fully restored at every level of the Chinese legal process.

Party–Legislative Relations

During the Deng Xiaoping era, the active legislative role played by the people's congresses at the national and local levels has relieved the overburdened Party committees of many law and order responsibilities, but it also weakened the control that the Party had traditionally wielded over lawmaking.[37] Although reformers have seen this as an inevitable and healthy trend toward a stable system of rule of law, conservatives have feared that the Party's dominance could be in real jeopardy. As legislatures and Party committees compete for lawmaking power, people often wonder which is superior, the Party or the

---

[36] *Zuzhi renshi xinxibao* 249 (Organization and Personnel Gazette) (March 8, 1990), p. 1.

[37] For a recent study of the erosion of the Party control over lawmaking, see Murray Scot Tanner, "The Erosion of the Communist Party Control over Lawmaking in China," *The China Quarterly* 138 (June 1994), pp. 381–403.

people's congress. This is the same question that was first asked during the "blooming and contending" in 1956–57. As we shall see later, the answer remains unclear despite repeated emphasis by the Party leaders on the supremacy of the people's congress.

The 1982 constitution stipulates that the national, provincial, and local people's congresses are the organs of the state power. The National People's Congress exercises legislative power, and the power to revise the constitution and to supervise the implementation of the constitution. Provincial and local people's congresses have the power to formulate and issue regulations of a local nature and exercise power within their jurisdiction to guarantee the implementation of the state constitution, laws and regulations. The Organic Law of the Local People's Congress specifies the powers of a local people's congress as: (a) legislation, (b) supervision of government, and (c) approval and removal of government officials.

Despite such constitutional and legal provisions, changes in Party–legislative relations are difficult and controversial. First, the Party core group system in the people's congress has continued to play a major role in ensuring the Party's control over the legislative process. It is worth noting that at the Thirteenth Party Congress, Party chief Zhao Ziyang proposed to retain Party core groups in the people's congress even though he advocated abolishing them in government administrative agencies. Because the NPC Standing Committee has assumed more legislative power under the 1982 constitution, the Party core group of the NPC Standing Committee is undoubtedly the most important channel through which Party leaders direct and monitor the national legislative process.[38] At the provincial, city, or county level, there is a Party core group inside every people's congress. It is appointed by, and directly reports to, the provincial, city, or county Party committee. As Party core groups in the people's congresses have to ask for instructions from the Party committees on legislative matters, provincial or local Party committees can often control the agenda of the people's congress.[39]

Second, the people's congresses still depend on the Party's organization department to provide background information about nominees for government positions and have to stick to the list of candidates recommended by the Party committee. Although one can imagine a scenario not too dissimilar to the

[38] Ibid., pp. 390–1.

[39] Zhao Baoxu, ed., *Minzhu zhengzhi yu difang renda: diaocai yu shikao ziyi* (Democratic Politics and Local People's Congress: Surveys and Thoughts, Part 1) (Shaanxi: Shaanxi renmin chubanshe, 1990), pp. 12–13.

process in the United States, where the President nominates the candidates, the FBI does the background check, and the Senate reviews and approves the nominations, it would require some major structural changes in China to straighten out the relations between the legislative and executive agencies on the one hand, and the Party committees on the other.

Third, provincial governors and city mayors usually are members of the Party committee, whereas chairpersons of the standing committees of the people's congresses often are not. Thus, although theoretically provincial or city governments should report to the people's congresses, in practice this is structurally hampered by the Party committee. When provincial or city Party committees hold meetings, governors or mayors are voting members of the Party committee, whereas chairpersons of the standing committees of the people's congresses are invited only to listen. This arrangement often makes it difficult for the people's congresses to exercise their oversight power over the government work. Only when a chairperson of the standing committee of a people's congress is concurrently the Party committee secretary is the status of the people's congress upgraded. In view of this, it is not surprising that some political scientists in China have argued that in order for people's congresses to function, it is better for a ranking member of the Party committee or even a deputy Party secretary to be concurrently chairperson of the standing committee of the people's congress.[40]

Although the people's congresses are far from being independent and autonomous, battles for lawmaking power have already begun. Before 1984, the people's congresses had routinely rubber-stamped government appointments decided by the Party committees. Sometimes, even before people's congresses approved the nominations, the appointments were already announced in the newspaper and the nominated officials were in their offices. In 1984, the Party center issued two documents (No. 8 and No. 9) that stipulated that appointments for government posts should be made by the people's congresses. Secret ballots were to be used and multiple candidates were to be nominated for offices.[41] Since then, there have been several cases where the people's congresses have opposed the nominations. In Shanghai, for instance, when one staff member from the Shanghai Municipal People's Congress complained at one government meeting that the people's congress still did not have enough power, Zhu Rongji, then Mayor of Shanghai, interrupted the complaint by

---

[40] Ibid., p. 85.   [41] Ibid., p. 9.

Table 7.1. *Career patterns of standing committee chairs of provincial people's congresses, 1992–95*

Province	Chair	Previous post(s)
Anhui	Meng Fulin	Deputy Party Secretary
Beijing	Zhang Jianmin	Vice Mayor
Fujian	Jia Qinglin	Governor, Party Secretary[a]
Guangxi	Zhao Fulin	Party Secretary[a]
Guizhou	Wang Chaowen	Governor
Hainan	Du Qinglin	Deputy Party Secretary
Hebei	Lu Chuanzan	Deputy Party Secretary
Henan	Li Changchun	Governor, Party Secretary[a]
Hubei	Guan Guangfu	Governor, Party Secretary[a]
Inner Mongolia	Wang Qun	Party Secretary[a]
Jiangsu	Shen Daren	Party Secretary
Jiangxi	Mao Zhiyong	Party Secretary
Jilin	He Zhukang	Governor, Party Secretary[a]
Liaoning	Quan Shuren	Party Secretary
Shaanxi	Zhang Boxing	Party Secretary
Shanxi	Lu Gongxun	Deputy Party Secretary
Sichuan	Yang Xizong	Chair, People's Congress of Henan
Tianjin	Nie Bichu	Mayor
Xizang	Raidi	Deputy Party Secretary
Yunnan	Yin Jun	Deputy Party Secretary
Zhejiang	Li Zemin	Party Secretary

[a]Concurrently holding the posts of the chair of the standing committee of the people's congress and secretary of the Party committee of that province.
Sources: Malcolm Lamb, *Directory of Officials and Organizations in China: A Quarter-Century Guide* (Armonk, NY: M. E. Sharpe, 1994); *The China Times Magazine* 203, November 19–25, 1995, pp. 50–51.

saying that the municipal people's congress already had too much power because several of his nominations for bureau chiefs had been turned down.[42]

Competition for lawmaking power between the Party and the legislature acquired a new twist after many senior leaders were "retired" to the national or provincial people's congresses. These so-called retirement arrangements were initially viewed as a political compromise aimed at persuading the veteran cadres to vacate leading posts in the Party and government for younger leaders,

[42] Interviews in Shanghai, January 1989.

while continuing to enjoy all the privileges usually reserved for officeholders. Few, however, had expected these retirement arrangements to turn the people's congress into a new arena of power struggle. After all, Chinese national and provincial legislatures had been known as rubber stamps for decades. Yet, after they went to the people's congresses, often reluctantly at first, the retired veteran cadres used their new institutional base to expand their power.

A brief survey of the career pattern of leaders of provincial people's congresses in the 1990s indicates that most of the new standing committee chairpersons were former provincial Party committee secretaries, governors, or both (see Table 7.1). They came to the people's congress after they had served in leading roles in the Party organization or government, not vice versa. Since the retired veteran cadres necessarily had more seniority than the younger leaders now in Party and government posts, the institution of people's congresses under their control has become an increasingly formidable contender for lawmaking power.

THE CONSTITUTIONAL CRISIS IN 1989

Although Deng Xiaoping had once inspired many people in China when he called for economic modernization and legal development, he often disappointed his supporters more than his opponents. In 1979, he ordered the crackdown on the Democracy Wall movement. In 1983, Deng launched the campaign against the so-called spiritual pollution. More shocking was Deng's decision in late 1986 to remove his hand-picked successor, Hu Yaobang, from his office as the Party general secretary, because of Hu's allegedly lenient attitude toward the student protests.

As Deng kept playing his game of balance of power between reformers and conservatives, the dynamism his reform had released and the frustration his retreats had created accumulated to a point where he could no longer dictate the situation. On April 15, 1989, when the news came that Hu Yaobang had died of heart attack, all hope was lost for those (largely intellectuals and students) who had been waiting for Hu to return to power. Saddened by Hu's sudden death and angered by Deng's decision not to remove the accusations made against Hu, students, intellectuals, and city residents poured into Tiananmen Square to mourn the death of Hu. As in the past, mourning the dead was also the most convenient way to make a protest. During the months of April and May, millions of the Chinese people, including many Party and government functionaries, took to the streets in Beijing and other major cities to call for political

177

reform and retirement of aging or incompetent leaders. The declaration of martial law in Beijing was unprecedented in the history of the PRC, yet it still could not deter people from joining the demonstration and hunger strikes. Then, the events occurring on June 3–4, 1989, shocked the world as fully equipped PLA field army soldiers went on the rampage in the capital city and killed hundreds, if not thousands, of innocent civilians.

Voices from Tiananmen Square

Since the suppression of the student and mass democracy movement, many books and articles have been written about this event. Emerging from these writings are several themes: a surprising realization of the inability of the Chinese government to manage a crisis; an optimistic view of the rise of a civil society in China; and an emphasis on the delegitimization of the Chinese Communist regime.[43] Yet there was a powerful and familiar voice that has often been neglected in the analysis of the Tiananmen Square crisis. Emerging from the hundreds of documents, newspapers, and leaflets written by students and intellectuals during this period, there was a persistent call for the Chinese people to stand up to "Defend the Republic!" and "Defend the Constitution!"[44]

In one leaflet from Beijing University entitled "The Republic Is Not Private Property," the author rebuked the view that because the Party had sacrificed more than twenty million lives to build a new China, the surviving Communist leaders should forever hold on to their power and privileges. Making the same argument first advocated by the non-Communists twenty-two years earlier, the author pointed out:

> When China was in the dark old days, the Chinese people were seek-
> ing an equal and fair world even at the price of sacrificing their own
> lives. They finally found an organization that could unite all the op-
> pressed people – the Chinese Communist party. The people gave all
> they had to the party, not to help those who later became the rulers to

---

[43] For examples, see David Bachman, "China's Politics: Conservatism Prevails," in *Current History* 88, no. 539 (September, 1989), pp. 257–60, 296–7; Chu-yuan Cheng, *Behind the Tiananmen Massacre: Social, Political and Economic Ferment in China* (Boulder CO: Westview Press, 1990); Cott Simmie and Bob Nixon, *Tiananmen Square* (Seattle: University of Washington Press, 1989); Liu Binyan, *"Tell the World": What Happened in China and Why* (New York: Pantheon, 1990); and Andrew Nathan, *China's Crisis: Dilemmas of Reform and Prospects for Democracy* (New York: Columbia University Press, 1990).

[44] The translated documents and materials are in Suzanne Ogden et al., eds., *China's Search for Democracy: The Student and Mass Movement of 1989* (Armonk, NY: M. E. Sharpe, 1992).

accumulate [power] for their own ease and comfort. . . . Those twenty
million lives sacrificed are not the private property of any individual
or any small group, but a price paid by the whole Chinese people.
This glorious republic belongs to the people.[45]

The protesters also raised the issue of legitimacy and legal procedure. Another handbill read:

Is it legitimate for Deng Xiaoping to be the country's sole decision
maker as chairman of the Military [Affairs] Commission? He places
himself above the party, the government, and the National People's
Congress. He orders people by gesture, and all bureaucrats around
him are obsequious. This proves the illegitimacy of his power. . . . We
loudly appeal to people; Immediately convene the special session of
the National People's Congress with elections based on democracy
and law. Elect real public servants who, under popular, strict, and
effective supervision, will observe, execute, and defend the solemn
constitution.[46]

After martial law was declared on May 19, emphasis on citizens' rights and
constitutional supremacy became a central focus of the protesters' demands.
Thus one wall poster in Tiananmen Square read:

The constitution should be respected as the foundation of the
state. . . . It should be clearly stipulated that the constitution is the final and highest expression of the will and interests of the Chinese
citizens, and that no [single] political party has the power to represent
the will of 1.1 billion Chinese nationals. . . . All public servants in the
government, especially high ranking ones and those in charge of political affairs, should swear an oath of office before the constitution. The
government should designate a day as Constitution Day, [so as to indicate to all] that our country is a "People's Republic," not a "party-
state."[47]

The clips cited here are only a small fraction of a huge amount of documents
and leaflets written during the 1989 democracy movement. Yet they clearly
indicate that in the late 1980s, thanks to Deng's emphasis on constitutional
supremacy and legal development, the Chinese students and intellectuals had

---

[45] Ibid., p. 338.   [46] Ibid., pp. 217–8.
[47] Ibid., p. 279.

become more confident in asserting their constitutional and legal rights. It is worth noting that many participants in the Tiananmen Square demonstrations came from Beijing's University of Political Science and Law. It was Deng's legal reform that had offered these students a chance to study law; now they used what they had learned to challenge Deng's decision to order the military crackdown.

The "Signature Incident"

Because legally only the NPC or its Standing Committee has the authority to declare or lift martial law, it is not surprising that the demonstrators turned to the NPC Standing Committee for support. On May 21, in a statement entitled "Declaration to Defend the Constitution," sixteen Chinese scholars made an appeal directly to the members of the Chinese national legislature. They stressed that in accordance with Article 67, Section 6, of the state constitution, the Standing Committee of the National People's Congress has the right to "supervise the work of the State Council, the Central Military Commission. . . . [A]n urgent session of the Standing Committee must be immediately convened to guarantee the supervisory power granted to it by the constitution. We believe that defending the constitution is an unshirkable duty of every Chinese citizen."[48]

Three days after the above declaration was issued, about 200 Chinese intellectuals published an open letter to the NPC Standing Committee. The open letter reads:

> Article 29 of the constitution stipulates that the military forces in our country belong to the people. . . . It violates the spirit of Article 29 to send the troops into Beijing to "carry out the task of imposing martial law" under circumstances where there is neither foreign invasion nor riots. Hence, we strongly appeal to the Standing Committee of the NPC to immediately convene a special session to repeal martial law. We also hope students will withdraw from Tiananmen Square after martial law is repealed.[49]

Meanwhile, some legislators had also taken actions. Between May 17 and May 24, several members of the NPC Standing Committee launched three petition drives, calling for an emergency session of the NPC Standing Committee to be

---

[48] Ibid., pp. 268–9.   [49] Ibid., p. 306.

convened "for the express purpose of repealing martial law."[50] According to one study, three petition drives had gathered at least fifty-one signatures, representing nearly one-third of the 156 NPC Standing Committee members.[51] What became known as the Signature Incident was so symbolically significant that an official investigation was immediately launched after the crackdown that resulted in several members being expelled from the NPC Standing Committee.

Unfortunately, the efforts to seek a peaceful solution to the crisis through the national legislature and legal means were aborted by gunfire on the night of June 3–4. One may even argue that these efforts represented the protesters' desperation more than their hope for the legislators to stand up to a paramount leader with the backing of guns. Yet, symbolic though they might have been at the time, the calls for defending the state constitution and the republic and for convening the emergency meeting of the NPC Standing Committee suggest that some profound changes are under way. Here we may have observed the unfolding of a difficult yet promising process whereby the Chinese people begin looking to the constitution for protection, protesting the abuse of power and privileges through legal procedures, and pledging loyalty to a political entity higher than the Party, that is, the republic. This process was first initiated by the Party leaders like Deng as they tried to respond to the lawlessness of the Mao era, but it soon moved ahead of the Party, and, indeed, brought the latter before the tribunal of legal opinion.

END OF THE CAMPAIGN AND THE BEGINNING OF LEGAL BATTLE

During the Mao era, the political witch-hunt was a part of daily life. Under the theory of "continuing the revolution under the dictatorship of the proletariat," there had been a consistent pursuit of "enemies" of the regime. Numerous political labels were invented to classify people into different categories, such as "counterrevolutionary," "bad element," "rightist," "capitalist roader," and "new bourgeois element." On the last day before the military crackdown in Tiananmen Square in June 1989, four hunger strikers made a special appeal to renounce the Mao-style class struggle mentality. "We must thoroughly give up

---

[50] Richard Baum, "The Road to Tiananmen: Chinese Politics in the 1980s," in Roderick MacFarquhar, ed., *The Politics of China, 1949–1989* (New York: Cambridge University Press, 1993), p. 452.

[51] Hu Shikai, "Representation Without Democratization: The 'Signature Incident' and China's National People's Congress," *The Journal of Contemporary China* 2, no. 1 (Winter–Spring 1993), p. 5.

the political culture of 'class struggle,' because hatred can only produce violence and autocracy."[52]

Yet, frightened by the massive scale of the demonstration and living in their own imaginary world, the veteran revolutionary leaders had returned to Mao's combative politics. In the aftermath of the Tiananmen crackdown, the hard-line leaders, with the endorsement of Deng, launched the largest political campaign of the reform era, trying to regain their lost political and ideological control over the populace.[53] To wage a new battle of class struggle, enemies had to be found. Thus Deng told the PLA officers on June 9, 1989: "In fact, we were dealing not only with people who merely could not distinguish between right and wrong, but there were a number of rebels and many persons who were the dregs of society. They tried to subvert our state and our Party."[54] So began the nationwide political witch-hunt. The public security apparatus, previously in disarray during the Tiananmen crisis, was mobilized to track down the dissidents. While about forty student leaders and dissident intellectuals managed to escape to the West, hundreds of thousands were arrested or detained for questioning.[55] In universities, research institutes, factories, army camps, and Party and government institutions, people were organized into small study groups and asked to report on each other's activities during the weeks of demonstration. Many were pressured to identify and inform on their colleagues. Old tactics of the Mao era were revived to classify those who were involved in demonstrations into different categories subject to condemnation, forced confessions, and imprisonment.

Second, there had to be enemies from Taiwan. As with any policy dispute among the top Party leaders in the previous four decades, the confrontation in Tiananmen Square was seen by the Party elders as a continuation of the sixty years of political and military struggle between the Communist Party and the Kuomintang. To prove this connection, some Taiwan spies were reportedly arrested after the crackdown.

Third, there had to be enemies in the West. The Chinese leaders have frequently warned that "Dulles-like" people in the West have not given up their hope for overthrowing the Chinese government. Since June 1989, opposition to

---

[52] Ogden et al., p. 358.

[53] For the Chinese official interpretation of the 1989 Tiananmen Square Incident and lines of propaganda, see David Shambaugh, ed., "The Making of the Big Lie: Content and Process in the CCP Propaganda System," *Chinese Law and Government* 25, no. 1 (Spring 1992).

[54] Deng Xiaoping, 1993, p. 295.

[55] Baum, "The Road to Tiananmen: Chinese Politics in the 1980s," in MacFarquhar, 1993, p. 462.

the "Western scheme of peaceful evolution" became one of the most important tasks of the Party committees at all the levels. Chinese universities and schools were asked to list as their top priority vigilance against peaceful evolution. Even though the Cold War was coming to an end, the veteran revolutionary leaders in China returned to the theme of "capitalist encirclement." Meeting with a visiting Tanzanian delegation on November 23, 1989, Deng suggested that the Western countries "are staging a third world war without gunsmoke."[56]

However, after more than ten years of reform, many people in China had neither stomach nor time for yet another Cultural Revolution-like campaign. In some cases, the political witch-hunt turned into a game of mutual protection. In others, the campaign was trivialized. Having learned important lessons from the previous mass campaigns, many simply refused to be the victimizers this time, much less to be the victims. Few, if any, wanted to be closely identified with Deng for bearing the responsibility for the bloody crackdown, for it is clear that after Deng dies it will only be a matter of time before the official verdict on the 1989 Tiananmen incident is reversed.[57]

As it became clear that the last campaign was going nowhere, the dramatic events in Eastern Europe and the Soviet Union must have shocked Deng out of his self-indulgence. The master bridge-player therefore tried his last game of balance of power by turning 180 degrees back toward market reform and open-door policies, this time no doubt to repair his tarnished image and save his place in history. During his much publicized southern China tour in early 1992, Deng advised the provincial leaders not to be worried about "too many elements of capitalist things" and to focus on promoting the growth of the productive forces.[58] With the new momentum of economic development, there was also a renewed emphasis on strengthening and improving the legal system.[59]

Lawyers and Lawsuits

One major development since 1992 has been the renewed effort to strengthen the system of lawyers. Lawyer service in China was abolished during the Anti-Rightist Campaign in 1957 and was not restored until 1980. At the beginning of

---

[56] Deng Xiaoping, 1993, p. 333.
[57] One only needs to be reminded of the reversed verdicts on similar dramatic events that had occurred before June 4, 1989, such as the 1957 Anti-Rightist Campaign and the April 5 Tiananmen Square Incident of 1976.
[58] Deng Xiaoping, 1993, pp. 360.
[59] Leng, 1994, p. 94.

the 1980s, China had no more than 1,000 lawyers.[60] During the next decade, the number of lawyers in China had stagnated at around 20,000 to 30,000.[61] In October 1993, Chinese Justice Minister Xiao Yang announced that the Ministry of Justice planned to triple the number of lawyers from the present 50,000 to 150,000 by the turn of the century. The legal reform package proposed by the Justice Minister also allowed lawyers to turn their law firms into self-regulating bodies such as legal partnerships.[62] Within less than two years, the number of Chinese lawyers had increased to 82,000 by August 1995. The 4,200 law firms in existence in 1993 had grown to 7,200, including cooperative and private firms.[63]

The renewed momentum in legal development reflects the reality of an increasing internationalization of the Chinese economy. Despite the lingering rhetoric of warnings against the Western scheme of peaceful evolution, the fact is that the Chinese leaders have neither the desire nor the ability to close the door of China again. China's integration with the world economy necessarily subjects legal procedure and practice in China to greater scrutiny by the international legal community. Chinese leaders often complain that the rules of the game are not fair and that they were set without China's participation. But this is the only game there is, and Chinese leaders will have to learn how to play it well. In December 1993, Tian Jiyun, vice chair of the NPC Standing Committee, told a group of legislators to "emancipate" their minds and learn from foreign laws so as to accelerate legal reform in China.[64] Increasing economic interaction among mainland China, Hong Kong, and Taiwan has also forced the leaders in Beijing to face the thorny issue of incompatibility of legal systems in the three Chinese societies. Learning about and understanding each other's legal systems and practices will lead to further demands for improving the PRC's legal system.

In the meantime, ordinary Chinese no longer lack legal tools. Among the many promulgated laws is the Administrative Litigation Law that went into effect in October 1990, which permits individuals to sue government agencies.[65] The Administrative Compensation Law passed in May 1994 also allows

---

[60] Xinhua News Agency, July 18, 1995.
[61] *The China Press,* August 30, 1994, p. 5.
[62] Xinhua News Agency, October 15, 1993.
[63] Ibid., August 15, 1995.
[64] Ibid.
[65] *South China Morning Post,* December 10, 1993, p. 10.

victims to be compensated for damage caused by government. Many Chinese and their lawyers no longer shy from suing the Party and government officials for wrongdoing. It is reported that since 1990, more than 70,000 lawsuits have been filed against the government, of which 37 percent were decided in favor of ordinary people.[66] Many participants in the 1989 demonstration have also concluded that their confrontational tactics were both costly and unproductive. Instead of demanding that one or two unpopular leaders step down or calling on the powerholders to give up power, it would be much wiser and more constructive to use legal means to pressure the Party leaders to keep their promises and to ensure that the Party and government officials behave within the constitution.[67] Indeed, if only a fraction of what has been already written into the Chinese constitution and laws could be achieved, the situation would be much different.

At a meeting attended by China's senior judicial officials in late 1993, the president of the Supreme People's Court, Ren Jianxin, promised to "put the entire adjudication process under the supervision of the masses through open investigation, open cross-examination, open debate and open sentencing." He also vowed to punish judicial officials and police for miscarriage of justice and wrongly adjudicating cases.[68] Undoubtedly, in the name of safeguarding state security, the authorities can, and have in many cases continued to ignore the constitutional rights of citizens and legal procedures, but they have also realized that ideological control and rule of man can neither deter corruption and crime nor ensure order and stability. Moving toward a true system of rule of law will shake the Party rule to its foundation, but promulgation of hundreds of laws and regulations with no intention to implement them is self-defeating. As Qiao Shi, the chairman of the NPC Standing Committee, recently told his colleagues in the NPC, "Enacting a law is not the ultimate objective, and the objective of enacting a law is to enforce it."[69] When it comes down to specific cases, "to enforce it or not to enforce it" is the classic institutional dilemma facing the Party leadership.

---

[66] For the English version of The Administrative Litigation Law and various Chinese views of the issue, see Pitman B. Potter, ed., "The Administrative Litigation Law of the PRC: Changing the Relationship Between the Courts and Administrative Agencies in China," *Chinese Law and Government* 24, no. 3 (Fall 1991).

[67] Xinhua News Agency, July 12, 1994.

[68] *South China Morning Post,* June 28, 1994, p. 19.

[69] Ibid., January 1, 1994, p. 1.

People's Congress: Rubber Stamp or Power Contender?

Legal battles are also waged in legislatures. As the people's congress has evolved from rubber stamp to a power contender, it has caused problems for both reformers and conservatives. For instance, between 1986–88, the NPC Standing Committee under the control of senior leaders like Peng Zhen more than once defeated the reformist leaders' attempts to get a bankruptcy law passed. When the controversial Three Gorges Project on the Yangtze River was put to a vote in 1992, the NPC deputies caused much embarrassment to Premier Li Peng; 177 voted against the project and as many as 664 abstained.[70] When the Commercial Bank Law was put for vote at the Third Session of the Eighth NPC in March 1995, only 66.5 percent of the 2,678 NPC deputies cast favorable votes, 19 percent (509) voted against it, and 13 percent abstained. Altogether, the objection votes accounted for nearly one-third of the total NPC deputies. There were also 689 NPC deputies (25 percent) who did not vote in favor of the Education Law.[71] Dissatisfied with the worsening situation of law and order, deputies to the Fourth Session of the Eighth NPC in March 1996 again cast objection votes in large numbers. Out of the 2,681 deputies, 242 voted against the approval of the work report by the Supreme People's Court, 208 abstained, and 63 did not bother to cast their votes. When the work report by the Supreme People's Procuratorate was put to the vote, 431 voted against the approval of it, 296 abstained, and 72 did not bother to cast their votes.[72]

The NPC deputies have become increasingly assertive not only in reviewing draft laws and work reports, but also in considering nominations for central government posts. At the First Session of the Seventh NPC in March 1988, 404 deputies voted against the nomination of Li Guixian to be state councilor, and 212 voted against Wang Zhen to be vice chairman of the state. Even Deng Xiaoping received 25 negative votes against his assumption of the chairmanship of the state Central Military Commission.[73] At the First Session of the Eighth NPC in March 1993, as many as 11 percent of the 2,960 deputies either voted against Li Peng's reelection to be the State Council premier or abstained.[74] Although Li Peng's four vice premiers received much higher per-

---

[70] Kevin O'Brien, *Reform Without Liberalization: China's National People's Congress and the Politics of Institutional Change* (New York: Cambridge University Press, 1990), pp. 133–5.
[71] *South China Morning Post,* March 18, 1995.
[72] *The Straits Times,* March 29, 1996.
[73] *World Journal,* March 18, 1996, p. A10.
[74] James C. F. Wang, *Contemporary Chinese Politics: An Introduction,* 5th edition (Englewood Cliffs, NJ: Prentice Hall, 1995), p. 90.

Table 7.2. *Votes for electing vice premiers of the State Council, March 1993*

Candidate	For	Against	Abstained
Qian Qichen	2,883	9	4
Zhu Rongji	2,826	51	19
Zou Jiahua	2,804	62	30
Li Lanqing	2,779	83	34

Source: Wen wei po, March 1993, p. 30, cited in John D. Friske, ed., *China: Facts and Figures, Annual Handbook,* vol. 18 (Gulf Breeze, FL: Academic International Press), pp. 43–44.

Table 7.3. *Candidates for central ministerial posts receiving the most negative votes, March 1993*

Candidate	Ministry/commission	Against	Abstained	Total
Li Tieying	Economic Restructuring	655	109	764
Li Guixian	Bank of China	358	79	437
Ai Zhisheng	Radio, Film & Television	158	43	201
Song Defu	Personnel	135	43	178
Zhang Haoruo	Internal Trade	116	37	153

Source: Wen wei po, March 1993, p. 30, cited in John D. Friske, ed., *China: Facts and Figures, Annual Handbook,* vol. 18 (Gulf Breeze, FL: Academic International Press), pp. 43–44.

centages of the votes, a few central ministers fared even worse than Li Peng. Some received as high as 22 percent of objection votes (see Tables 7.2 and 7.3).

At the Third Session of the Eighth NPC in March 1995, the Party's nominated candidates for the vice premiership of the State Council again met with strong opposition from the NPC deputies. Of 2,752 NPC deputies, there were 605 (22 percent) votes against Jiang Chunyun and 391 abstentions. There were also 210 votes against Wu Bangguo and 161 abstentions (see Table 7.4).[75] This was an unprecedented event in the forty-one-year history of the NPC not only because so many NPC deputies cast objection votes against the candidates favored by the CCP Politburo, but also because many NPC deputies openly talked about

[75] *South China Morning Post,* March 18, 1995, p. 1.

Table 7.4. *Votes for electing vice premiers of the State Council, March 1995*

Candidate	For	Against	Abstained	Void	Total
Jiang Chunyun	1,746	605	391	10	2,752
(%)	63.44	21.98	14.21	0.36	99.99
Wu Bangguo	2,366	210	161	15	2,752
(%)	85.97	7.63	5.85	0.55	100

Source: South China Morning Post, March 18, 1995, p. 1.

why they cast objection votes. Their complaints ranged from the candidate's incompetence, old age, and inadequate education to the lack of transparency in the election process.[76]

The rising influence of the people's congresses is attributable to several factors. As China has moved away from revolution and class struggle to economic reform and construction, the Party's ideological work and organizational control can no longer effectively meet the challenge of a new and dynamic economy and an increasingly diverse society. State-building, such as revitalizing the institution of the people's congress and enhancing the legal system, becomes necessary, if not inevitable.

Moreover, the recent increasing assertiveness of the NPC reflects a calculated move by NPC Standing Committee Chairman Qiao Shi and Vice Chairman Tian Jiyun. Since they were sidelined in 1993 into the NPC, Qiao and Tian have worked to build an institutional power base in the national legislature. Suddenly, the NPC looks like the perfect place to be. From there, one can claim that the national legislature is the "highest organ of state power" according to the 1982 state constitution and thus challenge the Party, the government, and everybody else to take the national legislature seriously. Indeed, if someone could effectively inspire and mobilize the fellow people's congress deputies all over the country, the NPC could become a potentially formidable force. According to the official Xinhua News Agency report, by November 1994, there were 3,501,811 deputies to people's congresses at various levels, one deputy for every 340 Chinese citizens on average.[77] People's congress deputies have

---

[76] Ibid., p. 7.
[77] Xinhua News Agency report, quoted in *World Journal,* February 12, 1995, p. A10.

188

an institutional interest to make sure that the constitutionally granted power of the people's congresses will be fully realized. After all, they could claim that they are elected (directly or indirectly) by the voters and therefore more representative than any other Party and government officials!

Furthermore, many deputies to the NPC are beginning to understand the logic and power of their votes: If you allow secret ballots and no longer try to track down who votes what way, some deputies will no longer hesitate to cast objection votes. If a nominee is unpopular, even if favored by the top Party leadership, he or she can well expect to receive many objection votes. To try to avoid the embarrassment, the top Party leadership will have to think twice about its choice of candidates and will have to please people's congress deputies. If you have multicandidate elections, some nominees will be defeated, and exactly for that reason, candidates will have to appeal to deputies for votes. As a result, it is not difficult to believe that more and more deputies will realize that they can not only use their voting rights to make a protest but also to change legislation and shape the formation and direction of government.

Twenty years after Mao's death, China has definitely moved away from lawlessness to rule by law. The confluence of societal revulsion against the political violence of mass campaigns, the ruling elite's felt need for a new basis of legitimacy, the increasing concern for social order and stability, and China's economic reform and integration with the world economy has carried China to a point of no return in legal development. Yet, while pushing for legal reform and rule by law, the Deng regime had not given up the principle of Party leadership over the legal system. The Party's Political and Legal Affairs Committee and the Party core group are still in charge of the state judicial and legislative institutions. The incompatibility of rapidly changing environment and slow legal reforms has inevitably led to tensions and conflicts, which was powerfully manifested in the crisis in May–June 1989. As Chinese citizens have begun to assert their constitutional rights and resort to legal means against power and privilege, Chinese central and provincial legislators have also become increasingly aggressive in using their prerogative either to make a protest or to force a change. Once the environment of revolution and class struggle changed into one of construction, Chinese legislators have gained more freedom in pushing for changes in the legal system. It seems that between reign of mass campaigns and law and order, China has already made its choice. But to move from the Party's rule by law to a system of rule of law, more institutional innovations are needed and therefore more conflicts and legal battles can be expected. Deng has led his regime halfway into the river of constitutional and legal reform. Now it is up to his successors to decide whether they want to cross the river or stay where they are, thus facing the danger of being swept away by the strong currents of economic and social changes.

8

Changing Party–Government Relations

A LONG with the renewed efforts at economic modernization, the post-Mao regime launched an equally ambitious program for reestablishing an effective and efficient government administrative system at both central and provincial levels. As the Chinese economy and society were undergoing dramatic transformation, the reformist Party leaders faced four institutional challenges: how to redefine the relations between the Party and government in a new situation; how to reorganize the government institutions; how to establish an effective civil service; and how to balance the interests of the center and localities. None of these challenges were new, but market reform and the rapid economic and social changes in China have rendered the old responses obsolete and demanded new innovations.[1] This chapter examines the CCP's responses to these challenges and evaluates the successes and failures of administrative state-building in the Deng era.

REFORM AND RETREAT

The Chinese state-building accelerated in 1979. At the central government level, the Finance and Economic Affairs Commission was the first to reemerge in the State Council. Two veteran central administrators, Chen Yun and Li Xiannian, quickly took the control of the national economy. Other central government agencies followed. Within less than two years, thirty-eight central administrative agencies were either restored or established. The State Council agencies grew from fifty-two in 1976 to seventy-six in 1978, and then ninety-

---

[1] According to Liu Yichang, vice president of the Chinese Public Administration Society, "Public administration plays an important role in modern states. Rapid economic growth and social development in any state depend on the effectiveness of public administration." Li Yichang, "An Insider's Perspective: The Development of Chinese Administrative Science," in Miriam K. Mills and Stuart S. Nagel, eds. *Public Administration in China* (Westport, CT: Greenwood Press, 1993), p. 135.

four in 1979 and ninety-eight in 1980 (including fifty-one ministries and commissions, forty-two administrative bureaus, and five State Council offices). By the end of 1981, a total of forty-eight agencies had been added to the State Council.

As a pragmatic leader, Deng Xiaoping was particularly concerned about having an effective and efficient government administration, mainly, if not exclusively, for the sake of carrying out his economic modernization programs. The 1982 state constitution reconfirms the legal status of the State Council as the central government of the PRC and the highest executive branch of the state. The State Council is accountable to the NPC and its Standing Committee. According to the stipulations of the constitution, the State Council has administrative authority over formulating the national plan of economic and social development, the budget, urban and rural construction, education, science, culture, public health, sports, family planning, civil administration, public security, the judiciary, administrative supervision, foreign affairs, minority affairs, overseas Chinese affairs, and defense. The 1982 constitution also established a responsibility system for the premier of the State Council and for the ministers of various central ministries and commissions.

The 1982 constitution defines three levels of local government administration: province, county, and village. These local administrative organs are the executive branch of the local people's congress and are responsible for organizing and managing local administrative affairs.[2] The 1982 constitution also authorized a separation of village government from people's communes, thus changing the basic administrative system that had existed in rural areas since the Great Leap Forward in 1958. Village government was to be reinstalled and the people's commune was to become a purely collective economic organization.[3] In June 1985, the official news agency announced that the process of separation had been completed and that more than 92,000 village and township governments had been set up.[4]

While the state institutions recovered from the devastation of the previous decade, the Party lost no time in regaining its organizational control. The

---

[2] Li Kangtai, "Administrative Law in China," in Mills and Nagel, eds., p. 87.

[3] *Quanguo renda jiqi changweihui dashiji, 1954–1987* (A Chronology of the National People's Congress and Its Standing Committee, 1954–1987) (Beijing: Falü chubanshe, 1987), pp. 21–3, 327. A full analysis of these new changes is found in Hsin-chi Juan, "New Departures in China's Constitution," *Studies in Comparative Communism* 1 (Spring 1984), pp. 53–68.

[4] Xinhua News Agency, June 4, 1985.

functional departments of the Party Central Committee resumed their work one after another. The CCP Secretariat was reestablished to supervise all government work.[5] In 1977, the CCP decided to reestablish the Party core group (PCG) system in state institutions. In 1980, the central and provincial Party committees reestablished their work departments to exercise direct leadership over the government agencies. For a while, the Party center did stress that any work within the jurisdiction of the government should be discussed and decided by the State Council and local governments. Related documents should be issued by the government. The central and the provincial Party committees would no longer send out instructions or make decisions concerning government work.[6] Yet the Party Central Committee after 1980 continued to send out joint documents and circulars with the State Council, particularly regarding agriculture, military reform, cadres, science and technology, and urban reform. For instance, there were fourteen jointly issued documents or circulars in 1980, eleven in 1981, seventeen in 1982, seventeen in 1984, sixteen in 1984, sixteen in 1985 and fourteen in 1986.[7] Indeed, once the PCGs and Party work committees regained their power, it was difficult for the administrative system to function without the Party center issuing the orders. Directives from the State Council alone were simply not authoritative enough, as the PCGs in central ministries did not report to the premier of the State Council and provincial Party work departments did not report to provincial governors.

Deng Xiaoping's Approach

The revival of Party control over government administration was not totally surprising. Deng had been managing the Party organization for many years. Before he was removed from his powerful Party post during the Cultural Revolution, Deng had performed a tremendous service to the Party in his role

[5] In his speech at the Fifth Plenum of the Eleventh Central Committee in February 1980, Deng Xiaoping pointed out that the Party Secretariat was responsible for taking overall charge of every major area of work, including the Party, government, military, school, industry, agriculture, and commerce. Jiang Huaxuan et al., eds., *Zhongguo gongchandang huiyi gaiyao* (Summaries of the Chinese Communist Party Conferences) (Liaoning: Shenyang chubanshe, 1991), p. 642.

[6] Nie Gaomin et al., eds., *Guanyu dangzheng fenkai de lilun tantao* (Theoretical Discussion on Separating the Party from the Government) (Beijing: Chunqiu chubanshe, 1987), p. 118.

[7] *Zhongguo gaige dacidian* (Dictionary of Chinese Reform) (Beijing: Zhongguo guoji guangbo chubanshe, 1992), pp. 885–974.

as the Party secretary-general (1954–67). As a veteran Party leader, Deng saw no alternative to the leading organizational role of the Party.[8] Moreover, despite the severe damage done to the Party apparatus during the Cultural Revolution, the Party remained the only organizational force in China. As thousands upon thousands of previously purged Party officials returned to power, the Party quickly regained its dominance of Chinese political life.

However, by emphasizing the Party leadership, Deng did not intend to suggest that the Party should take over the responsibilities of the government. In his major policy speech on "Reform System of Party and State Leadership" in August 1980, Deng stressed that it was time

> for us to distinguish between the responsibilities of the Party and those of the government and to stop substituting the former for the latter. . . . This will help strengthen and improve the unified leader-ship of the Central Committee, facilitate the establishment of an effec-tive work system at the various levels of government from top to bottom, and promote a better exercise of government functions and powers.[9]

Nothing of what Deng said in 1980 was new. Many CCP leaders had expressed the same views before. Indeed, as Chinese scholars remind us, Deng's speech in 1980 echoed what he had argued more than forty years earlier. On April 15, 1941, Deng wrote:

> [T]hese comrades misunderstand Party leadership, believing that "Party leadership is above everything else." They interfere in govern-ment work, change at will decrees promulgated by the government at a higher level, and transfer cadres who work in organs of political power without going through administrative procedures. . . . This has given the masses the impression that the government is incompetent and that it is the Communist Party that has the final say in everything, that the Party levies grain and other taxes, formulates all the decrees for the government and is responsible for all the mistakes made by the

---

[8] In 1979, Deng Xiaoping asked, "in reality, without the Chinese Communist Party, who would organize the socialist economy, politics, military affairs and culture in China, and who would organize the four modernizations?" Deng Xiaoping, *Selected Works of Deng Xiaoping 1975–1982* (Beijing: Foreign Languages Press, 1984), p. 178.

[9] Ibid., p. 303.

government. Hence, the government is not respected by the masses and the Party has alienated itself from them. What stupidity![10]

Stupid or not, the fact that Deng had to repeat himself in 1980 testifies to the persistence of the problems. For over four decades, the CCP had essentially failed to come up with a viable solution to the structural contradictions in its relations with the government. Overlapping authorities and confusing responsibilities of Party and government institutions had constantly troubled the Chinese leadership, forcing them to permit Party organization to take over the functions of the government only to find out later that Party organization often did a terrible job in managing state affairs.

Reform efforts up to the mid-1980s largely represented a restoration of the political structure that was destroyed in the Cultural Revolution. What could be characterized only loosely as political reform programs were mainly driven by a revulsion against the political chaos. Deng's speech in 1980 on reform of the Party and the state leadership system was ambitious and provoking, but the changes that followed fell well short of expectations. During the next few years, the CCP leaders seemed to have lost interest in political reform while busily pursuing economic reform. The efforts to reduce the Party's direct role in government administration were largely concentrated on changing the interlocking directorates in Party and government.

At the enlarged meeting of the CCP Politburo in August 1980, six senior members of the Politburo, including Deng, decided to give up their government posts as vice premiers of the State Council.[11] Deng explained:

> [I]t is not good to have too many people holding two or more posts concurrently or to have too many deputy posts. There is a limit to anyone's knowledge, experience and energy. If a person holds too many posts at the same time, he will find it difficult to come to grips with the problems in his work and, more important, he will block the way for other more suitable comrades to take up leading posts.[12]

At the Third Session of the Fifth NPC in 1980, it was announced that first secretaries of provincial, municipal, or county Party committees would no longer concurrently assume government posts as governor, mayor, or county magistrate. Directors of Party work departments should not concurrently as-

---

[10] *Selected Works of Deng Xiaoping (1938-1965)* (Beijing: Foreign Languages Press, 1992), pp. 17–18.

[11] Jiang Huaxuan et al., p. 647. [12] Deng Xiaoping, 1984, p. 303.

sume the leading posts of parallel government agencies. The change was said to enable Party secretaries to pay more attention to Party work and help the State Council and local governments establish an efficient government work system.[13] By the end of 1980, interlocking directorates at the provincial level had been reduced from twenty-one to seven. By 1984, there was only one interlocking directorate at the provincial level.

However, we must take caution not to exaggerate the significance of the change in interlocking directorates. Even in the Mao era, interlocking directorates showed a general trend of decline. It was only during the Cultural Revolution that interlocking directorates had reached the highest level, when the Party regained its organizational control over everything. During the Deng era, interlocking directorates were fewer, but they did not totally disappear. Moreover, as Chinese scholars have noted, merely separating the posts of Party secretary and government administrator was not enough to solve the problem of Party–government relations, if Party work departments still overlapped the government agencies and the PCGs still functioned in central ministries and provincial government bureaus.[14] Furthermore, merely dividing up the interlocking directorates not only resulted in a proliferation of Party and government posts, but also led to confusion over responsibilities and policy conflicts between the Party committee and government at the same level. This was often reflected in the personal relationship between Party secretaries and government administrators. For instance, personal relations were very tense between Rui Xingwen (Party secretary of Shanghai) and Jiang Zemin (mayor of Shanghai) in 1985–87, and subsequently between Jiang Zemin (Party secretary of Shanghai) and Zhu Rongji (mayor of Shanghai) in 1987–89.[15] What has happened in Shanghai appears to be the rule rather than the exception, for Party secretaries and mayors/governors in other cities and provinces have experienced the same problem.[16] Personal relations were reportedly tense between Li Ximing and Chen Xitong in Beijing, Tang Shaowen and Ni Bichu in Tianjin, Xing Chongzhi and Chen Weigao in Hebei, Yang Rudai and Zhao Haoruo in Sichuan, Hou Zongbin and Li Changchun in Henan, Guang Guangfu and Guo

---

[13] Nie Gaomin et al., p. 118.

[14] Ibid., p. 36.

[15] Personal interviews with officials in the organization department of the Shanghai Municipal Party Committee, January 1989.

[16] A former provincial official associated with the then Party General Secretary Zhao Ziyang confirmed the existence of the same tension in other provinces. Personal interview, Cambridge, MA, Fairbank Center for East Asian Studies, Harvard University, March 16, 1990.

Shuyan in Hubei, Deng Hongxun and Liu Jianfeng in Hainan, Wang Maolin and Hu Fuguo in Shanxi, and Sun Weiben and Shao Qihui in Heilongjiang, during their tenures in office.[17] The causes of these tensions are more likely to be structural than personal. Economic reform, administrative and fiscal decentralization have given provincial and local government administrators a much larger role to play in managing the local economy. Government administrators have become increasingly confident and assertive in exercising their respective authorities. Yet the institutionally embedded ambiguity in the Party–government relationship inevitably caused conflicts over the jurisdictions of governments and Party committees.

Zhao Ziyang's Agenda

In the summer of 1986, the issue of political reform had again become a major concern for the reformist leaders. Between July and August 1986 Deng talked about political reform several times and emphasized that the crucial aspect of political reform was to separate the Party from the government.[18] But his more conservative colleagues saw no need to hurry to reform the political system. Ironically, it took a major conservative maneuver, which unseated the reformist Party General Secretary Hu Yaobang, to prompt Deng to initiate a second round of political reform. Premier Zhao Ziyang and his associates seized the opportunity to prepare for a comprehensive political reform package to be presented to the upcoming Thirteenth Party Congress. In June 1987, Deng's 1980 reform speech was republished by the official Xinhua news agency. Whether it was Deng or Zhao's idea, this was a well calculated move to send a clear message.

High on Zhao's political reform agenda was to separate the Party from the government. On October 14, 1987, at a preparatory meeting for the Seventh Plenary Plenum of the Twelfth Central Committee, Zhao suggested that among the socialist countries, China was most seriously afflicted by the lack of separation of Party and government. This was a long-standing problem and to solve it was the "primary key to political structural reform."[19] Zhao also pointed out that since the 1950s, whether or not to accept the system of the Party's unified

---

[17] *The China Times Magazine* 203, November 19–25, 1995, p. 50.
[18] Deng Xiaoping, *Selected Works of Deng Xiaoping, (1982-1992)* (Beijing: Foreign Language Press, 1994), pp. 163, 166–7, 179.
[19] Zhao Ziyang, "On separating the party and government," The *People's Daily,* November 26, 1987, p. 1.

leadership had become the criterion for judging whether someone supported or opposed the leadership of the Party. Each time a campaign was launched, the system of a unified Party leadership was reinforced. Anticipating a strong resistance to his proposals for political reform, Zhao warned that it would be a tremendous turnaround from promoting the Party's unified leadership to stressing separation of Party and government.[20]

In his political report to the Party congress, Zhao presented his carefully crafted argument for separating the Party from the government. It was first justified by economic efficiency. Zhao argued that political reform was indispensable if economic reform were to continue and not grind to a halt.[21] This was because "China's existing political structure was born out of the war years, basically established in the period of socialist transformation and developed in the course of large-scale mass movements and incessantly intensifying mandatory planning . . . It fails to suit economic, political and cultural modernization under peacetime conditions or the development of a socialist commodity economy."[22] This was particularly so when a decentralized and market-oriented economy required flexibility, efficiency, and innovation. As the economic environment changed, the role of the Party should also change. Separation was also necessary because the "nature, functions, organizational forms, and ways of working of the party and state organs are different."[23] Zhao stressed that distinctions should be made between the functions of Party organization and those of state organs, and the relationships between the Party and people's congresses, government agencies, judicial organs, and all other non-CCP organizations should be correctly handled so that they could properly function. Zhao finally argued that the failure to separate the Party and government in the previous decades had "downgraded the party's leading position and weakened the party's leading role." The Party members allowed "their own land to go barren while tilling the land of others. "Lack of functional separation between the Party and the government also "has placed the party on the first front of administrative work, and has caused the party to become easily involved in contradictions or even become the center of contradictions."[24]

Zhao was certainly not the first one to recognize these problems. Many

[20] Jiang Huaxuan, at el., p. 756.
[21] Zhao Ziyang, "Advance Along the Road of Socialism with Chinese Characteristics," FBIS-CHI, October 26, 1987, pp. 10–34.
[22] Ibid., p. 28.
[23] Ibid., p. 24.
[24] Ibid., pp. 24–5.

government administrators had discovered the defects in the system long before Zhao did. It was only when economic development became the top priority of the Party that it became possible for Zhao to acknowledge the defects
in front of the delegates to the Party congress. The most important reform
measure proposed by Zhao was to reduce Party work departments and abolish
PCGs in state administrative agencies. Zhao stressed that the Party committee
at a given level should not "designate a full-time secretary or member of its
standing committee, who holds no government post, to take charge of government work. . . . Party departments that overlap their counterpart government
departments should be abolished, and the administrative affairs they are now
managing should be transferred to competent government departments." Zhao
further stressed that the existing system of PCGs in the government agencies
"is not conducive to unity and efficiency in government work; such groups
should therefore be gradually abolished."[25]

Since the PCGs had long been the organizational device for the Party to
control state agencies, putting an end to them would mean a major reduction in
the Party's influence in state affairs. Thus the abolition of PCGs in the central
government could not be expected to happen quickly. It was not until August 1,
1988, that the Party Organization Department formally announced that the
PCGs would gradually be abolished in the central ministries and commissions,[26] a process that was supposed to be completed by the end of 1988,
although, according to one source, by the spring of 1989, PCGs in only about a
quarter of the agencies in the State Council had been dismantled.[27] Some
provinces responded to Zhao's proposal much more enthusiastically. Newslet-
ters of Party organization departments indicated that in early 1988 several
provinces began to dismantle the PCGs in local government institutions.[28] In
January 1988, authorities in Guangdong province announced that all bureau-
level PCGs would be abolished by the end of the year.[29] Another report from
Sichuan indicated that by the end of 1988 Sichuan province had abolished
PCGs in eleven provincial government bureaus, committees, and offices, and
had plans to abolish a further twelve PCGs within a few months.

Zhao's proposals represented some fundamental changes in the Party–state
relations, and their implications were not difficult for Party officials to under-

---

[25] Ibid., p. 16.
[26] The *People's Daily,* August 1, 1988, p. 1.
[27] *Jingji baodao* 2134 (Hong Kong) (August 25, 1989), p. 8.
[28] *Zuzhi renshi xinxibao* 141 (Organization and Personnel Gazette), February 11, 1988, p. 1.
[29] *Wenhui bao* (Hong Kong), January 18, 1988.

stand. One article published a few days after the Thirteenth Party Congress reported that some Party officials believed that after the Party's functions were separated from those of the government, "there will not be anything to do," and they were "at a loss."[30] The Party secretary of Sichuan province admitted that some Party officials in his province worried that after the separation, "power will be lost" and "prestige will be lost."[31] However, after the purge of Zhao in June 1989, some of the political reform measures were halted. The decision to abolish PCGs in government agencies was revoked in mid-August 1989. Where they had been abolished they were restored.[32] Through the 1990s, therefore, the PCG system has been well entrenched in government institutions from the central ministries of the State Council down to bureaus in provincial and local governments. This has remained an unresolved issue in the Party–state relationship.

GETTING THE CENTRAL GOVERNMENT RIGHT

During the four decades of the PRC, several major institutional reforms have been implemented in order to achieve administrative efficiency. The classic challenge to any Chinese leader, Communist or otherwise, has always been how to keep a centralized administrative system efficient in such a vast and diverse country. The approaches to institutional reforms by the CCP leaders, however, are problematic and sometimes counterproductive. The frequent institutional reforms and structural changes of the highest organ of the state administrative power – the State Council – best illustrates these problems.

Since 1958, the State Council has been trapped in cycles of "reduction–expansion," which have occurred almost chronically and aborted several administrative reforms.[33] Whereas certain central ministries such as Foreign Affairs, Defense, and Public Security have to remain constant, many economic ministries and commissions have been highly unstable; minor changes occurred every year and major expansion or reduction occurred every two or three years (see Table 8.1). Most central ministries and commissions have been abolished or merged at least once, if not more (see Table 8.2).

---

[30] *Liaowang* 45 (Outlook), FBIS-CHI, November 10, 1987, p. 35.
[31] *Guangming ribao,* translated in FBIS-CHI, November 20, 1987, p. 17.
[32] *Jingji baodao* 2134 (Hong Kong), August 25,1989, p. 8.
[33] Sometimes the cycle is referred to as "swelling–simplifying–swelling again–simplifying again." Li Yichang, "An Insider's Perspective: The Development of Chinese Administrative Science," in Mills and Nagel, p. 140.

Table 8.1. *Changing size of the State Council, 1949–1994*

Year	Number of agencies	Year	Number of agencies
1949	35	1972	35
1950	36	1973	42
1951	36	1974	42
1952	42	1975	52
1953	42	1976	52
1954	64	1977	56
1955	70	1978	76
1956	81	1979	94
1957	80	1980	99
1958	68	1981	100
1959	60	1982	61
1960	61	1984	65
1961	62	1984	65
1962	64	1985	67
1963	73	1986	72
1964	77	1987	72
1965	79	1988	72
1966	78	1989	72
1967	78	1990	68
1968	78	1991	80
1969	78	1992	86
1970	32	1993	59
1971	34	1994	59

Note: The State Council was established in 1954. Its predecessor was the Government Administrative Council that existed between 1949 and 1954.

Sources: Zhongguo guoqing baogao (Report on the National Conditions of China) (Shenyang: Liaoning renmin chubanshe, 1990); *Zhonghua renmin gongheguo dang zheng jun qun lingdaoren minglu* (Directory of the Leaders of the Party, Government, Military and Mass Organizations in the People's Republic of China) (Beijing: Zhonggong dangshi chubanshe, 1990); and *China Times Business Weekly,* 1993–94.

Table 8.2. *Changes in central government ministries*

Ministry	Established	Abolished	Merged[a]	Split[b]	Reestablished
Agriculture	1949	1970	1979		
			1982		1987
Building Materials	1956		1958		
		1974			1979
			1982		
Coal Industry	1955	1970			1975
		1988			1993
Education	1949		1966		1975
			1985		
Food	1952		1970		1978
			1982		
Light Industry	1954		1956	1965	1970
				1978	
			1993		
Petroleum Industry	1955		1970	1978	
			1988		
Textile	1949		1970	1978	
		1993			
Water Resources	1949		1958	1979	
			1983	1988	

Notes:

[a]"Merged" means the ministry either absorbed, or amalgamated with, others.

[b]"Split" means the ministry was divided into two or more separate ministries or separated from the previous amalgamation.

Sources: Malcolm Lamb, *Directory of Officials and Organizations in China: A Quarter-Century Guide* (Armonk, NY: M. E. Sharpe, 1994); Zhang Tianrong, Xiao Donglian, and Wang Nianyi, eds., *Zhongguo gaige dacidian* (Grand Dictionary of Chinese Reform) (Beijing: Zhongguo guoji guangbo chubanshe, 1992).

Cycles of Reduction–Expansion

In late 1952, as China was about to launch its first Five-Year Economic Plan, the central government administration was to become more centralized and specialized, following the Soviet model of economic management.[34] Six regional governments were abolished, and Beijing exercised its direct control over the provinces. By the end of 1953, the agencies of the central government had increased to 42 from 36 in 1950. In 1954, the State Council was authorized to establish 64 agencies, which had further grown to 81 in 1956. Since 1958, however, the State Council has undergone four major waves of streamlining and reorganization. Due to these reduction–expansion cycles, the State Council frequently changes its composition.

Mao Zedong Wave of 1958–60. In 1956, Mao concluded that the power was overcentralized in the center. Following Mao's call for a two-thirds cut in the central government apparatus, the first wave of reduction in 1958–60 reduced the number of the State Council agencies (ministries, commissions, direct bureaus, and offices) from 81 in 1956 to 60 in 1959. The three "adverse years" (1960–62) of economic difficulties following the failed Great Leap Forward movement dealt another severe blow to the central administration. Within the nine months between September 1960 and June 1961, the central ministries had abolished or merged a total of 89 bureaus, a reduction by 15 percent. Between 1961 and 1963, 800,000 cadres were either transferred to lower levels or sent to do manual work in factories or countryside.[35] As the economy gradually recovered after 1963, however, centralized control of the national economy was reemphasized, particularly over economic planning, basic construction, finance, bank loans, and resource allocation. The State Council managed to restore some of the abolished agencies. By the end of 1965, shortly before the Cultural Revolution broke out, the State Council again had 79 agencies, almost back to its size in 1956 before the massive reductions started. This completed the first round of reduction–expansion.

Lin Biao Wave of 1970. During the Cultural Revolution, the State Council agencies were drastically cut under Lin Biao's order for preparing for war. The

[34] For instance, the Ministry of Heavy Industry had split into four industrial ministries: Civilian Industry, Military Industry, Construction, and Geology. Yin Jingzhi, *Jigou gaige qishilu* (Lessons of the Institutional Reforms) (Beijing: Zhongguo zhengfa daxue chubanshe, 1994), p. 4.
[35] Ibid., p. 12.

number of the central ministries, commissions, and offices was reduced from a total of 78 to only 32, of which Lin Biao's military controlled 13. The number of the central government agencies had declined to the lowest point in the history of the PRC. Lin Biao's downfall in 1971 offered Premier Zhou Enlai a golden opportunity to reverse the trend. The State Council managed to restore or regain control over forty-two agencies in 1973. After the Cultural Revolution was declared to be over in 1977, efforts were made to overcome the chaos and to restore normal economic production. Consequently, many previously abolished central administrative agencies were restored. Meanwhile, the modernization program also required new agencies to be established. By the end of 1981, the State Council had grown to a total of 100 agencies, the highest point of growth in PRC history. This completed the second round of reduction–expansion.

Deng Xiaoping Wave of 1982. As the central administrative agencies expanded, the new paramount leader Deng Xiaoping came to the conclusion that the government bureaucracy had grown too large. He stressed that the situation of the "present over-staffed and overlapping party and state organizations" should not continue and that "streamlining organizations constitutes a revolution."[36] The CCP's Twelfth Party Congress endorsed Deng's diagnosis and decided to streamline the State Council again. In 1982, the number of the State Council agencies was reduced from 100 to 61 and the number of central ministers, commissioners, and directors was reduced from 540 to 180.[37] Yet, within a year or two, the State Council began to expand again. By 1986, it had expanded to a total of 72 agencies, thus completing the third round of the reduction–expansion.

Zhao Ziyang Wave of 1988. After the Thirteenth Party Congress in October 1987, new Party General Secretary Zhao Ziyang initiated yet another round of administrative reform. Following the principle of fixing establishment, personnel, and ranks of agencies, Zhao sought to use legal and budgetary measures to control the government administration. Also, the State Council was asked to shift its main economic responsibility from direct management of economic enterprises to macro supervision and regulation.[38] This administrative reform

---

[36] Deng Xiaoping, "Streamlining Organizations Constitutes a Revolution" in Deng Xiaoping, 1984, p. 374.

[37] Yin Jingzhi, p. 22.

[38] Zhao Ziyang, "Advance Along the Road of Socialism with Chinese Characteristics," p. 26.

reportedly shrank the State Council employees by one-fifth, abolished 20 percent of the administrative bureaus and ad hoc committees, and reduced the agencies of the State Council from 76 to 66.[39] After 1989, however, the State Council agencies expanded again, and by 1992, the agencies of the State Council had grown to 86. This completed the fourth round of the reduction–expansion.

Zhu Rongji Wave of 1993. After Deng's southern China tour in 1992, the central economic czar Zhu Rongji, who was in charge of economy, trade, finance, and economic restructuring, decided to streamline the central government agencies again. The official publications explained that the principal goals of this structural streamlining were to "change functions, straighten relationships, obtain better staff and simpler administration, and raise efficiency."[40] The focus was to strengthen coordination and supervision functions and reduce direct economic management responsibilities of the central government. According to the final reform package approved by the Eighth NPC in 1993, seven central ministries were abolished. Some of their responsibilities have been taken over by newly organized general associations under the State Council, such as the General Association of Light Industry and the General Association of Textiles. Six central ministries or commissions were reorganized and a number of administrative bureaus were downgraded in their status. The size of the State Council was reduced from 86 to 59.[41] According to Chen Jinhua, Minister of the State Planning Commission, one major task of the streamlining was to reduce the government work force by about 25 percent.[42] Out of more than 9.2 million cadres working in the central government agencies, this meant 2.3 million people would have to change their jobs.[43] Despite these efforts, whether this new round of administrative reform can break the reduction–expansion cycle remains uncertain.

---

[39] Yin Jingzhi, p. 32.

[40] *Zhongguo jingji tizhi gaige* (April 1993), p. 8.

[41] *Zhongyang zhengfu zuzhi jigou* (The Organization of the Central Government), eds., by the Bureau of Secretarial Work of the General Office of the State Council and the Bureau of Comprehensive Work of the Central Establishment Commission (Beijing: Zhongguo fazhang chubanshe, 1995), pp. 15–18.

[42] Ibid., p. 6.

[43] Ibid., p. 137.

Causes of the Reduction–Expansion Cycles

The restructuring of the central government was often due to the attempts by a new leader of the State Council in order to consolidate his power base and minimize the institutional authority of his potential opponents. As the experience of administrative reform in other countries tells us, organizational streamlining is a political process and China is no exception. The expansion part of the cycle may be explained by the natural tendency of government bureaucracy to seek larger budgets, expand its establishments, and acquire more responsibilities. Given the primitive nature of the Chinese state institutions, launching new programs would also make it necessary to set up certain government agencies. Furthermore, because there was no basic division of power nor clear definition of responsibilities, tensions and deadlock between government agencies often forced the State Council leaders to set up intermediate, ad hoc committees to handle disputes.

Major reductions were often initiated because the paramount Party leader so demanded during decentralization and antibureaucracy campaigns. No one, of course, dared to question whether the paramount leader's order was reasonable or practicable; nor could anyone adventure asking how the paramount leader had reached his conclusion. Inevitably, the process became arbitrary and the central government agencies frequently changed according to the will of the paramount leader. For one more example, in December 1981, the State Council established fourteen administrative bureaus under its direct control. Eight months later, during the Deng Xiaoping wave, all of these bureaus were either abolished or merged.

Furthermore, the cycle of reduction–expansion reflects a lack of regularization and institutionalization. During several reduction and streamlining campaigns, the main focus was on numerical reduction of the administrative agencies and employees. There was no economic or budgetary basis for deciding how many agencies should be cut or what size would be appropriate. When the government agencies needed to expand, there was no specific legislative authorization nor strict budgetary controls. In 1988, legal and budgetary measures were introduced by Zhao Ziyang, but they were soon disrupted after the purge of Zhao in June 1989. The 1993 administrative reform had fixed the number of bureaus and number of employees for each ministry and commission of the State Council. It holds out a promise, but no guarantee that the unstable State Council will finally stabilize.

PARTY, BUREAUCRACY, AND CIVIL SERVICE

China's problem of governance in a changing society is exacerbated by the fact that the Party organization that has controlled China for decades has been losing its effectiveness. Frequent efforts to get the central government right during the past sixteen years have reflected an emerging sense of urgency. Whereas Mao relied on the Party organization during the Great Leap Forward movement and the military during the Cultural Revolution, the reformers in the 1980s and 1990s have to rely more on the government administration because the problems generated by market reform and economic development are beyond the capabilities of the Party, whose ideological and organizational control has greatly eroded.

First, the Party's organizational growth has reached a crisis point. Because China has been facing a serious problem of population explosion,[44] the CCP also suffered from a problem of membership expansion. Since the end of the Cultural Revolution, more than 20 million more members have been added to the Party.[45] As the Party grew larger and larger, managing the Party organization became increasingly difficult. In the early 1970s, Chalmers Johnson pointed to the organizational constraints on the CCP caused by the sheer size of the country and its population. "The Chinese Communist Party is itself the world's largest Communist Party, but its effective party-to-population ratio is smaller than that of all but one other established Communist system (Cuba)."[46] In the 1980s and 1990s, this organizational problem has only worsened. On the one hand, the CCP membership accounts for only 4.3 percent of China's total population, which represents the lowest party-to-population ratio among all the major Communist parties in the world.[47] The Party is too small a political force to control the Chinese population effectively, especially when the Communist

[44] The Chinese population increased by roughly 15 million each year in the recent decade.

[45] During the reform period of 1978–90, the annual rate of recruitment was 2.8 percent, but this low percentage translates into an average of 1.1 million new members each year. See Appendix A in this book.

[46] Chalmers Johnson, "The Changing Nature and Locus of Authority in Communist China," in John M. H. Lindbeck, ed., *China: Management of a Revolutionary Society* (Seattle: University of Washington Press, 1971), p. 47.

[47] The party-to-population ratio in thirteen Communist countries in 1988 was as follows: Romania (16.1), East Germany (14.0), North Korea (11.4), Czechoslovakia (10.9), Bulgaria (10.4), Yugoslavia (8.8), Hungary (7.7), USSR (6.8), Poland (5.8), Cuba (4.8), Albania (4.7), China (4.3), and Mongolia (4.3). Richard F. Starr, ed., *Yearbook of International Communist Affairs 1989* (Stanford, CA: Hoover Institution Press, 1989).

regimes with higher party-to-population ratios had all collapsed (except in North Korea and Cuba) by the early 1990s. On the other hand, the sheer size of the CCP already makes it hopeless as an efficient and effective political organization. With a 57 million membership that is still growing, the CCP has become organizationally unmanageable.

Second, the problem of growing membership has been aggravated by the fact that the Party has lost its organizational purpose. If the state constitution provided the general political framework, people's congresses made the laws, the legal apparatus maintained law and order, and the State Council and provincial governments ran the country, what was left for the Party to do? What role or function was there for the Party to perform that the state institutions could not do?

In a booming economy with huge opportunities for profiteering created by piecemeal or partial reforms, a ruling party that had a bankrupt ideology, poor discipline, and no organizational purpose inevitably became a party of corruption.[48] For instance, between 1983 and 1987, the Party expelled 150,000 members for corruption and disciplined a further 500,000.[49] In December 1988, the authorities announced that, during the first eight months of the year they had investigated 11,000 cases of corruption.[50] In 1989, 32,000 members were expelled from the Party, 99,000 were disqualified, and 22,000 gave up their memberships voluntarily.[51] In the anticorruption campaign of 1990–92, 707,000 cases were investigated, and more than 600,000 Party cadres were punished, including 16,005 cadres above the rank of county magistrate.[52] Between September 1993 and June 1995, 244,913 cases were investigated, and 237,627 individuals were punished, including 35 cadres at the rank of minister/

---

[48] Corruption and official profiteering was one of the primary causes of massive protests in Tiananmen Square during April–June 1989. For some handbills that reflect the anger of the populace, see Han Minzhu, *Cries for Democracy: Writings and Speeches From the 1989 Chinese Democracy Movement* (Princeton, NJ: Princeton University Press, 1990), pp. 28–31. For some documented evidence of escalating corruption, see Xiaoxia Gong, ed., "Corruption and Abuses of Power During the Reform Era" in *Chinese Sociology and Anthropology* 26, no. 2 (Winter 1993–1994) (Armonk, NY: M. E. Sharpe). For analyses of the Chinese corruption problem, see Nan-shong Lee, *Bureaucratic Corruption During the Deng Xiaoping Era* (Hong Kong: Chinese University of Hong Kong, 1991); Ting Gong, *The Politics of Corruption in Contemporary China: An Analysis of Policy Outcomes* (New York: Praeger Publishers, 1994).

[49] Xinhua, August 11, 1988, in FBIS-CHI, August 11, 1988, p. 18.

[50] *Wenhui bao* (Hong Kong), December 26, 1988.

[51] The *People's Daily* (Overseas Edition), June 28, 1990. The 1989 figure should include those Party members who participated in the Tiananmen Square demonstration and were subsequently disciplined.

[52] *Zhongguo jingji tizhi gaige* (September 1993), p. 20.

208

provincial governor, 546 cadres at the rank of bureau chief, and 6,582 at the rank of county magistrate/division chief.[53] In April 1995, Wang Baosen, Deputy Mayor of Beijing, committed suicide as he was about to be charged with embezzling more than 3 billion Chinese yuan (about 37 million dollars). Wang's patron, Chen Xitong, Beijing Party boss and a member of the CCP Politburo, was forced to resign. In September 1995, Chen became the first Politburo member and the highest ranking Party official ever ousted for corruption in the history of the PRC. Although serious warnings against corruption are repeated almost every day in the official newspaper, corruption in China seems to have continued unabated. The reason is that the widespread and epidemic official corruption in China is structural rather than personal. It reflects the hard truth that a political party that has ruled China for decades now has no way to control its members, no ability to discipline its cadre corps, and no vision to inspire the people.

Chinese Bureaucracy in Question

Although the Party cadres have recently become synonymous with corruption or incompetence, the government bureaucracy has long been condemned. From the CCP elite in the Zhongnanhai compound to ordinary people in the streets, everyone seems to hate the bureaucracy. Conservatives and reformers alike, the Chinese leaders in both the Mao era and Deng era agreed on one thing: The government is too big and too bureaucratic. During the Mao era, various methods were adopted to deal with the so-called bureaucratism, ranging from attempts at rationalization and control to mass campaigns, Party rectification, and purges.[54] Antibureaucracy continued to constitute an important ingredient of Deng's reform agenda. In his 1980 speech on reforming the Party and state systems, Deng summarized the defects of Chinese bureaucracy into five categories: bureaucratism, overconcentration of power, paternalism, life tenure, and the existence of all forms of special privileges. These resulted in chronic problems such as the abuse of power, inefficiency, overstaffing, redundancy of organizations, corruption and irresponsibility.[55]

Who are the "notorious" Chinese bureaucrats? Table 8.3 presents information about the cadre corps in sixteen ministries and commissions of the State

---

[53] The *People's Daily,* January 2, 1996.
[54] Harry Harding, *Organizing China: The Problem of Bureaucracy, 1949–1976* (Stanford, CA: Stanford University Press, 1981), pp. 327–59.
[55] Deng Xiaoping, 1984, pp. 309–17.

Table 8.3. *Types of cadres in State Council ministries and commissions,*
1987

Agency	Total no. of cadres	Party (%)	Administrative (%)	Technical (%)	Service (%)
Foreign Affairs	2,290	3.1	33.3	63.6	–
Foreign Trade	1,970	2.8	14.3	76.0	6.8
Agriculture	1,709	4.0	22.0	55.0	19.0
Public Security	1,393	4.4	9.2	71.4	15.0
Communications	1,206	6.5	13.0	66.5	14.0
Finance	1,191	4.3	12.3	80.0	2.8
Planning	1,125	2.9	10.1	86.9	–
Culture	1,015	7.0	53.2	32.0	7.0
Water Conservancy	907	6.6	23.5	61.4	5.8
Space Industry	732	6.7	26.0	51.9	15.2
Labor & Personnel	681	3.0	27.0	66.6	3.4
Petroleum Industry	602	8.5	17.3	67.1	7.1
Civil Affairs	441	3.3	17.0	71.2	8.5
Justice	427	3.5	28.3	57.6	28.3
Science & Technology	389	3.3	68.3	28.3	–
Nationalities Affairs	168	11.0	26.0	52.0	5.0

Source: Compiled by the author from information in the reform proposals of these agencies, in Wu Peilun, ed., *Woguo de zhengfu jigou gaige* (The Government Institutional Reform in Our Country) (Beijing: Jingji ribao chubanshe, 1990).

Council. "Party" cadre here refers to Party officials and functionaries. They are specially assigned to manage the Party organization and affiliated mass organizations in the government agencies, and they generally do not hold government posts. The size of this "nongovernmental part" of the government ranged from 2.8 percent (the Ministry of Foreign Trade) to 11 percent (the State Nationalities Affairs Commission). "Administrative" cadre refers to ministers and commissioners, and bureau and division chiefs below them. "Technical" cadre refers to specialists and experts hired for their special skills. As Deng was pushing for administrative efficiency, the size of this group should have presumably been enlarged. Ironically, the Ministry of Culture and the State Science and Technology Commission had the lowest percentage of technical cadres.[56] "Service" cadre refers to those in charge of logistical supplies. Over

[56] Wu Peilun, ed., *Woguo de zhengfu jigou gaige* (The Government Institutional Reform in Our

210

the decades, Chinese government agencies had developed a tendency toward what was called "big and complete" or even "small but complete." This meant that each government agency attempted to become supplies-independent by seeking control of as many resources as possible. This was partly due to scarcity of resources, but more because the Chinese distribution system was distinguished by vertical control at the center (through each ministry) and horizontal control at the provinces (through provincial Party committees). Thus rear service became an important task of each government agency. Many government agencies have their own dining halls, kindergartens, clinics, and transportation services. Some even have their own shops, schools, and construction companies. The percentage of rear service cadres ranged from 2.8 percent (the Ministry of Finance) to 28.3 percent (the Ministry of Justice). About one-fourth of the total employees of the State Council worked for the rear service.[57]

Is the Chinese bureaucracy too big? This simple question deserves no simple answers. In 1951 there were 3.85 million cadres in China;[58] by 1979 the overall size of the cadres had reached 17 million;[59] and by 1988 it had reached 27 million.[60] Judging by these numbers, we can easily conclude that the Chinese bureaucracy has grown too big and too fast. On the other hand, is the Ministry of Foreign Affairs of 2,291 people (including Party cadres and service cadres), the Ministry of Foreign Trade of 1,970 people, or the Ministry of Justice of 427 people too big for a country of 1.2 billion people? It is perhaps fair to say that the Chinese government is overstaffed in certain areas and understaffed in others. What the numbers in Table 8.3 also tell us is that if the central bureaucracy is deemed too big and inefficient, then the real focus should be on improving the service sector and reducing the officials exclusively engaged in Party and mass organization work in the central government.

It is important to note that the numbers about the overall size of the Chinese bureaucracy can be deceiving. For instance, the 17 million cadres in 1979 included 5 million Party and government officials, 4 million cadres of economic management, and 3 million elementary and high school teachers.[61] A

Country) (Beijing: Jingji ribao chubanshe, 1990), p. 55.

[57] Ibid.

[58] Among them, there were 1 million military cadres and 1.1 million cultural and educational cadres. *China's Labor and Personnel Yearbook, 1949–10, 1987,* p. 1,421.

[59] Jiang Huaxuan et al, p. 633.

[60] Hong Yung Lee, "China's New Bureaucracy?" in Arthur Lewis Rosenbaum, ed., *State and Society in China: The Consequences of Reform* (Boulder, CO: Westview Press, 1992), p. 60.

[61] Jiang Huaxuan et al., p. 633.

Table 8.4. *Distribution of cadres in China, 1987*

Category	Number	Percentage
Government administration	4,000,000	14.81%
Legislative/judicial branches	350,000	1.30
Service units[a]	10,800,000	40.00
Economic enterprises	10,300,000	38.15
Others (parties, mass organizations,[b] etc.)	1,550,000	5.74
Total	27,000,000	100.00

Note: [a]Service units include those of education, public health, science and technology. [b]Mass organizations include trade unions, youth leagues, and women's federation.
Source: Xinhua News Agency, November 18, 1987, in FBIS-China (November 18, 1987), pp. 17–18.

close look at the distribution of the cadres in 1987 further suggests that a sweeping condemnation of the Chinese bureaucracy for being too big is hardly justified. As Table 8.4 indicates, cadres working in institutions of education, health, culture, science and technology and economic enterprises comprised 78.15 percent of the total of 27 million Chinese cadres in 1987. This was the result of many years of a highly centralized planning economy. As China continued to implement economic reform and decentralization of authority to social and economic units, this portion of the bureaucracy was expected to be reduced. Having 5.74 percent of all cadres in Party and mass organizations meant 1.55 million people. Is that number too big and should it be cut? Cadres in government administration, legislative, and judicial institutions together comprised only 16.11 percent of the total number of the Chinese cadres. An administrative and judicial bureaucracy of 4.35 million people for a big country like China would seem anything but too big. Indeed, a legislative and judicial cadre corps of 350,000 was too small and needed to be expanded.

Establishing a State Civil Service

Reforming the government bureaucracy through the establishment of a state civil service constituted the core of Deng's administrative reform program in 1987–88. This was based on several factors. First, since the early 1980s, China has undergone a massive generational change of leadership. As Hong Yung Lee points out, the drive for economic modernization has led to a major

212

replacement of old revolutionary cadres by younger technocrats.[62] By the end of 1986, 1.37 million old cadres who joined the CCP before 1949 had officially retired. Meanwhile, during 1982–87, 550,000 younger and middle-aged cadres assumed the leading positions at the county level and above.[63] Second, the old cadre management system, which dated back to the pre-1949 revolutionary years, was no longer functioning in a new environment. Old criteria and methods for recruitment, appointment, evaluation, promotion, transfer, or removal were nonproductive and in many cases obstructive to reform programs.[64] Third, facing the declining ability of the Party organization to control and rising social and economic problems, the Chinese leaders hoped that an efficient and effective administrative state staffed by competent civil servants might provide the answer.[65]

At the Thirteenth Party Congress in 1987, Zhao Ziyang announced that a state civil service system would be introduced, under which cadres working in government agencies would be divided into two categories: "political civil servants," who were elected for fixed terms of office by people's congress on the recommendation of the Party, and "professional civil servants," who were openly recruited through competitive examinations to permanent positions in government agencies.[66] In 1988, there were 27 million cadres in government, Party and mass organizations, economic enterprises, education, and research institutions. The new civil service system would be applied to 4.2 million cadres working in government agencies, including 500,000 at central and provincial government levels.[67] Zhao also announced that a separate state agency of personnel management – the Ministry of Personnel – would be established to implement the state civil service system. In June 1988, the

[62] Hong Yung Lee, *From Revolutionary Cadres to Party Technocrats in Socialist China* (Berkeley: University of California Press, 1991).

[63] *Zuzhi renshi xinxibao* 180 (November 10, 1988), p. 1.

[64] For the study of the Chinese cadre system in Mao's China, see A. Doak Barnett, *Cadres, Bureaucracy, and Political Power in Communist China* (New York: Columbia University Press, 1967); for changes in post-Mao China, see Cao Zhi, *Zhonghua renmin gongheguo renshi zhidu gangyao* (Outline of the Personnel System of the People's Republic of China) (Beijing: Beijing daxue chubanshe, 1985); Melanie Manion, "The Cadre Management System, Post-Mao: The Appointment, Promotion, Transfer, and Removal of Party and State Leaders," *The China Quarterly* 102 (June 1985), pp. 203–33; and Hong Yung Lee, 1991.

[65] Gu Yunchang, "China to Gradually Implement the Civil Service System," FBIS-CHI, November 24, 1987, pp. 25–9.

[66] FBIS-CHI, October 26, 1987, p. 26.

[67] *Zuzhi renshi xinxibao* 196 (March 2, 1989), p. 1.

Provisional Regulations of State Civil Servants (the fifteenth draft) was adopted to provide a legal basis for constructing the new system.[68]

To establish a state civil service system in China, the major political obstacle is the issue of Party leadership.[69] Zhao Ziyang's political reform package called for a major redefinition of the Party and state relationship, including the authority of cadre control and management. However, after Zhao was purged in June 1989, his successors were much less committed to having a clear division of labor between the Party and state over the control of government administrators. The idea that civil servants only serve the state, not any political party, is fundamentally contradictory to the idea of Party leadership. After the collapse of the Communist regimes in Eastern Europe and the Soviet Union, the last thing that the CCP leaders wanted was the emergence of an independent organizational force, military or civilian. Although a competent government civil service was essential to the modernization programs, it could also become an alternative force for reorganizing China. Thus, the process of establishing a state civil service system proceeded at a snail's pace. Four years after Zhao Ziyang made the proposal at the Thirteenth Party Congress, one deputy Minister of Personnel announced in October 1991 that a primitive civil service system would be established in the central and provincial governments in five or more years.[70] In late September 1994, the Xinhua News Agency reported that 462 civil servants below the level of division chief would be recruited for twenty-six agencies in the central government.[71] At this pace, it is quite an optimistic view that a new civil service system in China will be established before the end of this century.[72]

The slow pace of establishing a government service contrasts sharply with the fast changes in the Chinese economy and society. Market reform and China's integration with the global economy has opened many channels of opportunity for the best and brightest in China. Government jobs with lower salaries were no longer among the most attractive careers. In terms of net

---

[68] For the English translation of the Civil Service Regulations, see John P. Burns and Jean-Pierre Cabestan, eds., "Provisional Chinese Civil Service Regulations," *Chinese Law and Government* 23, no. 4 (Winter 1990–91).

[69] For some of the problems in establishing a civil service reform in China, see Thomas G. McCarthy, "Rebirth of Civil Service in China," *Bureaucrat* 18, no. 2 (Summer 1989), pp. 24–6; and Li Weiqiang, "Reform in the Chinese Public Personnel System," *Public Personnel Management* 19 (Summer 1990), pp. 163–74.

[70] The *People's Daily* (Overseas Edition), October 12, 1991.

[71] The *China Press,* August 1, 1994.

[72] The last civil service system in China was abolished at the beginning of this century (1905).

income from fixed salaries, government administrative cadres, who were the highest paid of all occupation groups in the mid-1950s, have been among the losers during the reform. Of eleven major occupation groups that employed administrative cadres, the income of those employed in government during the mid-1980s ranked no higher than ninth place. Survey data from Beijing indicate that administrative cadres in enterprises earn from 22 percent to 28 percent more than those working in government, a disparity that is even higher in Shanghai.[73] It is not surprising, therefore, that many government workers have simply resigned from their government jobs to pursue business opportunities, which is called "jumping into the sea," or have taken on a second job as consultants for a fee to supplement their meager income.[74] Less honest but powerful ones have indulged themselves in all kinds of corruption, ranging from bribery, embezzlement, profiting for personal interest with public power, eating at public expense, extravagance and waste. Frequent anticorruption campaigns have so far achieved only modest progress. How to recruit and keep a large number of competent and disciplined administrators in government service remains one of the most daunting challenges for the Chinese leaders.

CHANGING CENTRAL–PROVINCIAL RELATIONS

In 1920, a young man argued:

> The foundation of a big country is its small localities. Without first constructing small localities, there is no way to build a big country. . . . Big organizations are ultimately hopeless; small organizations offer boundless hope. The people of Hunan are truly capable and talented. Let us dare to build a Republic of Hunan that shines like the rising sun. Break down the foundationless big China and build up many small Chinas "starting with Hunan."[75]

An elder Mao Zedong, however, did not faithfully practice what a younger Mao had preached. The central–local relations in the Mao era were plagued with cycles of "centralization–decentralization–recentralization." Mao's successors, however, seemed to have understood a young Mao's logic better, and

[73] Zhang Wei, "Thought Concerning the Wages of Office Cadres," *World Economic Herald,* June 27, 1988, in FBIS-CHI, July 15, 1988, p. 40.
[74] *Ganbu renshi yuebao* (Cadre and Personnel Monthly) (September 1993), pp. 18–19.
[75] Stuart R. Schram, ed., *Mao's Road to Power: Revolutionary Writings, 1912–1949,* vol. 1, *The Pre-Marxist Period, 1912–1920* (Armonk, NY: M. E. Sharpe, 1992), pp. 546–7.

the post-Mao economic reform has placed at its core policies of decentralization to promote local economy and regional development.

Decentralization in the 1980s

The CCP's decentralization policies can be broadly grouped as fiscal and administrative.[76] Fiscal decentralization began in 1980, which permitted each provincial government to negotiate revenue-sharing contracts with the central government and to retain profits above the contracted amount for local purposes. Known as "eating in separate kitchens," this fiscal reform was aimed at making provinces financially self-sufficient. Revenue-sharing formulas would have been insignificant to provinces if they had not been granted administrative authority and autonomy in revenue-generating management. Economic reform, particularly the urban reform since 1984, has shifted considerable control over imports and exports, foreign investment, resource allocation, bank credit, local industry, and enterprise from the Party organization and central government to local governments, which have now become "primary economic agents" for their own investment and production.

Provinces in the coastal regions have particularly benefited from these reforms. In 1979, four Special Economic Zones were set up in Guangdong and Fujian provinces, which have enjoyed customs exemptions and preferential policy treatment to attract foreign capital, advanced technology, and equipment.[77] In 1984, fourteen port cities were given preferential tax status to attract foreign business and investment. In early 1988, a Coastal Regional Economic Development Strategy was adopted, which was aimed at turning some 284 cities and counties in some fourteen coastal provinces into export zones.[78] Provincial and local governments in these areas were given greater authority in investment and resource-allocation decisions.

Consequences of Decentralization

While the decentralization policies won political support for Deng's reform, boosted the local economy, particularly in the coastal areas, and sustained an average growth rate of 9 percent for the past sixteen years, they have also

---

[76] Susan L. Shirk, *The Political Logic of Economic Reform in China* (Berkeley: University of California Press, 1993), chap. 9, pp. 149–96.

[77] James C. F. Wang, *Contemporary Chinese Politics: An Introduction,* 5th edition (Englewood Cliffs, NJ: Prentice Hall, 1995), p. 310.

[78] Ibid., p. 147.

produced serious consequences for the center. First is the declining central revenue. As Christine Wong points out, the central government budget share of national income decreased from 35.3 percent in 1980 when the decentralization began to 24.7 percent in 1989.[79] So far as its revenue is concerned, the central government is the loser in the economic reform. Despite rapid economic growth, the revenue base of the central government has shrunk and Beijing's economic capacity has declined.

Second is the weakening macroeconomic control. Fiscal and administrative decentralization gave local officials strong incentives to accelerate local industrial growth, sometimes ignoring the repeated warnings from the central government about an overheated economy. This often created serious problems of inflation, shortage of materials and energy, budget deficit, excessive investment, land and real estate speculation, price-gouging competition for export markets, and chaotic bidding wars for foreign investors. Because provincial officials could use some extrabudgetary sources of capital – including users' fees and ad hoc levies imposed on consumers and local enterprises, foreign loans and credits, and bond issuance to finance economic growth – the austerity policy and antiinflationary measures of the central government often achieved only limited results.[80]

Third is the rising local protectionism. While competing with each other, provinces often use various administrative means to protect their revenue-generating industries and local market. This has not only segmented the national market, but also led to an outbreak of interprovincial or interregional trade wars over silkworms, wool, tea, tobacco, coal, cotton, pigs, and grain.[81] In some instances, trade blockades were erected by local authorities to prevent or curtail incoming goods desired by local consumers.[82]

---

[79] Christine P. W. Wong, "Central–Local Relations in an Era of Fiscal Decline: The Paradox of Fiscal Decentralization in Post-Mao China," *The China Quarterly* 128 (December 1991), pp. 691–2.

[80] Jia Hao and Lin Zhimin, eds., *Changing Central–Local Relations in China: Reform and State Capacity* (Boulder, CO: Westview Press, 1994), p. 97. In 1992, the municipal government of Shanghai with its largest stock market in China was able to raise more than 20 billion Chinese Yuan of funds for local projects through stocks and bonds issuance, far more than its revenue income of 16.5 billion in the same year. *Liberation Daily,* December 16, 1992, quoted in Jia Hao and Lin Zhimin, p. 5.

[81] Chen Kang, "The Failure of Recentralization in China: Interplay Among Enterprises, Local Governments, and the Center," in Arye L. Hillman, ed., *Markets and Politicians: Politicized Economic Choice* (Holland: Kluwer Academic Publishers, 1991), pp. 109–229.

[82] Jia Hao and Lin Zhimin, pp. 107, 126.

Fourth, fiscal decentralization has gradually transformed a hierarchical relationship between the central and provincial governments into an equal partnership, or a bargaining relationship. Administrative decentralization has devolved decision-making power on a wide array of economic activities from central to provincial and local authorities. As a result, provincial government officials are better positioned to pursue their local interests, sometimes at the expense of the center. Negotiation of revenue-sharing contracts often turned into a process of arm-twisting, and any adjustment to the fixed contracts asked by the center meant a tough bargaining battle with the province concerned.[83]

Negotiation was not easy; recentralization of power was even more difficult. After the 1989 Tiananmen crackdown, the hard-liners in the center attempted to recentralize some of the decentralized authority. However, provincial governors who were called to Beijing to discuss the Eighth Five-Year Plan demanded there be no reversal of the decentralization reforms.[84] During the recent debate about tax reform, provincial officials insisted that further decentralization would lead to more reforms despite the fact that central leaders argued that only recentralization could ensure the deepening of the reform.[85]

As a further reminder of the history of localism, outside influences and interests also join the Chinese center–local conflicts. Whereas foreign and not so foreign (Hong Kong and Taiwan) businessmen and investors find in local officials much greater enthusiasm for making deals, local officials see incoming foreign investment to their areas as a valuable bargaining chip in negotiation with Beijing. Such emerging regional economies as Guangdong–Hong Kong, Fujian–Taiwan, Shanghai–Japan, and Shandong–South Korea links only exacerbate the headache of the central leaders.[86]

---

[83] No one knew the pains better than Vice Premier Zhu Rongji, who had to be engaged in rounds and rounds of negotiation with provincial officials over the issue of tax reform. In a speech at Qinghua University in July 1993, Zhu claimed that he had lost more than ten pounds by going down to negotiate with local officials from one province to another. *China Times Business Weekly* 157 (January 1–7, 1995), p. 8.

[84] Jia Hao and Lin Zhimin, p. 159.

[85] *China Times Business Weekly* 157 (January 1–7, 1995), p. 8.

[86] On the subject of Chinese regional economic integration with the outside world, see Gerald Segal, "The Middle Kingdom? China's Changing Shape," *Foreign Affairs* 73, no. 3 (May/June 1994), pp. 43–58; David Shambaugh, ed., *Greater China: The Next Superpower?* (New York: Oxford University Press, 1994); Thomas P. Lyons and Victor Nee, eds., *The Economic Transformation of South China: Reform and Development in the Post-Mao Era* (Ithaca, NY: East Asia Program, Cornell University, 1994); Reginald Yin-Wang Kwok and Alvin Y. So, eds., *The Hong Kong–Guangdong Link: Partnership in Flux* (Armonk, NY: M. E. Sharpe, 1996); and Murray Weidenbaum and Samuel Hughes, *The Bamboo Network: How Expatriate Chinese*

Changing Party–Government Relations

To be sure, Deng had no intention to "break down the foundationless big China and build up many small Chinas," but the consequences of the decentralization remind one of a centralized empire breaking up into many small kingdoms. The fiscal and administrative decentralization seems to have "uplifted" the central government into the status of a United Nations and the center has to negotiate with 30 quasi-sovereign province-states constantly. Moreover, the membership keeps growing. From 1983 to 1991, the center extended provincial-level economic authority to fourteen so-called central cities; more cities are demanding similar status with special economic authorities.[87]

Playing into the Hands of the Provinces

Susan Shirk suggests that by decentralization, the reformers in the 1980s adopted a strategy of "playing to the provinces" pioneered by Mao Zedong in the Great Leap Forward movement. "Mao sought to overcome the resistance of stodgy central bureaucrats to his vision of accelerated growth and revolutionary collectivism and egalitarianism by appealing to provincial officials and building up their power within the Central Committee." Similarly, Deng and his allies gave power and money to the provinces to build up support for economic reform.[88]

However, as I have argued in Chapter 4, the decentralization in 1958–60 was not a transfer of power from the central bureaucracies to local governments or economic enterprises, but to provincial Party committees. Centralization or decentralization, the Party leadership was not weakened; it was the power of the central administrators that had been drifting into the hands of provincial Party committees. Because of this, Mao could boast to Field Marshal Montgomery that when there was too much centralization, he decentralized the power; and when there was too much decentralization, he centralized the power. By maintaining the Party's organizational control, the initiative to launch campaigns against localism, and political purges, Mao could play to the provinces without worrying too much about losing control.

It was a different ball game in the Deng era. First, the decentralization was a transfer of power vertically from the center to the provinces and horizontally from the Party committees to provincial governments. The fiscal and admin-

Entrepreneurs Are Creating a New Economic Superpower in Asia (New York: The Free Press, 1996).

[87] Shirk, p. 180.
[88] Ibid., pp. 150–1.

istrative authorities of both central ministries and provincial Party committees have been drifting into the hands of provincial governments. As a result, provincial Party committees no longer have as much power to control the local economy. Second, launching political campaigns to curtail the rising localism is no longer in the cards. Recentralization through Mao-style antilocalism campaigns only serves to jeopardize economic development.[89] Since economic growth (at a fast rate) and an open-door policy had been the cornerstones of Deng's reforms, whatever the center intended to do must not contradict these two goals. Beijing would be foolish to kill the goose (the coastal provinces and their connections with the outside world) that lays the golden eggs. This gave the localities an overall protection for seeking more autonomy and independence in the name of promoting the local economy and attracting more foreign investment. Under these circumstances, playing to the provinces was actually playing into the hands of the provinces.

Beijing's Tools of Control

While the Mao-style method of managing the center–local relations – oscillations between centralization and decentralization through Party organizational control and mass campaigns – is no longer relevant, the leaders in Beijing are at a loss about what can be put in place to maintain a balance between the need for central control and economic dynamism in localities. Not surprisingly, while mobilizing the official news media to emphasize the need for strengthening the central authority,[90] the leaders in Beijing often resorted to the last organizational tool that the Party center still has, namely, the centrally controlled nomenklatura system, especially by reshuffling provincial leaders.[91]

Exchange of officials as a method of control was not a new invention. The imperial rulers and Mao had often used this method to prevent local officials from plotting an opposition to the center.[92] In recent years, however, exchange

---

[89] In fact, one may even wonder whether the center is capable of launching such campaigns nowadays.

[90] See The *People's Daily* commentator's article, "Zijue weihu zhongyang de quanwei" (conscientiously safeguard the central authority), The *People's Daily,* November 29, 1994, p. 1.

[91] John P. Burns, ed., *The Chinese Communist Party's Nomenklatura System: A Documentary Study of Party Control of Leadership Selection, 1979–1984* (Armonk, NY: M. E. Sharpe, 1989).

[92] In the early 1960s, the CCP established a regular exchange system of Party and government officials aimed at preventing localism and factionalism. In September 1962, the Tenth Plenum

or rotation of central and provincial leaders has become unusually frequent. For instance, between 1990 and 1994, fourteen provincial governors and Party secretaries were asked to go to Beijing to take up posts in the central ministries. In 1993, five ministers (or vice ministers) were sent down to provinces to be governors or Party secretaries. Also during 1990–94, seventeen provinces had new leaders (governors, Party secretaries, or standing committee chairs of the provincial people's congresses) who were transferred from another province (see Table 8.5). It should be pointed out that not all the transfers were aimed at consolidating the central control over the localities. Personnel changes can be explained by many other factors. Nevertheless, it was no coincidence that frequent transfers occurred as the center–provincial conflicts intensified.

Frequent transfers of Party and government officials across regions and between Beijing and the provinces may help break regionalism and local protectionism. However, given the changing nature of center–local relations, one has to wonder whether the traditional control method of nomenklatura could solve the conflicts. The central leaders hope that they can reap a larger share of the golden eggs, but frequent transfer of the goose herders is unlikely to achieve that goal. Moving provincial governors around is particularly troublesome, for they are supposedly removable only by the provincial people's congress that elect them in the first place. Legally, provincial people's congresses could (and perhaps do) question and challenge the Party center's choice of their governors.

A huge and diverse country like China ultimately cannot be governed the way it used to be, particularly when China's social, economic, and international environment has been changing so dramatically. Changes call for strengthening the government administration, changing the way government administrators are recruited, and redesigning a framework for balancing the needs for central control and local autonomy. The Deng regime has taken important steps in all these areas, but they are far from adequate. First, the basic relationship between the Party organization and state administration needs to be redefined. If an effective and responsible administrative system is needed for directing the economic reform and social development, the role and status of PCG in state

---

of the Eighth Party Congress passed the *Decision Regarding Exchange of Leading Party and Government Cadres*. But there is evidence that this system had not been effectively implemented. After the Tenth Plenum, only two provinces had exchanged their leaders in 1962 (Fujian and Qinghai), three in 1963 (Tianjin, Shandong, and Shaanxi), and three in 1964 (Guizhou, Tibet, and Shaanxi).

221

Table 8.5. *Transfer of central and provincial officials, 1990–94*

Name	Old post	New post	Year
Province to Beijing			
Doje Cering[a]	Governor, Tibet	Vice Minister, Civil Affairs	1990
Guo Zhenqian[a]	Governor, Hubei	Vice Governor, People's Bank	1990
Jiang Zhuping[a]	Vice Governor, Jiangxi	Director, State Civil Aviation Administration	1991
Jin Jipeng	Governor, Qinghai	Deputy Auditor-General, State Auditing Administration	1992
Wang Zhongyu[a]	Governor, Jilin	Deputy Director, Office of Economy and Trade, State Council	1992
Chen Guangyi[a]	Party Secretary, Fujian	Director, State Civil Aviation Administration	1993
Guo Shuyan[b]	Acting Governor, Hubei	Vice Minister, State Planning Commission	1993
Li Boyong	Deputy Party Secretary, Sichuan	Minister, Labor	1993
Liu Jianfeng[a]	Governor, Hainan	Vice Minister, Electronics	1993
Wu Jichuan	Deputy Party Secretary, Henan	Minister, Post and Telecommunications	1993
Zhang Haoruo	Governor, Sichuan	Minister, Internal Trade	1993
Deng Hongxun	Party Secretary, Hainan	Deputy Director, Development Research Center, State Council	1994
Mao Rubo	Vice Governor, Tibet	Minister, Construction	1994
Sun Jiazheng[b]	Deputy Party Secretary, Jiangsu	Minister, Radio, Film & Television	1994
Beijing to Province			
Chen Shineng	Vice Minister, Light Industry	Governor, Guizhou	1993
Gao Dezhan[a]	Minister, Forestry	Party Secretary, Tianjin	1993
Hu Fuguo[a]	General Manager, General Coal Mine Corp.	Party Secretary, Shanxi	1993
Ma Zhongchen[b]	Vice Minister, Agriculture	Governor, Henan	1993

continued

Table 8.5. *continued*

Name	Old post	New post	Year
Ruan Chongwu[a]	Minister, Labor	Governor & Party Secretary, Hainan	1993
Zheng Silin	Vice Minister, Foreign Trade	Acting Governor, Jiangsu	1994

Province to Province

Name	Old post	New post	Year
Shen Daren[a]	Party Secretary, Ningxia	Party Secretary, Jiangsu	1990
Cheng Weigao[a]	Governor, Henan	Governor, Hebei	1990
Li Changchun[a]	Governor, Liaoning	Governor, Henan	1990
Hou Zongbin[a]	Governor, Shaanxi	Party Secretary, Henan	1990
Huang Huang[a]	Vice Governor, Jiangxi	Party Secretary, Ningxia	1990
Yue Qifeng[a]	Governor, Hebei	Governor, Liaoning	1990
Chen Kuiyuan	Vice Governor, Inner Mongolia	Party Secretary, Tibet	1992
Du Qinglin[b]	Deputy Party Secretary, Jilin	Chair, Standing Committee, Hainan People's Congress	1993
Gu Jinchi[a]	Party Secretary, Gansu	Party Secretary, Liaoning	1993
Jia Zhijie[a]	Governor, Gansu	Governor, Hubei	1993
Liu Fangren[b]	Deputy Party Secretary, Jiangxi	Party Secretary, Guizhou	1993
Sun Wensheng[b]	Deputy Party Secretary, Hunan	Governor, Shanxi	1993
Wang Maolin[a]	Party Secretary, Shanxi	Party Secretary, Hunan	1993
Yang Xizong	Chair, Standing Committee, Henan People's Congress	Chair, Standing Committee, Sichuan People's Congress	1993
Hui Liangyu[b]	Deputy Party Secretary, Hubei	Governor, Anhui	1994
Liu Minzhu[b]	Chair, Standing Committee, Guangxi People's Congress	Party Secretary, Inner Mongolia	1994

Notes: [a]Elected member of the Fourteenth CCP Central Committee in October 1992.
[b]Elected alternate member of the Fourteenth CCP Central Committee in October 1992.
Source: Compiled by the author from biographical information in the following: Malcolm Lamb, *Directory of Officials and Organizations in China: A Quarter-Century Guide* (Armonk, NY: M. E. Sharpe, 1994); *China Directory,* 1990, 1991, 1992, 1993, 1994 (Tokyo: Radio Press).

institutions must be changed. Second, the agencies of the "highest organ of state administrative power" – the State Council – have to be stabilized. Frequent changes and waves of streamlining only serve to weaken the state administrative capacity. Third, China urgently needs to train and recruit a large number of competent government administrators. Yet, due to political hurdles and financial difficulties, the government is losing China's best and brightest to the private sector, joint ventures, and foreign companies. Finally, the center–local power relationship built on the old system needs an overhaul. Some of the most serious institutional challenges facing the post-Deng leadership are whether China should adopt a federal system; how power is to be shared between the center and provinces; how the Chinese national legislature can effectively reflect and balance the local, regional, and national interests; and how the resources and wealth should be allocated.

9

Military Modernization and Party Politics

MILITARY modernization was one of the fundamental issues during the Deng Xiaoping era. Deng first intended to tackle the problems in the People's Liberation Army (PLA) in 1975 when he returned from disgrace and assumed the posts of vice chairman of the Party Central Military Commission (CMC) and chief of the PLA General Staff. In January 1975, Deng pointed to two major problems in the army: factionalism and lack of discipline.[1] He concluded that the PLA did not "act like an army."[2] Deng's efforts to rectify the army were soon aborted when he was purged for the second time in April 1976. After he returned to power in 1977, Deng had placed army rectification high on his agenda. In a speech to the Party CMC in August 1977, Deng, in his resumed official capacity as the new vice chairman of the Party CMC, pointed out: "Now we simply have to admit that by international standards, our science and technology have a long way to go. We must also admit that our army is not sufficiently capable of conducting modern warfare, and that although it is numerically strong, it is of relatively poor quality."[3] Deng's worries were mostly confirmed by the PLA's poor performance in the 1979 "punitive war" against Vietnam. The Vietnam War was for Deng what the Korean War was for Mao. Deng painfully realized that as the Soviet military threat to China was perceived to be on the rise, the PLA's combat readiness had eroded to the point where China's national security was at risk. Deng was also concerned about the PLA's political orientation. Loyal followers of Mao and the disgruntled subordinates of Lin Biao posed a serious threat to Deng's efforts to reform the army. In March 1980, Deng identified four problems in the PLA: (1) the "bloatedness" in the army and lack of combat effectiveness; (2) overstaffing of the military leadership structure; (3) lack of training in modern warfare; and (4)

---

[1] Deng Xiaoping, *Selected Works of Deng Xiaoping, 1975–1982* (Beijing: Foreign Languages Press, 1984), p. 12.
[2] Ibid., pp. 12–13.   [3] Ibid., p. 75.

5

poor political and ideological work.[4] If Deng's diagnosis was accurate, the PLA was indeed in bad shape; it was neither militarily competent nor politically reliable. This chapter analyzes Deng's successes in rehabilitating and reorganizing the PLA and his failure in institutionalizing the military command. The PLA's tragic involvement in the bloody crackdown in Tiananmen Square in 1989 is the primary example of this failure. This chapter also underscores two major challenges that the post-Deng leadership faces in the 1990s: how to control an army business empire and how to command the guns without the paramount leader.

MILITARY REFORM OF THE 1980s

Deng's agenda of military reform was best summarized by his call in 1981 to build "powerful, modern and regularized revolutionary armed forces."[5] Powerful meant the capacity to fight actual battles. Modernization referred to improvement of weapons systems and military equipment. Regularization involved "clarification of mission; coordination of organization, weapons procurement, training, and operations to meet that mission; and optimization of management personnel and resources."[6] A continued emphasis on revolution was meant to "make the armed forces a model" for carrying out the Party's line and policies.[7] It was certainly not to "depoliticize," but to "repoliticize" the PLA away from Mao's politics of class struggle toward Deng's politics of economic modernization.

Rehabilitation

Deng began to rectify the army by rehabilitating a large number of political victims in the PLA. Beginning in March 1979, the Party CMC issued a series of circulars officially reversing unjust verdicts on many senior military leaders purged before or during the Cultural Revolution. In addition, all the 5,799 Rightists and 11,000 middle-Rightists in the PLA who were persecuted in 1958 were rehabilitated. So were 17,000 military personnel purged in the 1959 Anti-Rightist Tendency campaign. These measures served to consolidate Deng's

---

[4] Ibid., pp. 269–75. [5] Ibid., p. 372.
[6] Richard J. Latham and Kenneth W. Allen, "Defense Reform in China: The PLA Air Force," *Problems of Communism* (May–June 1991), p. 31.
[7] Deng Xiaoping, 1984, p. 373.

power base in the military as well as to pave the way for correcting the political orientation of the PLA.[8]

While rehabilitating veteran military leaders, Deng was keenly aware of the incompatibility of aging military commanders and a modernizing army. In 1981, Deng suggested that the PLA set age limits for regiment-, division-, and army-level officers around 30, 40, and 50, respectively.[9] However, to force many recently rehabilitated military leaders to retire would have been politically unwise. Thus the reform in this area had to proceed gradually, and the age limits were flexible to allow many exceptions. Two major personnel changes came in 1983 and 1985 that substantially promoted younger officers to leading posts. By 1986, the average age of regiment-level officers had been reduced from 39.1 years in 1982 to 37.2, division-level officers from 48.3 to 43.5, army-level commanders from 56.8 to 49.6, and military region-level commanders from 65.3 to 57.1.[10]

Reorganization

During the 1980s, the PLA military corps and armed services had undergone massive reorganization. In 1983–84, the Capital Construction Engineering Corps was abolished, the PLA units of internal security and patrol were reorganized into the Chinese People's Armed Police, the Railway Corps was merged into the Ministry of Railways, and the Engineering Corps, Armored Force, and Artillery (First) Force became three departments of the PLA General Staff.[11] In May–June 1985, the Party CMC decided to reduce the four million strong PLA troops by one million. This resulted from Deng's assessment that China could expect a relatively long-term peaceful international environment and his belief that economic growth had to precede defense modernization.[12] By the end of 1986, thirty-one army-level units and 4,054 division-level units had been eliminated. Eleven military regions were consolidated into seven, which in turn

---

[8] *Guanyu xinshiqi jundui zhengzhi gongzuo de jueding zhushiben* (The Annotated Book for the Resolution Concerning the Political Work in the Military in the New Era) (Beijing: Jiefangjun chubanshe, 1987), pp. 158–60.

[9] Deng Xiaoping, 1984, p. 364.

[10] Ma Yuping and Huang Yuchong, eds., *Zhongguo zuotian yu jintian: 1840–1987 nian guoqing shouce* (China's Yesterday and Today: Handbook of National Conditions: 1840–1987) (Beijing: Jiefangjun chubanshe, 1989), p. 804.

[11] Ibid.

[12] Deng Xiaoping, *Selected Works of Deng Xiaoping*, vol. 3 (Beijing: Foreign Languages Press, 1993), pp. 131–3.

commanded twenty-seven provincial military districts and 9 military garrisons in major urban centers.[13] Thirty-six corps of the PLA's 5 field armies had been reorganized into 24 group armies under the command of 7 military regions. These group armies, each of which commanded about 50,000 troops, had fully integrated infantry, armor, field artillery, antiaircraft artillery, surface-to-air missile batteries, and engineering units.[14] In terms of manpower, Beijing Military Region was the strongest, commanding 6 group armies, followed by Shenyang Military Region (5), Jinan Military Region (4), Nanjing Military Region (3), Guangzhou Military Region (2), Chengdu Military Region (2), and Lanzhou Military Region (2).[15]

Although it was not unprecedented in PLA history, this massive reduction of the military forces was by no means easy. By the end of 1987, the PLA had managed to retire some 600,000 military officers who had failed to meet the new age limits or education requirement or both.[16] By the early 1990s, the Chinese military forces had included a standing army of 2.93 million – ground force (2.2 million), navy (260,000), and air force (470,000), plus a reserve force of 1.2 million and an armed police force of 1.2 million.[17]

Education

In 1977, Deng stressed that military education and training were of strategic importance.

> Historically, our army was tempted and grew through long years of war, and cadres were promoted mainly on the basis of the test of the battlefield. But now that we are not at war, how are we to test our cadres, raise their level, and improve the quality and combat effectiveness of our troops? How else if not through education and training?[18]

---

[13] Malcolm Lamb, *Directory of Officials and Organizations in China: A Quarter-Century Guide* (Armonk, NY: M. E. Sharpe, 1994), pp. 586–604; James C. F. Wang, *Contemporary Chinese Politics: An Introduction,* 5th edition (Englewood Cliffs, NJ: Prentice Hall, 1995), p. 176.

[14] Paul H. B. Godwin, "A Tentative Appraisal of China's Military Reforms," in Leng Shao-chuan, ed., *Reform and Development in Deng's China* (Lanham, MD: University Press of America, 1994), p. 110; *Guanyu xinshiqi jundui zhengzhi gongzuo de jueding zhushiben,* p. 185.

[15] A list of these group armies and their military regional commands can be found in Michael D. Swaine, *The Military and Political Succession in China: Leadership, Institutions, Beliefs* (Santa Monica, CA: RAND), 1992, p. 243.

[16] Paul Godwin, "A Tentative Appraisal of China's Military Reforms," in Leng, 1994, pp. 109–10.

[17] *The Military Balance* (London: International Institute for Strategic Studies, 1994).

[18] Deng Xiaoping, 1984, p. 74.

Following Deng's instruction, the PLA has placed great emphasis on military training. Since the early 1980s, combined arms training has become standard in military exercises, involving both ground and air force units and including logistical support and intelligence preparation.[19]

In 1982, the majority of the PLA officers had received only junior high school education: 92.8 percent of army-level officers, 86.9 percent of division-level officers, and 75.6 percent of regiment-level officers.[20] A poorly educated army was not capable of conducting combined arms training for modern warfare. To meet the need of military education, many military academies and schools were restored. In 1984, the Party CMC decided to recruit PLA officers mainly among graduates of colleges and military technical academies and schools.[21] In 1985, parts of the PLA Military Academy, the PLA Political Academy, and the PLA Logistics Academy merged to form the PLA National Defense University – China's equivalent of West Point. By the early 1990s, the PLA had established a comprehensive education and training system that consisted of more than one hundred military academies and schools, offering programs in areas of military command, political work, science, cultural learning, and civilian technology. It is a three-tier system under which military schools are responsible for training junior officers at platoon level; the Army Command, Navy Command, and Air Force Command Academies are responsible for training mid-level officers at the division and regiment levels; and the National Defense University is responsible for training senior officers at group army level. In October 1991, it was announced that new urban recruits for the army must be high school graduates and rural recruits must be junior high school graduates.[22] The official Xinhua News Agency reported that by 1994, a majority of PLA officers had received college education, a dramatic change from the situation in 1982 (see Table 9.1).

Modernization

Some China observers suggest that Deng Xiaoping assigned a relatively low priority to modernizing the PLA's military hardware.[23] Yet it must be pointed

---

[19] Godwin, "A Tentative Appraisal of China's Military Reforms," in Leng, 1994, pp. 110–11.

[20] Ma Yuping and Huang Yuchong, p. 803.

[21] Godwin, "A Tentative Appraisal of China's Military Reforms," in Leng, 1994, p. 109.

[22] *Los Angeles Times,* November 12, 1991, p. 1.

[23] June Teufel Dreyer, *China's Political System: Modernization and Transition* (New York: Paragon House, 1993), p. 255.

Table 9.1. *PLA officers having received college education (%)*

Command level	1982	1986	1994
Army/group army	1.2	58.4	87.0
Division	1.6	66.4	90.0
Regiment	2.2	41.4	75.0

Sources: Ma Yuping and Huang Yuchong, eds., *Zhongguo zuotian yu jintian 1840–1987 nian guoqing shouce* (China's Yesterday and Today: Handbook of National Conditions: 1840–1987) (Beijing: Jiefangjun chubanshe, 1989), p. 803; Xinhua News Agency report, December 19, 1994.

out that defense modernization was ranked third place in Deng's Four Modernizations, after industry and agriculture, but before science and technology. In Zhou Enlai's work reports to the NPC in 1954 and 1964 and in Hua Guofeng's work report to the NPC in 1978, modernization of national defense had consistently been ranked third place. Deng did nothing to change the ranking. The need for modernizing the Chinese military weaponry was obvious. As one article in the army newspaper, The *Liberation Army Daily,* put it: "Modern wars will be more acute, complicated, and cruel than any previous wars. Thus the army is required to improve its fighting quality, that is, to combine the forces of various armed services and to combine modernized men with modernized weaponry in a scientific manner."[24] The official army newspaper admitted that the level of modernization of the PLA was still rather low. Except for a few advanced weapons, the PLA was generally ten to twenty years behind the developed countries.[25]

Modernizing military armaments and equipment, however, was more difficult than many other military reform programs. Deng had been constrained by two factors: lack of hard currency to finance massive procurement of advanced military hardware and concern over the Chinese armed forces' dependence on foreign weapons and equipment. Deng therefore tried hard to convince the military leaders that modernization of national defense could not be achieved without a strong economic base. In a speech in November 1984, Deng urged the army to serve the needs of national economic development.[26]

[24] FBIS-CHI, December 20, 1987, p. 18.
[25] Ibid.
[26] Deng Xiaoping, 1993, p. 105.

230

In June 1985, Deng again discussed the issue of military weaponry and equipment upgrading. He reasoned, "Only when we have a good economic foundation will it be possible for us to modernize the army's equipment." Deng asked the military to "wait patiently for a few years" and promised more resources for weapon and equipment upgrading at the end of the century.[27] Thus during the 1980s, Chinese military spending was kept at a relatively low level even though the PLA was allowed to finance its R&D programs and some weaponry upgrading with the proceeds from overseas sales of Silkworm antiship missiles, F-7 fighter jets, and ballistic missiles.[28]

However, after the victory of Western advanced military technology and air power over a numerically superior Iraqi army with outmoded weaponry during the Gulf War in 1991, the Chinese military spending increased steadily – by 12 percent in 1991, 13.8 percent in 1992, and 13 percent in 1993.[29] The Party and military leaders seemed to have concluded that weaponry and equipment upgrading could no longer be delayed. At the Fourth Session of the Seventh NPC in 1991, when the military budget hike was approved, PLA deputies to the NPC stressed that with the gradual improvement in the economy, it was necessary to increase the military spending and upgrade the equipment. They also argued that economic construction and national defense were interdependent and could reinforce each other.[30] It was reported that Party Chief Jiang Zemin proposed to set up a state-of-the-art air defense system whose components would include radar, advance warning systems, surface-to-air missiles, jet fighters, intelligence and telecommunications.[31] The PLA group armies also "strengthened the training and drills of antiaircraft, antielectronic, antichemical and antinuclear warfare."[32] In the 1990s, the PLA has been closing the gap of military technology much faster than was the case in the 1980s, with help from countries like Russia and Israel.[33]

THE TRAGEDY OF 1989

The military modernization in the 1980s led many to conclude that the PLA had become an increasingly "professionalized" army. PLA officers were also

---

[27] Ibid., p. 133.
[28] Wang, p. 196; *The New York Times,* May 24, 1994, p. A-6.
[29] Dreyer, pp. 264–5; Wang, pp. 190–1.
[30] Xinhua News Agency report, March 30, 1991.
[31] *South China Morning Post,* June 14, 1991, p. 13.
[32] Xinhua News Agency report quoted in *Los Angeles Times,* November 12, 1991, p. 1.
[33] *Jane's Defence Weekly* 21, no. 7 (February 19, 1994), p. 28.

reportedly led to believe that "factional political exploitation of the PLA was a thing of the past."[34] Yet, as the tragic events of 1989 demonstrated, this optimism might be premature, and our conceptualization of military professionalism in the PLA may need some fine tuning.

The term "professionalism" is a confusing one in the Chinese context because there is simply no equivalent Chinese word for it. The Chinese military publications use the terms "regularization" (*zhengguihua*), "modernization" (*xiandaihua*), or "specialization" (*zhuanyehua*), but not "professionalization" or "professionalism." Nonetheless, we can still begin with Western literature on the subject as a reference point. According to some scholars, military professionalism can be measured by four criteria: (1) specialization in military training and education; (2) sense of military corporateness; (3) internal codes of conduct or professional ethics; and (4) noninvolvement in domestic political affairs.[35] Chinese military modernization in the 1980s indicates that the PLA should have no problem meeting some of these criteria. Specialization in military training and education, as well as forging internal codes of conduct, should be well covered by what the Chinese military refers to as regularization and modernization. In the recent decade, because most military officers received formal education in more than one hundred military academies and schools, we can also reasonably expect the development of a sense of military corporateness. But in the Chinese case, there is little correlation between military modernization and political disengagement, and the PLA has always been structurally centered in Chinese politics. As noted earlier in Chapter 5, from its birth in 1927, the Red Army had been an integral part of the Party and a vital tool for achieving political purposes. After 1949, the PLA continued to play an extremely important role in Chinese politics, much in contrast to the imperial tradition.[36] As the events of 1989 demonstrate, there is no evidence for us to conclude that the PLA will become disengaged from politics as it makes progress, slowly but progressively, toward military modernization.

---

[34] Harlan W. Jencks, "Civil–Military Relations in China: Tiananmen and After," *Problems of Communism* (May–June 1991), p. 16.

[35] Samuel P. Huntington, *The Soldier and the State: The Theory and Politics of Civil–Military Relations* (Cambridge, MA: The Belknap Press of Harvard University Press, 1957); Bengt Abrahamsson, *Military Professionalization and Political Power* (Beverly Hills, CA: Sage Publications, 1972).

[36] The imperial tradition was that once founding emperors had exhausted the utility of military generals in building a new dynasty, military force would be kept as far away as possible from the capital and palace politics.

What Has Professionalism Got to Do with It?

It was widely reported that during the Tiananmen crisis, 150 active and retired senior officers petitioned the Party CMC not to spill the people's blood.[37] A group of seven retired military generals appealed to the General Headquarters of the Martial Law Troops and the Party CMC "not to open fire on the people."[38] Lieutenant General Xu Qinxian, commander of the 38th Group Army, reportedly refused to carry out the martial law order.[39] As many as 110 army officers and 1,400 PLA soldiers did not obey orders or observe army discipline.[40] All these examples have been cited as evidence that a professionalized part of the PLA had become increasingly unwilling to serve as a political tool of the Party.[41] In other words, military modernization in the 1980s made the PLA increasingly professional, and military professionalism explained the PLA's reluctance to enforce the martial law order.

Although many PLA officers and soldiers did "run away," the PLA as an institution ultimately carried out the martial law order and bloodily suppressed the civilian resistance. There was some suggestion that the troops that participated in the bloody crackdown were mobilized from the remote provinces and therefore were somehow less educated or less professionalized. Yet there is not enough evidence to confirm the involvement of any army unit from the two remote military regions – Chengdu Military Region and Lanzhou Military Region. Perhaps these two military regions had already been overburdened by each having only two group armies and to guard huge territories. Second, the June 4th crackdown was not a small military action by a few units of the PLA, but a massive military deployment involving more than 150,000 soldiers from twelve group armies of five military regions, and employing tanks, heavy

---

[37] Harlan Jencks, "The Military in China," *Current History* (September 1990), p. 266.

[38] Their petition is translated and included in Suzanne Ogden et al., eds., *China's Search for Democracy: The Student and Mass Movement of 1989* (Armonk, NY: M. E. Sharpe, 1992), p. 292.

[39] Harlan W. Jencks, "China's Army, China's Future," in David S. G. Goodman and Gerald Segal, eds., *China in the Nineties: Crisis Management and Beyond* (New York: Oxford University Press, 1991), p. 135. General Xu's story was printed on a handbill distributed in Tiananmen Square in late May 1989. For the translation of the handbill, see Ogden et al., eds., pp. 340–1.

[40] Sources are quoted in David Shambaugh, "The Soldier and the State in China: The Political Work System in the People's Liberation Army," *The China Quarterly* (September 1991), p. 552.

[41] For a brief discussion of this issue, see A. James Gregor, "The People's Liberation Army and China's Crisis," *Armed Forces & Society* 18, no. 1 (Fall 1991), p. 19.

artillery, antiaircraft weapons, paratroopers, and missiles.[42] Third, all the six group armies under the Beijing Military Region – a region that had been the leader in military training and modernization – were involved in the crackdown. Using the same professionalism argument, Ellis Joffe thus suggested that the PLA intervened in the Tiananmen crisis because it was "a disciplined, professional army."[43] David Shambaugh also asked, "What could be more professional than to ensure national security as directed by the commander-in-chief and other members of the CMC?"[44]

However, if we accept these arguments of "military professionalism" on both sides, we will arrive at a strange conclusion: It is military professionalism to either enforce or not enforce the martial law order. Obviously, we cannot have it both ways. The confusion, we may suggest, arises from an insistence on explaining the PLA's role in the Tiananmen crisis in terms of "politicization versus professionalism." In doing so, we ask ourselves an impossible question: Is it or is it not professional for the army to carry out orders to resolve domestic political conflicts?

Under the circumstances, those PLA generals who refused to carry out the martial law order did what they believed to be right. Yet their actions had less to do with military professionalism and more to do with the PLA's traditional emphasis on inseparable relations between the people and the people's army. Military generals refusing to carry out orders on the basis of their own political judgment is not the best example of military professionalism.[45] For those who did shoot their way into Tiananmen Square, it was an agonizing and frightening experience. Unlike an army dashing toward enemy targets on the battleground, the people's army was ordered to fight an army of people in the streets of the capital city. In this unprecedented political crisis in the history of the People's Republic of China, it was a divided Party leadership and the decision by one man that put the PLA in a classic dilemma: The PLA was damned if it intervened and damned if it didn't. What has military professionalism got to do with it?

Like the Peng Dehuai incident and Lin Biao affair during the Mao era, the army's involvement in the bloody Tiananmen crackdown in 1989 was the single most important event that affected the army in the Deng era. It not only

---

[42] Sources are quoted in Wang, pp. 199–208.
[43] Ellis Joffe, "The Tiananmen Crisis and the Politics of the PLA," in Richard H. Yang, ed., *China's Military: The PLA in 1990/1991* (Boulder, CO: Westview Press, 1991), p. 27.
[44] Shambaugh, "The Soldier and the State in China," p. 528, n2.
[45] Huntington, 1957, p. 71.

destroyed the image of the People's Liberation Army as an army of the people, but plowed deep seeds of division between those who followed orders and those who did not. For many years to come, the PLA will have to live with the shame and burden of the June 4th crackdown. The Tiananmen Square Incident was a tragedy in the true meaning of the word. It was a tragedy for those who lost their lives or their loved ones. It was a tragedy for the PLA as a modernizing national defense force. It was also a tragedy for Deng Xiaoping, who had been until then the champion of China's reform and open-door policy. Historians in the future will be in a better position to judge whether Deng was misinformed, irritated by selective and exaggerated reports, and pressured by his elder colleagues to order the bloody crackdown, or acted willingly and consciously.

The Rise and Fall of Yang Baibing

The June 4th crackdown was followed by a massive purge in the PLA. Some Western observers believed that by the spring of 1990, as many as 400 officers and 1,600 soldiers had been disciplined.[46] It was estimated that as many as 3,500 military and armed police officers were placed under investigation.[47] For a while, Mao's revolutionary politics seemed to have returned to the PLA camps. Military officers were ordered to study Mao's writings and oppose bourgeois liberal ideas. Lei Feng, the model soldier of the Mao era, was revived to set an example for the soldiers of the Deng era to follow. Standing "in the forefront of the effort at repoliticization" was General Yang Baibing, the director of the PLA General Political Department (GPD).[48]

Yang was promoted to be director of the GPD from political commissar of the Beijing Military Region in December 1987. After the June 4th crackdown, Yang was further promoted to be the secretary-general of the Party CMC while continuing his control of the GPD. Until his quite unexpected demotion three years later, Yang Baibing was thought to be the "most powerful individual among the central PLA elite."[49] Michael Swaine suggested that there were at least three reasons to believe so. First, Yang Baibing had strong patronage connections. He belonged to Deng's Second Field Army and his elder half-

---

[46] Sources quoted in Wang, p. 208, n158.
[47] Gregor, "The People's Liberation Army and China's Crisis," p. 19.
[48] Michael D. Swaine, "China Faces the 1990's: A System in Crisis," *Problems of Communism* (May–June 1990), p. 33.
[49] Ibid., p. 62.

brother, Yang Shangkun, was the first vice chairman of the Party CMC and was believed to exercise actual power over the military. It was also believed that the Yang brothers had long enjoyed Deng's support. Second, Yang Baibing, in his new post as the secretary-general of the Party CMC, managed the PLA command and control apparatus. Third, as the director of the GPD, Yang Baibing was largely responsible for military personnel matters.[50] Yet, after the Fourteenth Party Congress in October 1992, Yang Baibing (along with his elder half-brother) was removed from all his military posts.

If Yang Baibing were so powerful, how could he fall so easily? Although information about Yang Baibing's downfall is still sketchy, we can try to piece together some possible, albeit tentative, explanations. It seems almost certain that Yang Baibing's political patron, Deng Xiaoping, had decided to withdraw his support. Much less clear is why Deng had lost his full confidence in Yang Baibing. We have no evidence to believe that Deng himself felt threatened by the rising influence of the Yangs in the PLA. It is more likely that Deng decided to sideline the Yangs in order to calm the strong resentment against the "Yang family gang" and to keep some balance among different factions in the PLA.

After the June 4th crackdown, Yang Baibing had been in charge of correcting the problems in the military. With support from Yang Shangkun, Yang Baibing was said to have purged many military officers at the rank of deputy army commander. The 1990 military reshuffle was primarily, if not exclusively, politically motivated. It therefore can be argued that Yang Baibing had gone too far in promoting his associates and removing his opponents, thus upsetting the balance of power among various factional groups and offending some senior generals such as Zhang Aiping. Undoubtedly, Yang Baibing had his political ambitions and his opponents, but to give Yang Baibing the most blame for the post-Tiananmen purge is to exaggerate his authority, because any major military dismissal or appointment had to have gone through the Party CMC and, ultimately, Deng himself. Nonetheless, by being overzealous about "purifying" the army, Yang Baibing became a target that his opponents could afford to attack and a scapegoat that his patron could afford to make.

It is also likely that Deng decided to suppress the Yangs in order to safeguard his succession plan. It was reported that Yang Baibing did not get along well with new Party CMC Chairman Jiang Zemin.[51] Jiang not only felt threatened by the Yangs' rising influence, but was also concerned by rising resentment against the Yangs. For a designated successor who had no military background

[50] Ibid., pp. 63–6.   [51] Ibid., p. 196.

whatsoever, to be acceptable to all the major factions in the PLA was more important than anything else for his own survival. So Jiang must have seized on some of Yang Baibing's mistakes to persuade Deng to take action. The Yangs' ouster was followed by another major military reshuffle. Many supporters of the Yang brothers faced the fate of early retirement, reassignment, or demotion.[52] A few "defected" in time to save themselves.[53] But this would have required walking on a highly risky, political fine line that military officers ultimately are not trained to do.

MONEY GROWS OUT OF THE BARREL OF A GUN

The challenge to the PLA becoming a professional army also comes from an inevitable, if unanticipated, consequence of the sixteen years of economic reform: the money-making and "getting rich first" frenzy that has spread into the military. Since the 1980s, the PLA has become deeply involved in large- and small-scale business activities. All three services (army, navy and air force) and all military regions, provincial military districts, and field armies have set up their own business companies.[54] An army of businessmen has gradually emerged within an army of soldiers.

Army of Business

Military business activities include two broad categories: defense conversion industries and army-owned enterprises that make and sell everything from ships and planes to motorcycles, bicycles, refrigerators, and wristwatches and that manage hotels, restaurants, resort areas, discos, and real estate.[55] Defense

---

[52] June Teufel Dreyer, "The People's Army: Serving Whose Interests?" *Current History* (September 1994), p. 267.

[53] Michael Swaine suggests that General Yu Yongbo, a close supporter of the Yangs, succeeded General Yang Baibing as the director of the GPD in 1992 perhaps because he abandoned the Yangs. Swaine, p. 198. It was reported that Yang Baibing, without Jiang Zemin's knowledge, had compiled a new list of appointments of commanders and political commissars to the seven PLA military regions. Before the Fourteenth Party Congress, Yu Yongbo, deputy director of the GPD, got a copy of Yang's new list of appointments and immediately reported to Jiang Zemin. *World Journal (Shijie Ribao)* (December 14, 1992), p. 2.

[54] *Ming Pao* (Hong Kong), February 2, 1994, p. A-10, quoted in BBC Summary of World Broadcasts, February 10, 1994.

[55] On a field research trip back to Shanghai in May 1995, I saw a new building of considerable size. The big Chinese characters on the front nameplate said: "The Shanghai Accounting Center of the People's Liberation Army." It is not difficult to imagine that if the PLA needs such a large accounting center in Shanghai, there must be a lot of business transactions to reckon with.

conversion to civilian output began in the early 1980s when Deng tried to reduce the size of the army and cut the military budget. By early 1995, the total value of civilian production accounted for some 75 percent of the defense industry's overall output production, compared to less than 10 percent in 1979.[56] The Xinhua News Agency reported that the electronics enterprises in China's military industry have formed more than fifty enterprise groups consisting of more than 18,000 companies. By early 1995, they accounted for about 30 percent of China's total output of color TV sets, and one half of China's total exports of refrigerators.[57] China North Industries Group, the country's leading weapons manufacturer, planned to produce about 2.33 million motorcycles, 60,000 minivans, and 44,700 minicars in 1995.[58] Army factories produce more than half of China's cameras, 65 percent of its bicycles, and 75 percent of its minicabs.[59]

Moreover, there are more than 20,000 military-run businesses in almost every field.[60] The largest among them are directly affiliated with the PLA General Headquarters under the Party CMC. China Poly Corp. under the PLA General Staff conducts business in arms sales, infrastructure property, electronics, shipping, and trading; China Xinxing Corp. under the PLA General Logistics Department conducts business in clothing, food, construction, materials, fuel, and vehicles; and Kaili Corp. under the PLA General Political Department conducts business in communication equipment.[61]

Besides the reasons for defense conversion, income-seeking is one of the most important driving forces behind army businesses. During the 1980s, the military was repeatedly told by Deng to be patient and to endure difficulties because the Chinese state treasury could not afford a large increase in defense spending. Although many prospered during the economic reform, the central government had not become richer. In fact, the purse of the state had shrunk because of fiscal decentralization and high inflation. Financially strapped, the central government had no choice but to let the military "jump into the sea" of business to make their own ends meet. Not surprisingly, given the PLA's privileged status in China, army-run enterprises have turned out to be the most

[56] *Asiaweek,* April 28, 1995; *Jane's Defence Weekly* 21; no. 7 (February 19, 1994), p. 28.

[57] Xinhua News Agency report, February 12, 1995, quoted in BBC Summary of World Broadcasts, March 15, 1995.

[58] The *China Daily,* January 19, 1995.

[59] Reuters World Service, March 28, 1995.

[60] *International Herald Tribune,* July 10, 1995.

[61] *The Nikkei Weekly,* October, 1994, p. 24; *Financial Times,* November 28, 1994, p. 19.

successful business group in China.[62] Mao Zedong had often insisted that the PLA should be "an army of production" as well as "an army of national defense."[63] But if he were alive today, Mao would probably be shocked to see how productive "PLA Inc." is.

Consequences

The PLA's involvement in business is a double-edged sword. Although it gives the military more money to spend and better cars to drive, it also has a serious negative impact on the morale, discipline, and training of the PLA. In July 1993, the Party CMC Vice Chairmen Liu Huaqing and Zhang Zhen, two Long March veterans, warned in an article in the Party newspaper: "All sorts of unhealthy attitudes and negative phenomena from society are continuously using all paths and routes to infiltrate the military, putting army construction in danger."[64] Among the cited examples of adverse consequences were low troop morale, officers' resistance to Party orders, competition between PLA units and government units to get a bigger slice of the market, smuggling, speculative financial dealings, profiteering and corruption, and many other illegal activities.[65]

Corruption is the most visible consequence of the army's involvement in business. Members of the PLA are suspected of smuggling computer equipment, electronic appliances, and other luxury goods. In the mid-1980s, the PLA naval units on Hainan Island colluded with local officials to smuggle more than $500 million in Japanese vehicles.[66] A South Korean newspaper reported that in July 1993, forty-three army units involving 300 military officials were found to be smuggling cars from South Korea to the northeastern province of Liaoning.[67]

Low morale and declining fighting ability are other direct consequences. That military officers are more familiar with a Mercedes-Benz than with a tank

---

[62] For instance, the PLA had controlled an extensive transportation network. Few traffic policemen dare to stop trucks bearing the PLA's license plates.

[63] *Jianguo yilai Mao Zedong wengao, 1949, 9–1950, 12* (Mao Zedong's Manuscripts Since the Founding of the People's Republic of China: September 1949–December 1950) (Beijing: Zhongyang wenxian chubanshe, 1987), pp. 182–3.

[64] *Far Eastern Economic Review,* October 12, 1994, p. 66.

[65] Quoted by Yojana Sharma, "China: Army's Economic Ventures Threaten Fighting Ability," in Inter Press Service, July 11, 1994.

[66] *Far Eastern Economic Review,* October, 14, 1993, p. 66.

[67] The *Korean Economic Daily,* March 24, 1995.

or armored vehicle is anything but comforting news for the national defense. On April 3, 1995, the *Liberation Army Daily* reported that a recent survey showed that an increasing number of soldiers were spending more time than allowed on vacation and weekends, attending to private business or going sightseeing at the expense of their military training.[68] One Western expert on the PLA gave a rough estimate that about half the members of the PLA were engaged in nonmilitary activities.[69] Faced with the enormous temptation of money-making, soldiers have found it hard to concentrate on their basic mission: defending the country. Too preoccupied with deal-making, many military units can no longer keep their military training programs on track, maintain discipline, and keep morale up.

The booming army businesses is a reflection and a result of the declining control of the Party center over the military. Although the military modernization programs are aimed at transforming the PLA into a more integrated fighting force, army business interests are working in the opposite direction, localizing and fragmenting the PLA. Various army units have established so many entrenched business connections with local governments and markets and with Hong Kong and foreign companies that their loyalty to the central Party leadership is highly questionable.

Vested interests and economic power have boosted the PLA's confidence and influence. On a trip to Beijing in May 1995, I asked one officer from the PLA General Headquarters why the military these days seemed to have a strong voice in foreign affairs. He said that if the military did not speak out, no one would take the military seriously. To be sure, the world is now taking the PLA very seriously. It is widely suggested that the PLA generals were behind China's tough stance on issues of arms sales and nuclear nonproliferation, the confrontational approach toward Washington, and China's recent missile tests aimed at intimidating Taiwan.[70] There are also reports that the military has become a strong critic and rival of the Ministry of Foreign Affairs.[71]

The Chinese leaders are fully aware of the negative consequences of the army's involvement in business. If the PLA's extensive involvement in politics

---

[68] The *Liberation Army Daily,* April 3, 1995.
[69] Gerald Segal, a military analyst at the International Institute for Strategic Studies (IISS), made this estimate during an address to the Foreign Correspondents' Club in Hong Kong on July 8, 1994, reported in *The Straits Times* (Singapore), July 9, 1994.
[70] *South China Morning Post,* July 11, 1995, p. 9; *The Independent,* August 6, 1995, p. 13; *The Christian Science Monitor,* August 22, 1995, p. 1; and Inter Press Service, September 6, 1995.
[71] *Cheng Ming* (Hong Kong), July 25, 1994.

during the Cultural Revolution made Deng Xiaoping conclude in 1975 that the army did not "act like an army," the PLA's extensive involvement in business during the reform makes the army look like anything but an army. However, it is easier to talk about the problems than to solve the problems. Western analysts have suggested that China should try to privatize the nonmilitary operations of the PLA whereas Chinese scholars believe that the Chinese state should assume more responsibility for "supporting the armed forces with tax revenues." Hu Angang and Kang Xiaoguang, two researchers from the Chinese Academy of Sciences, specifically suggested: (1) strictly prohibiting the armed forces from engaging in business; (2) increasing the military budget substantially; (3) separating most military enterprises from the regular establishment of the armed forces; and (4) redefining the armed forces' tasks and reducing excessive nonmilitary expenditures.[72]

However, it appears that neither the market approach nor the statist approach appeals to the Party leaders. What has evolved is what we may call the "centralized, better management" approach. In 1994, the Party CMC and PLA Commission for Disciplinary Inspection held several meetings on curbing corruption and cutting down on irregular business activities. Among recommended measures were plans to close down PLA-run business under the level of group army and place most army corporations under the direct control of the PLA General Logistics Department.[73] On January 1, 1995, the Provisional Regulation on Economic Accountability and Auditing for Leading Army Cadres went into effect. Jointly signed by the PLA chief of the General Staff, the director of the General Political Department, and the director of the General Logistics Department, the Provisional Regulation would subject officers and cadres at the regiment level or above to "auditing and supervision."[74] On April 24, 1995, the Party CMC issued an order to promulgate the PLA Regulations on Auditing, which stipulates that auditing departments at various levels in the army are responsible for auditing the incomes, expenditures, and state-owned assets of various military departments, enterprises, and business units and supervising the actual operations, lawfulness, and efficiency of their economic activities.[75] The "centralized and better management" approach thus holds some promise of putting the house of "PLA Inc." in order, but the army

---

[72] *Ming Pao,* February 2, 1994.
[73] *South China Morning Post,* January 5, 1995, p. 1.
[74] Ibid.
[75] The *Liberation Army Daily,* April 25, 1995, p. 1, quoted in BBC Summary of World Broadcasts, May 9, 1995.

business is unmistakably here to stay. Indeed, given the limited financial capacity of the central government, it is impossible to persuade the military not to seek other sources of income for supporting itself. Nor is it realistic to ask the rich and powerful to give up their wealth and influence. "PLA Inc." will continue to operate, perhaps in a more centralized and better-managed way, and whether the negative impact on the army can be controlled or minimized remains to be seen.

ARMY OF THE PARTY OR ARMY OF THE STATE?

While calling for military reform, the *Liberation Army Daily* makes it clear that the Party's leadership over the army must be maintained. One commentator in December 1987 pointed out: "As our army is an armed group dealing with arms, it should absolutely be placed under the Party's leadership."[76] The PLA publication has defined the Party's leadership over the army as follows:

(1) The PLA must completely and unconditionally place itself under the leadership of the Party.
(2) The supreme military command is centralized in the Party Central Committee and Central Military Commission.
(3) Every military operation must follow the order of the Party Central Committee and Central Military Commission.
(4) No one is allowed to seek independence from the Party.
(5) No other political parties are allowed to set up their organizations and conduct activities in the PLA.
(6) No one is allowed to contend with the Party for the control over the army.
(7) Without the authorization from the Party Central Committee and Central Military Commission, no one is allowed to meddle in military affairs or mobilize and direct troops presumptuously.[77]

These are very specific and strict rules, and given the fact that these rules have long existed, one has to wonder why the issue of the Party's command of the gun remains unresolved.

To be sure, Deng Xiaoping has discouraged the military from taking over the Party, and until the June 4th crackdown in 1989, he was able to persuade the military leadership to support his economic modernization program. The Party leadership also has tried to maintain political control over the PLA through the

---

[76] FBIS-CHI, December 16, 1987, p. 23.
[77] *Guanyu xinshiqi jundui zhengzhi gongzuo de jueding zhushiben,* p. 270.

traditional political work system.[78] From the top down to the company level, this system consists of a hierarchy of Party committees and political commissars or instructors running parallel to the different ranks in the army hierarchy.[79] There is also a certain degree of political disengagement in terms of interlocking directorates.[80] For instance, PLA commanders or political commissars of military regions, districts, and garrisons no longer concurrently hold posts as provincial governor or provincial Party secretary, whereas in 1975, 68 percent of provincial leaders and 47 percent of provincial Party secretaries were PLA commanders and political commissars.[81] Indeed, during the Deng era, the pattern of interlocking directorates seems to have been reversed. Instead of PLA regional commanders or political commissars assuming leading roles in provincial Party organization and government, now the secretary of the provincial Party committee automatically becomes the first secretary of the Party committee of the provincial military district.[82] The purpose is to place provincial military districts and subdistricts under dual control – military control from higher command and political control from the Party committee at the same level.

However, the PLA's structural political role has remained essentially unchanged during the Deng era. First, every four or five years, the PLA sends hundreds of delegates to attend the National People's Congress. The PLA delegation is always the largest of all. For instance, at the recently convened Eighth NPC (March 1993), Sichuan, the largest province in China with more than 100 million people, sent a delegation of 205 members to the NPC. Yet the PLA with 3.5 million personnel sent a group of 267 delegates to the NPC, which was about 9 percent of the total number of delegates (2,978).[83] The presence of a large number of uniformed military officers in the U.S. Congress

[78] For recent studies of the political work system in the PLA, see Shambaugh, "The Soldier and the State in China," pp. 527–68; Nan Li, "Changing Functions of the Party and Political Work system in the PLA and Civil–Military Relations in China," *Armed Forces & Society* 19, 3 (Spring 1993), pp. 393–409; and Fang Zhu, "Political Work in the Military from the Viewpoint of the Beijing Garrison Command," in Carol Lee Hamrin and Suisheng Zhao, eds., *Decision-Making in Deng's China: Perspectives from Insiders* (Armonk, NY: M. E. Sharpe, 1995), pp. 118–29.

[79] *Guanyu xinshiqi jundui zhengzhi gongzuo de jueding zhushiben*, pp. 486–9.

[80] For an analysis of the Party and military elites holding interlocking positions, see Monte R. Bullard, *China's Political Military Evolution: The Party and the Military in the People's Republic of China, 1960–1984* (Boulder, CO: Westview Press, 1985).

[81] Wang, pp. 184–5.

[82] *Guanyu xinshiqi jundui zhengzhi gongzuo de jueding zhushiben*, pp. 415–6.

[83] *China Directory 1994* (Tokyo: Radio Press, Inc., 1994), p. 75.

Table 9.2. *Military representation in the CCP Central Committee and the Politburo*

Party Congress	Year	Central Committee (%)	Politburo (%)
Eighth	1956	35.2	35.0
Ninth	1969	45.0	52.0
Tenth	1973	24.0	40.0
Eleventh	1977	29.5	57.0
Twelfth	1982	21.5	43.0
Congress of Delegates	1985	14.9	18.0
Thirteenth	1987	18.6	11.1
Fourteenth	1992	22.7	10.0

Source: Michael D. Swaine, *The Military and Political Succession in China: Leadership, Institutions, Beliefs* (Santa Monica, CA: RAND, 1992), p. 159.

would make everyone wonder if the U.S. Army had staged a coup. In China, people have become so accustomed to the military presence in the national legislature that few would bother to ask why they are there.

Second, PLA's significant presence in the Party is also too obvious to ignore. In discussing the increasing or decreasing influence of the military in politics, a frequently cited indicator is the military representation in the Party Central Committee and Politburo. As Table 9.2 shows, the military representation reached its peak in 1969 during the military takeover of the country. Since then, the trend has declined, although the military representation of the Fourteenth Central Committee in 1992 increased again.

What is more telling than the changing percentages of military representation in the Party central leading bodies is the inclusive or comprehensive nature of the military representatives. Michael Swaine has identified sixty-four military members of the Fourteenth Central Committee (forty-three full and twenty-one alternate members).[84] They include two vice chairmen of the Party CMC, director of the CMC General Office, the defense minister, the director of the State Commission of Science, Technology, and Industry for National Defense, the PLA general chief of staff, the director of the PLA General Political Department, the director and political commissar of the PLA General

---

[84] Swaine, pp. 254–6.

Logistics Department, the director of the central guard bureau, commanders and political commissars of PLA air force and navy, commanders and political commissars of all seven military regions,[85] seven commanders and four political commissars of ten group armies, the commandant and political commissar of the National Defense University, the commandant of the PLA Academy of Military Sciences, and directors of the army newspaper and the PLA General Hospital. In a way, the Party Central Committee looks like a high-level military club joined by the military leaders of the PLA General Headquarters, of all the armed services, and of all the military regions. The pattern that has emerged in the Fourteenth Central Committee may also suggest that the military presence in the Party Central Committee has been somewhat institutionalized in that whoever assumes a certain leading military post will be a member of the Central Committee either before or after.

Army of the State?

The intricate structural linkage between the Party and the army has always been a source of controversy and conflict. Indeed, the most important issue in the military reform in the 1980s was whether the Chinese army should belong to the Party or the state. Nerve-racking for elder revolutionary leaders, this had long been a forbidden area. The fact that in the 1980s one could question whether it was appropriate for the army to continue to be under the sole dominion of the Party suggests that much had changed since Mao. The call for separating the Party from the army at first seemed a logical step following the overall reform measures to separate the Party from the government initiated by none other than Deng Xiaoping. If the Party were not going to manage state affairs directly, not take over the government administration, not make laws in place of the people's congress, and not interfere in the judicial processes, why then could the Party not remove itself from directly commanding the army? Deng's military reform, of course, did not follow logic, but politics.

Deng has never given up the idea of the Party leadership over the military, but when faced with the challenge of stabilizing this leadership in the early 1980s, he had to come up with certain institutional adaptations, for the existing

[85] Zhang Wannian, who was Commander of Jinan Military Region before the Fourteenth Party Congress, immediately became the chief of the PLA General Staff after the Party Congress. Zhang Wannian is a full member of the Fourteenth Central Committee, but Zhang Taiheng, who succeeded Zhang Wannian as Commander of the Jinan Military Region, is neither a full, nor an alternate, member of the Central Committee.

system under which the Party chairman was concurrently the commander-in-chief of the armed forces could no longer be sustained. First, Mao-style military leadership ran directly contradictory to Deng's critique of Mao's over-centralization of power. Second, Deng himself had no intention of being the Party chairman, but he trusted no one other than himself to command the army. Third, because the reformist Party leadership intended to apply laws and regulations to ruling the country, some legal basis must also be found to justify the Party's command of the military forces.

In December 1982, the newly adopted state constitution installed a Central Military Commission of the People's Republic of China. According to Article 93, the state CMC "directs the armed forces of the country." Article 94 also stipulates, "The Chairman of the Central Military Commission is responsible to the National People's Congress and its Standing Committee."[86] To many it was a promising sign that the Party was finally beginning to transfer formal control of the military to the command of the state. Indeed, Premier Zhao Ziyang had hoped that this would prove to be true. In an interview with Japanese TV reporters in June 1982, Zhao commented that the state CMC was necessary because "the army is an important component of the state."[87]

In September 1982, the Party convened its Twelfth Party Congress, three months before the Fifth National People's Congress ratified the state constitution. The timing was important. The Twelfth Party Central Committee elected a new Party CMC whose members were all military generals in active duty except Deng Xiaoping (as the chairman of the Party CMC). Three months later, the same group of people became members of the newly established state CMC. The respective jurisdictions of the Party's CMC and the newly established state CMC turned out to be exactly the same. In fact, it is misleading to talk about them as if they were two separate institutions, because they were the same people holding the same office with two different names. The PLA publications made it clear that after the state CMC was established, the Party CMC would continue to exercise its leadership over the military and the existing management system and procedures would remain unchanged.[88]

Under the same command system that was established in 1954, all the armed services and military regions now report to the PLA General Staff, the PLA

---

[86] For the English version of the 1982 state constitution, see Appendix A in Wang, pp. 321–42.
[87] Interview with Premier Zhao Ziyang, NHK-TV (Tokyo), June 4, 1982, translated in FBIS-CHI, June 7, 1982, pp. D/1–2.
[88] *Guanyu xinshiqi jundui zhengzhi gongzuo de jueding zhushiben*, p. 273.

General Political Department, and the PLA General Logistics Department, which in turn directly report to the Party CMC, bypassing the Ministry of Defense, the State Council, and the National People's Congress. Not only does the state CMC exist on paper only, but the Ministry of Defense exercises no actual control over military affairs. With such bureaus as American and Oceanic Affairs, Asian Affairs, European Affairs, Foreign Affairs, West Asian and African Affairs, Conscription, and Military Production, the Ministry of Defense looks more like the Ministry of Foreign Affairs of the PLA.[89] In sharp contrast, the departments of the PLA General Staff include: Antichemicals, Armament, Artillery, Cartography, Engineering, Intelligence, Joint Tactical Training, Management, Military Affairs, Military Training, Mobilization, Operation, Political Work, Radar, Second Artillery, Signals, and Surveying.[90] Most of these departments of the General Staff are responsible for supervising the special troops that now account for 60 percent of the PLA.[91]

Because the Party's CMC has continued to function as the highest command of all the military forces in China, the idea of a "state army" never stood a chance, and the legislative control over the military was only true on paper. Thus, in many ways the fuss over the establishment of the state CMC seems to have been much ado about nothing. However, the window dressing was by no means unnecessary. Because the Party CMC and the state CMC are in fact one and the same institution, Chinese publications thus suggest that the principle of the Party exercising absolute leadership over the army is consistent with the 1982 constitutional articles stipulating that the State Central Military Commission commands all the armed forces in China.[92] Deng might have been pleased that he could "have his cake and eat it, too" – the Party CMC's actual control over the military with a facade of legitimacy through the state CMC. But the odd institutional arrangement of the Party and state CMC only invites more questions about the legitimacy of the Party CMC and calls for straightening the military command system.[93]

---

[89] *Zhongguo gaige dacidian* (Dictionary of Chinese Reform) (Beijing: Zhongguo guoji guangbo chubanshe, 1992), pp. 478–9.

[90] Ibid., p. 492.

[91] Xinhua News Agency report, July 23, 1992.

[92] *Guanyu xinshiqi jundui zhengzhi gongzuo de jueding zhushiben,* pp. 273–4; *Zhongguo Gaige Dacidian,* p. 492.

[93] It was reported that in 1988 the PLA Academy of Military Science completed a secret study that recommended that the powers of the State CMC and the Defense Ministry be strengthened. *South China Morning Post,* November 22, 1989, p. 19.

Central Military Commission and Paramount Leader

During Mao's time, the control over the Party CMC was affirmed by the Party constitutional provision that the Party chairman was concurrently the chairman of the Party CMC. Since Mao retained his Party chairmanship until he died in 1976, there was an even match between the formal institutional power and the informal personal power of the paramount leader. When Mao's hand-picked successor, Hua Guofeng, assumed both posts of the chairman of the Party and chairman of the Party CMC, a gap emerged between his official posts (or formal authority) and personal power (informal power or lack of it). The military leaders in the Party CMC who exercised actual control over the military began to undermine the rules of the game. In 1981, Deng Xiaoping, who did not assume the Party chairmanship became the chairman of the CMC. The new Party constitution adopted in 1982 had to accommodate reality, so the provision that "the chairman of the Military Commission must be the Party chairman" was changed into "the chairman of the Military Commission must be a member of the Standing Committee of the Politburo."

In 1987, the rule was further amended to meet Deng's desire to retain his chairmanship of the Party CMC while preparing to give up all his leading posts in the Party Central Committee, including membership in the five-member Standing Committee of the Politburo. At the Thirteenth Party Congress, Paragraph 5 of Article 21 of the 1982 Party constitution – "The members of the Military Commission of the Central Committee are decided on by the Central Committee. The Chairman of the Military Commission must be a member of the Standing Committee of the Politburo" – was changed into: "The members of the Military Commission of the Central Committee are decided on by the Central Committee."[94] This justified Deng's continuing assumption of the chairmanship of the Party CMC even though he was theoretically only one of the 50 million Party members. This change highlighted Deng's personal power at the expense of institutionalization of the military command, the consequences of which were clearly manifested in the 1989 Tiananmen crisis, when Deng personally persuaded the military regional commanders to send troops into Beijing to impose martial law against strong opposition from Party Chief Zhao Ziyang and without the prior approval of the National People's Congress.

After Mao, Deng was able to assert his control over army generals mainly because of his many years of active leadership in the military. Since the Party

---

94 FBIS-CHI, November 2, 1987, p. 28.

CMC was reestablished in 1954, Deng has been the only member of the CMC besides Mao, who was not a military general. Deng was a member of the Party CMC from 1954 to 1966, its vice chairman in 1975–76 and 1977–81, and its chairman from 1981 to 1989. This was roughly a total of twenty-five years of service on the Party CMC. In fact, Deng stayed on the Party CMC longer than anybody else, including Mao. Deng had certainly come a long way in preparation for controlling the army after Mao.

Chairman Jiang: The Commander in Chief?

In late 1989, Shanghai Party boss Jiang Zemin was chosen to succeed Deng as the chairman of the Party CMC. An engineer by training, Jiang Zemin had neither military experience nor strong personal connections in the PLA before he became the designated successor. Surrounded by military generals on the Party CMC, Chairman Jiang, the commander in chief, is perhaps only a nominal leader of this military group. To be sure, Jiang wasted no time in trying to build up his power base in the military. Indeed, as Deng was leaving the political scene, Jiang Zemin has in recent years accelerated his efforts.

First, Jiang frequently reminds his generals of Mao's maxim: "Party commands the gun, and the gun must never be allowed to command the Party." But military generals also remember Mao's other maxim: "Every Communist must grasp the truth, 'Political power grows out of the barrel of a gun.' " Mao further stressed that, "having guns, we can create Party organizations."[95] Quoting Mao perhaps is not going to help Jiang get very far. Nonetheless, Jiang needs whatever legitimacy he can hope to get from resorting to the CCP's orthodoxy.

Second, since November 1989, Jiang has visited hundreds of platoons, brigades, military bases, and regional command headquarters all over the country.[96] Jiang has also sought to win support from a new generation of top generals. In June 1993, June 1994, and January 1996, Jiang thrice pinned generals' stars on the nation's top twenty-nine military leaders.[97] These new promotions reflect a well-thought-out balance among various factions, armed

---

[95] Mao Zedong, *Selected Works of Mao Tse-tung,* vol. 2 (Beijing: Foreign Languages Press, 1965), p. 224.

[96] *The Independent,* August 6, 1995, p. 13.

[97] *The New York Times,* December 4, 1994, p. 24; *World Journal,* January 24, 1996, p. A10; Lin Changsheng, "Dang yao zhihui qiang; qiang yao zhihui dang" (Party seeks to command the gun and gun seeks to command the Party) *China Times Business Weekly* 155 (December 18–24, 1994), p. 7. There are now altogether forty-six generals in China.

Table 9.3. *Reshuffling of military leaders, 1990–94*

Name	Old post	New post
	1990	
Cao Pengsheng[a]	Deputy Commissar, Jinan MR	Commissar, Lanzhou MR
Liu Xinzeng	Deputy Commissar, Lanzhou MR	Deputy Commissar, Guangzhou MR
Pang Weiqiang	Commander, Hainan MD	Commander, Hunan MD
Pei Jinzhou	Deputy Commissar, Lanzhou MR	Deputy Commissar, Nanjing MR
Wang Chengbin[a]	Deputy Commander, Nanjing MR	Commander, Beijing MR
Wen Guoqing	Commander, Hunan MD	Commander, Guangxi MD
Wu Yuqian[b]	Commander, 67th GA Jinan MR	Commander, 23rd GA Shenyang MR
Xiao Xuchu	Commissar, Guangxi MD	Commander, Hainan MD
Zhang Haiyun	Commissar, South China Sea Fleet	Commissar, North China Sea Fleet
	1991	
Ai Weiren	Deputy Commissar, Chengdu MR	Deputy Commissar, Shenyang MR
	1992	
Gu Shanqing[a]	Commissar, Chengdu MR	Commissar, Beijing MR
Liu Anyuan[a]	Commissar, 2nd Artillery Corps	Commissar, Nanjing MR
Liu Jingsong[a]	Commander, Shenyang MR	Commander, Lanzhou MR
Jiang Hongquan	Deputy Commander, Chengdu MR	Deputy Commander, Beijing MR
Shi Yuxiao[a]	Commissar, Nanjing MR	Commissar, Guangzhou MR
Wang Ke[a]	Deputy Commander, Lanzhou MR	Commander, Shenyang MR
Zhang Zhijian	Deputy Commander, Jinan MR	Deputy Commander, Beijing MR
	1993	
Geng Quanli[b]	Commissar, Tibet MD	Commissar, Sichuan MD
Qu Zhenmou	Deputy Commander, Jinan MR	Deputy Commander, Nanjing MR
Zhang Taiheng	Deputy Commander, Nanjing MR	Commander, Jinan MR
Zhang Yujiang	Commissar, Jiangxi MD	Commissar, Fujian MD
Zhao Lianchen	Commissar, Qinghai MD	Commissar, Shaanxi MD
Zheng Shichao	Commissar, Fujian MD	Commissar, Jiangxi MD
	1994	
Dong Xuelin	Deputy Commander, Beijing MR	Deputy Commander, Jinan MR
He Daoquan	Commander, 40th GA Shenyang MR	Deputy Commander, Beijing MR

continued

Table 9.3. *Continued*

Name	Old post	New post
Jiang Futang	Director, Political Dept., Jinan MR	Deputy Commissar, Chengdu MR
Li Xinliang	Deputy Commander, Guangzhou MR	Commissar, Shenyang MR
Tan Neida[b]	Commissar, 39th GA Shenyang MR	Director, Political Dept. Jinan MR
Wang Jiying	Commander, North China Sea Fleet	Commander, East China Sea Fleet
Wu Guangyu[b]	Deputy Commissar, Air Force Nanjing MR	Commander, Air Force Jinan MR
Wu Runzhong	Commissar, 38th GA Beijing MR	Deputy Commissar, Chengdu MR
Xie Decai	Deputy Commander, Air Force Chengdu MR	Commander, Air Force Nanjing MR
Zhang Gong[a]	Commissar, Chengdu MR	Commissar, Academy of Military Sciences
Zhang Zhijian	Deputy Commander, Beijing MR	Commissar, Chengdu MR
Zhao Bingyao	Commissar, Air Force Beijing MR	Commissar, Air Force Guangzhou MR

Notes: [a]Elected member of the Fourteenth CCP Central Committee in October 1992.
[b]Elected alternate member of the Fourteenth CCP Central Committee in October 1992.
MR = Military Region; MD = Military District; GA = Group Army
Sources: Compiled by the author from biographical information in the following: Malcolm Lamb, *Directory of Officials and Organizations in China: A Quarter-Century Guide* (Armonk, NY: M. E. Sharpe, 1994); Michael D. Swaine, *The Military and Political Succession in China: Leadership, Institutions, Beliefs* (Santa Monica, CA: RAND, 1992); Lin Changsheng, "Dang xiang zhihui qiang; qiang xiang zhihui dang" (Party seeks to command the gun and the gun seeks to command the Party), *China Times Business Weekly* 155 (December 18–24, 1994), pp. 6–10.

services, and military regions. The Party CMC under Jiang also authorized an increase in officers' salaries and in food subsidies for soldiers.[98]

Third, Jiang (with Deng's permission) has conducted several reshuffles of military commanders and political commissars. Transferring of military leaders of course is not new. The recent military reshuffling, however, is much

[98] *The New York Times,* December 4, 1994, p. 24.

more frequent and massive than routine personnel changes. After the 1989 Tiananmen crackdown, there has been major military reshuffling every year except in 1991. As we can see from Table 9.3, within a four-year period, at least ten military districts changed their commanders (and deputy commanders) or political commissars (and deputy commissars), and all seven military regions have had at least one of their leaders transferred. In 1994 alone, four regional commanders and four political commissars were transferred. Moreover, between 1993 and 1995, more than 150 cadres from the three departments of the PLA general headquarters were transferred to combat or grassroots units.[99]

Fourth, Jiang has also tried to institutionalize and regularize the military service. Under his tenure as the chairman of the Party CMC, several major military laws and regulations were adopted or revised, including the Military Service Law of the People's Republic of China, the Law on Reserve Officers of the People's Republic of China, the Regulations on PLA Officers on Active Service, the Regulations Guiding the Active Service of Servicemen, the Provisional Regulations on Non-Military Cadres, and the Provisional Regulations Guiding the Enrollment of the Institutions and Academies of the Chinese People's Liberation Army.

Finally, Jiang has tried to institutionalize the military retirement system to bring about more desirable personnel changes in the military. The Regulations on PLA Officers on Active Service revised in May 1994, set new age limits for officers at or below military regional levels (see Table 9.4). In 1995, several senior military leaders were retired upon or after their sixty-fifth birthday, including Li Jing, the deputy chief of the PLA General Staff; Zhou Keyu, the political commissar of the PLA General Logistics Department; Zhao Nanqi, the commandant of the PLA Academy of Military Sciences; Liu Mingpu, the deputy director of the PLA General Logistics Department; Zhang Bin, the deputy director of the PLA General Logistics Department; and Li Wenqing, the political commissar of the National Defense University.[100] More senior military leaders were retired in 1996, including General Li Xilin, the commander of the Guangzhou Military Region, General Gu Hui, the commander of the Nanjing Military Region, and General Cao Pansheng, the political Commissar of the Lanzhou Military Region, all were born in 1930.[101]

Despite what Jiang has done in recent years, there are indications that his command of the gun is still far from assured. Jiang holds all the most important

[99] Xinhua News Agency report quoted in *South China Morning Post,* January 15, 1996.
[100] *World Journal,* August 29, 1995, p. A-10.
[101] Ibid., February 1, 1996, p. A-10.

Table 9.4. *Age limits for military, political, and logistics officers of combat units*

Level	Age limits
Major Military Region	
Principal leading officer	65
Deputy officer	63
Army	55
Division	50
Regiment	45
Battalion	40
Company	35
Platoon	30

Source: Xinhua News Agency report (Domestic Service), May 13, 1994.

posts of the Party, the state, and the army. He has been in power for more than six years now, longer than any of the successors-designate before him. Deng's support for Jiang, although at times wavering, has never been fully withdrawn. Jiang has had more time and better opportunity than other previously chosen successors to consolidate his power. Yet, the picture of succession remains unclear and much still depends on Jiang's relations with the military leadership.

During the Deng era, the PLA made noticeable progress toward military modernization, but the structural political role of the army has remained significant. The lessons from the past convinced many military officers that the PLA should not be used to suppress demonstrating civilians in May–June 1989 or to solve an intraparty political crisis. Yet those who followed this conviction and refused to carry out the martial law order were later punished for being politically unreliable and disloyal to the Party. Those military leaders who were actively involved in the bloody crackdown, however, only had a short time to celebrate. Before long, those responsible for the post-Tiananmen purge in the military were themselves purged. The PLA in the Deng era thus still faced its classic political dilemma: It was structurally difficult to disengage from CCP politics, and yet its active political role often brought more humiliation than glorification to the military institution.

The difficulty of transforming the PLA into a modern standing army of the Chinese state has been exacerbated by the central government's declining financial capacity to support the military and by the booming army business in pursuit of wealth and power. The most challenging task for Jiang Zemin or anyone else is how to command an army without a paramount leader. Our analysis demonstrates that the Party commanding the gun has always been a myth. For the past decades, it was the paramount leader like Mao and Deng who commanded the gun through the military generals in the Party CMC. The time of the paramount leader is gone, and a continuous emphasis on Party command of the army is only self-deceiving when in reality neither the Party Central Committee nor the Party chief can hope to control the gun. The solution to the institutional dilemma is to transfer the command of the military forces to the state institutions and to manage the army through legal and institutionalized procedures. This requires a fundamental transformation in Party–army relationship, including making the State Central Military Commission actually in command of the military and empowering the Ministry of Defense. This is no easy choice, but there isn't much choice. As the PLA is becoming militarily stronger, economically richer, and politically ambitious, lack of an effective system of commanding the army is not good news for the Party, the country, and the army itself.

Conclusions

THE main theme in this book is that the Chinese Communist Party has become the major obstacle to state-building in post-1949 China. After the imperial institutions collapsed in the first decades of this century, China was plunged into social chaos and political disintegration. In a desperate search for a modern form of state, the Chinese political elite and intellectuals experimented with many opposing ideological and organizational discourses. However, severe socioeconomic conditions, structural problems of governance, and frequent foreign invasions overwhelmed China. By 1949, only a strong revolutionary mass party had emerged from the civil war as the organizational force of China.

As the social and economic situation in China changed from war and revolution to economic construction, state institution-building became necessary, if not inevitable. The CCP leaders in the 1950s recognized this need and embarked upon ambitious plans for building a new Chinese state. Meanwhile, in a new environment, the Party's revolutionary ideology, organizational principle, and methods of mass mobilization, which had spelled the Party's success before 1949, became increasingly counterproductive to economic construction and political institutionalization. These features, however, proved to be difficult to change because they had been deeply built into the Party organization over many years of revolutionary warfare. Because the revolutionary party and the state institutions followed different organizational rationale and logic, the development of the state inevitably challenged the leading status and power of the Party, which in turn prompted the Party's reaction or overreaction to suppress and even destroy the state institutions that the Party had initially built. Thus the CCP leaders during the Mao era were constantly troubled by the institutional dilemma: The Party cannot live without the state and it cannot live with the state.

In the late 1970s and the 1980s, as China moved away from Mao's political campaigns to Deng's economic modernization, building the state legislative, judicial, administrative, and military institutions became essential, especially when the Party was losing its relevance and predominance due to the rapidly changing socioeconomic environment. Yet, although the Deng regime needed the benefits of legitimacy, stability, and efficiency associated with the state constitution, legislative and judicial system, government administration, civil service, and a modernized standing army, it failed to fundamentally redefine the status and the role of the Party in the Chinese political process. The institutional reforms and adaptations under the Deng regime were therefore inconsistent and contradictory, reflecting the regime's dilemma of trying to "have its cake and eat it, too." This only intensified the institutionally embedded conflicts between the state institutions and the Party organization.

CHINESE STATE-BUILDING IN RETROSPECT

This study has demonstrated that the post-1949 Chinese state-building is a difficult and still unfolding process. In retrospect, several strands to the main argument seem to stand out. First, the assumed "statist" tradition and the CCP's pre-1949 experience did not help build a modern state in post-1949 China. The Chinese imperial state functioned more like a big family, and as an empire of Confucian culture, it offered only a limited foundation upon which a modern state could be constructed. The revolutionary ideology of the CCP provided no easy answer to the question of state-building. From a Marxist-Leninist perspective, a state is something that would either wither away or be swept away. During the CCP's years of managing their base areas in Jiangxi and Yan'an, the organizational principles of the Party's unified leadership and methods of mass mobilization were established, which later greatly conditioned the CCP's responses to new institutional challenges.

Second, the 1950s were a major turning point in Chinese state-building. Because the rapidly changing balance of forces on the battleground gave the CCP leaders little time to prepare for state-building, the new state institutions of the PRC in the early 1950s were primitive and underdeveloped. The CCP leaders therefore had no choice but to rely on the army to run the country and to use the traditional method of mass campaigns to implement policies. Thus, even though the CCP leaders had changed their headquarters from Yan'an to Beijing, China experienced a continuation of revolutionary struggle and mass mobilization. In the mid-1950s, there was an opportunity for the CCP leaders to move away from war-style management of the economy and society. The end of the Korean War, three years of economic recovery, and restoration of social stability made it possible for China to move from revolution to construction. Changes in China's domestic and international environment challenged the CCP's ability to make necessary institutional innovations. Mao Zedong's initial responses were not much different from those of many leaders of newly independent nations: namely, glorifying and constructing state institutions to deal with the problems of legitimacy, organization, integration, and economic development.

The Anti-Rightist Campaign of 1957 suddenly reversed the course of state-building. The Party's revenge against its critics trampled upon the first state constitution, paralyzed the newly established national legislature, and destroyed the emerging legal system. During the Great Leap Forward movement in 1958–60, the Party committees took the responsibilities for economic management away from the central administrators and provincial governments. Revolutionary zeal replaced caution and reasoning, and political consideration took command over economic calculation. Under the Party leadership, economic production was organized like guerrilla warfare. In 1959, the dispute over economic policy at Lushan caused a major split among the top Party leadership, which unexpectedly resulted in a severe blow to the military institution. Like a dependent child, the Chinese state, after receiving crippling blows in its early life, was slow to recover and had tremendous difficulty growing up under a revolutionary party.

Third, the reformist Deng regime was characterized by a deep ambivalence toward state-building. By the time of Mao's death in 1976, what had artificially sustained Mao's revolution after 1949 ultimately buried it. Having recognized the legitimacy crisis, the CCP under Deng sought to build up the legitimacy of the new regime through the legal system and economic modernization. During the sixteen years of post-Mao reform, the most important change was the overall situation of moving from revolution to construction. Despite several major setbacks, not the least of which was the June 4th crackdown in 1989, reform and economic development have characterized the Deng era. This provided a favorable environment under which the process of state-building had unfolded. In the area of organizational principles and norms, such concepts as legislative supremacy, judicial independence, and separation of the Party and government, which had been condemned during the Mao era, could now be advocated. Some of them have even been officially endorsed.

Reforms and state-building required a basic redefinition of the relationship between the Party and state. Here, however, the Deng regime has largely failed to get the Chinese state institutions right. In 1980, Deng delivered a major speech on the reform of the Party and state systems. But the subsequent changes were piecemeal and disappointing due to Deng's concessions to the resisting conservative Party veterans. Zhao Ziyang's proposal of political reform in 1987 would have led to major structural changes, but Zhao's purge and the June 4th crackdown in 1989 aborted the political reform program. At the end of the Deng era, the principle of Party leadership is still guarded against any challenge. Key Party organizational units, such as the Party's Political and Legal Affairs Committee, Party core groups, and Party Central Military Commission, are still kept in place, even though the Party organization is rapidly losing its ability to discipline its members and to control the populace.

Finally, during the more than four decades from Mao to Deng, the Chinese Communist leaders failed to come up with a viable solution to the state-building problem. The "A or B" (either party or state) approach was destructive and antistate. The experience in China and other socialist countries also proved that the "A = B" (party supersedes state) approach is not constructive. Because the revolutionary party and the state are essentially two different types of political organization, using one to control the other necessarily led to conflicts and tensions. The CCP leaders had hoped that the "A & B" (both party and state) approach could work, but this was possible only in circumstances where the Party elite agreed to provide some real space for those who went into the state bureaucratic sphere and only if the limits of the role of the Party and of the state were carefully delineated and adhered to. Yet the emphasis on overall Party leadership and continuation of the Party organizational control created formidable obstacles to institutionalization that would have delineated one sphere for the Party, another for the state. The Party–state relationship in China has therefore remained ill defined and conflict ridden.

THE INSTITUTIONAL PERSPECTIVE ON STATE-BUILDING

As the analysis in this book demonstrates, changes in the broader socioeconomic environment do not automatically lead to institutional innovations. Human agents functioning within the constraints of their organizational environment may choose to respond, or not to respond, to changes. What made it impossible for the veteran Party leaders to agree on a few rules that might give the state institutions a minimum opportunity to develop? One could argue that, like the founding emperors of the imperial dynasties before them, the CCP leaders regarded the People's Republic as their own dynasty, in which any rule was nothing but an instrument serving the need of the Party and, above all, the will of the paramount leader. As such, rules and procedures were disposable and could be amended or abandoned if necessary. Nonetheless, even though the "dynastic" interpretation underscores certain "neotraditional" elements of the Communist elite, the CCP as a revolutionary party built on an ideology of class struggle and mass mobilization was something that no imperial dynasty could possibly match. Moreover, living in a world where the modern nation-state had become the dominant form of polity, the CCP leaders were no less enthusiastic than leaders of any newly independent nation about establishing constitutional legitimacy, enhancing government administration, and building a modern national army.

Following the institutional approach, this study suggests that the sequence of institutional development in China had a significant impact: The political party had emerged after an old regime collapsed, but before a new state had been established. In discussing the sequential development of parties and constitutional rule, Giovanni Sartori points out: "Perhaps the polity must exist first, perhaps unification has to precede party 'partition,' and perhaps this is the condition that makes parties a subdivision compatible with unity rather than a division that disrupts it."[1] The Communist Party in China, however, was not born into an existing institutional order. On the contrary, it emerged in political chaos and grew strong in violence and guerrilla warfare. While the Communist revolutionary movement gained momentum, the Nationalist-sponsored state-building achieved very limited results. In 1948–49, when more than two million military, financial, and administrative personnel of the Nationalist government fled to Taiwan, the state of the Republic of China also moved to Taiwan, leaving a state vacuum on the mainland for the CCP to fill.

Revolutionary or right-wing fascist political parties usually emerged in the midst of a prolonged political crisis and were designed to "organize the chaotic public will."[2] But as Leonard Schapiro and John Lewis point out, "Mussolini and Hitler were both concerned to impose the rule of their movements on an existing state structure, which they modified and dominated, but did not or could not destroy."[3] Their parties "were designed not so much for administra-

---

[1] Giovanni Sartori, *Parties and Party Systems: A Framework for Analysis,* vol. 1 (Cambridge: Cambridge University Press, 1976), p. 16.

[2] Sigmund Neumann, ed., *Modern Political Parties* (Chicago: University of Chicago Press, 1956), p. 397.

[3] Leonard Schapiro and John Wilson Lewis, "The Roles of the Monolithic Party Under the Totalitarian Leader," in John Wilson Lewis, ed., *Party Leadership and Revolutionary Power in China* (New York: Cambridge University Press, 1970), p. 117.

tion, as for bending the existing institutions of the administration, political and economic, to their will."[4] In contrast, the CCP as the most powerful organizational force in 1949 did not need to bend the existing state institutions to its will, for there was not much left to bend; in fact, the Party could establish new state institutions at will.

The point that a revolutionary party of twenty-seven years was responsible for building a new state in China is too important to miss. By the time the People's Republic was being created, the CCP had already become the dominant political and military force. The CCP's rich experience in mobilizing masses into guerrilla warfare and land reform naturally shaped the Party leaders' perceptions of what was desirable and how things should be done in post-war China. The Party's revolutionary ideology and organizational skills of mass mobilization, once proven successful, had later become an integrated part of the post-1949 organizational norms, thus limiting the options of the CCP leaders as they faced the challenge in a new environment.

In the Soviet Union, the process of industrialization had presumably made the Communist Party more bureaucratic and less revolutionary. This has led Jerry Hough to suggest a prefectural role performed by the Communist Party in the Soviet industrial decision-making; The local Party organs assumed the economic responsibility for fulfillment of the development program while maintaining their political responsibility for maintaining stability and order.[5] Yet evidence underscores the ignorance of the revolutionary idealists who fail to understand that every state institution implies an internal logic of its action. Efforts to create party structures to oversee governmental and administrative procedures are a form of wanting to have one's cake and eat it, too. The problem is really one of incompatible roles. With a Party cadre corps more urbanized and educated than the CCP cadre corps, the Soviet Communists still achieved only limited efficiency in managing the economy.[6] In China, Mao's

---

[4] Ibid., p. 118.

[5] Jerry F. Hough, *The Soviet Prefects* (Cambridge, MA: Harvard University Press, 1969), p. 256.

[6] In an assessment of the Communist Party's economic role, Peter Rutland points out that "the extensive activity by party officials and members on the Soviet shopfloor is not motivated purely and simply by a desire to promote economic efficiency, but that it has a distinct organizational and political logic of its own which frequently clashes with what managers and workers perceive to be economically rational." *Studies of Comparative Communism* 21, no. 1 (Spring 1988), pp. 25–43. Gorbachev's reform in the late 1980s was aimed at transferring a significant amount of power from the regional and local Party organs to the Soviets. Vladimir Brovkin, "First Party Secretaries: An Endangered Soviet Species?" *Problems of Communism* (January–February 1990), pp. 15–6.

guerrilla-style mass mobilization for economic drives only produced disastrous consequences, as horribly manifested in 1958–60.

This study also suggests that organizational features are particularly influenced by critical moments or extraordinary events in history. The CCP's rise to national political power was through a long process of fierce armed struggle against the Nationalist government. Massacres, bloody battles, and death by the thousands were no news to the CCP members. Given the life-and-death nature of that power struggle, it is no surprise that the CCP was the most antistate among the world's communist parties. While even the Russian Bolsheviks had a brief experience with electoral competition within a parliamentary system (Duma), the CCP had been fighting against the existing state for more than two decades before it seized political power. After some twenty-seven years of trying to survive, the revolutionary leaders of the CCP came to the strong belief that they had paid a high price for establishing the new state and that they had earned the right to control it. Fresh in their minds were the many years of suffering, hardships, sacrifice, and armed struggles. This experience of gaining control over state power through a long, violent, and bloody process undoubtedly had a profound impact on the CCP's internal organizational structure as well as on the human agents working in it.

Here, a brief comparison with the Kuomintang may further highlight the CCP's ideological and organizational constraints. The two political parties in China once had much in common. Both were explicitly built on the Leninist model of a revolutionary party. Both had strong leaders (Chiang Kai-shek and Mao Zedong). Both came to assert that their party bore the sole responsibility of saving China. From 1928 to 1948, the KMT maintained a single-party regime that was then replaced by the similar single-party regime of the CCP after 1949. However, three major differences are noteworthy. First, even though the KMT had in fact dominated the state of the Republic of China for decades, the official ideology claimed that the one-party rule was only temporary. According to Dr. Sun Yat-sen, the founding father of the party, the KMT assumed the task of ruling the nation only because of the enormous social and political problems that China was facing at the time. When conditions were appropriate, the KMT regime was to move from the stages of "Military Rule" and "Political Tutelage" to that of "Constitutional Government." After all, Dr. Sun expected the stage of Political Tutelage to last for only six years. The insertion of the period of "Suppression of Communist Rebellion" in 1948 much prolonged the stage of Political Tutelage, but it could not (and did not) indefinitely rule out the possibility that the stage of "Constitutional Government" would ultimately arrive. Thus, at least theoretically, there was to be a foreseeable end to the KMT's control of the state. In contrast, there is no similar time limit in Communist ideology to the CCP's rule. The Party would "wither away" along with the state, only when or if all human beings enter a Communist society.

Second, the CCP under Mao insisted that class struggle should continue in post-1949 China. One campaign after another had to be launched to eliminate class enemies, thus artificially recreating a revolutionary environment in which the state institutions and legal system were difficult to develop. Even the Deng regime, although rejecting the Mao-style mass campaigns, continued to stress the ideological and political struggle against "bourgeois liberalization" and the "Western scheme of peaceful evolution." In contrast, although ideological control and political repression had continued in Taiwan until 1986, internal class struggles and mass campaigns were not characteristic of the KMT regime.

Third, a major difference lay in the fact that the legitimacy of the KMT's rule in Taiwan was dependent on the state of the Republic of China (ROC). The KMT was forced to leave the mainland after the nationalist revolution failed to modernize or unify China. To the Taiwanese, the KMT was an alien regime imposed on the local society. Thus, only by claiming to represent all China within the framework of the ROC could the KMT regime hope to justify its residence in Taiwan. During thirty-eight years of martial law, it was not uncommon for KMT officials to manipulate the state institutions, but these were examples of an authoritarian regime abusing the state's authority to suppress its opponents rather than a revolutionary regime attacking the state itself. The CCP, on the other hand, gained its legitimacy through its revolutionary victories. In the name of "continuing the revolution," the CCP could afford to, and did, attack the state institutions directly.

This study further suggests that paramount leaders like Mao and Deng played an extremely important role in shaping the organizational environment. Since 1957, Mao had tried to reverse the state-building process by artificially recreating a revolutionary environment. In doing so, Mao not only served his own purpose, but also helped preserve an environment with which a revolutionary party would feel most comfortable. Continuing the revolution through mass campaigns reinvigorated the Party's revolutionary ideology, legitimized the Party's unified leadership, and defined the Party's organizational purpose. In this way, mass campaigns became a mechanism of "political reproduction" that served to prolong the triangular system of the paramount leader, revolutionary ideology, and Party organizational control. Although Mao constantly purged Party officials, the way he did it – through numerous mass campaigns – effectively created an environment conducive to the regeneration of the revolutionary party and devastating to state institution-building.

Deng had tried to do the impossible: keeping the Party while creating an environment not conducive to the Party and rebuilding the state institutions while maintaining the Party organizational dominance of the state. On the one hand, Deng was determined to move away from Mao-style class struggle and toward economic modernization. On the other hand, Deng insisted that the Party's leadership must not be weakened and Party organizational control over the state must be maintained. In other words, Deng had decided to "get off the horse," but he was reluctant to abandon the horse and was unable to move on with a new life. It was not surprising, therefore, that the Deng regime appeared contradictory and half-hearted in making the institutional innovations and adaptations required by the fundamental changes in the Chinese economy and society.

THE FUTURE OF THE CHINESE STATE

Because rapid economic development and social changes are unleashing many dynamic forces, how to reorganize China has again become an urgent issue. The future of China may be as unpredictable as the past of China, and predicting the unpredictable is often unrewarding. However, to try to understand where China is going is of tremendous significance for our world.

It seems clear that by the mid-1990s, the CCP, once the only organizational force of China, can no longer be an effective force for reorganizing China. Despite the repeated emphasis in the official media, the Party's unified leadership is neither possible nor desirable. The so-called neo-authoritarianism that characterized the regimes in South Korea and Taiwan of the 1960s and 1970s is no longer relevant to China because China today does not have a strongman like Park Chung Hee or Chiang Kai-shek. Indeed, after ten years of the Cultural Revolution under Mao and sixteen years of market reform under Deng, the Chinese society has already moved beyond the time of a one-strongman dictatorship. Once the paramount leader is gone, the revolutionary ideology becomes bankrupt, and the organizational discipline erodes, the Party as we know it is over. The final end of mass campaigns in Chinese politics removes the mechanism of political reproduction, making it all the more certain that a revolutionary environment can never be recreated again. Any attempt to revitalize the Party organization in order to control a fast-changing society is likely to fail miserably. The Party may be "saved" only if post-Deng leaders fundamentally redefine the power relationship between the Party and the state, reestablish certain basic rules of the game, and more important, try to learn how to play by the rules.

It also seems likely that we are going to see a "segmented state" of China in which multiple centers of power emerge among the state legislative, judicial, and administrative institutions vis-à-vis the Party organization. Sixteen years of state-building under the Deng regime have given the state institutions more legitimacy and authority. Given the changed socioeconomic environment, it is no longer possible to reverse the course of state-building as Mao did during the Anti-Rightist Campaign and the Cultural Revolution. As the Party's Politburo with its Standing Committee becomes a less collective decision-making body, key political players in post-Deng China are likely to hold on to their institutional power base in the legislature, the government administration, the military, and the provinces. Thus we can expect more debates and conflicts involving the power relationships among various political institutions.

China today has also become more decentralized than it used to be. On many occasions, the center pretends to command provinces whereas provinces don't even recognize the center. In reality, many regions and provinces are largely on their own. Allocation of authorities over tax, investment, construction, foreign trade and source utilization often has to be negotiated between Beijing and thirty provincial capitals. Frequent transfer of provincial leaders only leads to more discontent and resistance. If economic modernization continues to be the top priority for the post-Deng regime, we are going to see more divergent interests between the center and localities and among various regions. Given the declining extractive capacity of Beijing and the continuing tensions between the center and provinces, some major institutional adaptations may have to be made. One way to deal with these problems would be to rearrange the central–local power relationship within a more or less federal framework. The Chinese National People's Congress has already become a forum for different regions to express their concerns, and it is likely that China will move further toward a federalist solution to the country's chronic problem of oscillation between central control and local autonomy. A political or even military crackdown on rebellious regions is not impossible, but it can be orchestrated only at the expense of economic prosperity, thus leading to more regional conflicts and social tensions.

Short of the outbreak of civil war, a military takeover of China is unlikely to happen, however. It is not because the Party or Party CMC Chairman Jiang Zemin has a firm command over the guns. On the contrary, the PLA, with the passing of the paramount leader, has already become more assertive and independent than ever before. The army will continue to show its nominal loyalty to the Party center because the current leadership essentially gives what the army wants. The army, therefore, has no reason to take the risk of upsetting the power relationship while it continues to push for military modernization. Without redefining the Party–army relationship and changing the Chinese military command system, there is little chance for the PLA to remain neutral should a major power struggle break out in the top leadership. It is still possible that someone in the military would try to play with fire in changing political winds. Because the PLA is structurally centered in the political process, there are always incentives for someone, regardless of his background as political commissar or military commander, to try to take advantage of the changing political situation to maximize his influence. Moreover, if a divided center and semiautonomous provinces prove to be unable to maintain stability or handle riots, turmoil, massive violence, or independence movements, some Party leaders in desperation may seek help from the military, as happened during both the Mao and the Deng eras. Institutionally speaking, the PLA could attempt to play an interventionist role in post-Deng power struggles, at the risk of falling easy prey to factional politics or to exercise self-discipline and limit its political role to a minimum in exchange for protection from attacks against the military following a political showdown. It is a delicate balancing act that the PLA as a whole has to perform.

The institutional crisis in China today also presents a danger, as well as an opportunity, for the opposition. The danger is that by opposing the so-called Party-state, those who hope to change the Party rule in China may mistakenly weaken the very state institutions that a fast-changing society needs. In the absence of a system of rule of law and a government that can actually govern, a civil society is less likely to emerge. In the wake of political institutional breakdown in the former Yugoslavia and Soviet Union, what we have seen is not civil societies but civil wars. The opportunity is that by separating the state from the Party, one can discover and pursue various actual and potential institutional alternatives to the Party rule. Thus, opposition does not have to be obstructive, and democracy does not have to be destructive.

China today can no longer be governed the way it was before under Mao Zedong or under Deng Xiaoping, but how it can be governed is far from certain. Citing the historical example of the development of modern Europe,

Arthur Waldron comments: "Europe's new economy and new society demanded new state structures – with constitutions, legal systems, and citizen participation – and Europe got them, but only at the cost of much turmoil."[7] China's fast-changing economy and society also demand similar state institutions. The question is: How high a cost does China have to pay before it gets them? Regrettably, after more than four decades of Communist Party rule, China today is still confronted with the century-old problem of how to build a modern Chinese state. As the world is preparing for the arrival of the twenty-first century, the Chinese leaders and people have yet to meet the most serious challenge of the twentieth century. Failure to reorganize China in a dramatically changing domestic and international environment will almost certainly lead to disastrous consequences for China, the Asia-Pacific region, and the world.

[7] Arthur Waldron, "After Deng the Deluge," *Foreign Affairs* (September/October 1995), p. 149.

Appendix A

CCP Membership Changes, 1921–96

Year	Total membership	Gross change	% of change
1921	57[a]	57	100.0
1922	195[b]	138	242.0
1923	420[c]	225	115.4
1924	994[c]	574	136.7
1925	3,000[c]	2006	201.8
1926	18,500[c]	15,500	516.7
1927 (Apr.)	57,967[c]	39,467	213.3
1927 (Aug.)	10,000[b]	−47,967	−82.7
1928	40,000[a]	30,000	300.0
1929	69,000[c]	29,000	72.5
1930	122,318[c]	53,318	77.3
1931	68,000[a]	−54,318	−44.4
1932	107,000[a]	39,000	57.4
1933	200,000[d]	93,000	86.9
1934	300,000[c]	100,000	50.0
1935	40,000[c]	−260,000	−86.7
1936	30,000[d]	−10,000	−25.0
1937	40,000[a]	10,000	33.3
1938	200,000[d]	160,000	400.0
1939	300,000[d]	100,000	50.0
1940	800,000[a]	500,000	166.7
1941	700,000[d]	−100,000	−12.5
1942	730,000[a]	30,000	4.3
1943	700,000[d]	−30,000	−4.1
1944	900,000[a]	200,000	28.6
1945	1,211,128[c]	311,128	34.5
1946	2,200,000[d]	988,872	81.6
1947	2,759,000[c]	559,000	25.4
1948	3,000,000[a]	241,000	8.7

continued

Appendix A: CCP membership changes, 1921–96

CCP membership changes, 1921–96

Year	Total membership	Gross change	% of change
1949	4,488,000[b]	1,488,000	49.6
1950	5,000,000[b]	512,000	11.4
1951	5,800,000[c]	800,000	16.0
1952	6,001,698[e]	239,405	4.2
1953	6,369,000[c]	367,302	6.1
1954	7,859,473[e]	1,490,473	23.4
1955	9,393,394[e]	1,533,921	19.5
1956	10,730,000[c]	1,336,606	14.2
1957	12,720,000[a]	1,990,000	18.5
1958	12,450,000[a]	−270,000	−2.1
1959	13,960,000[g]	1,510,000	12.1
1961	17,380,000[b]		
1964	18,010,000[c]		
1965	18,710,000[c]	700,000	3.9
1966	20,000,000[c]		
1969	22,000,000[b]		
1971	17,000,000[g]		
1972	20,000,000[g]	3,000,000	17.6
1973	28,000,000[b]	8,000,000	40.0
1976	35,070,000[c]		
1977	35,000,000[c]	−70,000	−2.0
1979	37,000,000[c]		
1980	38,000,000[h]	1,000,000	2.7
1981	38,923,569[g]	923,569	2.4
1982	39,657,212[a]	733,643	1.9
1983	40,950,000[i]	1,292,788	3.3
1984	41,000,000[g]	50,000	0.1
1985	42,000,000[f]	1,000,000	2.4
1986	44,000,000[j]	2,000,000	4.8
1987	46,011,951[c]	2,011,951	4.6
1988	48,000,000[i]	1,988,049	4.3
1989	49,000,000[i]	1,000,000	2.1
1990	50,000,000[i]	1,000,000	2.0
1991	50,320,000[i]	320,000	0.6
1992	51,956,000[k]	1,636,000	3.3
1993	52,800,000[i]	844,000	1.6
1994	54,000,000[i]	1,200,000	2.3
1995	56,781,000[l]	2,781,000	5.2
1996	57,000,000[l]	2,190,000	3.9

continued

*b*Zhongguo gongchandang lishi dashiji* (A Chronology of the Chinese Communist Party History) (Beijing: Renmin chubanshe, 1989).

*c*Feng Wenbin et al., eds., *Zhongguo gongchandang jianshe quanshu 1921–1991* (Encyclopedia of the Construction of the Chinese Communist Party, 1921–1991), vols. 4, 9 (Shanxi: Shanxi renmin chubanshe, 1991).

*d*Li Tianmin, ed., *Zhonggong wenti lunji* (Essays on the Problems of the Chinese Communist Party) (Taipei: Institute of International Studies, 1974), pp. 9–12.

*e*Current Background* (Hong Kong: U.S. Consulate General), 428, p. 1.

*f*Cheng Baoshan, ed., *Zhongguo gongchandang zhuzhi gongzuo dacidian* (The Dictionary of the Organizational Work of the Chinese Communist Party) (Jinan: Jinan chubanshe, 1992), p. 2,089.

*g*Hong Yung Lee, *From Revolutionary Cadres to Party Technocrats in Socialist China* (Berkeley: University of California Press, 1991), pp. 16–17.

*h*Hongqi* (Red Flag) (1980), No. 5, p. 1.

*i*The *People's Daily,* August 27, 1984; June 25, 1991; September 30, 1994.

*j*Daigong bao*(Hong Kong), September 26, 1986.

*k*John D. Friske, ed., *China: Facts & Figures, Annual* 17 (Gulf Breeze, FL: Academic International Press, 1994), pp. 36, 40.

*l*Xinhua News Agency, June 14, 1996.

Sources: *a*Ma Yuping and Huang Yuchong, eds., *Zhongguo zuotian yu jintian 1840–1987 nian guoqing shouce* (China's Yesterday and Today: Handbook of National Conditions: 1840–1987) (Beijing: Jiefangjun chubanshe, 1989), pp. 685–6.

Appendix B

Campaigns in China: 1950–89

Year	Campaign	Scope
1950	Party/Army Rectification	Party organization
1950–52	Agrarian Reform	Newly liberated areas
	Suppression of Counterrevolutionaries	Nationwide
1950–53	Resist-U.S. and Aid-Korea	Nationwide
1951	Party Rectification & Building	Party organization
	Criticizing Wu Xun	Cultural & ideological areas
1951–54	Mutual Aid Teams	Countryside
1951–52	Democratic Reform	Industrial enterprises
	Thought Reform	Intellectuals, teachers
	Three-Antis	Nationwide
1952	Five-Antis	Urban industrialists
1952–54	Party Member Registration	Party organization
1953	New Three-Antis	Party & government officials
	Organizing Primitive APCs	Countryside
	Study of Marxism-Leninism	Rural cadres
	Study of the Party's General Line	Nationwide
	Criticizing Yu Pingbo and Hu Shi	Areas of literature
1953–54	Opposing Gao-Rao Anti-Party Alliance	High-ranking Party officials
1955	Agricultural Collectivization	Countryside
1955–56	Anti-Hu Feng	Nationwide
	Anti-Idealism	Academic & cultural areas
	Socialist Reform of Private Business	Private entrepreneurs
1955–57	Exposing "Hidden Counterrevolutionaries"	Party, government & army
1957	"Hundred Flowers"	Intellectuals
1957	Party Rectification	Party organization
1958	Criticizing Ma Yinchu	Colleges/universities

continued

Campaigns in China: 1950–89

Year	Campaign	Scope
1957–58	Anti-Rightists	Nationwide
1958–59	Great Leap Forward	Nationwide
	Socialist & Communist Education	Countryside
1959	Criticizing Bourgeois Literature & Art	Literature & art areas
1958–60	People's Commune	Countryside
1959–60	Anti-Rightist Deviation	Party organization
1960	Setting Up Communal Mess Halls	Countryside
	Learn from Anshan Steel Company	Enterprises & large cities
	Strengthening Ideological Work	Army & government institutions
1961	Rectification of People's Communes	Countryside
	Reeducation of Party Members	Party organization
1963	Learn from Lei Feng	Nationwide
	Criticizing Art & Academic Authorities	Art & academic areas
1963–64	Five-Antis Campaign	Party & government agencies
	Art and Literature Rectification	Professional associations
1964	Learn from Daqing	Sectors of industry & transportation
	Learn from Dazhai	Countryside
	Party Rectification	Party organization
1964–66	Socialist Education	Rural cadres
1965	Preparing for War	Nationwide
1966–69	Cultural Revolution	Nationwide
1969	Party Rectification	Party organization
1970	Criticizing Chen Boda & Rectification	Party organization
1971–74	Criticizing Lin Biao & Confucius	Nationwide
1975	Studying Theory of Proletarian Dictatorship	Nationwide
	Commenting on the Book, *Water Margin*	Nationwide
1975–76	Anti-Rightist Tendency to Reverse Verdicts	Nationwide
1976	Criticizing Deng Xiaoping	Nationwide
1976–77	Criticizing the "Gang of Four"	Nationwide
1978	Debate on Criterion of Truth	Nationwide
1979	Criticizing "Xidan Democracy Wall"	Capital city
1981	Anti-Bourgeois Liberalization	Areas of ideology & art
1982	Anti-Corruption	Coastal cities

continued

Campaigns in China: 1950–89

Year	Campaign	Scope
	Strengthening the Social Order	Party organization
	Anti-Economic Crimes	Economic areas
1982–83	Sorting Out Three Kinds of People	Cadres
1983	Party Rectification	Party organization
	Anti-spiritual Pollution	Areas of theory & art; Party
1983–84	Anticrime	Nationwide
1983–87	Party Rectification	Nationwide
1985	Rural Party Rectification	Rural Party members
1987	Antibourgeois Liberalization	Party organization
1989	Socialist Education Campaign	Urban & rural areas

Sources: Zhongguo gongchandang lishi dashiji (A Chronology of the Chinese Communist Party History), Party History Research Office of the CCP Central Committee (Beijing: Renmin chubanshe, 1989); *Dangshi yanjiu yu jiaoxue* (Research and Teaching of Party History), published by the Party History Teaching and Research Office of the Central Party School.

Bibliography

CHINESE PERIODICALS AND NEWSPAPERS CITED

China Times Magazine. Taiwan and USA.
China Times Business Weekly. Taiwan and USA.
Dangde wenxian (Party Documents). Beijing.
Dangshi yanjiu yu jiaoxue (Research and Teaching of Party History). Beijing.
Diaocha yu yanjiu (Investigation and Research). Beijing.
Guangming Daily. Beijing.
Jingji baodao (Economic Reporter). Hong Kong.
Jiushi niandai (*The Nineties*). Hong Kong.
Liaowang (Outlook). Beijing.
Liberation Daily. Shanghai.
Minzhu yu fazhi (Democracy and Legal System). Shanghai.
People's Daily. Beijing.
Wen wei po. Hong Kong.
World Journal. USA.
Zhongguo jingji tizhi gaige (China's Economic Structure Reform). Beijing.
Zuzhi renshi xinxibao (Organization and Personnel Gazette). Shanghai.

ENGLISH-LANGUAGE REFERENCES

Abrahamsson, Bengt. *Military Professionalization and Political Power.* Beverly Hills, CA: Sage Publications, 1972.

Allison, Graham T. *Essence of Decision: Explaining the Cuban Missile Crisis.* Boston: Little, Brown, 1971.

Anderson, Benedict. *Imagined Communities: Reflections on the Origin and Spread of Nationalism.* London: Verso, 1983.

Aron, Raymond. *Democracy and Totalitarianism: A Theory of Political Systems.* Ann Arbor: The University of Michigan Press, 1965.

Bachman, David. *Bureaucracy, Economy, and Leadership in China: The Institutional Origins of the Great Leap Forward.* Cambridge: Cambridge University Press, 1991.

Barnett, A. Doak. *Cadres, Bureaucracy, and Political Power in Communist China.* New York: Columbia University Press, 1967.

Bibliography

Bartlett, Beatrice S. *Monarchs and Ministers: The Grand Council in Mid-Ch'ing China, 1723–1820.* Berkeley: University of California Press, 1991.

Baum, Richard, and Teiwes, Frederick C. *Ssu-ch'ing: The Socialist Education Movement of 1962–1966.* Berkeley: Center for Chinese Studies, University of California, 1968.

Baum, Richard. *Burying Mao: Chinese Politics in the Age of Deng Xiaoping.* Princeton, NJ: Princeton University Press 1994.

Bedeski, Robert E. *State-Building in Modern China: The Kuomintang in the Prewar Period.* Berkeley: Institute of East Asian Studies, University of California, 1981.

Bennett, A. Gordon. *Yundong: Mass Campaigns in Chinese Communist Leadership.* Berkeley: Center for Chinese Studies, University of California, 1976.

Binder, Leonard et al., eds. *Crises and Sequences in Political Development.* Princeton, NJ: Princeton University Press, 1971.

Blaustein, Albert P., ed. *Fundamental Legal Documents of Communist China.* South Hackensack, NJ: Fred B. Rothman & Company, 1962.

Bowie, Robert R., and Fairbank, John K., eds. *Communist China 1955–1959: Policy Documents with Analysis.* Cambridge, MA: Harvard University, 1962.

Brady, James P. *Justice and Politics in People's China: Legal Order or Continuing Revolution?* New York: Academic Press, 1982.

Braibanti, Ralph, ed. *Political and Administrative Development.* Durham, NC: Duke University Press, 1969.

Brzezinski, Zbigniew. *The Soviet Bloc: Unity and Conflict.* Cambridge, MA: Harvard University Press, 1960.

Brugger, Bill, and Kelly, David. *Chinese Marxism in the Post-Mao Era.* Stanford, CA: Stanford University Press, 1990.

Bullard, Monte R. *China's Political Military Evolution: The Party and the Military in the People's Republic of China, 1960–1984.* Boulder, CO: Westview Press, 1985.

Burns, John P., and Rosen, Stanley, eds. *Policy Conflicts in Post-Mao China: A Documentary Survey with Analysis.* Armonk, NY: M. E. Sharpe, 1986.

Burns, John P., ed. *The Chinese Communist Party's Nomenklatura System: A Documentary Study of Party Control of Leadership Selection, 1979–1984.* Armonk, NY: M. E. Sharpe, 1989.

Cell, Charles P. *Revolution at Work: Mobilization Campaigns in China.* New York: Academic Press, 1977.

Chang, David Wen Wei. *China Under Deng Xiaoping: Political and Economic Reform.* New York: St. Martin's Press, 1988.

Chang Hao. *Liang Chi'-ch'ao and Intellectual Transition in China, 1890–1907.* Cambridge, MA: Harvard University Press, 1971.

Chang King-yuh. *Mainland China After the Thirteenth Party Congress.* Boulder, CO: Westview Press, 1990.

Chang, Parris H. *Power and Policy in China.* University Park: Pennsylvania State University Press, 1978.

Chen, Theodore H. E. *Thought Reform of the Chinese Intellectuals.* Hong Kong: Hong Kong University Press, 1960.

Bibliography

Chen Yung-fa. *Making Revolution: The Communist Movement in Eastern and Central China, 1937–1945.* Berkeley: University of California Press, 1986.

Ch'en, Jerome. *The Military-Gentry Coalition: China Under the Warlords.* Toronto: University of Toronto–York University, Joint Centre on Modern East Asia, 1979.

Cheng Chu-yuan. *Behind the Tiananmen Massacre: Social, Political and Economic Ferment in China.* Boulder, CO: Westview Press, 1990.

Cheng Hsiao-shih. *Party-Military Relations in the PRC and Taiwan: Paradoxes of Control.* Boulder, CO: Westview Press, 1990.

Chi Hsi-sheng. *Warlord Politics in China, 1916–1928.* Stanford, CA: Stanford University Press, 1976.

Chi Wen-shun. *Ideological Conflicts in Modern China: Democracy and Authoritarianism.* New Brunswick: Translation Books, 1986.

Ch'ien Mu. *Traditional Government in Imperial China: A Critical Analysis.* Translated by Chün-tu Hsüeh and George O. Totten. Hong Kong: The Chinese University Press. 1982.

Deng Xiaoping. *Selected Works of Deng Xiaoping 1975–1982.* Beijing: Foreign Languages Press, 1984.

Deng Xiaoping: Speeches and Writings, 2nd and expanded edition. Elmsford, NY: Pergamon Press, 1987.

Dittmer, Lowell, and Kim, Samuel S., eds. *China's Quest for National Identity.* Ithaca, NY: Cornell University Press, 1993.

Domes, Jürgen. *Peng Te-huai: The Man and the Image.* Stanford, CA: Stanford University Press, 1985.

Dreyer, June Teufel. *China's Political System: Modernization and Tradition.* New York: Paragon House, 1993.

Eastman, Lloyd F. *Seeds of Destruction: Nationalist China in War and Revolution, 1937–1949.* Stanford, CA: Stanford University Press, 1984.

The Abortive Revolution: China Under Nationalist Rule, 1927–1937. Cambridge, MA: Harvard University Press, 1990.

Eckstein, Alexander. *China's Economic Revolution.* New York: Cambridge University Press, 1977.

Elster, Jon. *Making Sense of Marx.* New York: Cambridge University Press, 1985.

Fairbank, John King. *The United States and China,* 4th and enlarged edition. Cambridge, MA: Harvard University Press, 1983.

The Great Chinese Revolution, 1800–1985. New York: Harper & Row, 1987.

China: A New History. Cambridge, MA: The Belknap Press of Harvard University Press, 1992.

Falkenheim, Victor C., ed. *Citizens and Groups in Contemporary China.* Ann Arbor: Center for Chinese Studies, University of Michigan Press, 1987.

Friedrich, Carl J., and Brzezinski, Zbigniew. *Totalitarian Dictatorship and Autocracy.* Cambridge, MA: Harvard University Press, 1956.

Getty, J. Arch. *Origins of the Great Purges: The Soviet Communist Party Reconsidered, 1933–1938.* New York: Cambridge University Press, 1985.

Gittings, John. *The Role of the Chinese Army.* New York: Oxford University Press, 1967.

Bibliography

Goldman, Merle. *China's Intellectuals: Advise and Dissent.* Cambridge, MA: Harvard University Press, 1981.

Goldman, Merle, with Cheek, Timothy, and Hamrin, Carol Lee, eds. *China's Intellectuals and the State: In Search of a New Relationship.* Cambridge, MA: Council on East Asian Studies, Harvard University, 1987.

Goncharov, S. N., Lewis, John W., and Xue Litai. *Uncertain Partners: Stalin, Mao, and the Korean War.* Stanford, CA: Stanford University Press, 1993.

Gong Ting. *The Politics of Corruption in Contemporary China: An Analysis of Policy Outcomes.* New York: Praeger Publishers, 1994.

Goodman, David S. G., ed. *Groups and Politics in the People's Republic of China.* Armonk, NY: M. E. Sharpe, 1984.

Centre and Province in the People's Republic of China: Sichuan and Guizhou, 1955–1965. Cambridge: Cambridge University Press, 1986.

Goodman, David S. G., and Segal, Gerald, eds. *China in the Nineties: Crisis Management and Beyond.* New York: Oxford University Press, 1991.

China Deconstructs: Politics, Trade and Regionalism. London: Routledge, 1994.

Gray, Jack. *Rebellions and Revolutions: China from the 1800s to the 1980s.* New York: Oxford University Press, 1990.

Gray, Jack, ed. *Modern China's Search for a Political Form.* New York: Oxford University Press, 1969.

Greenblatt, Sidney, Wilson, Richard, and Wilson, Amy, eds. *Organizational Behavior in Chinese Society.* New York: Praeger Publishers, 1981.

Greenstein, Fred I., and Polsby, Nelson W., eds. *Handbook of Political Science,* vol. 3, *Macropolitical Theory.* Reading, MA: Addision-Wesley, 1975.

Guillermaz, Jacques. *The Chinese Communist Party in Power, 1949–1976,* translated by Anne Destenay. Boulder, CO: Westview Press, 1976.

Hamrin, Carol Lee. *China and the Challenge of the Future: Changing Political Patterns.* Boulder, CO: Westview Press, 1990.

Hamrin, Carol Lee, and Zhao Suisheng, eds. *Decision-Making in Deng's China: Perspectives from Insiders.* Armonk, NY: M. E. Sharpe, 1995.

Han Minzhu. *Cries for Democracy: Writings and Speeches From the 1989 Chinese Democracy Movement.* Princeton, NJ: Princeton University Press, 1990.

Harding, Harry. *Organizing China: The Problem of Bureaucracy, 1949–1976.* Stanford, CA: Stanford University Press, 1981.

China's Second Revolution: Reform After Mao. Washington, DC: The Brookings Institution, 1987.

Heuser, Robert. *The Legal Status of the Chinese Communist Party.* Baltimore, MD: School of Law, University of Maryland, 1987.

Hillman, Arye L., ed., *Market and Politicians: Politicized Economic Choice.* Holland: Kluwer Academic Publishers, 1991.

Hinton, Harold, ed. *Government and Politics in Revolutionary China: Selected Documents, 1949–1979.* Wilmington, DE: Scholarly Resources, 1982.

Holmes, Leslie. *The End of Communist Power.* New York: Oxford University Press, 1993.

Hough, Jerry F. *The Soviet Prefects.* Cambridge, MA: Harvard University Press, 1969.

276

Hsü, Immanuel C. Y. *The Rise of Modern China.* 4th edition. New York: Oxford University Press, 1990.

Huntington, Samuel P. *The Soldier and the State: The Theory and Politics of Civil-Military Relations.* Cambridge, MA: The Belknap Press of Harvard University Press, 1957.

Political Order in Changing Societies. New Haven, CT: Yale University Press, 1968.

Jia Hao and Lin Zhimin, eds. *Changing Central-Local Relations in China: Reform and State Capacity.* Boulder, CO: Westview Press, 1994.

Joffe, Ellis. *Party and Army: Professionalism and Political Control in the Chinese Officer Corps, 1949–1964.* Cambridge, MA: The East Asian Research Center, Harvard University, 1965.

The Chinese Army after Mao. Cambridge, MA: Harvard University Press, 1987.

Johnson, Chalmers A. *Peasant Nationalism and Communist Power; The Emergence of Revolutionary China.* Stanford, CA: Stanford University Press, 1962.

Johnson, Chalmers, ed. *Change in Communist Systems.* Stanford, CA: Stanford University Press, 1970.

Kallgren, Joyce K., ed. *Building a Nation-State: China After Forty Years.* Berkeley: Institute of East Asian Studies, University of California, 1990.

Karnow, Stanley. *Mao and China: A Legacy of Turmoil.* New York: Penguin Books, 1990.

Kataoka, Tetsuya. *Resistance and Revolution in China: The Communists and the Second United Front.* Berkeley: University of California Press, 1974.

Kau, Michael Y. M. *The Lin Biao Affairs: Power, Politics and Military Coup.* White Plains, NY: International Arts and Sciences Press, 1975.

Kau, Michael Y. M., and Leung, John K., eds. *The Writings of Mao Zedong: 1949–1976,* vol. 1. Armonk, NY: M. E. Sharpe, 1986.

Kim, Ilpyong J. *The Politics of Chinese Communism, Kiangsi Under the Soviets.* Berkeley: University of California Press, 1973.

Kwok, Reginald Yin-Wang, and So, Alvin Y., eds. *The Hong Kong-Guangdong Link: Partnership in Flux* Armonk, NY: M. E. Sharpe, 1996.

Lamb, Malcolm. *Directory of Officials and Organizations in China: A Quarter-Century Guide.* Armonk, NY: M. E. Sharpe, 1994.

Lampton, David M., ed. *Policy Implementation in Post-Mao China.* Berkeley: University of California Press, 1987.

Lane, David, ed. *Elites and Political Power in the USSR.* U.K.: Edward Elgar Publishing Limited, 1988.

LaPalombara, Joseph, and Weiner, Myron, eds. *Political Parties and Political Development.* Princeton, NJ: Princeton University Press, 1966.

Lee, Hong Yung. *From Revolutionary Cadres to Party Technocrats in Socialist China.* Berkeley: University of California Press, 1991.

Lee Nan-shong. *Bureaucratic Corruption During the Deng Xiaoping Era.* Hong Kong: Chinese University of Hong Kong, 1991.

Lee Su-hoon. *State-Building in the Contemporary Third World.* Boulder, CO: Westview Press, 1988.

Bibliography

Leng Shao-chuan, and Hongdah Chiu. *Criminal Justice in Post-Mao China: Analysis and Documents.* Albany, NY: State University of New York Press, 1985.

Leng Shao-chuan, ed. *Reform and Development in Deng's China.* Lanham, MD: University Press of America, 1994.

Lenin, V. I. *State and Revolution.* New York: International Publishers. 1971.

Leung, John K., and Kau, Michael Y. M., eds. *The Writings of Mao Zedong: 1949–1976,* vol. 2. Armonk, NY: M. E. Sharpe, 1992.

Levine, Steven I. *Anvil of Victory: The Communist Revolution in Manchuria, 1945–1948.* New York: Columbia University Press, 1987.

Lewis, John Wilson, ed. *Party Leadership and Revolutionary Power in China.* New York: Cambridge University Press, 1970.

Lieberthal, Kenneth. *A Research Guide to Central Party and Government Meetings in China, 1949–1975.* White Plains, NY: International Arts and Science Press, 1976. *Governing China: From Revolution Through Reform.* New York: W. W. Norton & Company, 1995.

Lieberthal, Kenneth, and Oksenberg, Michel. *Policy Making in China: Leaders, Structures, and Processes.* Princeton, NJ: Princeton University Press, 1988.

Lieberthal, Kenneth, and Lampton, David M. *Bureaucracy, Politics, and Decision Making in Post-Mao China.* Berkeley: University of California Press, 1992.

Liew, K. S. *Struggle for Democracy: Sung Chiao-jen and the 1911 Chinese Revolution.* Berkeley: University of California Press, 1971.

Lifton, Robert Jay. *Revolutionary Immortality; Mao Tse-tung and the Chinese Cultural Revolution.* New York: Random House, 1968.

Lin Yu-sheng. *The Crisis of Chinese Consciousness: Radical Antitraditionalism in the May Fourth Era.* Madison, University of Wisconsin Press, 1979.

Lindbeck, John M. H., ed. *China: Management of a Revolutionary Society.* Seattle: University of Washington Press, 1971.

Liu Binyan. *"Tell the World": What Happened in China and Why.* New York: Pantheon, 1990.

Liu Shaoqi. *Collected Works of Liu Shao Ch'i: 1945–1957.* Hong Kong: Union Research Institute. 1969.

Lyons, Thomas P., and Nee, Victor, eds. *The Economic Transformation of South China: Reform and Development in the Post-Mao Era.* Ithaca, NY: East Asia Program, Cornell University, 1994.

MacFarquhar, Roderick, ed. *The Hundred Flowers.* London: Stevens, 1960.

MacFarquhar, Roderick. *The Origins of the Cultural Revolution, I: Contradictions Among the People 1956–1957.* New York: Columbia University Press, 1974. *The Origins of the Cultural Revolution, II: The Great Leap Forward 1958–1960.* New York: Columbia University Press, 1983.

MacFarquhar, Roderick, Cheek, Timothy, and Wu, Eugene, eds. *The Secret Speeches of Chairman Mao, From the Hundred Flowers to the Great Leap Forward.* Cambridge, MA: Council on East Asian Studies, Harvard University, 1989.

MacFarquhar, Roderick, ed. *The Politics of China 1949–1989.* New York: Cambridge University Press, 1993.

Bibliography

Mao Zedong. *Selected Works of Mao Tse-tung,* vol. 4. Beijing: Foreign Languages Press, 1961.

Selected Works of Mao Tse-tung, vols. 1–3. Beijing: Foreign Languages Press, 1965.

Selected Works of Mao Tse-tung, vol. 5. Beijing: Foreign Languages Press, 1977.

March, James G., and Olsen, Johan P. *Rediscovering Institutions.* New York: The Free Press, 1989.

Metzger, Thomas A. *The Internal Organization of Ch'ing Bureaucracy: Legal, Normative, and Communication Aspects.* Cambridge, MA: Harvard University Press, 1973.

Migdal, Joel S., *Strong Societies and Weak States: State-Society Relations and State Capabilities in the Third World.* Princeton, NJ: Princeton University Press, 1988.

Mills, Miriam K., and Nagel, Stuart S., eds. *Public Administration in China.* Westport, CT: Greenwood Press, 1993.

Moody, Peter R., Jr. *The Politics of the Eighth Central Committee of the Communist Party of China.* Hamden, CT: The Shoe String Press, 1973.

Naquin, Susan, and Rawski, Evelyn. *Chinese Society in the Eighteenth Century.* New Haven, CT: Yale University, 1987.

Nathan, Andrew. *China's Crisis: Dilemmas of Reform and Prospects for Democracy.* New York: Columbia University Press, 1990.

Nee, Victor, and Mozingo, David, eds. *State and Society in Contemporary China.* Ithaca, NY: Cornell University Press, 1983.

Nelson, Harvey W. *The Chinese Military System: An Organizational Study of the People's Liberation Army,* 2nd and revised edition. Boulder, CO: Westview Press, 1981.

Neumann, Sigmund. *Permanent Revolution: Totalitarianism in the Age of International Civil War,* 2nd edition. New York: Praeger Publishers, 1965.

Neumann, Sigmund, ed. *Modern Political Parties.* Chicago: University of Chicago Press, 1956.

Nordlinger, Eric A. *Soldiers in Politics: Military Coups and Government.* Englewood Cliffs, NJ: Prentice-Hall, 1977.

O'Brien, Kevin J. *Reform Without Liberalization: China's National People's Congress and the Politics of Institutional Change.* New York: Cambridge University Press, 1990.

Ogden, Suzanne, et al., eds. *China's Search for Democracy: The Student and Mass Movement of 1989.* Armonk, NY: M. E. Sharpe, 1992.

Papp, Daniel S. *Contemporary International Relations: Frameworks for Understanding,* 4th edition. New York: Macmillan College Publishing Company. 1994.

Perrolle, Pierre M. *Fundamentals of the Chinese Communist Party.* White Plains, NY: International Arts and Science Press, 1976.

Poggi, Gianfranco. *The Development of the Modern State: A Sociological Introduction.* Stanford, CA: Stanford University Press, 1978.

The State: Its Nature, Development and Prospects. Stanford, CA: Stanford University Press, 1990.

Potter, Pitman B., ed. *Domestic Law Reforms in Post-Mao China.* Armonk, NY: M. E. Sharpe, 1994.

Bibliography

Pye, Lucian W. *Warlord Politics: Conflict and Coalition in the Modernization of the Republic of China.* New York: Praeger Publishers, 1971.

China: An Introduction. Boston: Little, Brown, 1972.

Rakowska-Harmstone, Teresa, ed. *Communism in Eastern Europe,* 2nd edition. Bloomington: Indiana University Press, 1984.

Resolution on the History of the Chinese Communist Party (1949–81). Beijing: Foreign Languages Press. 1981.

Riskin, Carl. *The Political Economy of Chinese Development Since 1949.* New York: Oxford University Press, 1986.

Rosenbaum, Arthur Lewis, ed. *State and Society in China: The Consequences of Reform.* Boulder, CO: Westview Press, 1992.

Sartori, Giovanni. *Parties and Party Systems: A Framework for Analysis.* vol. 1. Cambridge: Cambridge University Press, 1976.

Scalapino, Robert, and Yu, George T. *Modern China and its Revolutionary Process: Recurrent Challenges to the Traditional Order, 1850–1920.* Berkeley: University of California Press, 1985.

Schapiro, Leonard. *The Communist Party of the Soviet Union,* 2nd edition. New York: Vintage Book, 1971.

Totalitarianism. New York: Praeger Publishers, 1972.

Schram, Stuart R., ed. *Chairman Mao Talks to the People.* New York: Pantheon Books, 1974.

Foundations and Limits of State Power in China. London: The School of Oriental and African Studies, University of London, 1987.

Mao's Road to Power: Revolutionary Writings, 1912–1949, vol. 1, *The Pre-Marxist Period, 1912–1920.* Armonk, NY: M. E. Sharpe, 1992.

Schurmann, Franz H. *Ideology and Organization in Communist China.* 2nd and enlarged edition. Berkeley: University of California Press, 1968.

Schwartz, Benjamin I. *Chinese Communism and the Rise of Mao.* Cambridge, MA: Harvard University Press, 1951.

In Search of Wealth and Power: Yen Fu and the West. Cambridge, MA: The Belknap Press of Harvard University Press, 1964.

Selden, Mark. *The Yenan Way in Revolutionary China.* Cambridge, MA: Harvard University Press, 1971.

Shambaugh, David, ed., *Greater China: The Next Superpower?* New York: Oxford University Press, 1994.

Shaw Yu-ming, ed. *Power and Policy in the People's Republic of China.* Boulder, CO: Westview Press, 1985.

Shirk, Susan L. *The Political Logic of Economic Reform in China.* Berkeley: University of California Press, 1993.

Shue, Vivienne. *The Reach of the State: Sketches of the Chinese Body Politic.* Stanford, CA: Stanford University Press, 1988.

Simmie, Cott, and Nixon, Bob. *Tiananmen Square.* Seattle: University of Washington Press, 1989.

Skocpol, Theda. *States and Social Revolutions: A Comparative Analysis of France, Russia and China.* New York: Cambridge University Press, 1979.

Bibliography

Skowronek, Stephen. *Building a New American State: The Expansion of National Administrative Capacities 1877–1920.* New York: Cambridge University Press, 1982.

Solinger, Dorothy J. *Regional Government and Political Integration in Southwest China, 1949–1954: A Case Study.* Berkeley: University of California Press, 1977.

Spence, Jonathan D. *The Search for Modern China.* New York: W. W. Norton & Company, 1990.

Starr, John Bryan. *Continuing the Revolution: The Political Thought of Mao.* Princeton, NJ: Princeton University Press, 1979.

Starr, Richard F., ed. 1989. *Yearbook on International Communist Affairs 1989.* Stanford, CA: Hoover Institution Press, 1989.

Stepan, Alfred. *The State and Society.* Princeton, NJ: Princeton University Press, 1978.

Sun Yat-sen. *San Min Chu I,* translated by Frank W. Price. Shanghai: China Committee of the Institute of Pacific Relations, 1927.

Swaine, Michael D. *The Military and Political Succession in China: Leadership, Institutions, Beliefs.* Santa Monica, CA: RAND, 1992.

Tan, Chester C. *Chinese Political Thought in the 20th Century.* Newton Abbot: David & Charles, 1971.

Taras, Raymond. *Leadership Changes in Communist States.* Boston: Unwin Hyman Publishers, 1989.

Teiwes, Frederick C. *Politics and Purges in China: Rectification and the Decline of Party Norms, 1950–1965.* 2nd edition. Armonk, NY: M. E. Sharpe, 1993.

Politics at Mao's Court: Gao Gang and Party Factionalism in the Early 1950s. Armonk, NY: M. E. Sharpe, 1990.

Thaxton, Ralph. *China Turned Rightside Up: Revolutionary Legitimacy in the Peasant World.* New Haven, CT: Yale University Press, 1983.

Tien Hung-mao. *Government and Politics in Kuomintang China, 1927–1937.* Stanford, CA: Stanford University Press, 1972.

The Great Transition: Political and Social Change in the Republic of China. Stanford, CA: Hoover Institution Press, Stanford University, 1989.

Tilly, Charles, ed. *The Formation of National States in Western Europe.* Princeton, NJ: Princeton University Press, 1975.

Townsend, James R., and Womack, Brantly. *Politics in China.* Boston: Little, Brown, 1986.

Tsou Tang. *The Cultural Revolution and Post-Mao Reforms: A Historical Perspective.* Chicago: The University of Chicago Press, 1986.

Tucker, Robert C. *The Soviet Political Mind: Stalinism and Post-Stalin Change,* revised edition. New York: W. W. Norton & Company, 1971.

Tucker, Robert C., ed., *Stalinism: Essays in Historical Interpretation.* New York: W. W. Norton & Company, 1977.

Tung, William L. *The Political Institutions of Modern China.* The Hague, Netherlands: Martinus Nijhoff, 1968.

Uhalley, Stephen, Jr. *A History of the Chinese Communist Party.* Stanford, CA: Hoover Institution, Stanford University, 1988.

Bibliography

Von Laue, Theodore H. *Why Lenin? Why Stalin? A Reappraisal of the Russian Revolution, 1900–1930,* 2nd edition. New York: J. B. Lippincott Company, 1971.

Waller, Derek J. *The Kiangsi Soviet Republic: Mao and the National Congress of 1931 and 1934.* Berkeley: Center for Chinese Studies, University of California Press, 1973.

Wang, James C. F. *Contemporary Chinese Politics: An Introduction,* 5th edition. Englewood Cliffs, NJ: Prentice Hall, 1995.

Wakeman, Frederic, Jr. *The Fall of Imperial China.* New York: The Free Press, 1975.

Weidenbaum, Murray, and Hughes, Samuel. *The Bamboo Network: How Expatriate Chinese Entrepreneurs Are Creating a New Economic Superpower in Asia.* New York: The Free Press, 1996.

White, Gordon. *The Chinese State in the Era of Economic Reform: The Road to Crisis.* Armonk, NY: M. E. Sharpe, 1991.

Whitson, William W. *The Chinese High Command: A History of Communist Military Politics, 1921–71.* New York: Praeger Publishers, 1973.

Whyte, Martin King. *Small Groups and Political Rituals in China.* Berkeley: University of California Press, 1974.

Wilson, Amy Auerbacher, Greenblatt, Sidney Leonard, and Wilson, Richard W., eds. *Methodological Issues in China Studies.* New York: Praeger Publishers, 1983.

Wong Young-tsu. *Search for Modern Nationalism: Zhang Binglin and Revolutionary China, 1869–1936.* New York: Oxford University Press, 1989.

Wortzel, Larry M., ed. *China's Military Modernization: International Implications.* Westport, CT: Greenwood Press, 1988.

Yang, Richard H., ed. *China's Military: The PLA in 1990/1991.* Boulder, CO: Westview Press, 1991.

Yang, Winston, et al., eds. *Tiananmen: China's Struggle for Democracy, Its Prelude, Development, Aftermath, and Impact.* Baltimore, MD: School of Law, University of Maryland, 1990.

Yang Zhongmei. *Hu Yaobang: A Chinese Biography.* Armonk, NY: M. E. Sharpe, 1988.

You Ji, and Wilson, Ian. *Leadership Politics in the Chinese Party-Army State: The Fall of Zhao Ziyang.* Canberra: Research School of Pacific Studies, 1989.

Young, Graham, ed. *China: Dilemmas of Modernization.* Dover, NH: Croom Helm, 1985.

Yu, George T. *Party Politics in Republican China: The Kuomintang, 1912–1924.* Berkeley: University of California Press, 1966.

Zhou Enlai. *Selected Works of Zhou Enlai.* Beijing: Foreign Languages Press, 1981.

CHINESE-LANGUAGE REFERENCES

An Ziwen. *An Ziwen zuzhi gongzuo wenxuan* (Selected Works by An Ziwen on Organization Work). Beijing: Zhonggong zhongyang dangxiao chubanshe, 1987.

Bo Yibo. *Ruogan zhongda juece yu shijian de huigu* (Some Major Policy-Decisions and Events in Retrospect), vol. 1. Beijing: Zhonggong zhongyang dangxiao chubanshe, 1991.

Bibliography

Cao Zhi. *Zhonghua renmin gongheguo renshi zhidu gangyao* (Outline of the Personnel System of the People's Republic of China). Beijing: Beijing daxue chubanshe, 1985.

Chen Xuewei. *Lishi de qishi: shi nian jianshe yanjiu, 1957–1966* (Revelations of History: Research on the Ten Years of Construction, 1957–1966). Beijing: Qiushi chubanshe, 1989.

Sishi nian huigu (Remembrance of Forty Years). Beijing: Zhongyang dangxiao chubanshe, 1990.

Chen Yizi. *Zhongguo: shi nian gaige yu baijiu minyun* (China: Ten Years of Reform and 1989 Democracy Movement). Taipei: Lianjin chuban gongsi, 1990.

Chi Fulin et al., eds. *Zhengzhi gaige jiben wenti tantao* (Discussion on the Basic Questions in the Reform of the Political System). Beijing: Chunqiu chubanshe, 1988.

Dang de shiyijie sanzhong quanhui yilai zhengzhi tizhi gaige de lilun yu shijian (Theories and Practices of Reform of the Political System Since the Third Plenum of the Eleventh Party Congress). Beijing: Chunqiu chubanshe, 1987.

Dangdai zhongguo de gongan gongzuo (China Today: Public Security Work). Beijing: Dangdai zhongguo chubanshe, 1992.

Dangdai zhongguo de haijun (China's Navy Today). Beijing: Zhongguo shehui kexue chubanshe, 1987.

Dangdai zhongguo jundui de junshi gongzuo (China Today: The Military Work of the Chinese Army). Beijing: Zhongguo shehui kexue chubanshe, 1989.

Dangshi jiaoxue cankao zhiliao (Reference Materials for Teaching the History of the Chinese Communist Party), vol. 3. Beijing: Renmin chubanshe, 1979.

Dong Biwu. *Dong Biwu xuanji* (Selected Works of Dong Biwu). Beijing: Renmin chubanshe, 1989.

Faxue gailun ziliao xuanbian (Selected Materials for Introduction to Legal Theories). Beijing: Falü chubanshe, 1983.

Feng Zhibin et al., eds. *Zhongguo gongchandang jianshe quanshu, 1921–1991* (Encyclopedia of the Construction of the Chinese Communist Party, 1921–1991), vol. 6. Shanxi: Shanxi renmin chubanshe, 1991.

Guanyu xinshiqi jundui zhengzhi gongzuo de jueding zhushiben (The Annotated Book for the Resolution Concerning the Political Work in the Military in the New Era). Beijing: Jiefangjun chubanshe, 1987.

Huang Yao, Li Zhijing, and Yang Guoqing. *Luo Ronghuan yuanshuai zuihe de shiwu nian* (The Last Fifteen Years of Marshal Luo Ronghuan). Beijing: Renmin chubanshe, 1987.

Jiang Huaxuan et al., eds. *Zhongguo gongchandang huiyi gaiyao* (Summaries of the Chinese Communist Party Conferences). Liaoning: Shenyang chubanshe, 1991.

Jiang Zhaoyuan. *Dang de shenghuo zhishi shouce* (Handbook of Information on the Party Life). Beijing: Zhongguo liaowang chubanshe, 1988.

Jianguo yilai Mao Zedong wengao: 1949, 9–1950, 12 (Mao Zedong's Manuscripts Since the Founding of the People's Republic of China: 1949, 9–1950, 12), vol. 1. Beijing: Zhongyang dangan chubanshe, 1987.

Jianguo yilai Mao Zedong wengao: 1953, 1–1954, 12 (Mao Zedong's Manuscripts

Bibliography

Since the Founding of the People's Republic of China: 1953, 1–1954, 12), vol. 4. Beijing: Zhongyang dangan chubanshe, 1990.

Li Fuyu, Tang Jian, and Zhang Xuelian, eds. *Zhongguo xingzheng guanli jiangzuo* (Lectures on the Administrative Management in China). Shenyang: Liaoning renmin chubanshe, 1985.

Li Rui. *Lushan huiyi shilu* (True Record of the Lushan Plenum). Beijing: Chunqiu chubanshe and Hunan jiaoyu chubanshe, 1989.

Li Weihan. *Huiyi yu yanjiu* (Recollections and Research). Beijing: Zhonggong dangshi ziliao chubanshe, 1986.

Liu Kegu et al., eds. *Dangzheng jigou gaige yanjiu* (Research on the Reform of the Party and Government Institutions). Beijing: Renmin ribao chubanshe, 1988.

Liu Shaoqi. *Liu Shaoqi xuanji* (Selected Works of Liu Shaoqi), vol. 2. Beijing: Renmin chubanshe, 1988.

Luo Ronghuan zhuan (Biography of Luo Ronghuan). Beijing: Dangdai zhongguo chubanshe, 1991.

Ma Ge, Pei Pu, and Mao Taiquan. *Guofang buzhang fuchen ji* (The Rise and Fall of the Defense Minister). Beijing: Kunlun chubanshe, 1988.

Ma Yuping and Huang Yuchong, eds. *Zhongguo zuotian yu jintian 1840–1987 nian guoqing shouce* (China's Yesterday and Today: Handbook of National Conditions: 1840–1987). Beijing: Jiefangjun chubanshe, 1989.

Mingfan huiyi (Reflections of Blooming and Contending). Hong Kong: *Zhanwang* Magazine, 1966.

Nie Gaomin et al., eds. *Guanyu dangzheng fenkai de lilun tantao* (Theoretical Discussion on Separating the Party from the Government). Beijing: Chunqiu chubanshe, 1987.

Peng Dehuai zhuan (Biography of Peng Dehuai). Beijing: Dangdai zhongguo chubanshe, 1993.

Quanguo renda jiqi changweihui dashiji, 1954–1987 (A Chronology of the National People's Congress and Its Standing Committee, 1954–1987). Beijing: Falü chubanshe, 1987.

Shanghai dangzheng jigou yange, 1949–1986 (The Evolution of the Party and Government Institutions in Shanghai, 1949–1986). Shanghai: Shanghai renmin chubanshe, 1988.

Shi nian gaige dashiji, 1978–1987 (A Chronology of the Ten Years of Reform, 1978–1987). Beijing: Xinhua chubanshe, 1988.

Shi Zhongquan. *Mao Zedong de jianxin kaituo* (The Arduous Path-Finding by Mao Zedong). Beijing: Zhonggong dangshi zhiliao chubanshe, 1990.

Sishi nian huigu yu shikao (Remembrance and Thoughts on the Forty Years). Beijing: Zhongyang dangxiao chubanshe, 1991.

Tan Fangzhi. *Dang de tongzhan gongzuo cidian* (Dictionary of the Party's United Front Work). Beijing: Zhongguo zhanwang chubanshe, 1988.

Wang Jueyuan. *Zhongguo dangpai shi* (The History of Parties and Groups in China). Taibei: Zhengzhong shuju, 1983.

Wen Lü, ed. *Zhongguo "zuo" huo* (The "Leftist" Calamities in China). Beijing: Zhaohua chubanshe, 1993.

Bibliography

Wu Lei, ed. *Zhongguo sifa zhidu* (The Chinese Judiciary System). Beijing: Zhongguo renmin daxue chubanshe, 1988.

Wu Peilun, ed. *Woguo de zhengfu jigou gaige* (The Government Institutional Reform in Our Country). Beijing: Jingji ribao chubanshe, 1990.

Xiao Xiaoqin and Wang Youqiao, eds. *Zhonghua renmin gongheguo sishi nian* (Forty Years of the People's Republic of China) Beijing: Beijing shifan xueyuan chubanshe, 1990.

Xinhuashe wenjian ziliao xuanbian (Selected Documents and Materials of the Xinhua News Agency), vol. 2, 1949–1953. Beijing: Xinhua chubanshe, 1987.

Xuexi lishi jueyi zhuanji (Studies of the Resolution on the CCP History). Beijing: Research Department of the Chinese Communist Party History, the Chinese Communist Party Central Committee, 1982.

Yin Jingzhi. *Jigou gaige qishilu* (Lessons of the Institutional Reforms). Beijing: Zhongguo zhengfa daxue chubanshe, 1994.

Yue Qingping. *Jiaguo jiegou yu zhongguoren* (Family-State Structure and Chinese). Hong Kong: Zhonghua shuju, 1989.

Zhang Qingfu, ed. *Fazhi jianshe shinian* (Ten Years of Legal Construction). Beijing: Lüyou jiaoyu chubanshe, 1988.

Zhang Zhanbin et al., eds. *Xin zhongguo qiye lingdao zhidu* (The Leadership System of Enterprises in New China). Beijing: Chunqiu chubanshe, 1988.

Zhao Baoxu, ed. *Minzhu zhengzhi yu difang renda: diaocai yu shikao ziyi* (Democratic Politics and Local People's Congress: Surveys and Thoughts, Part 1). Shaanxi: Shaanxi renmin chubanshe, 1990.

Zheng Qian et al., eds. *Dangdai zhongguo zhengzhi tizhi fazhang gaiyao* (Outline of the Development of Contemporary Chinese Political System). Beijing: Zhonggong dangshi zhiliao chubanshe, 1988.

Zhonggong dangshi zhong de shijian yu renwu (Events and Personages in the History of the Chinese Communist Party). Shanghai: Shanghai renmin chubanshe, 1983.

Zhongguo gaige dacidian (Dictionary of Chinese Reform). Beijing: Zhongguo guoji guangbo chubanshe, 1992.

Zhongguo gongchandang dangwu gongzuo dacidian (Dictionary of Chinese Communist Party Work). Beijing: Zhongyang dangxiao chubanshe, 1990.

Zhongguo gongchandang lishi dashiji (A Chronology of the Chinese Communist Party). Beijing: Renmin chubanshe, 1989.

Zhongguo gongchandang shanghai shi zhuzhi shi zhiliao, 1920, 8–1987, 10 (Organizational Data of the Chinese Communist Party in Shanghai, 1920, 8–1987, 10). Shanghai: Shanghai renmin chubanshe, 1991.

Zhongguo gongchandang zhizheng sishi nian (Forty Years of the Chinese Communist Party in Power). Beijing: Zhongyang dangxiao chubanshe, 1988.

Zhongguo guoqing baogao (Report on the National Conditions of China). Shenyang: Liaoning renmin chubanshe, 1990.

Zhongguo guoqing daiquan (Comprehensive Book of the Chinese National Conditions). Beijing: Xuewang chubanshe, 1990.

Zhongguo renmin jiefangjun liushinian dashiji (A Chronology of Sixty Years of the People's Liberation Army). Beijing: Junshi kexue chubanshe, 1988.

Bibliography

Zhongguo renmin jiefangjun jiangshuai minglu (Biography of the People's Liberation Army Marshals and Generals), vol. 7. Beijing: Jiefangjun chubanshe, 1988.

Zhongguo sheng shi zizhiqu ziliao shouce (Handbook of Reference of the Provinces, Municipalities and Autonomous Regions in China). Beijing: Shehuikexue wenxian chubanshe, 1990.

Zhongguo zhengzhi fazhan yu duodang hezuo zhidu (Chinese Political Development and the System of Multi-Party Cooperation). Beijing: Beijing daxue chubanshe, 1989.

Zhonghua renmin gongheguo dang zheng jun qun lingdaoren minglu (Directory of the Leaders of the Party, Government, Military and Mass Organizations in the People's Republic of China). Beijing: Zhonggong dangshi chubanshe, 1990.

Zhonghua renmin gongheguo sheng zizhiqu zhixiashi dang zheng qun jiguan zuzhi jigou gaiyao (An Outline of the Party, Government and Mass Organizations of Provinces, Autonomous Regions and Municipalities Under the Direct Jurisdiction of the Central Government of the People's Republic of China). Beijing: Zhongguo renshi chubanshe, 1989.

Zhonghua renmin gongheguo quanguo renda zhongyang he difang zhengfu quanguo zhengxie Lijie fuzeren renming lu (Directory of the Former Responsible Persons of the National People's Congress of the People's Republic of China, the Central and Local Government, and the National People's Political Consultative Conference). Beijing: Renmin chubanshe, 1984.

Zhonghua renmin gongheguo yaoshilu, 1949–1989 (Major Events of the People's Republic of China, 1949–1989). Jinan: Shandong renmin chubanshe, 1989.

Zhou Enlai zhuan, 1898–1949 (A Biography of Zhou Enlai, 1898–1949). Beijing: Renmin chubanshe and Zhongyang wenxian chubanshe, 1989.

Index

administration, PRC: 39–40, 59, 99; Administrative Committee, 45; dual rule, 81–2; Military Administrative Committee, 45; Military Control Commission, 54; military, 45, 145–6; regional government, 45, 99, 100, 149, 203
Administrative Compensation Law, 184–5
Administrative Litigation Law, 184
agriculture, 91, 93, 101, 133, 193
air force, PLA, 106, 107, 108–9, 151, 228, 229
Alliance Society, 32
Anderson, Benedict, 46–7
Anti-Japanese War, 35–6, 43, 112
Anti-Rightist Campaign, 20; attacks on judicial system, 57, 73–4; attacks on legislative system, 69, 71–3, 77; governors dismissed in, 70–1; intellectuals as victims, 69, 81; issues in, 64–7; ministers dismissed in, 69; Party in, 67–8, 74–7; rightists designated in, 67–8
Anti-Rightist Tendency Campaign, 94, 118, 124, 226
antibureaucracy campaign, 154, 206, 209
Aristotle, 26
armored force, PLA, 227
arms, Chinese sales of, 231, 240
army business, 237–42; consequences of, 239–41; types of, 237–9

"backyard furnaces," 93
Bedeski, Robert E., 36
Beidaihe, meeting, 97–8
Beijing Military Region, 228, 234
big character posters, 68, 144
"blooming and contending," 64, 75, 77, 91, 174
Bolshevik revolution, 32
bourgeois liberalization, campaign against, 262
Buddhism, 25

bureaucracy, attacks on, 209; size of, 211
bureaucratism, campaign against, 46, 64, 209

cadres, distribution of, 212; exchange of, 220–3; management system of, 213; promotion of younger, 212–13; rehabilitated, 162–3; salaries of, 214–15; types of, 210–11
campaigns, 270–2 (Appendix), consequences of, 156; functions of, 154–5. *See also* specific campaigns
Cao Diqiu, 136
Capital Construction Engineering Corps, PLA, 227
CCP, *see* Chinese Communist Party
Central Party Secretariat, 84, 115, 193
Central Committee, functional departments of, 86, 115, 192–3; work departments of, 18, 86–8, 193, 195, 196, 199
Central Leading Group of Political and Legal Affairs, 73–4, 76
Central Military Commission (CMC), CCP, 107, 109, 112–16, 130–1, 238, 248–9
Central Military Commission, PRC, 246–7
Central People's Government Council (CPGC), 41
Central People's Revolutionary Commission, 55, 115
centralization-decentralization cycles, 99–104, 215; case of Shanghai, 101, 102–3; state-society perspective of, 98–9
Chen Boda, 153
Chen Jinhua, 205
Chen Pixian, 172
Chen Weigao, 196
Chen Xitong, 196, 209
Chen Yun, 95–6, 124, 133, 191
Chengdu Military Region, 228, 233
Chiang Kai-shek, 42, 261, 263; and purge of Communists, 35, 84; comparison with Mao, 128

287